French Philosophy Today

French Philosophy Today

New Figures of the Human in Badiou, Meillassoux, Malabou, Serres and Latour

CHRISTOPHER WATKIN

EDINBURGH
University Press

For Alison, my joy

Edinburgh University Press is one of the leading university presses in the UK. We publish academic books and journals in our selected subject areas across the humanities and social sciences, combining cutting-edge scholarship with high editorial and production values to produce academic works of lasting importance. For more information visit our website: www.edinburghuniversitypress.com

Edinburgh University Press Ltd
The Tun – Holyrood Road
12(2f) Jackson's Entry
Edinburgh EH8 8PJ

First published in hardback by Edinburgh University Press 2016

Typeset in 11/13 Adobe Garamond by
Servis Filmsetting Ltd, Stockport, Cheshire,
and printed and bound in Great Britain by
CPI Group (UK) Ltd, Croydon CR0 4YY

A CIP record for this book is available from the British Library

ISBN 978 1 4744 1473 9 (hardback)
ISBN 978 1 4744 2583 4 (paperback)
ISBN 978 1 4744 1474 6 (webready PDF)
ISBN 978 1 4744 1475 3 (epub)

Contents

Acknowledgements

This book has been a long time in the writing, and I am glad to be able to record here how grateful I am to those who have helped it on its way. Thanks are due to Martin Crowley and Ian James for their encouragement in the project's early days and for their insightful comments on a paper to the Cambridge Modern French Research Seminar in March 2011. I am grateful to the anonymous reviewers for Edinburgh University Press who sharpened my discussion of Malabou and, in particular, made me engage more closely with *The Heidegger Change*. I am privileged to work alongside colleagues at Monash University who maintain a stimulating intellectual environment and who have encouraged me in the thinking that led to these chapters, with a special mention to Benjamin Andréo, Phillip Anderson and Kate Rigby. I am also grateful to Monash for granting me the period of research leave during which the bulk of this book was drafted.

I continue to benefit from the excellent, timely and encouraging support of Carol Macdonald at Edinburgh University Press, and it is once more thanks to her that this book has been guided smoothly through both the storms and the doldrums of the publication process. I am hugely grateful to Kenneth Watkin, my father, for proofreading a late draft of this book, spotting myriad small errors, and saving my blushes by correcting some rather more obvious mistakes. His witticisms and poetic asides in the proofing notes also made me smile. All remaining mistakes and all failed jokes are, I am afraid, mine alone. Little Benjamin, who is yet too young to know it, put a spring in my step during the final stages of drafting.

Words can only betray the ocean of gratitude I owe to Alison, my wife, whose influence on these pages, both in encouragement and insight, is too broad to capture and too deep to tell. This is our book. 'When I consider your heavens, the work of your fingers, the moon and the stars, which you have set in place, what is mankind that you are mindful of them, human beings that you care for them?' (Psalms 8: 3–4).

Abbreviations

Badiou

RE	*La Relation énigmatique entre politique et philosophie*
RP	*La République de Platon*
S	*Le Siècle*
Sem91–2	Séminaire: La Politique
Sem96–8	Séminaire: Théorie axiomatique du sujet
Sem01–2	Séminaire: Images du temps présent (1)
Sem03–4	Séminaire: Images du temps présent (Qu'est-ce que vivre?)
Sem04–5	Séminaire: S'orienter dans la pensée, s'orienter dans l'existence (2004–5)
Sem06–7	Séminaire: S'orienter dans la pensée, s'orienter dans l'existence (2006–7)

Meillassoux

AF	*Après la finitude*
AfF	*After Finitude*
CAA	'Contingency & the absolutization of the One'
CEA	'Contingence et absolutisation de l'un'
ExID	'Excerpts from "L'Inexistence divine"', in Harman, *Quentin Meillassoux*
ID	'L'Inexistence divine'
IntDT	'Interview with Quentin Meillassoux', in Dolphijn and Tuin (eds), *New Materialism*
IRR	'Iteration, reiteration, repetition'
IWB	'The immanence of the world beyond'

Malabou

AD	*Avant demain*
ADH	*L'Avenir de Hegel*
CCM	'A conversation with Catherine Malabou'
CDM	*La Chambre du milieu*
EOW	'The end of writing? Grammatology and plasticity'
FOH	*The Future of Hegel*
Hum	'The future of the Humanities'
LCH	*La Change Heidegger*
LNB	*Les Nouveaux Blessés*
LNBc	'Les Nouveaux Blessés'
OdA	*Ontologie de l'accident*
OoA	*Ontology of the Accident*

PAS   *La Plasticité au soir de l'écriture*
PDW   *Plasticity at the Dusk of Writing*
PFPT   'Plasticity and the future of philosophy and theology'
Pla   *Plasticité*
PLR   'Catherine Malabou: pour la rencontre entre philosophie et neuro-sciences'
PT   'Post-trauma: towards a new definition?'
QF   *Que faire de notre cerveau?*
SEL   *Self and Emotional Life*
THC   *The Heidegger Change*
TNW   *The New Wounded*
WSD   *What Should We Do With Our Brain?*

Serres

AP   *L'Art des ponts: Homo pontifex*
BP   *The Birth of Physics*
BPP   'Le Balancier, la pierre philosophale'
CN   *Le Contrat naturel*
Conv   *Conversations on Science, Culture and Time*
Dis   *La Distribution: Hermès IV*
Ec   *Eclaircissements*
EH   'Exact and human'
Ge   *Genèse*
Gen   *Genesis*
H3   *La Traduction: Hermès III*
HN   'L'Homme nouveau'
Hom   *Hominescence*
Inc   *L'Incandescent*
LP   *Le Parasite*
NC   *The Natural Contract*
NP   *La Naissance de la physique dans le texte de Lucrèce: fleuves et turbulences*
Ram   *Rameaux*
RH   *Récits d'humanisme*
SP   'Sciences et philosophie (entretien)'
SR   'The science of relations'
TH   'Le Temps humain: de l'évolution créatrice au créateur d'évolution'
TP   *The Parasite*
TU   'Temps, usure: feux et signaux de brume'

Latour

AIME	*An Inquiry into Modes of Existence*
AT	'Another turn after ANT: an interview with Bruno Latour'
ATA	'Anthropology at the time of the Anthropocene'
BoI	'Biography of an inquiry: on a book about modes of existence'
CM	*Sur le culte moderne des dieux faitiches*
CO	'Coming out as a philosopher'
CP	'A cautious Prometheus'
EME	*Enquête sur les modes d'existence*
EP	*L'Espoir de Pandore*
FD	*La Fabrique du droit*
FF	'Factures/fractures. De la notion de réseau à celle d'attachement'
FFe	'Factures/fractures: from the concept of network to the concept of attachment'
FG	'Facing Gaia'
FMOF	'From "matters of facts" to "states of affairs". Which protocol for the new collective experiments?'
IDS	'"It's development, stupid!" or: how to modernize modernization'
IMEg	'An inquiry into modes of existence: glossary': online glossary. References followed by relevant glossary entry title
JEM	*Nous n'avons jamais été modernes*
Jub	*Jubiler ou Les tourments de la parole religieuse*
LB	'Les Baleines et la forêt amazonienne: Gabriel Tarde et la cosmopolitique. Entretien avec Bruno Latour'
MC	*On the Modern Cult of the Factish Gods*
MOL	*The Making of Law*
MP	*Un monde pluriel mais commun*
NBM	*We Have Never Been Modern*
ŒBL	'L'Œuvre de Bruno Latour: une pensée politique exégétique. Entretien avec Bruno Latour'
OTM	'On technical mediation'
PES	'A plea for earthly sciences'
PF	*The Pasteurisation of France*
PGP	*Pasteur: guerre et paix des microbes.* Suivi de *Irréductions*
PH	*Pandora's Hope*
PN	*Politiques de la Nature*
PNe	*Politics of Nature*
PNEW	'Politics of nature: East and West perspectives'

Ref	'Reflections on Etienne Souriau's *Les Différents modes d'existence*'
Rej	*Rejoicing, or the Torments of Religious Speech*
RPDP	'From Realpolitik to Dingpolitik, or how to make things public'
RTSL	'Redefining the social link'
SUL	'Sur un livre d'Etienne Souriau: *Les Différents Modes d'existence*'
TME	'To modernize or to ecologize? That's the question'
WFG	'Waiting for Gaia'
WWL	'"We would like to do a bit of science studies on you . . ." An interview with Bruno Latour'

Introduction

French philosophy today is laying fresh claim to the human. This is not to be mistaken for an exercise in winding back the clock, nor is it a return to previous ideas of the human, much less a coordinated 'human turn'. It is a series of fundamentally independent and yet strikingly simultaneous initiatives arising across the diverse landscape of French thought to transform and rework the figure of the human. Whereas the latter decades of the twentieth century adopted a decidedly critical and cautious approach to the question of 'the human', imprisoning it within the iron bars of scare quotes and burying it under caveats warning against its false universalism and dangerous totalitarianism, now we find ourselves entering a new moment of constructive transformation in which fresh and ambitious figures of the human are forged and discussed, and in which humanism itself is being reinvented and reclaimed in multiple ways. These new figures of the human take diverse and sometimes mutually antagonistic forms, but what unites them all is that they cannot be plotted on the spectrum running between twentieth-century humanism and antihumanism. Each in its own way rejects the assumptions that humanism and antihumanism share. By tracing these varied transformations of the human we can discern one of the most widespread, most surprising and potentially most transformative trends in contemporary French thought.

The aim of this book is threefold: to make visible, to critique and to highlight the dangers and possibilities of this important contemporary trend. I will make these diverse transformations of the human visible as an important feature of contemporary French thought for the first time by bringing them together in one volume and discussing them comparatively. The chapters of this book are not presented as a series of isolated studies but as a cumulative account and progressive critique of different contemporary transformations of the human. This comparative critique opens the way to offering a taxonomy of the current and future ways in which the human is being and can be transformed, as well as showing what is at stake in the reception of these different accounts of the human and how they can shape the future of French thought.

Beyond the trichotomy of humanism, antihumanism and posthumanism

The latter decades of the twentieth century were characterised by a suspicion of 'the human', the culmination of the first adumbrative rumblings of misgiving that came in the form of Nietzsche's death of God. The human as traditionally conceived was revealed as a correlative of the now defunct deity,[1] a microcosm of the vanishing divinely ordered macrocosm, and the 'self' was nothing more than a temporary placeholder that would inevitably go the way of its divine counterpart.[2]

A second wave of suspicion came in the form of the post-Second World War 'humanism debate'[3] in which battle lines were drawn in the exchange between Sartre and Heidegger.[4] For Sartre, 'Existentialism is a humanism' because

> we remind man that there is no legislator but himself, that he himself, thus abandoned, must decide for himself, also because we show that it is not by turning back upon himself, but always by seeking, beyond himself, an aim which is one of liberation, of some particular realisation, that man will realise himself precisely as human.[5]

For a not dissimilar set of reasons, Heidegger firmly denounces humanism. To speak of humanism is to presuppose a metaphysical human essence to which, after the death of God, we have no right:

> every humanism remains metaphysical. In defining the humanity of the human being, humanism not only does not ask about the relation of being to the essence of the human being; because of its metaphysical origin humanism even impedes the question by neither recognising nor understanding it.[6]

Nevertheless, both Sartre's embrace of humanism and Heidegger's rejection of the label continue to affirm the uniqueness of the human form of being in the world in contradistinction to nonhuman being, and continue to be determined by the Nietzschean moment of the death of God.

In the wake of the events of May 1968, a third wave of suspicion broke on European shores when post-Nietzschean ideas found new expression in the structuralist and poststructuralist discourses of Althusser, Foucault,

Barthes, Derrida, Deleuze and others, and in which the death of God was consummated, though not unproblematically,[7] in the recognition that Nietzsche had discovered 'the point at which man and God belong to one another, at which the death of the second is synonymous with the disappearance of the first'.[8] Discussions of the human in these decades take place, in one way or another, within these Nietzschean parameters.[9] Humanism is seen as indebted to religion[10] and as instituting a falsely universalising category which does violence to differences and singularities.[11]

Today, however, something new is happening. Late twentieth-century figures of the human stand in the shadow of the twin disappearances of God and man, but the contemporary philosophers discussed in this volume are no longer determined either positively or negatively by the antihumanism debates of the past century or by the 'death of man', although their different ways of escaping from the terms of these debates are, as we shall see, radically divergent. The new figures of the human discussed in this volume see the antihumanism of the twentieth century and the 'end of man' that it proclaimed as an insufficiently radical response to the crisis of Cartesian and Kantian modernity, and they judge that the antihumanism of the second half of the twentieth century still shares the most fundamental assumptions of the humanism it seeks to challenge.

What unites the thinkers discussed in these chapters is that their thought resists the easy dichotomy of traditional humanism and twentieth-century antihumanism. Badiou returns to this story to reject both the humanism of modernity and the antihumanism of the late twentieth century, elaborating a 'formalised inhumanism' (S 251/Cen 178) that cannot be understood on the spectrum between Sartre and Foucault (S 241/Cen 172), or indeed between Sartre and Heidegger. Quentin Meillassoux works within the assumptions of Kantian 'correlationism' neither to praise Kant nor to bury humanism but to set forth what he claims is simultaneously a rigorously anti-anthropocentric philosophy and also the first account ever to give the human its rightful supreme and ultimate value (ExID 209). Catherine Malabou rejects both the 'cognitivist' reduction of the mind to the brain and also the 'Continental' rejection of any necessary relationship between mind and brain (CDM 230), embracing the language of the human while seeking to transform the way we understand the relation between brain, mind and self. Michel Serres, in his recent work, sets out the case for a new universal humanism which, for the first time, radically situates humanity within its ecological milieu, with its objects, and in the 'Great Story' of the universe, rather than founding the claims of humanism on some purported human specificity or uniqueness. Finally, Bruno Latour follows Serres in rejecting not only the humanism of modernity but also the antihumanism that shared modernity's reliance on the subject–object dichotomy and on the related dualisms of nature and culture, matter and meaning, the absurd clash of a world indifferent to human concerns and an active and meaning-giving subject. For Latour, to peddle the death of God and the death of man today is the self-indulgent fancy of 'epicurean tourists' (FG 110) who ignore the real question of the contemporary ecological crisis. In rejecting the humanism of modernity Latour claims not to be jettisoning the human but, quite to the contrary, to be allowing us to 'become ordinary humans again' (FMOF 8). There has been talk in recent years, in the subdiscipline of Continental philosophy of religion, of 'returning to God after God'.[12] What we are witnessing in French thought today is a series of returns to the human after the human.

If these new figures of the human are neither humanist nor antihumanist in the way in which those terms are usually used, then neither are they posthumanist. In the current volume I resist the discourse of posthumanism for two main reasons. The first is the thundering lack of sustained attention paid to the term by the five thinkers in the book, and a similarly overwhelming lack of approbation when, on occasion, they do mention it. I have only been able to find one reference to posthumanism or transhumanism in Badiou, in a lecture course from 2004–5 where he talks of the divine as 'a place it is philosophy's very task to build, a place consequently in-human or trans-human [. . .] It is in philosophy's nature to refer to the trans-human capacity of humanity' (Sem04–5). However, in his published work the transhuman drops away and he privileges the motif of the inhuman, and even Badiou's evocation of the transhuman here cannot reasonably be thought as an instance of human enhancement as that term is commonly understood within the discourse of transhumanism.[13] The term is absent from both Meillassoux's and Malabou's published work, though it is parsimoniously scattered across the secondary literature on Malabou.[14] Of all the thinkers treated in this volume, the one to have been most closely associated with posthuman thought is Michel Serres. The blurb to the 2007 edition of the English translation of Serres's *The Parasite* proclaims the volume to be '[t]he foundational work in the area now known as posthuman thought',[15] and the edition includes a preface by Cary Wolfe entitled 'Bring the noise: *The Parasite* and the multiple genealogies of posthumanism'. In addition, Serres is frequently quoted in volumes purporting to argue from a posthumanist perspective. Nevertheless, despite the importance of Serres for posthumanism, posthumanism does not appear to be important for Serres.[16] In the same way that Badiou refuses posthumanism and (eventually) transhumanism in favour of the inhuman, Claire Colebrook insists that Serres's thought is best understood in terms of the inhuman in explicit opposition to the posthuman. For Colebrook, posthumanism 'renounces human privilege or speciesism but then fetishises the post-human world as man-less'[17] while some of its guises perversely 'attribute all the qualities once assigned to man – qualities such as mindfulness, connectedness, self-organizing dynamism – to some supposedly benevolent life in general that needs to be saved from the death of merely calculative systems'.[18] As opposed to such posthumanisms (which Colebrook says are more rightly classed as ultra-humanisms), Serres's work on the parasite and pollution focuses 'on the inhuman multiplicities of systems',[19] an approach which does not follow the posthumanism for which 'once man is abandoned as a distinct system or inflection he returns to characterize nature or life in general'.[20] Finally, of the five thinkers considered in these pages Latour is the one who employs the term 'posthumanism' most often, and always to distance his own thought from it. In 'Anthropology at the time of the Anthropocene' he is very dismissive of the term, quipping: 'Remember the old concept of "posthuman"? Posthuman! Just at the time when the Anthropocene brings the human back with a vengeance!' (ATA 8),[21] and the question with which Latour prefers to engage is 'What does it mean to redistribute human agency without being humanist, or post-human, or anti-humanist?' (ATA 13).

A second reason I avoid the language of posthumanism is the frequently problematic way in which posthumanism retrojects the humanism against which it defines itself. To the extent that much posthumanism seems to be inveighing against the affirmation (by whom, nowadays?) that humans are at the apex of the Great Chain of Being, it risks tilting at windmills. This is akin to persisting in framing the debate around the human in terms of the deaths of God and man, and it is exactly what the thinkers in this book refuse to do. Colebrook voices this concern in her treatment of Serres when she argues that '[t]he man of the humanities was already post-human, possessing no being other than his reflexive capacity to read his own ungrounded and utterly flexible becoming',[22] and Latour advances a similar argument when he says that 'there is nothing necessarily posthuman in enveloping, folding, veiling humans into their life supports' and that his own emphasis on matters of concern as opposed to matters of fact 'is every bit as removed from the post-human dreams of cyborgs' as it is from classical humanism (CP 11).[23] Humanism and posthumanism have much more in common than either of them would like to admit, and Latour is seeking to rethink their shared legacy, rather than positioning himself at a point on the spectrum between them. The problem with posthumanism is that it tends to seek to reject a 'traditional' or 'classical' figure of the human that then serves as a benchmark to be surpassed, but part of the argument of the present book (particularly in Chapters 1, 3 and 6) is that the classical or traditional account of the human is always already one of self-surpassing or non-self-identicality, and therefore to suggest that the human has only recently hit upon the idea of moving beyond itself is historically unaware.

In addition, posthumanism also inscribes itself within the logic of emancipation (and therefore of progress) which also characterises both modernism and postmodernism. The rhetoric of emancipation is woven into much of the discourse around posthumanism, for example when it characterises its own prefix 'post-' as a step forward or a step beyond the human.[24] Given that this ideology of progress is, particularly in the final two chapters of this book, precisely what is at stake, it is imprudent to load the dice by introducing the term posthumanism in our analysis.

Thirdly, much discourse that identifies itself as posthuman is intent upon blurring the boundary between the human and the animal, or between the human and technology, but this blurring of boundaries goes too far for Badiou and Meillassoux and not half far enough for Serres and Latour. They are not concerned with upsetting the distinction between the human and the nonhuman (animal or object) but, variously, with rethinking and reaffirming it (Chapters 1 and 2), or rendering it an out-dated curio of philosophical history (Chapters 5 and 6). Even if 'posthu-manism' means nothing more than moving beyond 'traditional' figures of the human, then it still does not quite fit the analysis of this book, which argues that contemporary French thought is not dreaming up new figures of the human *ex nihilo* but transforming and re-purposing existing motifs and accounts.

There is one final reason (as if we needed another) why it is imprudent to cast contemporary French thought in the mould of the posthuman. The term has become, like 'postmodernism' a passe-partout signifier drained of determinate content which, without a much greater elaboration than I am able to give it in these pages, brings very little clarity and adds very little analytical value.[25] If some posthumanists feel irate that my first three reasons for dismissing the term do not apply to them, then they help to prove my fourth point, that the notion is so diverse as to have lost its criti-cal incisiveness. If I were to seek to do justice to the fifty-seven varieties of posthumanism in terms of contemporary French philosophy then this book would have to treat as its main focus a term mentioned by only a few of the thinkers it discusses and endorsed by none of them. For all of these reasons, it is profoundly misguided to characterise the current prolifera-tion of figures of the human in French thought as a posthuman turn.

French philosophy today

One of the features that makes the contemporary transformations of the human so interesting – and so important – to consider in relation to each other is that they are not taking place only in one corner of the contemporary French philosophical scene, but in and through the writings of a remarkably diverse range of thinkers. Indeed, the five philosophers discussed in this volume have been chosen not because of their temperamental or political affinities, nor because of any shared philosophical approach. Some are atheist (Badiou, Meillassoux, Malabou) while others situate themselves in a religious tradition (Serres, Latour). Badiou is unambiguously aligned with the political left but it is impossible to throw the same political blanket over the other thinkers in this volume. Nor can we talk about a 'new generation' of French philosophers reclaiming the language of the human. If anything there are three generations represented in this book, with Michel Serres (b. 1930) and Alain Badiou (b. 1937) born pre-war in the generation of the so-called Lucky Few, Bruno Latour (b. 1947) and Catherine Malabou (b. 1959) as baby boomers, and Quentin Meillassoux (b. 1967) a member of Generation X. The return to the language of the human is certainly happening in many philosophical loci at once, but not as a concerted or coordinated effort driven by any particular philosophico-political agenda. It is, for that reason, all the more remarkable. It is precisely because of their differences, not in spite of them, that the diverse transformations of the human are illuminating when studied comparatively.

Indeed, there is a case to be made that characterising the contemporary landscape and direction of French thought in terms of a series of attempts to rethink and transform the figure of the human is one of the least forced and most productive ways to draw together the diversity of approaches within the contemporary landscape of French philosophy today, after the heyday of the so-called linguistic turn. Other recent attempts to map the current trajectories of French philosophy have highlighted certain trends and family resemblances, but have been able to discern no clear 'movement'. Among those volumes which take a particular interest in the overall direction of French philosophy in recent years, John Mullarkey's *Post-Continental Philosophy* and Ian James's *The New French Philosophy* distinguish themselves for the clarity of their presentation and the incisiveness of their analysis. Opening his 2006 *Post-Continental Philosophy* with the Nietzschean gesture (today well on its way to being vindicated) that 'this book may well have been written too early',[26] John Mullarkey argues that 'the thesis of the book, and the thing which draws all the writers together, is an embrace of absolute immanence over transcendence'.[27] What unites the four thinkers he considers in the book (Deleuze, Badiou, Henry and Laruelle) is that 'all these writers carve up reality as an inside with no outside'.[28] Mullarkey's identification of the trends against which these thinkers position themselves signals a propensity to rethink philosophy in intimate relation to other disciplines:

> Rejecting both the phenomenological tradition of transcendence (of Consciousness, the Ego, Being, or Alterity), as well as the post-structuralist valorisation of Language, they instead take the immanent categories of biology (Deleuze), mathematics (Badiou), affectivity (Henry), and science (Laruelle) as focal points for a renewal of philosophy.[29]

The 'non-reductive' naturalism that Mullarkey's chosen thinkers elaborate is rightly identified by Iris van der Tuin as an important contribution to the ongoing elaboration of a 'new materialism',[30] and although Mullarkey's book does not contain the term 'new materialism' itself, an earlier version of some of the material in its opening chapter on Deleuze originally appeared under the title 'Deleuze and materialism: one or several matters?'[31] and he sums up the different approaches of the thinkers he considers by stating that 'taken together, these strategies amount to a rekindled faith in the possibility of philosophy as a worldly and materialist thinking'.[32]

Published six years after *Post-Continental Philosophy*, Ian James's *The New French Philosophy* discusses seven thinkers (Marion, Nancy, Stiegler, Malabou, Rancière, Badiou and Laruelle) all of whom distance themselves from the linguistic paradigm of (post)structuralism.[33] James concurs with Mullarkey in discerning a materialism in contemporary thought, arguing that the philosophers he discusses 'seek to rethink the relation of thought both to worldly existence or appearance and to what might be termed "the outside"',[34] and that their thought can be seen as a 'systematic attempt to radically rethink questions of materiality and the concrete'.[35] He does use the term 'new materialism' in relation to his seven thinkers as a whole and to Catherine Malabou in particular, noting that she uses the term as a self-description and glossing it as 'what one might also call a metamorphic materialist ontology'.[36] Although he 'broadly reaffirms Mullarkey's arguments relating to the realignment of French thought with a non-reductive naturalism and the life sciences, with mathematics and with a worldly and materialist thinking',[37] James nevertheless characterises the 'new' philosophers in terms broader than Mullarkey's focus on immanence alone, arguing that they bring

> a re-engagement with the question of ontology [. . .], but also a sustained renewal with the question of the subject and of subjectivity, with questions of community, politics and political change, and with questions relating to the aesthetic and aesthetics.[38]

The idea that contemporary French thought is characterised by a certain focus on materiality also emerges in Alexander Galloway's *Les Nouveaux Réalistes*.[39] Galloway's analysis, originally presented as a series of seminars at the Public School in New York in October 2010, treats five French thinkers that are not readily accessible in translation to an English readership (Catherine Malabou, Bernard Stiegler, Mehdi Belhaj Kacem, Quentin Meillassoux and François Laruelle), and for the French publication he adds an 'intermission' on Badiou. While he actively resists any idea that he is offering a new canon of emerging French philosophers, he nevertheless identifies certain themes that run, if imperfectly, through the work of the five thinkers he discusses. He situates contemporary French thought as reclaiming a 'new reality' now that 'post-structuralism and its incisive anti-realism have long since passed their zenith',[40] a new reality that digs below 'the antirealist stratum of subjects and cultures' in order to reach the 'realist substrate of material and things'.[41] What this amounts to is a 'renaissance' of materialism.[42]

There are indeed new forms of materialism emerging in French thought today, and my focus on the human in this volume is by no means intended to challenge that thesis. In fact, each of the thinkers discussed herein offers an account of materiality in the process of articulating the notion of the human. My focus on transformations of the human sits alongside, not against, the idea that much contemporary French thought is characterised by a series of new materialisms, and it fleshes out what is at stake in those materialisms and what motivates their newness. Both James's and Galloway's focus on the material and my own choice of the motif of the human have one important feature in common: they are plural. James is prudent in not herding all of contemporary French thought into the paddock of a capitalised 'New Materialism'. Badiou's materialism is not Latour's, and neither of them can be equated with Meillassoux's or Malabou's. In the same way, what emerges in contemporary French thought is not one new figure of the human but a series of transformations irreducible one to the other but that still admit of certain prudent comparisons.

What about common enemies? Although there is a widespread rejection of the so-called linguistic philosophy of the late twentieth century, it is by no means the case that contemporary French thinkers uniformly turn their back on it. Malabou's relation to Derrida is far from one of rejection, and the same could be said of Stiegler's. To the attentive ear, there are also subtle borrowings and adaptations of linguistic paradigms to be heard whispering beneath the fanfare of the rejection of linguistic philosophy.[43] Similarly, though the thinkers discussed in these pages do share a rejection of many aspects of Cartesian and Kantian thought, this common profession by no means serves as an unproblematic article of allegiance. Meillassoux, for example, articulates his philosophical position in terms of a rejection of what he characterises as an insidious 'correlationism', where the correlation in question is 'the idea according to which we only ever have access to the correlation between thinking and being, and never to either term considered apart from the other', and 'correlationism' is 'any current of thought which maintains the unsurpassable character of the correlation so defined' (*AF* 18–19/*AfF* 5). The term has since gained general currency as a designation for a 'focus on discourse, text, culture, consciousness, power, or ideas as what constitutes reality', amounting to 'something resembling ethereal idealism'.[44] This rejection of correlation cannot do duty as a general theme running across all our philosophers, however, as Latour would read Meillassoux's rejection of correlationism as a more fundamental agreement with the assumptions underlying correlationist thought, and he would conclude that therefore Meillassoux still works within a correlationist framework.[45] Furthermore, Malabou argues in *Avant demain* that Kant is not so far from Meillassoux as Meillassoux himself may think.

It is not simply materialism that contemporary French thinkers have in common, then, and it is not the same rejection of Descartes and Kant. Could it be argued that what contemporary French thinkers share is a cross-disciplinary itch? Mullarkey notes Badiou's recourse to mathematics,[46] and we can easily add Meillassoux's profound engagements with mathematics and theology, Malabou's ongoing conversation with neuroscience, Serres's rampant cross-disciplinary engagements with the 'northwest passages' between literature, science, mathematics, philosophy, music and art, and Latour's work on the border of sociology and philosophy. James argues that the move away from the postmodern linguistic paradigm 'dictates a re-alignment of philosophy', in many cases with the natural sciences,[47] and Paul Ennis asserts that 'Continental realism is a middle path that accepts, contra traditionalist continental philosophy, that the natural sciences, realism, and analytic philosophy are not a threat, but aids in the task of first science: metaphysics.'[48] Nevertheless, there is a great deal of difference between a recourse to pure mathematics and to the sciences, as Adrian Johnston points out persuasively in his critiques of Badiou and Meillassoux.[49] In addition, this propensity to engage deeply and at length with other scientific and non-scientific disciplines does not distinguish contemporary French thought from that of previous generations: Foucault's history, Deleuze's biology, Pascal's theology or Descartes' *Optics* and *Meteorology* do not look out of place in this constellation.

The trend identified and clarified in the present book is hinted at by Ian James when he puts at the heart of the new French philosophy 'a sustained attempt to re-engage with the question of the subject and to resituate something which might still be called subjectivity within a pre-symbolic/ linguistic and material dimension'.[50] It is only an oblique hint, however, as the motif of the 'subject' with its implication of subject–object dyad is very ill-fitting indeed for Serres and Latour, who labour fervently to dismantle that particular Cartesian opposition. Given the ill-fittingness of the frameworks of anti-Kantianism or cross-disciplinarity to characterise the general direction of contemporary French thought, it can be argued – and with some cause I think – that the transformations of the human discussed in this volume themselves provide one of the least partial and most comprehensive ways to characterise the trajectory of contemporary French thought, spanning writers of different generations, temperaments, religious outlooks and politics.

Human: the very idea(s)

One of the features shared by the thought of Badiou, Meillassoux, Malabou, Serres and Latour is that their figures of the human are not *ex nihilo* inventions but draw on themes and motifs from the history of Western thought, both theological and philosophical. What we are seeing today are not reinventions of the human but transformations and some-times subversions of some of the oldest classical motifs. In order to aid us in forming comparative critiques of these transformations, and as an attempt to offer the reader a framework for evaluating both current and future figures of the human, I will be guided in this book by a threefold taxonomy. As with all such taxonomies it is a bad master, but nevertheless it remains a good servant. I purposefully draw it not from the immediate context of the 'postlinguistic' French philosophical scene, nor from the death of man and antihumanism which contemporary thought rejects, for some comparisons between contemporary accounts only take shape when we gain a little more historical altitude and dare to strike out beyond the twentieth century.

In order to edge towards a comparative critique of contemporary trans-formations of the human it is meet to begin by considering the peculiar phenomenon (we might almost say 'fetish') of the *homo* or *animal* epi-thet.[51] The history of Western thought is littered (not to say polluted) with a string of adjectival adjuncts to the Latin noun *animal* (or *homo*) and its Greek equivalent *zoon*, claiming to discern and isolate this or that qual-ity of humanity that sets it apart from the other 'lower' animal species, and promising to yield the secret of 'what makes us human'.[52] The phe-nomenon of the *homo* epithet can be subdivided into three tendencies:[53]

substance, capacity and relation.[54] In each of these three guises its function is to identify a trait or property of humanity that distinguishes it from the nonhuman, either in terms of a human specificity (a descriptive difference with no necessary ethical or ontological implications) or human uniqueness (a property that sets humanity apart from the nonhuman in a qualitative way).[55]

The first group of *homo* epithets seek to locate human specificity in human substance, either in the material of the human body or in the form which that material takes. The definition of humanity as the 'featherless biped' falls into this category,[56] along with *Homo erectus* (upright man) and Thomas Aquinas's view in the *Summa Theologica* that bipedalism befits humans as 'a posture more suited to the contemplation of the heavens'.[57] More contemporary examples of routing human specificity through a substance would be Jean-Pierre Changeux's 'neuronal man'[58] and Joseph LeDoux's affirmation that 'you are your synapses',[59] which I shall discuss at length in Chapter 3. A focus on human specificity in terms of substance can also be seen in modern and contemporary emphases on the importance of embodiment.

A second group of *homo* epithets – *Homo habilis* (skilful man), *Homo faber* (man the creator) and *Homo sapiens* (wise man) – distinguish humanity in terms of particular capacities, as does Heidegger's reading of Aristotle in terms of a *zoon logon echon* ('animal with a rational principle', or 'speaking animal') and its Latin cognate *animal rationale*.[60] In the Christian tradition, appeals to rationality as the basis of the *imago dei* abound. For Anselm the mind is 'the true image of that being which, through its memory and intelligence and love, is united in an ineffable Trinity',[61] and the contemporary theologian J. Wentzel van Huyssteen considers 'quintessentially human' qualities to be the capacity to function 'biologically as a centre of self-awareness, identity, and moral responsibility'.[62] Variations on the capacity for speech or reason include the *animal symbolicum* of Ernst Cassirer[63] or Friedrich Schiller's adumbration of *Homo ludens* (playful man)[64] further developed by Johan Huizinga in the book of that name,[65] and Hans Jonas's *Homo pictor* (man the artist).[66] In each of these cases, the most salient quality of humanity is thought to be found in a capacity which, it is claimed, humanity alone possesses.

Finally, a third category of *homo* epithets discerns human specificity not, in the first instance, in a unique human substance or capacity, but in how humans relate to each other or to the nonhuman, often stemming from the conviction that 'there is a persistent Augustinian/Cartesian error made when we presume that human uniqueness necessarily lies within us, rather than between us'.[67] This emphasis emerges in Aristotle's *zoon politikon* (the political or state-building animal),[68] as well as the *Homo oeo-*

conomicus of John Stuart Mill[69] and the *Homo socius* of sociologists Peter Berger and Thomas Luckmann.[70] Gabriel Marcel's *Homo viator* (pilgrim man, or man in search of God)[71] can also be considered a variation on this relational theme. In theological accounts of the *imago dei* motif, the most famous twentieth-century proponent of the relational view is Karl Barth, for whom the image of God 'does not consist in anything man is or does' but resides in humanity being a 'counterpart to God', such that 'the image is the relationship itself, not the capacity for relationship'.[72] A cursory consideration of this threefold taxonomy reveals that the categories are not mutually exclusive. *Homo sapiens* gains its capacity for abstract reasoning (function) from its highly developed pre-frontal cortex and temporal lobes (substance), and no animal can entertain relationships unless it has the capacity to do so. The three categories are not sorting boxes, but they are nevertheless indicative of real tendencies both in the history of Western thought and, as we shall also see, in contemporary French philosophy as well.

These three broad and flexible emphases can be deployed in a number of different ways. Perhaps the bluntest way is to designate one substance, one capacity or one relation as the sole bearer of human distinctiveness: humans may share many characteristics in common with other entities, but what it means to be 'properly human' is to be understood in terms of one particular determinate trait. Throughout this book I call such a gatekeeper property a 'host' (host substance, host capacity or host relation). Any such 'host' is that without which, according to a given account, there is no humanity, and that by virtue of which, if a being possesses or enjoys it, that being is considered human. The term is a development of the notion of the 'host property', taken from John E. Coons and Patrick M. Brennan's history of the idea of equality in Western thought,[73] where it denotes 'some uniquely important characteristic' the possession of which grants to its bearer moral equality.[74] As the peg on which human dignity is hung, Coons and Brennan's 'host property' is a contemporary equivalent of the more classically articulated *locus humanus*, that quality or property of humans which, among all their other qualities and properties, distinguishes them from all other entities. Each of capacity, substance or relation can act as a 'host' of the human when it is taken to be the one defining characteristic of human uniqueness. A particular theoretical discourse can also act as a 'host' when it is considered to be the one non-metaphorical form of expression that gives access to the human as such, and by comparison with which all the other ways of speaking about human beings are secondary and figurative. One example of a host discourse would be Jean-Pierre Changeux's *Neuronal Man, Homo neuronalis*. For Changeux, the discipline of cognitive neuroscience unveils the human as such, the human degree zero, whereas all other discourses (including mathematics[75]) are either derivative or metaphorical in contrast to the direct and literal language of cognitive neuroscience.

Finally, the capacity–substance–relation taxonomy can also function as a means for the rejection of any particular determinate 'host'. This is achieved by making one of the aspects reflexive, turning it into a 'meta' version of itself. For example, rather than identifying human specificity with a particular capacity, it can be argued that humans uniquely have a capacity to change and alter their capacities: a capacity for self-transcendence or a capacity for freedom from determinate capacities. The idea that the distinctive human trait is the lack of fixed capacities and the possibility for self-transformation has a long tradition in the West, commonly accepted to begin with Cappadocian Father Gregory of Nyssa's (c. 335–395) *On The Making of Man*. For Gregory it is humanity's very indeterminacy and 'incomprehensibility of essence' that renders it, uniquely among all the animals, *in imago dei*.[76] The theme is later given a humanist twist by Pico della Mirandola who proclaims in the work known as the *Oration on the Dignity of Man* that when God made humanity 'there was nothing among His archetypes from which He could mould a new progeny'[77] and so the human is a 'creature of indeterminate image',[78] addressed as 'constrained by no limits' and 'shaper of yourself',[79] having in its possession 'every sort of seed and all sprouts of every kind of life'.[80] For Giorgio Agamben Pico's *Oration* is seen as offering a 'definition of man by his lack of a face', and Agamben claims that its 'central thesis' is that man 'can have neither archetype nor proper place'.[81]

This apophaticism dons more modern garb in Sartre's insistence that for humans uniquely, existence precedes essence and the human is distinguished because it 'is not what it is',[82] as well as in Nietzsche's characterisation of humanity as 'the unfinished animal'.[83] We could also place in this category those posthumanisms that emphasise the human capacity to enhance itself and give itself new capacities. As this final example illustrates, it is not only capacities that can be turned into second-degree or self-reflexive indicators of human distinctiveness. As well as the capacity to change capacities, humans can be thought as uniquely able to alter and transform their substance, or rather than being in a set of fixed relations with others of their kind and with the features of their habitat, humans can be thought unique in being able to change and manipulate their relations. We will encounter this self-reflexivity particularly in relation to Malabou and Serres. These three categories of substance, capacity and relation will provide our preliminary orientation in the transformations of the human in contemporary French thought. Pointing out the dangers and shortcomings of various 'hosts' along with their reflexive variants will be a regular feature of the analysis in the chapters that follow. By undertaking the read-ings contained in this book in relation to this threefold schema I hope to show that contemporary French thought is reworking, not reinventing the human. The old emphases are still there, but they have been transposed and sometimes hidden in new configurations in which various 'hosts' still vie with each other for primacy.

The argument

Armed with the emphases of substance–capacity–relation and equipped with the notion of host properties, this book weaves the accounts of the human that emerge in Badiou, Meillassoux, Malabou, Serres and Latour together into one unfolding narrative of the new figures of the human in contemporary French thought. The reader will not need to be reminded that these five philosophers have not been chosen for their resemblance to each other! Quite to the contrary, I have chosen to discuss these think-ers and not others in order to plot a particular course through the three emphases of capacity, substance and relation, and to open possibilities of combining them.[84]

The first chapter probes the limits of Badiou's 'formalised inhuman-ism'. It argues that it is wrong to characterise the figure of the human that emerges in Badiou's thought as radically new, and traces its similarities with other figures which Badiou rejects. For both Badiou and his antago-nists, the human is irreducibly composite: it cannot be what it is with-out a constitutive relation to an instance of inhumanity or nonhumanity outside itself. Badiou's split anthropology of the 'human animal' and the 'immortal' faces one major structural and ethical problem, which arises in the way in which he seeks to understand the relation between the animal and immortal: he makes fidelity to a truth, and therefore humanity in its full sense, contingent upon an individual's possession of what he calls 'the one and only uniquely human capacity' (*AMP* 111/*MetP* 97–8), namely the capacity for affirmative thought. Such thought functions for Badiou as a host capacity, a boundary marker or a gatekeeper of the uniqueness of humanity among animal, organic and non-organic entities. Despite attempting several creative ways to overcome the problem of this host capacity in Badiou, it remains a thorn in the flesh of his claim that 'several times in its brief existence, every human animal is granted the chance to incorporate itself into the subjective present of a truth' (*LM* 536 n11/*LW* 514 n11).

Chapter 2 continues exploring the contemporary permutations of the host capacity account of humanity with a close reading of Quentin

Meillassoux's transformation of the human. The place of the human in Meillassoux's thought is complex. On the one hand, he maintains a strong and consistent rhetoric of anti-anthropocentrism, and his fundamental philosophical project can be summarised as an attempt to break free from what he sees as the anthropocentric straitjacket of Kantian and post-Kantian 'correlationist' thought. On the other hand, however, Meillassoux evinces (especially in his work subsequent to *After Finitude* and nowhere more strikingly than in 'The Divine Inexistence') a very high view of the human indeed, not hesitating to call his philosophy a humanism and asserting the value of the human as ultimate. I seek to show, in the first half of the chapter, that Meillassoux's humanism is less humanist than he thinks and, in the second part, that his attempt to disengage from anthropocentrism is more anthropocentric than he thinks. As in the case of Badiou, it is Meillassoux's insistence on tethering the value of humanity to its capacity for thought that lies at the root of many of the problems of his anthropology, and it is in an attempt to move beyond this host capacity approach that I consider, in Chapter 3, the thought of Catherine Malabou.

The transition from Badiou and Meillassoux to Malabou leads us away from a host capacity and to a host substance, namely the human brain. Chapter 3 argues that Malabou manages to avoid a host capacity account of the human by laying out, in her reading of Hegel, a notion of plasticity not as a uniquely human trait but as the possible transformation of all traits. This position harbours an irreducible ambiguity, however, between an escape from the host capacities approach and its hyperbolisation, and according to this latter reading what Malabou offers us is nothing more than a host meta-capacity. Nevertheless, her notion of plasticity does allow her to develop a figure of the human that is universal, material, monist and immanent to itself. In the second half of Chapter 3 I explore Malabou's determination to initiate a new plastic encounter between philosophy and neuroscience, eschewing both the 'cognitivist' position of neuroscientist Jean-Pierre Changeux and the 'Continental' resistance to neuroscience of Paul Ricœur, in order to elaborate her own 'neuronal materialism' (*QF* 162/*WSD* 69) in terms of what she calls 'destructive plasticity'. In an attempt to develop this neuronal materialism in a way that avoids plasticity becoming one more defunct metaphor of the human, I offer a reading of Malabou's self not as a metaphor but as a movement or tension of metaphoricity.

Chapter 4 turns to the question of human identity over time in Malabou. After setting out the stakes of her recent work on epigenesis in *Avant demain* I point out some shortcomings of her previous accounts of identity over time, particularly in relation to the famous case of Phineas

Gage and her experience of her own grandmother's Alzheimer's disease. Malabou's account of epigenesis provides us with a powerful way to re-read this earlier work. Although she moves away from a host capacity account of the human she is – at least in her work prior to *Avant demain* – trapped in a paradigm which forces her to regard cerebral matter as the 'host substance' of human identity and personhood: just as rational thought acted as a gatekeeper of humanity for Badiou and Meillassoux, personal memory as it is encoded in the individual's brain is the gatekeeper of personhood and identity for Malabou. However, in her recent work she elaborates what she calls an 'epigenesis of the real' (*AD* 261) according to which epigenesis and hermeneutics are extensions of each other, breaking down the division between nature and culture. I draw out the implications of this exciting recent move, using Paul Ricœur's account of narrative identity as a sounding board for what I call Malabou's eco-synaptic self-hood: a self understood neither wholly in internal (cerebral) nor utterly in external (narrative) terms.

With Michel Serres's universal humanism (Chapter 5) the argument returns to the question of host capacities in order, finally, to go beyond it. Rather than Badiou's and Meillassoux's determinate capacity for thought and rather than Malabou's meta-capacity of plasticity, Serres seeks to elaborate a figure of the human that accommodates both determinate qualities (like Badiou and Meillassoux) and de-differentiation (like Malabou). This is judged to be the most adequate way of dealing with capacities encountered thus far, because it marries singularity and determinacy with genericity and plurality, yielding neither an undifferentiated and abstract notion of humanity nor a diversity of individuals with nothing in common. The second half of the chapter explores how Serres develops further the continuity between epigenetics and hermeneutics which Malabou begins to elaborate in *Avant demain*. Humanity is best understood, for Serres, as part of the 'Great Story' (*Grand Récit*) of the universe, a story not only about but also told by the natural world in a way that emphasises the continuity between 'human' language and 'nonhuman' processes. This insistence upon continuity between the human and the nonhuman also positions Serres very differently to Badiou, Meillassoux and Malabou, who all continue to assume that humanity inhabits a meaningless and indifferent universe, and continue to maintain that to think otherwise is anthropocentric. The combination of Serres's Great Story and his introduction of the two figures of multi-coloured Harlequin and all-white Pierrot gives him a multi-modal account of humanity (capacities plus narrative), and this makes the figure of the human that emerges from his work richer, as well as more situated in its landscape and its history, than in the accounts considered in previous chapters. There is, however, a danger that Serres's

Great Story becomes a 'host story' for his account of the human, forcing all humans into a single narrative mould in the same way that a host capacity or a host substance routes all discourse about the human through one single characteristic or quality. It is in order to resist this tendency that we turn in the final chapter to Bruno Latour.

Chapter 6 considers the figure of the human that emerges in Bruno Latour's *An Inquiry into Modes of Existence* and his 'Facing Gaia' lectures. Like the other thinkers discussed, Latour neither repeats nor discards previous notions of humanity but translates them in a gesture that can be traced all the way back to his doctoral work on the theologian of demythologisation Rudolf Bultmann. In his attempts to elaborate a figure of the human that follows neither the structure nor the emancipation narrative of modernity, Latour (like Serres) develops a multi-modal approach. The human is an amalgam of multiple modes of existence, and cannot be isolated within, or adequately narrated in, any single one. This dispersal mitigates the danger of Serres's singular Great Story acting as a host narrative of humanity. In addition, Latour avoids the problems inherent in a host capacity approach by distributing both capacities and substance across human and nonhuman actors in unatomisable collectivities. Whereas the host capacity and host substance approaches seek to understand the human by looking within, Latour insists that the human only becomes comprehensible when we look outside and around. His 2013 Gifford Lectures both develop and challenge themes from the Modes of Existence project, reasserting the centrality of the human now in the new form of the 'Earthbound', a non-modern *anthropos* defined in terms of its limits and its multiple attachments to its world.

This book goes searching in contemporary French thought for figures of humanity no longer in thrall to the death of man. What does it find? The human remains.

Chapter 1

Alain Badiou: Formalised Inhumanism

L'homme est un animal enfermé à l'extérieur de sa cage. Il s'agite hors de soi.
Valéry, *Œuvres complètes*[1]

For Alain Badiou the twentieth century was 'haunted by the idea of changing man, of creating a new man' (*S* 20/*Cen* 8) with communism and fascism, humanism and antihumanism each offering its vision of a transformed humanity. At the beginning of the twenty-first century Badiou offers us his own account of transformation that both remains (or so he claims) within a materialist frame and yet dusts off and reworks motifs seemingly from a bygone religious age: immortality, grace, resurrection and miracle. If, as these terms already hint, Badiou's reworking of the human is not a simple case of either accepting or rejecting a historical legacy, then neither is his relation to materialism. Along with Quentin Meillassoux, Badiou is the contemporary French thinker most commonly identified with the 'new materialist' tendency in contemporary thought,[2] but as we shall see in this chapter he insists on a double understanding of materialism: Badiou introduces two very different figures of the human, and qualifies both as materialist. The well-known distinction in *Logics of Worlds* between the 'democratic materialism' (for which there are only bodies and languages) and 'materialist dialectics' (for which there are bodies, languages and truths) shapes Badiou's anthropology in terms of the twin figures of the 'human animal' and the 'immortal', but we shall discover that the relation between these two figures is far from straightforward.

The first half of this chapter introduces these two major figures of Badiou's anthropology, showing how they relate to the irreducibility of the inhuman in his formalised and generic account of humanity. Although

Badiou does demonstrate how materialist humanity can be transformed, his account is more continuous with traditional figures of the human than is often acknowledged in the literature on his work.[3] In the second half of the chapter the focus tightens from a discussion of the importance of the inhuman Idea in Badiou's anthropology to the question of the relation between the human animal and what Badiou calls 'living as an immortal'. How is a human animal incorporated into a truth or an Idea, and how is that incorporation best described? The relation between the human animal and the immortal seems uncompromisingly to emphasise both the passivity of grace and the activity of heroism, and a number of commentators have tried in various ways to square the circle of grace and heroism in Badiou's account of the subject. At the heart of this difficulty is what Badiou calls 'the one and only uniquely human capacity' (*AMP* 111/*MetP* 97–8) for affirmative thought. In the final section of the chapter I show why this capacity is not merely a local problem for Badiou's account of the human but a structural one: in other words, the problem is not with thought per se, but with the very idea that Badiou routes his account of the human through a determinate host capacity.[4]

Badiou's figures of the human

Badiou transforms the figure of the human in a way that is both ancient and contemporary. The fault line between the understanding of humanity which Badiou considers inadequate (which belongs to what in *Logics of Worlds* he calls 'democratic materialism') and that which he commends (belonging to the 'materialist dialectic') is not temporal: he is not arguing for a modern or contemporary account of the human as opposed to an ancient or outdated one. The fault line upon which he insists runs through the history of philosophy parallel to time's arrow, dividing Plato from Aristotle, Voltaire from Rousseau, Sartre from Foucault and Althusser. In order to understand Badiou's own refiguring of the human we first need to appreciate the nature of this fault line, and why Badiou considers it to be the most important factor in understanding the place and possibilities of the human today.

From classical humanism to democratic materialism

Throughout the Western tradition as it is reconstructed in Badiou's published work and unpublished seminars, humanity has been understood constitutively to require a relation with, or incorporation into, something other than itself. In other words, there is no 'pure' humanity without some irreducible relation to the nonhuman. Humanity is what it is not, and is not what it is,[5] and the human is always irreducibly and simultaneously 'human+'[6] (in that it requires a constitutive relation to the nonhuman or the inhuman in order to be 'human' at all) and 'human-' (in that it is never entire unto itself, because it lacks in itself this relation to the inhuman or the nonhuman which makes it what it is). We can see this very clearly in the comments Badiou makes about the figure of the human in what he calls classical humanism.

The picture of the human that emerges from classical Western humanism, Badiou argues, is reliant upon God and irreducibly complicit with the divine. Classical humanism is the 'knotting together' (*nouage*) of God and Man,[7] and he insists that we have no right to continue speaking of 'humanity', classically understood, without God. The very concept of humanity in classical humanism relies for its coherence on the God of whom the human is a microcosm, and the human is only human insofar as it is convoked by and potentially incorporated into the divine, thereby fully realising for the first time its true humanity. Badiou argues that this structure – according to which humanity is not what it is apart from relation to that which is outside itself – runs through the modern Western tradition. We might call it a 'grammar' of the human, in the sense of a structural rule governing the composition of humanity, whatever happens to be the particular 'nonhuman' or 'inhuman' to which humanity is constitutively related. Badiou sums up the history of this grammar in *The Century* in a breathtaking tour that advances, by his own admission, 'at the speed of a historic steam engine' (*S* 236/*Cen* 167). Descartes requires God as the guarantor of truth, and it is truth that 'ties God and man together' ('fait nœud de l'homme et de Dieu') (*S* 235/*Cen* 166). In Kant's critical philosophy, the link with God is found in the limits of human reason: 'Man has no purely theoretical access to the supersensible. The Good, and not the True, opens man to God' (*S* 236/*Cen* 167). With Hegel, the destiny of humanity is to be the absolute becoming of subjective spirit, and this is also what completes the self-realisation of God. For Hegel, Badiou argues, the knot between God and man is immanent: 'God is the process of a supposedly complete man' (*S* 236/*Cen* 167). Finally, for Comtean positivism the human–divine knot is tied more tightly than ever: God is humanity itself, a humanity that is re-baptised as the 'great Being' (*S* 237/*Cen* 168). In each of these cases there is an undecidability between 'man' and 'God', between a divinisation of man and a humanisation of the divine. In summary, Badiou concludes: 'We should say that the essence of classical metaphysical humanism is the construction of a predicate which is undecidable between the human and the divine' (*S* 237/*Cen* 168).

The problems and the possibilities opened up by this undecidability come to the surface when the same tradition turns its back on God. The God of monotheism, Badiou argues, has been dead for at least two hundred years (*S* 234/*Cen* 166), and given the complicity of the human with the divine throughout the history of the modern West it is hardly surprising that any attempt to do away with the divine would also signal the end of the 'man of humanism'. Humanity cannot be thought in isolation – it cannot be what it is – without its relation to the divine. Adapting the anarchist motto 'neither God nor Master' Badiou insists on the intertwined fate of humanity and deity: the tradition must reconcile itself to retaining 'neither God nor Man' (*S* 234 n1/*Cen* 216 n53). Once more, there is no concept of humanity *simpliciter*; either man is intertwined with the divine or is not at all.

Slowing the pace of his whistle-stop tour, Badiou argues that the West's abandonment of God and of the 'passion for the real' which drove early twentieth-century attempts to 'change what is deepest in man' (*S* 21/*Cen* 9) left it faced, in the mid-twentieth century, with the choice between Sartre's radical humanism in the 1958 'Questions of Method'[8] and Foucault's radical antihumanism from the final pages of *The Order of Things* (1966).[9] For Foucault and Sartre alike, humanity is not simply human; for Sartre it becomes more than human and for Foucault it becomes less. For Sartre, humanity is its own foundation (*fondement*) and the only possible foundation (*S* 241/*Cen* 172); it is the historical creator of its own absolute essence, and human consciousness is absolute freedom. Given that absolute creation and absolute freedom have been traditionally understood as attributes of God alone, Badiou concludes that, for Sartre, 'godless man must take the place of the dead God' (*S* 239/*Cen* 169). The essence of man becomes the ultimately unrealisable project to occupy the place left vacant by the now absent God. In other words, deprived of the reality of God, humanity continues to think itself in irreducible relation to the divine, but this relation is now in the mode of seeking to occupy the place of the absent deity. It is a usurpation which forever remains a necessary impossibility.

Despite his rejection of classical humanism, Sartre keeps the fundamental grammar according to which the human, in order to be itself, requires something outside itself. Without communism and its project of complete equality, humanity for Sartre 'is an animal species of no more interest than ants or pigs' (*S* 246/*Cen* 175; see also *Circ4* 135), and no more interesting than any animal species living in a collectivity (Sem06–7). We also note that, for Badiou's Sartre, the idea of communism itself occupies the place of God in one particular and important way: in raising Sartre's porcine humanity above its uninteresting animal existence it provides the same function achieved by a relation to the divine in theological humanism: it is that which, though not itself human, is nevertheless required for the human to be what it is.

The second mid-century response to the disappearance of God is Foucault's radical antihumanism, for which humanity stands on the brink of its own disappearance (*S* 246–7/*Cen* 172). Although Badiou does not quote from it directly, he clearly has in mind the famous passage from the final section of *The Order of Things* in which Foucault proclaims that 'man is an invention of recent date. And one perhaps nearing its end.'[10] In contrast to Sartre's humanity which, *per impossibile*, occupies the empty space left by God, Foucault argues that there is a second empty space soon to be left by humanity itself, an imminent disappearance which means that '[i]t is no longer possible to think in our day other than in the void left by man's disappearance' (*S* 241–2/*Cen* 171). For Foucault, those who persist in proclaiming the reign or the liberation of man deserve only to be the butt of 'philosophical laughter' (*S* 242/*Cen* 171). Nevertheless, once more the grammar of the human is left unchanged by Foucault. As we saw in the case of Sartre, the principle that humanity cannot be thought without that which is exterior to it remains constant also in Foucault's thought. Sartre seeks to transform the '+' of 'human+' from God to communism while Foucault, refusing any substitute for the absent God, finds himself renouncing the idea of humanity as well, a humanity once more mirroring God this time in the mode of an absence mirroring an absence. Both Sartre and Foucault ask the question 'what becomes of man without God?' (*S* 242/*Cen* 171), and they both agree that 'man, if he is not the infinite programme of his own absoluteness, deserves only to disappear' (*S* 247/ *Cen* 175). The programme of thinking humanity without God leads either down the path of man as his own 'historical creator and his own absolute essence' or 'the man of inhuman beginning', of the discontinuity that marks the end of humanity (*S* 246–7/*Cen* 174). In neither case does the twentieth century offer any possibility of thinking the human *simpliciter*, without any relation to that which it is not.

Today, however, in the opening decades of the twenty-first century, Badiou notes that both radical humanism and radical antihumanism have withered on the vine and what we are left with is the sorry spectacle of an eviscerated humanity both without God and also without a project or possibility in the absence of God: lacking that without which it cannot be itself. It is important to recognise that, for Badiou, this simple humanity stripped of the 'vitality' of deity (*S* 246/*Cen* 174) is no humanity in the full sense of the term at all; humanity without the divine, humanity without a project is not humanity properly speaking but mere 'human animality' with its mode of being of 'democratic materialism' and its reduction of man to his animal body (*S* 246/*Cen* 174). Humanity is not what it is: in the absence of the divine or the infinite project – which for Sartre sets man the impossible task of occupying the place of the divine – humanity is not humanity but 'quite simply, a species' (*S* 246/*Cen* 174). Those who still hold to an idea of humanity by itself, without any relation to that which it is not, Badiou notes, are the Thermidorian 'new philosophers', the authors of *Why We Are Not Nietzscheans* (*S* 247/*Cen* 175).[11] If we join with them in rejecting the twin programmes of radical humanism and radical anti-humanism, we will also ineluctably find ourselves with the figure of the human as just one more animal species, and with a mixture of mysticism and sensual gratification, the blend of universal sex and oriental wisdom that Badiou witheringly calls the regime of 'Tibetan pornography' (*Circ2* 92/*Pol* 139).

So at the beginning of the twenty-first century the death of God has in fact led neither to the (radical humanist) exaltation of humanity as its own foundation and project, nor to the (radical antihumanist) rupture marking the transition from humanity to the inhuman, but to the damp squib of an essential animality which emasculates and denatures the human. If we search for the human today we find only that 'the odour of the animal suffocates him' (Sem01–2; my translation). Badiou's verdict on this species-humanity is, to say the least, unflattering. Even allowing for a splash of rhetorical colour, if we say that Badiou has little time for the human animal we need be in no fear of having overstated our case. Recalling Sartre's condemnation of porcine humanity, Badiou writes that this 'systematic killer' pursues 'interests of survival and satisfaction neither more nor less estimable than those of moles or tiger beetles' (*E* 80–1/*Eth* 58), while having the distinction of being among all the animals 'the most obstinately dedicated to the cruel desires of his own power'. A '"featherless biped" whose charms are not obvious' (*E* 27–8/*Eth* 12), humanity is a 'crafty, cruel and obstinate animal' (ASR 237) who, in 'the simple reality of his living being', is 'contemptible' (*E* 28/*Eth* 12).

Furthermore, this contemporary species-humanity comes hand in hand with an 'animal humanism' that reduces the human to its victimary body and enshrines as its only quality its capacity to be pitied: humanity is defined in animal humanism as 'the being who is capable of recognizing himself as a victim' (*E* 12/*Eth* 10). Animal humanism equates man with what Badiou calls his 'animal substructure', the 'humanity-' that supports the superstructure of a relation with the divine in classical humanism or the infinite project of communism in Sartre's radical humanism. Badiou, it is important to note, is not denying that animality is a necessary condition of humanity; he is arguing that it is not sufficient. Of course he is not denying that 'humanity is an animal species', he insists, and it is by all means 'mortal and predatory', but 'neither of these attributes can distinguish humanity within the world of the living' (*E* 13/*Eth* 11). This animal humanism is all that is meant by 'humanism' traditionally understood, and this, for Badiou, is the great humanist swindle: the more 'humanist' we are (in the sense of seeing nothing in the human but its animal nature and rejecting antihumanist formalisation or its insistence on the inhuman in the human), the more we dehumanise the human and reduce it to a quivering and impulsive animal; worst of all, we are proud of our own evisceration and inoculated against any true humanism. Winner loses.[12]

Too much has sometimes been made of Badiou's dismissal of the human animal. It is important to note that what he finds contemptible in the human animal is not its animality per se but that it is domesticated and lacking a programme. It offers no resistance to the forces that would seek to manipulate and control it, which for Badiou are primarily the forces of market capitalism. What should we do, Badiou asks in *The Century*, about the fact that genetic engineering and other scientific advances mean that finally we can now make a new humanity? As long as there is no project, he warns, it is the logic of profit that alone will step in to answer that question (*S* 22/*Cen* 9). 'Animal' is that which does not resist, which adheres to no programme but lets itself drift on the currents of its own immediate physical desires and the plans of those who, for their own reasons, have designs upon it. The human animal has therefore no possibility of self-surpassing (*RE* 53/*PM* 45). It is what it is, and in being what it is it is no longer human. What is more, animal humanism has built into itself an immunity against the possibility of being other than what it is, for its great argument is that 'the political will of the overhuman (or of the new type of man, or of radical emancipation) has engendered nothing but inhumanity' (*S* 250–1/*Cen* 177). The world of the human animal is composed exhaustively of bodies and languages in a mode of being that the Badiou of *Logics of Worlds* brands as 'democratic materialism', an existence summed up by the desire for physical survival and comfort, and the endless communication and exchange of ephemeral opinions. In *Plato's Republic* he describes animality as freedom without a norm, freedom 'reduced to the compulsory gratification of personal desires through the objects available on the market' (*RP* 63/*PR* 274). The great maxim of democratic materialism is 'Live with no Idea' ('Vis sans Idée') (*S* 250/*Cen* 177; translation altered), or 'let's loyally go about the business and transactions of the city, let's keep the shop doors open' (Sem03–4; my translation). It reduces the dreams and horizons of humanity to the desire for physical survival trusting that, all the while, 'ecology and bioethics will provide for our "correct" development as pigs or ants' (*S* 246/*Cen* 175). What is therefore at stake in Badiou's human animality is not a denigration of nonhuman life as such, but its impossibility of resistance, its yielding to a future that is nothing but the logical, controlled and inexorable unfolding of the market-governed present.

Formalised inhumanism

Faced with the passive impotence of this human animality and its failed attempt to resuscitate a disembowelled classical humanism, Badiou turns his attention to the need to overcome godless animality: 'Let us call our philosophical task, on the shores of the new century, and against the animal humanism that besieges us, that of a *formalized inhumanism*' (*S* 251/*Cen* 178). In this call for a new inhumanism Badiou is following the Nietzsche who defined the human as that which must be overcome:

> 'God is dead' means that man is dead too. Man, the last man, the dead man, is what must be overcome for the sake of the overman. What is the overman? Quite simply man without God. Man as he is thinkable outside of any relation to the divine. The overman decides undecidability, thus fracturing the humanist predicate. (*S* 238/*Cen* 168)

The innovation of Badiou's own account of the human, then, is to 'fracture' the necessity of thinking the human in relation to God. But it does not, for all that, challenge the idea that humanity can only be thought as constitutively related to something outside itself. Like Sartre before him, Badiou does not in fact think humanity *simpliciter*, but humanity as irreducibly related to the inhuman Idea. So whereas there is a fundamental change in the 'content' of humanity (it is no longer to be thought in relation to the divine but to the inhuman Idea), its fundamental grammar (it is irreducibly related to that which is other than itself) remains constant. For Badiou it is only if we 'begin from the inhuman' that we can envisage the overhuman which, following Nietzsche, is nothing other than the human pure and simple (*S* 250/*Cen* 177–8).

The 'inhuman' to which Badiou is referring sinks its roots deep into the Western tradition, drawing upon an Aristotelian motif. In the seminar[13] 'Qu'est-ce que vivre?' ('What is it to live?') from 2003–4, Badiou frames a discussion of Aristotle in terms of the passage from a 'two' to a 'three', the passage that marks the distinction later expressed in *Logics of Worlds* between democratic materialism and Badiou's own materialist dialectics (Sem03–4). The distinction emerges in the course of a discussion of two passages from Aristotle. The first situates the Athenian firmly as the philosopher of 'life' and characterises the human animal as a living being. It is the famous claim at the beginning of the *Politics* that humanity is the political animal (*zoon politikon*). Badiou understands this to mean that, for Aristotle, the human is political *as an animal*, not in a way that transcends or transfigures its animality: the political is not a supplement to animality; it is the mode of that animality. The political animal engages in politics, as it participates constructively in the affairs of the city rather than seeking any truth beyond the circulation of ideas and opinions within the polis. In Badiou's reading of Aristotle, the human is not an animal that contingently happens to engage in politics but an animal whose singular life is in its essence political: for humanity, to live is to live in the *polis*, and to live the good life is to live politically. In the light of the *zoon politikon*, then, Aristotle's politics is all about finding an adequate language for the political being of the human animal. The humanity of the *Politics* is human animality, existing in the mode of democratic materialism.

The second passage stands in stark contrast to the claim that humans are political animals. In the *Nicomachean Ethics* (X, 7) Aristotle writes:

> If the intellect, then, is something divine compared with the human being, the life in accordance with it will also be divine compared with human life. But we ought not to listen to those who exhort us, because we are human, to think of human things, or because we are mortal, to think of mortal things. We ought rather to take on immortality as much as possible, and do all that we can to live in accordance with the highest element within us; for even if its bulk is small, in its power and value it far exceeds everything.[14]

As the one who 'takes on immortality as much as possible', the human is no longer rightly described as a political animal. Why not? Because if there is one thing immortals care precious little about it is politics understood as the circulation of opinions within the city. To live as an immortal in this way is to live with a certain essential immobility, like Aristotle's divine Unmoved Mover. Whereas the political animal circulates within society interminably exchanging language and opinions, the immortality which Aristotle's human 'takes on [. . .] as much as possible' moves all things while itself remaining unmoved and unmoving. In the 2003–4 seminar Badiou calls these unmoving exceptions to the circulation of bodies and languages 'principles'; in *Being and Event* they are called 'truths', and in *Logics of Worlds* they are called 'Ideas'.

In a revealing passage from *Logics of Worlds*, Badiou argues that 'attaining the True is the calling of the immortal part of men, of the inhuman excess that lies in man' (*LM* 533/*LW* 511). By equating the immortal with the inhuman and the inhuman with an excess in man Badiou is arguing that the human cannot be what it is without being more than it is and without being other than it is: 'man is the species that needs the idea in order to dwell reasonably in its own world' (*PE* 45; my translation). It is by neglecting the inhuman in the human, Badiou continues in *Logics of Worlds*, that contemporary scepticism reduces man to the animal. It is clear: for Badiou the decisive anthropological distinction is not between the human and the animal, but between the human animal and that 'highest element within us', the unmoving, inhuman Idea.

Badiou insists on the inhuman within the human, and on the necessity of the inhuman to any humanity 'worthy of the name' (*LM* 534/*LW* 511). It is because of this necessity, he insists, that Lyotard argues that human rights are the rights of the infinite, 'For humanity, to the extent that the inhuman is a creative part of it, is not reducible to animality' (*RE* 47/*PM* 41–2). It is the inhumanity of the idea that opens up a gap, hole or fracture in human 'nature', that opens the human as that which 'does not yet exist but must become' (*RE* 47–8/*PM* 42). Humanity as a 'natural totality' does not exist, Badiou insists, for it is only ever a series of victories over its animal nature[15] in the name of the Idea. The inhuman is not the opposite or the negation of the human; quite to the contrary, it is the condition of possibility 'of every human – which is to say inhuman – life' (*LM* 534/*LW* 511):

> It is impossible to possess a concept of what is 'human' without dealing with the (eternal, ideal) inhumanity which authorizes man to incorporate himself into the present under the sign of the trace of what changes. If one fails to recognize the effects of these traces, in which the inhuman commands humanity to exceed its being-there, it will be necessary, in order to maintain a purely animalistic, pragmatic notion of the human species, to annihilate both these traces and their infinite consequences. (*LM* 533/*LW* 511)

Badiou sees this fault line running through the history of Western philosophy, dividing the humanity of the inhuman Idea from the human animal that lives with no idea. He sees it in the opposition between Rousseau's 'courage' and the 'humanitarian mediocrity' of Voltaire's 'we must cultivate our garden' (*S* 177/*Cen* 125); he sees echoes of Aristotle's 'live as an immortal' in Spinoza's beatitude and Nietzsche's overman (*PE* 149), as well as in Sartre's communism. In the light of such precedents it is potentially misleading to argue that 'Badiou is bringing about a significant transformation in the philosophical grammar for thinking about the human'.[16] It is in fact Badiou's grammar – if we are to understand by 'grammar' the structure and possibilities of combination of which his thought admits – that remains remarkably consonant with Aristotle's 'live as an immortal' and indeed remarkably consonant with the classical humanism for which man is unthinkable without God. In each case the human is understood as requiring an irreducible nonhuman or inhuman supplement in order to be what it is. What Badiou changes is not the grammar of the human but its content, for he claims to be articulating an account that is for the first time both atheistic and non-reductively materialistic.

Badiou's insistence on the irreducibility of the inhuman in the human raises a question: if the Idea is necessary for humanity as such, then in what sense is the idea inhuman? Badiou makes it abundantly clear that there are no other animals apart from human beings who can become immortal by being incorporated into an Idea. If the Idea is only ever received or instantiated by humans and by no other species, then why is it inhuman? If immortality is true human life (the argument of Sem03–4), then why is immortality inhuman? It is surely only inhuman if humanity is equated with human animality, in which case the idea is inhuman because it is universal and generic whereas human animality is particular and specific. In a section of 'What is love?' entitled 'Conditions of existence of human-ity', Badiou expresses humanity as 'H(x)', where x is one of the four truth procedures identified in *Being and Event* (politics, science, art and love). Humanity is the function of a truth, and there is no 'H' by itself; there is no humanity apart from its potential or actual relation to these procedures:

> By 'humanity' I mean that which provides support to the generic or truth procedures. There are four types of such procedures: science, politics, art and – precisely – love. Humanity can be attested if and only if there is (emancipatory) politics, (conceptual) science, (creative) art and love (not reduced to a mix of sentimentality and sexuality). Humanity is what sustains the infinite singularity of truths that fall within these types. Humanity is the historical body of truths. (*C* 258/*Con* 184)

If there is such a thing as humanity 'as such' it is as a virtual mixture of these four truth conditions and not a unitary humanity which precedes them: humanity as a fourfold product and not as a unitary cause. But Badiou nevertheless maintains that there is only one humanity, for every truth is indifferent to the particularities of its 'corporeal support': the sub-ject of a truth is always generic, and admits of no internal distinction of qualities. Whereas human animals take pleasure only in particularity, in the transitory fluctuations of the desires and drives that individuate them, overhumanity ('la surhumanité') abolishes particularity (*S* 277/*Cen* 161). It is the fascist New Man that is loaded with predicates – Nordic, Aryan, warrior . . . (*S* 99/*Cen* 66); in contrast the immortal subject of a truth takes on the universality and the genericity of the Idea itself. In a memorable turn of phrase Badiou insists that the truth sports no dreadlocks, nor an absence of dreadlocks (*Circ2* 121–2). He is firm in maintaining that humanity does not exist independently of a universal and generic truth: 'Humanity, prior to the real forms of egalitarian politics, simply does not exist, either as collective, or as truth, or as thought' (*C* 250/*Con* 175). This, in summary, is Badiou's 'formalized inhumanism': formalised because the Idea is formal, generic and universal, eschewing all particularity, and inhuman because without the generic and universal Idea there is no humanity at all, only human animality.

My intention in reconstructing Badiou's generic humanity has been to highlight a fundamental but often overlooked continuity between what he calls 'classical humanism' and his own formalised inhumanism. Whereas for classical humanism there is no humanity apart from God, for formalised inhumanism there is no humanity apart from the Idea. For both classical humanism and formalised inhumanism there is no humanity *simpliciter*, for humanity is the animal that is in excess of itself, that is non-linear, that does not develop smoothly within a closed and predictable system. There is a difficulty with this non-linear relation of the human to the inhuman for Badiou, however, and it is to that difficulty we now turn.

'every human animal is granted the chance . . .'

Badiou's reworking of the humanity+ motif from the history of Western thought is an important contemporary transformation of the figure of the human, but it faces a major theoretical and ethical problem. The problem arises in the way in which Badiou seeks to understand the relation between the human animal and the immortal subject: he makes fidelity to a truth, and therefore humanity in its full sense, contingent upon an individual's possession of the capacity for affirmative thought, and this capacity functions for Badiou as a boundary marker or gatekeeper of the uniqueness of humanity among animal, organic and non-organic entities. In this second section of the chapter I will explore the problem of the relation between the human animal and the immortal, along with several solutions that have been suggested to it. I will conclude by suggesting why all such solutions have so far failed.

Thought as the 'the one and only uniquely human capacity'

Like many theories of human specificity, the relationship Badiou draws between the human animal and the immortal Idea relies on the possession of a particular quality or capacity. In the history of Western anthropology, candidates for this specifically human capacity are many and varied, from humanity's uniquely upright posture through rationality and intelligence to the human capacity for playfulness.[17] In *Logics of Worlds* Badiou denies that language use is a distinctive human capacity. At the end of the discussion of Lacan's insistence that humanity is the animal that lives in (*habite*) language, Badiou argues that 'the gap [*béance*] that results from the lingual marking of bodies' (*LM* 505/*LW* 478) is by no means the last word on human specificity. Just such a gap can be observed, he notes, in the water turtle that swims up to the aquarium glass when Badiou approaches, its little flippers thrashing about, waiting until the intimidated or guilt-ridden philosopher throws in its food for the day (*LM* 505/*LW* 478).[18]

For Badiou the significant capacity for determining the specificity of the human is not language but thought, and he defines the human in terms of this capacity:

> Thought is the one and only uniquely human capacity, and thought, strictly speaking, is simply that act through which the human animal is seized and traversed by the trajectory of a truth. Thus a politics worthy of being interrogated by philosophy under the idea of justice is one whose unique general axiom is: people think, people are capable of truth. (*AMP* 111/*MetP* 97–8)

Badiou has more in his sights here than brute cognitive capacity, but certainly not less. It is a particular way of thinking that he intends, an 'affirmative thought' of 'singular truths' which make man 'the most resilient [*résistant*] and most paradoxical of animals' (*E* 33/*Eth* 16), the capacity to remain faithful to an immortal Idea in the face of changing appetites and desires. In his fidelity to an inhuman truth, 'man is a tissue of truths' (*E* 28/*Eth* 12). This routes the materialist dialectic through the uniquely human capacity for thought, introducing an irreducible anthropocentrism into Badiou's philosophy: politics is a matter of truths, and incorporation into a truth relies on the uniquely human capacity for thought. Politics, therefore, is a human affair.

In his *Badiou: A Philosophy of the New*, Ed Pluth tussles against this stubborn anthropocentrism in Badiou's thought. He quite rightly insists that, for Badiou, 'subject' is not a subset of 'human', and that nonhuman entities can be the subject of a truth. He draws attention, quite correctly, to the point that, for Badiou, the subject of an artistic truth can be a series of works of art (*E* 64/*Eth* 44). But if the subject can be nonhuman, Pluth goes on, how can we ascribe what Badiou says about subjects to such nonhuman entities? Badiou insists that subjects decide 'to relate henceforth to the situation from the perspective of its eventual supplement' and that they invent 'a new way of being and acting in the situation' (*E* 62/*Eth* 42). 'Does it make any sense at all to say that these works believe in a truth?' Pluth asks.[19] He squares the circle by offering to tighten Badiou's language a little: it is not subjects but the 'inhabitants of situations' who decide, and 'the subjectivation of inhabitants is required in order to bring about the presence of real change in a situation (as the subject proper)'.[20]

The subject then becomes what the inhabitants make. This is a helpful clarification of the relation between subject and thought, but as far as the present argument goes it does not help us. Whether it is the 'subject' or the 'inhabitant' who decides, being seized by a truth is still contingent on the host capacity for affirmative thought. In fact, even if we were to allow (perhaps through a carnivalesque splicing of Badiou's inhumanism with Bruno Latour's Actor Network Theory) that for Badiou works of art can indeed think, it would not solve the problem of thought as a host capacity because however entities such as artworks may or may not be incorporated into an Idea, when it comes to human animals the capacity for affirmative thought remains the shibboleth without which no incorporation is possible.

Before going on to point out more problems with Badiou's reliance on the capacity for affirmative thought I want to dispel two possible misconceptions to which the present discussion could give rise. First, it is important to stress that Badiou's appeal to affirmative thought does not resolve to a warmed-over *animal rationale*. In the 1991–2 Seminar on 'Politics' he insists that the Idea is not the property of humanity, but precisely the inhuman into which the human animal can be incorporated:

> Man as a thinking being is not what is specific to humanity (that would be a humanist discourse), but the figure of the inhumanity of man arrives in the becoming reflexive of the Idea. The Idea places this other approach under the metaphor of constellation, of the starry sky, i.e. as an exception to the human, at a sidereal distance, which leaves us at an infinite distance from the natural (Sem91–2; my translation)

The Idea can never be said to belong to humanity or to be its possession, for it is the human animal which is incorporated into an inhuman and eternal Idea or truth, and not the other way round. The human animal becomes immortal; the inhuman Idea does not become finite. Nevertheless, although the inhuman is not possessed or domesticated by the human, incorporation into the inhuman still rests upon the capacity for affirmative thought and, if inhumanity itself is not a property of the human, then the capacity to be incorporated into such inhumanity most certainly is. Even if we take Badiou's point about the difference between his own position and a traditional *animal rationale*, his figure of the human still rests upon a determinate capacity, functioning as a 'host capacity' of humanity. While those human animals incorporated into an immortal subject may possess many qualities and capacities contingently (an upright posture, language use, the ability to play . . .), for Badiou they possess the capacity for affirmative thought necessarily. Insofar as incorporation into an Idea necessarily passes through the capacity for affirmative thought, and given that immortal existence is for Badiou the full expression of humanity (as opposed to human animality), Badiou's figure of the human is rightly described as a 'host capacity' account.

The second clarification that needs to be made is that, in the quotation from *Metapolitics* above, Badiou stresses that 'people think' is not a fact of politics but an axiom, and the claim is not that all people do in fact hold themselves in fidelity to truths but that all people are capable of truth. The distinction is important because it begins to address the status in Badiou's anthropology of those whose capacity for affirmative thought is greatly impeded or non-existent, such as neonates or those with dementia or a severe mental disability. Perhaps, we might think, the axiomatic status of the capacity for truth means that Badiou is arguing we should treat all people *as if* they are potential subjects and not just 'contemptible' human animals? Badiou means nothing of the sort, however, which he makes very clear in his seminar from 1996–8 in which he insists that a theory of the subject (as opposed to a moral or psychological account of the subject) 'must admit in a sense that the human animal can be not [*peut ne pas être*] a subject' (Sem96–8). He clarifies that it is the moral account of subjectivity, the account which he rejects, that issues the injunction to treat all human animals as if they were subjects.

Though he denies that that all human beings are or should be treated as subjects, Badiou does hold, axiomatically, that all human animals have the capacity to be incorporated into an Idea. In *Logics of Worlds* he boldly asserts that 'several times in its brief existence, every human animal is granted the chance to incorporate itself into the subjective present of a truth' (*LM* 536 n11/*LW* 514 n11) but it is far from clear how his philosophy can cash the cheque this sentence signs. If incorporation into a truth is contingent upon the capacity for affirmative thought, and if not all humans possess such a capacity in actuality, then how are we to understand the axiomatic claim that all are accorded the opportunity 'several times' to be incorporated into a truth? Surely it must either accord with the moral 'as if' which Badiou rejects, or be an empty gesture, or a Platonic noble lie. What of those without the capacity to think sufficiently to apprehend a truth and be seized by it? What about those with severe Alzheimer's disease (a condition close to Malabou's heart, as we shall see), or those who go through the whole of life with severe mental disability, or very young children who are to die before the development of their capacity for affirmative thought? What does this blanket affirmation mean for them? Though Badiou maintains that 'every human being [. . .] is capable of being this immortal' (*E* 28/*Eth* 14), it is also the case that not all human beings are or will ever be immortal, and one cannot but wonder whether some are more capable of it than others, for whatever reason. The inescapable conclusion is that some will only ever be human animals, with all that this implies for Badiou. For him it can be no other way, for it is truth procedures that constitute 'the singularly human' and humanity is defined in terms of a capacity.[21]

In vain does Badiou insist that 'anyone can be seized by a political event; anyone can be seized by love' (*Ent* 193–4; my translation); the universal affirmation carries the unspoken but crucial caveat: anyone *who can think*. The question of capacities is once again addressed in *Plato's Republic* with much the same outcome. Socrates affirms that 'we're justified in assuming that the same positive capacity for thinking exists in all people, without exception' (*RP* 374/*PR* 219). On what basis? Simply, it seems, on the back of the bald affirmation that if, through a 'surgical removal', we can turn people's eyes away from the trinkets of capitalism and fix them on eternal truths, thereby inciting each individual to incorporate themselves into a truth, we would find that in all of those individuals 'the same eye can see these truths with the same clarity that's currently turning it toward the utter worthlessness of bad things' (*RP* 374/*PR* 219). For those in possession of functioning (literal or metaphorical) eyes this is all well and good, but Badiou's conjectural affirmation is little better than the moral account of the subject he so strongly dismisses in his 1996–8 seminar, simply holding that we must treat all human animals 'as if' they were subjects. Where is the practical difference between the two?

Finally, it could be objected that we might consider human animals lacking the capacity for affirmative thought to be incorporated into a truth in a passive way, for example by being part of a revolutionary community or the object of another's ardent love, being carried along by the capacity for affirmative thought of those around them rather than exercising their own. However, if this is the case then the question must immediately be raised as to why this option of being 'carried' cannot also be extended to animals and, in principle, even further. As it is, Badiou offers no such option: 'There is only a particular kind of animal convoked by certain circumstances to *become* a subject' (*E* 67/*Eth* 40; original emphasis).

The problematic relation between the human animal and the immortal

The detail of the relation between the human animal and the immortal is at the very heart of Badiou's transformation of the figure of the human, and it is also the point at which that transformation is at its most problematic. In seeking to come to terms with Badiou's transformation of humanity it is now time to interrogate this relation directly. How does an animal become incorporated into a truth, and what does that mean for the animal in question? A number of different extrapolations have been suggested in the secondary literature on Badiou, and I will offer a brief survey below. There are two misunderstandings in this area. The first is that Badiou holds to a binary division between the human animal and the subject, leaving him with an immiscible oil-and-water anthropology. The second misunderstanding is over just how the human animal is incorporated into a truth, whether it is by what Badiou calls 'grace', or by heroic effort.

On the question of the relation between the human animal and the immortal, readers of Badiou fall into two camps. On one side, Adrian Johnston and Slavoj Žižek lead the ranks of those who think that there is a problematic, non-dialectical dichotomy of animal and immortal in Badiou:

> both Slavoj and I are very adamant that one of the things that's missing from Badiou is that you have the stark contrast between, on the one hand, the individual, the mere miserable human animal, and, on the other hand, you have the post-evental immortal subject that's faithful to a given evental truth.[22]

In Žižek's case this leads to looking for a pre-subjective subject in Badiou, holding that 'what Badiou misses is the simple fact that there is no human animal [. . .] with humanity proper, [. . .] it is only into such a distorted animal that an Event can inscribe itself'.[23] This way of reading Badiou finds his account of the subject question-begging: 'the subject *precedes itself* – in order to become subject, it already has to be subject, so that, in its process of becoming, it becomes what it already is'.[24] Nina Power levels the same accusation when she argues that Badiou has need of a 'pre-evental generic capacity' to give traction to his egalitarian politics.[25]

Those who hold in this way to a non-dialectical relation between the human animal and the immortal in Badiou tend to stress – and to have problems with – Badiou's notion of grace. Adrian Johnston argues that:

> Badiou's persistent use of the theologically saturated signifier 'grace' for a process of evental subjectification eerily resembling the Catholic notion of transubstantiation is one of the more visible symptoms of the return of the religious repressed once the vast majority of the sciences have been categorically prevented from informing what presents itself as a materialist ontology.[26]

For Johnston, this grace is 'the inexplicable catalyst for processes of subjectivation breaking with animality' that 'descends upon the human animal so as to denaturalize it in creating an evental subject wedded to a given truth, a subject with no real, delineable relation to the natural matter of animality'.[27]

There is another reading of Badiou, however, one that stresses not human/animal disjunction and grace but human/animal overlap and heroism. Foremost among the proponents of this second position is Bruno Bosteels, who in his *Alain Badiou, une trajectoire polémique* critiques Žižek's reading of the Badiouian event, holding that the Slovenian's insistence on the importance of the 'Truth-Event' (a term we will search for in vain in Badiou's own writing, he points out) blinds him to the arduous process of forcing and maintaining fidelity to a truth.[28] There is something 'embarrassing and clumsy' about the critique that there is a naïve, non-dialectical separation in Badiou between the spheres of the mortal animal and the immortal subject, Bosteels argues,[29] and Badiou himself insists that the innovation of the 'and' of *Being and Event* is that it is conjunctive, not disjunctive.[30]

Whereas Johnston, adopting the dichotomous interpretation of the animal/immortal distinction, saw in the Badiouian account of the human animal and the immortal a preponderance of grace, conversely Alberto Toscano, from a position that emphasises the continuity between human animal and immortal, emphasises the capacity of the human animal to become a subject:

> This immanent split and articulation between self, animal or individual, on the one hand, and subject, on the other, does not revolve around the question of *responsibility*, as in Critchley, but of *capacity*. As Badiou writes: 'the "some-one" was not in a position *to know that he was capable of this* co-belonging to a situation and to the hazardous course of a truth, this becoming-subject.'[31]

Toscano in fact tries to hold this capacity together with Badiou's clear refusal to abandon the lexicon of grace, evoking the two in an uneasy union as 'the production of a sameness (a generic truth) that exceeds the particular resources of the "human animal" but which, at the same time, can only be constructed with their aid'.[32]

In a variation on the contrasting positions claiming a dichotomy or continuity between the animal and the immortal, Ed Pluth seeks to split the horns of the dilemma by giving passivity and heroism each their moment in the sun: the arrival of an event is a moment of passivity, but fidelity to that event once the subject has been incorporated into it is active. As far as the arrival of an event is concerned, 'No individual chooses to be seized by an event, and no individual decides to begin a truth procedure';[33] grace is predominant in the event because '[t]he emergence of the new is not willed or decided on by anyone'.[34] What requires effort, by contrast, is 'sticking with a subjectivation that has already taken place or persisting in a subject-process that seems to be going nowhere',[35] and fidelity is needed not to create the new but to 'encourage the *durability* of the new'.[36] In

Pluth's account it is grace that primes the pump, but then fidelity must roll up its sleeves if it wants to draw water. However, even if '[n]o individual chooses to be seized by an event'[37] there is still the requirement that the subject be seized by the event. It does not follow from Pluth's argument (the argument that individuals cannot consciously bring about the inauguration of truth procedures as an act of will) that truth procedures can be inaugurated in the absence of human willing. I agree with Pluth that Badiou's position is that the creation of truths is not under the conscious supervision of affirmative thought, but the creation of truths is not possible in the complete absence of the exercise of the capacity for affirmative thought either. Thought remains the gatekeeper of humanity, even in the context of Badiouian grace.

The truth is not as black and white as Pluth paints it: truth procedures begin within a context of the exercise of the capacity for affirmative thought, but not because of it. The event of May 1968, for example, is not the logical product of an engineered exercise of thought, but neither did it arrive in the absence of dogged, determined efforts on the part of a number of human animals who, somewhere along the line, became incorporated into an Idea of communism. If none of the concerned actors had possessed the capacity for affirmative thought, then the event of May 1968 would not have happened. Becoming incorporated into a truth does not bestow the capacity for affirmative thought; it directs that pre-existing capacity to exercise itself upon an Idea. The active and passive are simply more co-implicated in Badiou than Pluth would like. Let us consider once more what Badiou says about thought: 'Thought is the one and only uniquely human capacity, and thought, strictly speaking, is simply that act through which the human animal is seized and traversed by the trajectory of a truth' (*AMP* 111/*MetP* 97–8). To be seized by a truth is to exercise thought; it is to act. There is passivity in being seized by a truth, to be sure, but the 'uniquely human capacity' and the activity associated with it are still the *sine qua non* of seizure. If, on the other hand, truth procedures were to begin in a way utterly unrelated to the peculiar human capacity for affirmative thought, then we would have to admit the possibility of nonhuman truth procedures on a pre-human earth, what following Meillassoux we might call 'ancestral' events. If a tree falls in the forest and there is no 'anonymous hero' to declare it, can it be an event? I am aware of no indication anywhere in Badiou's work to suggest that it can, and so I must conclude that, while truth procedures are not inaugurated under the conscious control of the capacity for affirmative thought, they are not inaugurated without it either.

Let us take a closer look at what Badiou says. In terms of the first question, namely whether there is an overlap between the human and the animal, he sides (so to speak) with Bosteels and Toscano against Žižek and Johnston. He could not be more explicit when, in the 'Qu'est-ce que vivre?' ('What is it to live?') seminar from 2003–4 he says of the three elements of bodies, languages and truths that 'certainly the first two remain, man does not stop being a political animal, so there is life and language, but there is also this paradigm of the immortal, in other words the principle' (Sem03–4). He is equally explicit when, in *Ethics*, he insists that the immortal does not destroy all trace of the animal, that subjecthood is always 'the being-subject of a human animal' (*E* 94/*Eth* 69) and that 'the Immortal exists only in and by the mortal animal' (*E* 112/*Eth* 84). In a passage worth quoting at length, he repudiates the goal of eliminating all animality:

> When Nietzsche proposes to 'break the history of the world in two' by exploding Christian nihilism and generalizing the great Dionysian 'yes' to Life; or when certain Red Guards of the Chinese Cultural Revolution proclaim, in 1967, the complete suppression of self-interest, they are indeed inspired by a vision of a situation in which all interest has disappeared, and in which opinions have been *replaced* by the truth to which Nietzsche and the Red Guards are committed. The great nineteenth-century positivists likewise imagined that the statements of science were going to *replace* opinions and beliefs about all things. And the German Romantics worshipped a universe entirely transfixed by an absolutized poetics. But Nietzsche went mad. The Red Guards, after inflicting immense harm, were imprisoned or shot, or betrayed by their own fidelity. Our century has been the graveyard of positivist ideas of progress. And the Romantics, already prone to suicide, were to see their 'literary absolute' engender monsters in the form of 'aestheticized politics'. For every truth presumes, in fact, in the composition of the subjects it induces, the preservation of 'some-one', *the always two-sided activity of the human animal caught up in truth.* (*E* 112/*Eth* 84)

There is no dichotomy between truth and opinion or between generic subject and particular animal. Rather than Pascal's characterisation of the human as 'neither angel nor beast', it would be more accurate to summarise Badiou's anthropology as 'both angel and beast': the beast of the human animal is not replaced or effaced by the immortal angel, but both persist in the human subject of a truth. But we can go further. This persistence of the animal is not merely a fact for Badiou, it is also a good thing:

> Every absolutization of the power of a truth organizes an Evil. Not only does this Evil destroy the situation (for the will to eliminate opinion is, fundamentally, the same as the will to eliminate, in the human animal, its very animality, i.e. its being), but it also interrupts the truth-process in whose name it proceeds, since it fails to preserve, within the composition of its subject, the duality [*duplicité*] of interests (disinterested-interest and interest pure and simple). (*E* 112/*E* 85)

To seek to eliminate all opinion is to seek to eliminate the vehicle of opinion, which is the human animal, and this for Badiou is an Evil. To seek the Idea at the cost of eliminating all opinion, or to seek the inhuman at the expense of eliminating all human animality, puts the Idea itself at risk. Just as there is no humanity without the inhuman, so also there is no inhumanity without the human. Badiou is here insisting on the difference between two modes of interest, the 'interest pure and simple' of the human animal and the 'disinterested-interest' of the immortal subject. The interest of the human animal is its perseverance in being, its desire for food, water, sleep and sex, but when it is incorporated into a truth,

> All my capacity for interest [. . .] has *poured out* into the future consequences of the solution to this scientific problem, into the examination of the world in the light of love's being-two, into what I will make of my encounter, one night, with the eternal Hamlet, or into the next stage of the political process, once the gathering in front of the factory has dispersed. (*E* 71–2/*Eth* 50)

The interest of the human animal 'has success as its only source of legitimacy', but when I am seized by an Idea 'I find myself compelled to measure life, my life as a socialized human animal, against something other than itself' (*E* 71/*Eth* 50) and my own interest is disorganised and reorganised by this inhuman intrusion. Crucially, Badiou warns that it is very hard to distinguish interest from disinterested-interest, and when they pull 'the being-subject of a human animal' in different directions, it is not clear from the outset which will prevail (*E* 94/*Eth* 78).

In the light of this ultimate inextricability of interest and disinterested-interest it is misleading to say that a human animal is transformed into an immortal subject. It would be more accurate to say that the multiplicity that is the animal is held together either by interest or by disinterested-interest. In short, there is no dichotomy between the human animal and the immortal because the latter is always two-sided; the immortal caught up in a truth remains, also, a human animal. Furthermore, the human animal living as an immortal and oriented by disinterested-interest can always regress once more to being organised by its animal interest. In an image reminiscent of Sartre's discussion of torture in *Being and Nothingness*,[38] Badiou argues that this is what happens to torture victims who yield to their interrogators:

> if the torturers and bureaucrats of the dungeons and the camps are able to treat their victims like animals destined for the slaughterhouse, with whom they themselves, the well-nourished criminals, have nothing in common, it is because the victims have indeed become such animals (*E* 26–7/*Eth* 11)

Badiou concedes that some exceptional souls may remain human 'through enormous effort' which resists assuming the identity of a victim, their humanity verified in their determination to 'keep going!' in their fidelity to an inhuman truth.

This ethic of resistance under torture brings us to the second of the two misunderstandings about the relation between human animal and immortal subject. Is the inhuman, immortal Idea received by grace or is it heroically snatched from the jaws of animality 'through enormous effort'? On this question, Badiou's own position is emphatically ambiguous. He seems, on occasion, to espouse an exclusivity of grace and at other times to propound unequivocally an ethic of heroism, both with equal vigour. In a way that responds to the thesis held by Johnston, Žižek and Power that Badiou assumes a pre-subjective event or pre-subjective subject, he insists that 'all imperatives presume that the subject of the imperative is already constituted, and in specific circumstances. And thus there can be no imperative to become a subject, except as an absolutely vacuous statement' (OE). There is no room, it seems, for heroism here, for there is no call to subjectivity to which a putative hero could respond, 'Here I am!' If there can be no imperative to become a subject then there is no room left, it would seem, for a heroic animal to seize its fleeting opportunity to become immortal (*LM* 536/*LW* 514). In the same paragraph from 'On Evil' Badiou is once again emphatic: 'The possibility of becoming a subject does not depend on us, but on that which occurs in circumstances that are always singular' (OE).

Nevertheless, Badiou is equally insistent elsewhere about the heroism of becoming a subject. In the 2007 preface to the new edition of *Le Concept de modèle*, for example, he insists that 'free and constrained, an individual can *overcome* [*surmonter*] his animal infrastructure and, *incorporating himself* into the construction of a truth, become in the future anterior the subject he should be' (*ConM* 24; my translation and emphasis), and in 'The Idea of Communism' we read that

> What is at issue is the possibility for an individual, defined as a mere human animal, and clearly distinct from any Subject, to decide to become part of a political truth procedure. To become, in a nutshell, a militant of this truth. In *Logics of Worlds*, and in a simpler manner in the *Second Manifesto for Philosophy*, I describe this decision as an incorporation. (*Circ5* 184/*CH* 13)

Once more, in *The Meaning of Sarkozy* Badiou identifies a 'heroic element' when we turn away from the pressing interests of our animal individuality (*Circ4* 99/*MOS* 74), and in *Philosophy for Militants* he puts flesh on the bones of this heroism: it is 'the luminous appearance, in a concrete situation, of something that assumes its humanity beyond the natural limits of the human animal' (*RE* 50/*PM* 26).

In summary, both grace and heroic capacity are brought onto the

Badiouian stage as the protagonist in the incorporation of the human animal into an Idea, and it would appear that the play is not big enough for both of them. What are we to do? The common solutions until now, as I have already sketched, have been to emphasise either grace (Žižek, Johnston, Power) or heroism (Bosteels, Toscano), or to find a way of separating them temporally (Pluth), but this will only ever yield a partial and awkward reading of Badiou, punctuated with a strategic silence around inconvenient passages. Toscano's attempt to reconcile the two by evoking a truth 'that exceeds the particular resources of the "human animal" but which, at the same time, can only be constructed with their aid'[39] risks doing justice neither to grace nor to heroism by seeking to accommodate them to each other in an uneasy compromise.

Michael O'Neill Burns explores whether there is a way to understand the animal/immortal relation in terms of Badiou's theory of affects, first sketched in *Theory of the Subject* and most fully elaborated in *Logics of Worlds*.[40] Badiou introduces two groups of affects in *Logics of Worlds*, each group with four members. One group describes the characteristic of the subject of each truth procedure: the political subject is characterised by the affect of enthusiasm, the scientific subject by joy, the artistic subject by pleasure and the amorous subject by happiness (*LM* 85/*LW* 76). The other group of four, terror, anxiety, courage and justice, 'signal the incorporation of a human animal into a subjective truth-process' (*LM* 96/*LW* 86). Terror 'testifies to the desire for a Great Point', a rupture or break that brings about a new world. Anxiety is a fear of terror, of 'everything that imposes a choice without guarantee between two hypotheses'. Courage affirms the acceptance of many points: discontinuity and rupture without guarantee will be the lot of the subject. Following on from courage's recognition of multiple points, justice is 'the desire for the subject to be a constant intrication of points and openings' (*LM* 96/*LW* 86), in other words the subject will not always prefer rupture to continuity or continuity to rupture, but it will subordinate the categories of its action to the contingency of worlds (it will do what it needs to do in order to remain faithful to its truth). Negotiation and violence are both its lot. All four of these affects must be present for a successful and sustained incorporation into an Idea (*LM* 98/*LW* 88). The affects do not create a truth or constitute in themselves fidelity to a truth, they are rather 'the immediate and immanent experience that one is participating, be it in an elementary fashion, in the becoming of a truth, in a creative body-subject' (*LM* 85/*LW* 76) and that by virtue of which the 'human animal recognizes that it participates, through its incorporated body, in some subject of truth' (*LM* 502/*LW* 480).

Prima facie, the four affects smooth over the tension between grace and heroism in the link between the human animal and the immortal: the animal is affected by the passing of a truth and the affects signal that it is heroically beginning to remain faithful to the truth it has encountered. For Burns, 'this theory of affects provides an account of how it is that the pre-subjective human animal finds itself drawn into the process of becoming-subject through an internal response to external affects'.[41] He explains that the affects provide an explanation of *how* the animal becomes incorporated into an Idea, rather than merely an indication *that* such an incorporation has taken place. However, complications arise when Badiou lets grace and affect bleed into one another: 'all affects are necessary in order for the incorporation of a human animal to unfold in a subjective process, *so that the grace of being immortal may be accorded to this animal*'.[42] Here, it appears that affects are not merely a signal of an incorporation that has already happened, but constitutive of that incorporation: without the affects the grace of being immortal may not be accorded to the animal. So the affects do not solve the problem of the place of capacity in Badiou's account of the human animal and immortal, but they double it: just as the capacity for affirmative thought is necessary for incorporation into a subject, so too are the affects.

In addition to this problem raised by the affects, Burns also comes up against the same issue encountered by Pluth in his discussion of the art-work: who or what has the capacity to be affected? Noting that Badiou has defined the subject as an 'operative disposition of the traces of the event and of what they deploy in the world',[43] Burns wonders 'just how does an operative disposition feel an affect?'[44] 'It seems', he continues, 'as if Badiou here wants to attribute specifically human forms of affect (i.e., anxiety, courage) to a purely formal structure.'[45] How do the affects give rise to the decision to remain faithful to an event? And who makes that decision: the animal, the immortal or a third intermediary figure? What is prevent-ing Badiou from advancing, Burns hypothesises, is in part his refusal of humanistic or anthropocentric philosophy,[46] but as we have already seen that refusal lands him with the equally difficult problem of accounting for how an artwork can be faithful to a truth or how an operative disposi-tion can feel. Affects complicate, but they do not solve the problem of the animal–immortal relation.

Pluth, for his part, takes a slightly different approach from Burns in emphasising the passivity of the affects, in the same way that he stresses the passivity of the inauguration of truth procedures, claiming that '[Badiou's] view of affects is about the impact that procedures have on individuals, and they also therefore involve a good degree of passivity.'[47] But this does not solve the problem of the grace/heroism dichotomy either because if affect is, as Pluth suggests, 'a signal to the "human animal" in question that he or she is "some subject of truth"[48] then it is downstream of the capacity for thought through which a human animal becomes incorporated into a truth procedure in the first place. Affects may explain how an individual knows that he or she is incorporated into a truth (though as Burns points out there are problems with that too), but they do not themselves effect that incorporation. In short, if affects are merely indications *that* incorporation has happened (as Pluth argues) then they do nothing to bridge the gap, and if they reveal *how* incorporation happens (as Burns thinks) then they merely repeat the problems inherent in Badiou's account of the capacity for affirmative thought.

I have laboured my point in this section (and beg the patient reader's pardon for having done so) because it is necessary to demonstrate that Badiou has no way out of the impasse of grace and heroism, and no way to circumvent the contingency of subjectivation on the 'the one and only uniquely human capacity' (*AMP* 111/*MetP* 97–8) for affirmative thought. By putting all his human eggs in the basket of this one capacity he leaves himself with an anthropology that cuts adrift some of the weakest human beings, those without the capacity to be seized by a truth and who are therefore forever condemned to the unenviable status of human animals. The problem is that there is no safety net for those deprived (either temporarily or permanently) of the capacity for affirmative thought. No detour via affects and no insistence on the importance of grace can alter this. The problem with Badiou's refiguring of the human is that he relies on the host capacity of affirmative thought.

Conclusion

In this opening chapter I have sought to set in motion two trains of thought that will guide us through the rest of this book. The first is that contemporary accounts of the human are not *ex nihilo* inventions but subtle and creative reworkings of motifs from the history of Western thought. In Badiou's case, he keeps the grammar of 'humanity+' and draws inspiration from Aristotle and, indirectly, from the Christian tradition,[49] in order to think humanity in its fullest sense only with an irreducible inhuman supplement. The second train of thought is that it is very problematic indeed to install a determinate capacity as the gatekeeper of humanity, but this is indeed what Badiou does, despite his and others' best efforts to explain things otherwise.

In his *Badiou: A Philosophy of the New*, Ed Pluth offers the most sustained reading to date on Badiou's relation to humanism, painting an attractive picture of Badiou's thought as 'an anti-humanism in defence of the human'.[50] It is only through the theoretical antihumanism of being seized by and holding oneself faithfully to the inhuman idea that practical humanism can be fostered, because it is only such an immortal existence that allows a human being to rise above its animal nature. As for the so-called humanism of democratic materialism, it leads only to a practical dehumanisation. In his fifth chapter, Pluth identifies what he calls the 'contact point' between Badiou's theoretical antihumanism and practical humanism.[51] That contact point is the subject, which 'serves as the bridge between the systematic part of Badiou's work and the ethical part'.[52] Though the subject can be many other things apart from an individual human being, it nevertheless 'has something to do with thought, with conscious activity, and even language, because it is in large part a product of such things'.[53] I have argued in this chapter that, despite the best efforts of Badiou criticism and Badiou himself in *Logics of Worlds*, his theoretical antihumanism and practical humanism never quite meet, because he has not yet made it clear how the human animal is incorporated into a truth. Furthermore I have shown that, even if Badiou could satisfactorily clarify this relation it would still not clear up the problem of the 'host' capacity for thought as a gatekeeper of humanity in the full sense, with the danger that some of those least able to raise their voices in protest are, at least in theory, left beyond the pale of the human.

Despite all the sophistication of Badiou's account of the human, and despite the theory of the affects in *Logics of Worlds* that seeks to respond to the gulf in *Being and Event* and *Ethics* between the pre-subjective animal and the faithful subject, there remains an unresolved amalgam of grace and heroism at the heart of Badiouian anthropology. If the human animal is incorporated into a truth by grace then why can nonhumans not be so incorporated? And if human animals are incorporated by virtue of a capacity which it is claimed they possess, then what of those human beings who do not possess the capacity in question? Furthermore, what can the affirmation that each human being is presented with a number of opportunities to incorporate itself into a truth amount to, other than wishful thinking, a noble lie, or attempt to brush the problem under the carpet? The problem of affirmative thought is the pineal gland of Badiou's anthropology: a necessary but ultimately inexplicable point of meeting and nothing more than a convenient placeholder for an unthinkable relation.

More broadly, Badiou's account of the human is beholden to the possession of a determinate capacity, and my aim is to show in the following chapters that this is by no means a problem exclusive to Badiouian thought. Any account of the human which rests on an individual's effective possession of a determinate capacity is problematic, because it can never be ruled out that liminal cases and exceptions will be cast outside the circle of humanity. Pluth claims that the aim of Badiou's formalised inhumanism is to 'think of the specificity of the human [. . .] better than other philosophical humanisms',[54] and Pluth calls the human specificity 'the capacity for truths'.[55] No doubt Badiou's focus on truth does discern the contours of the human better than many other theories, and it is not my purpose to quarrel with his truths per se. What I am uneasy with is that Badiou's anthropology rests on a capacity. The problems that dog Badiou are shared by all figures of the human that rest on a 'host', on a gatekeeper capacity of full humanity, and as we shall see in the next chapter it is a problem from which Quentin Meillassoux also finds it hard to escape.

Chapter 2

Quentin Meillassoux: Supreme Human Value Meets Anti-anthropocentrism

> What peculiar privilege has this little agitation of the brain which we call thought, that we must make it the model of the whole universe? Our partiality in our own favour does indeed present it on all occasions: But sound philosophy ought carefully to guard against so natural an illusion.
>
> Hume, *Dialogues Concerning Natural Religion*[1]

Reading the philosophy of Quentin Meillassoux gives one an appreciation of what it must be like to ride a donkey in a state of inebriation: in the attempt not to fall off on one side it is very easy to find oneself sliding down the other. It is easy to think, on the one hand, that Meillassoux's arguments are all spectacular, unheard-of and revolutionary, or to assume, on the other hand, that he is playing a game with his reader, and cannot possibly mean what he says in earnest. Neither of these readings is true or fair, and Meillassoux's approach to philosophy is nowhere more concisely summarised than in the following passage from *After Finitude*:

> Philosophy is the invention of strange forms of argumentation, necessarily bordering on sophistry, which remains its dark structural double. To philosophize is always to develop an idea whose elaboration and defence require a novel kind of argumentation, the model for which lies neither in positive science – not even in logic – nor in some supposedly innate faculty for proper reasoning. (*AF* 103/*AfF* 76–7)

Meillassoux is a purposeful contrarian, the lone face gazing skywards in a crowd of people looking down at their shoes,[2] precisely because everyone else is looking elsewhere. In this spirit, he frames the project of *After Finitude* as 'to understand how the most urgent question has come to be regarded as the most idle one' (IntDT 78).

In embarking therefore on an investigation of the figure of the human in Meillassoux's thought we shall seek to be neither beguiled nor hor-rified, to succumb to neither adulation nor derision. The place of the human in Meillassoux's thought is complex. On the one hand, he main-tains a strong and consistent rhetoric of anti-anthropocentrism, and his fundamental philosophical project can be summarised as an attempt to break free from what he sees as the anthropocentric straitjacket of Kantian and post-Kantian 'correlationist' thought. On the other hand, however, Meillassoux evinces (especially in his work subsequent to *After Finitude* and nowhere more strikingly than in 'The Divine Inexistence') a very high view of the human indeed, not hesitating to call his philosophy a human-ism and asserting the value of the human as ultimate. In this chapter I will consider these humanistic and anti-anthropocentric strands of his thought in turn. We shall see that Meillassoux's account of the human bears strik-ing resemblances to Badiou's (particularly in the importance of a 'host capacity' which underwrites the dignity of human beings), but that there are also important differences. My intention is to show, in the first part of this chapter, that Meillassoux's humanism is less humanist than he thinks and, in the second part, that his attempt to disengage from anthropocen-trism is more anthropocentric than he thinks.

Thought and human value

Meillassoux's factial humanism

Both among those thinkers associated with the 'new materialism' as well as among the 'speculative realists' – itself less a band of brothers and more a loose association of distant cousins – Meillassoux accords an unusually exalted place to the human being. Surrounded by thinkers who labour intensely to elaborate flat ontologies which argue for differences only of degree and not of kind between the human, the animal, the organic, the inorganic and the ideal, with a characteristically unabashed boldness Meillassoux delivers a vigorous and uncompromising humanism.

In a way that resonates with Badiou's survey and rejection of the place of humanity in religious and secular thought preceding his own, Meillassoux clears the way for his humanism by denouncing the way in which both religious and secular traditions have, until now, failed to do justice to the human being. He understands 'religion' in very broad terms, yet despite his generic definition it is clear that he has in mind princi-pally the Western, specifically Aristotelian–Thomistic, 'god of the phi-losophers'.[3] In 'The Divine Inexistence' he defines religion in terms of the claim that a necessary existence is possible (ExID 231), a definition which brings within the ambit of religion not only claims about God but all metaphysical systems that explicitly or implicitly rely on the existence of a necessary being or necessary laws. A second feature of religion for Meillassoux is that it 'consists in limiting the exercise of reason' (ExID 230).[4] For Meillassoux, these two features of religion conspire to condemn it to an irremediable failure to do justice to the human. First of all, the positing of any necessary existence, power or law above the human results in a humanity condemned always to subordinate itself to the nonhuman to which it owes its existence, condemned to 'desiring the manifestation of the power of being, and thereby desiring the inhuman' in a way which 'amounts once more to a religious subordination of the end to the origin, or of humans to the power that causes them to be born or reborn' (ExID 222). In terms of the limiting of reason, it issues in an 'incapacity to take the human for the end of action, an incapacity that ends in the submission of humans to the blind power of becoming, identified with a destinal mystery resulting in the incomprehensibility of transcendence' (ExID 222). When reason is limited rather than absolute, ultimate desire is never for the human because 'what the religious spirit desires is that there should be something *entirely other*: something inconceivable or absolutely inhuman' (ExID 222). In its metaphysical variant, religion subordinates humanity to a principle which exceeds it, for '[t]o claim that something surpasses the human is to condemn oneself to place the human under the despotism of the eternal, innocent, and amoral power of being qua being' (ExID 213). Religion (whether theological or metaphysical) therefore makes humans 'strangers to themselves' (ExID 213).

Atheism fares no better than religion for Meillassoux when it comes to doing justice to human beings. Atheism 'diminishes man, and humiliates him by dismantling what he takes to be a myth' but which turns out to be nothing other than 'the trace within man of his beautiful possibility, namely a possible father [*d'un père possible*] of the renaissance of man' (ID 384). Whereas religion crowbars humans into hoping in something utterly inhuman, atheism bludgeons out of them all hope for any future justice whatsoever. The atheist's cries against the crimes and outrages of the centuries simply echo back and forth down the endless hollow corridors of a meaningless universe, and all the innocent suffering of the generations is muffled and forgotten in the superbly impassive indifference of the cosmos.

Humanism joins religion and atheism in the dismal ranks of systems that fail to do justice to the human. Humanism for Meillassoux is merely a knock-off version of religion, taking the pure power ascribed by theologians to God and seeking to rework it in a human image: 'It is an idolization of power in humans: not power in God, but in humans become

God.'[5] This idolatrous or Promethean humanism is, if anything, even worse than religion, because it brings the inhumanity of human desire full circle: 'Prometheanism thinks it suppresses the alienation of humans when it reintegrates the transposed God back into humans. But in this way alienation is actually accomplished. Humans, instead of revering their own baseness in God, now venerate it in themselves' (ExID 213–14). What Meillassoux is referring to as 'baseness' here is the ascription to God of the horrors, injustices and outrages that litter the history of the world, particularly when coupled with a dogged insistence that the same God who allowed this suffering is to be thought of as supremely loving. Whereas he sees religion as vindicating a barbaric God, humanism merely goes one step further and vindicates a barbaric humanity. To think oneself equal to God, for Meillassoux, is not self-exaltation but self-abasement, and the renunciation along with God of the burning desire for universal justice has condemned the contemporary West to an 'infinite limitation of egalitarian demands' issuing from 'the criminogenic nature of the modesty of modern humanity, ferociously turned against the infinite and legitimate excess of universal justice' (IWB 454).

In the wake of the failure of religion, atheism and humanism to do justice to the human, Meillassoux proposes his own principle of factiality as the basis of the new – and the only authentic – humanism. Outdoing even the Badiou who proclaims his thought 'the most rigorously materialist in ambition that we've seen since Lucretius' (BBN 123), Meillassoux claims of human pre-eminence that '*no such thing has ever been seriously maintained*' (ExID 210; original emphasis) prior to his own humanism. Like his principle of factiality, Meillassoux's assertion of humanism (at least) resonates with and (at most) relies on a certain intuition for which he does not argue, namely 'The fact that the value of the human is ultimate seems to be such an insupportably banal assertion' (ExID 210). While many would consider the ultimacy of humanity to be anything but a banal assertion, it is sufficient for our purposes here to note that Meillassoux considers it so, and that it drives his attempt to counter 'the cynical and religious devaluations of the human by establishing *the essential ultimate status of the human*' (ExID 209; original emphasis).

Meillassoux's neo-humanistic project is to demonstrate the ultimate value of humanity with unprecedented rigour, and in order to accomplish this task he turns to his principle of factiality. It is the factial (the principle that only contingency is necessary) that for Meillassoux 'can *ontologically* establish the *value* of the human: the essential human dignity by which every act of justice always draws its legitimacy' (ExID 208; original emphasis). In what does this essential dignity consist for Meillassoux? The answer comes in two parts. First, dignity has to do not with human origins but with the untotalisable, mathematical absolute which the principle of factiality reveals as the ontological fabric of the universe:

> we propose to found the worth of the human in replacing the search for a first cause with the demonstration of a final effect: *the value of the human is not founded by the soil that sustains them, but by the void that outstrips them.* (ExID 210; original emphasis)

Secondly, human ontological dignity relies upon the particular relation which humans entertain with the necessary contingency of the universe. It is a relationship that exists by virtue of the human capacity to think this absolute. I shall return to this crucial capacity for thinking the absolute in the second subsection of this chapter.

Whereas 'the most up-to-date version of humanism [. . .] grants the human only a factual and descriptive knowledge of techniques and rules' (ExID 210) and therefore fails to ground human ontological dignity, for Meillassoux the object of human knowledge is neither the Other (God, life force, Nature . . .) nor mere facts about humanity itself and the world, but the one absolute truth of the universe: only contingency is necessary. This principle of factiality is admirably immunised against becoming just one more inhuman idol before which humanity abases and prostitutes itself, for the very good reason that it provides nothing to worship: factuality is not a law of contingency but the contingency of laws, not an immutable absence but the absence of immutability, not a substantial void but a voiding of all eternal substance.

In a move which is utterly in line with his rejection of religious accounts of the human,[6] Meillassoux insists upon what he calls human divinisation (ExID 232). In order to understand this divinisation we need to place it, and Meillassoux's transformation of the human more broadly, within the frame of his four-step account of the origin and destiny of the world. Thus far in the history of the world there have been three moments of *ex nihilo* emergence (*surgissement*), three 'essential ruptures of becoming' (ExID 187), each of which creates a radical and qualitatively irreducible 'before' and 'after' in the history of the world. These three moments are the emergence of matter from the non-material void, the emergence of life from matter and the appearance of rational thought from life. Each of these *ex nihilo* appearances for Meillassoux constitutes a new world (ExID 187).

Given that rational thought already provides access to the absolute through thinking the principle of factiality, now that humans have become beings of rational thought 'there can be no further being incommensurable with our humanity, but only additional contingent variations of life or matter' (ExID 190). Meillassoux's is not a philosophy of post- or transhuman enhancement, and no super-intelligence or other human modification could bring a change equal to the emergence of rational thought from life, because 'humans have access to the eternal truth of the world' (ExID 190), and 'only a thought reaching a higher truth than that of contingency could re-enact the rupture inaugurated by thought with respect to animality' (ExID 190). Nevertheless, there is for Meillassoux one final world yet to arrive, a world that will fulfil not the human desire for absolute knowledge (which is already satisfied by the principle of factiality) but that for ultimate, universal and exhaustive justice. It is a justice for the dead as well as for the living in a world in which humans are reborn: 'That is why the fourth World ought to be called the World of justice: for it is only the World of the rebirth of humans *that makes universal justice possible, by erasing even the injustice of shattered lives*' (ExID 190; original emphasis). Justice requires both that God does not presently exist (if he did he would be unjust and responsible for the atrocities of the world) and that God will exist in the future (in order to facilitate the resurrection of the dead and the inauguration of universal justice).

It is in relation to the modalities of the advent of this fourth world that Meillassoux speaks of the divinisation of the human: 'To be deified is to turn oneself into a demon: a *metaxu*, an intermediary, a living passage between the thinking of this world and the justice of the ultimate world' (IWB 478). To be divinised is to have one foot already in the world of justice, in a way that Meillassoux never fully explains but that seems to have much in common with upholding the Republican value of universal equality in a way that anticipates the justice to come. The structure of this anticipatory living, which Meillassoux (with his apologies for the inelegant neologism) calls 'eschaological', mirrors similar injunctions of the apostle Paul in his letters to the church in Rome and Thessalonica:

> The night is nearly over; the day is almost here. So let us put aside the deeds of darkness and put on the armour of light.[7]

> But you, brothers and sisters, are not in darkness so that this day should surprise you like a thief. You are all children of the light and children of the day. We do not belong to the night or to the darkness. So then, let us not be like others, who are asleep, but let us be awake and sober.[8]

Like the apostle's, Meillassoux's anticipatory living takes place in community with the aim '[t]o turn oneself and the universal people into a yonder self and a yonder people, between here and now, that is the coming task of eschaological becoming' (IWB 478). Those who live in this way are baptised by Meillassoux 'vectorial subjects',[9] highlighting that their existence is now 'neither only "here" (world 3) nor already "there" (world 4)' but 'already between here and there – this in-between for which the English language has a beautiful world [sic]: yonder' (IWB 478). Like Badiou's immortal, the vectorial subject is defined in terms of its relation to a truth, in Meillassoux's terms the absolute possibility of the advent of a world of justice. The vectorial subject is the one who is liberated both from the disillusionment of the theist whose God has permitted all the atrocities of world history and also from the despair of the atheist who can hope for no universal future justice. In a way that once more bears compari-son with the disinterested-interest of Badiou's immortal under the maxim 'Keep going!', the vectorial subject is therefore 'magnetically attracted by the vector of the emancipation to come' (IWB 463) at the advent of the fourth world of justice, and is characterised by 'the ardour of an eman-cipatory orientation insofar as this orientation distinguishes itself from both cynicism and fanaticism' (IWB 471). Slipping into the first person, Meillassoux explains that this ardour is 'the affect which dominates us and by which we are the heirs of all the emancipatory and eschatological move-ments of the past' (IWB 471). This is a crucial moment of self-realisation, and once more it shows how his contemporary refiguring of the human is not the *ex nihilo* appearance of a completely new set of concerns but a creative transformation of motifs and ideas – a 'grammar' – with the oldest heritage in the Western tradition: the human as an agent and object of emancipation, and a community united by hope in a future deliverance. Finally, in a way that again draws his figure of the human close to Badiou's resistance to 'animal humanism' and undirected 'interest', Meillassoux's vectorial subject has to resist the 'ultimate temptation' of understanding itself in terms of finitude and being-for-death (IWB 473) rather than desiring ultimate and universal justice, even for the dead.

Many questions could be and have been asked about Meillassoux's description of the world of justice: why is this the only New World that can now emerge? How do we know that this will be the final world to emerge? How does living in anticipation of the coming of justice make any difference whatsoever to the future possibility of the resurrection of the dead? These questions are not unimportant, but they are also not central to my project in this chapter, which is to come to terms with Meillassoux's understanding of the human being. Indeed, it is by grasping the dimen-sions of Meillassoux's understanding of the human that we begin to see how he might answer these questions. If the human is indeed ultimate, then its project must reflect the best and noblest of its hopes and aspira-tions. If those hopes and aspirations strive for ultimate, universal and perfect justice, then seeking to elaborate a project which has as its goal anything less than this justice is an insult to humanity:

> It is a mocking enterprise of demystification that only allows our species a few mediocre projects compared with what we are capable of envisaging. It

is a sarcasm of humans toward humans, and thus a hatred of oneself. But the project of humans has to be worthy of humans, and if the philosopher conceives God as this project, it is because he knows that one cannot limit what humans want, *because one cannot limit what a world can do.* (ExID 234; original emphasis)

Whatever one thinks of the details of Meillassoux's figure of the human, this principle repays reflection: how can a project which ignores or diminishes the greatest and noblest desires of humanity be thought worthy of the humanity that desires it? Nevertheless, compared with the elegant simplicity of the principle of factiality Meillassoux's discourse on the divine takes on the appearance of a Heath Robinson cartoon.

One important question does remain outstanding for our understanding of Meillassoux's humanism, however: in what sense is anticipatory living a 'divinisation' of humanity? Meillassoux gives us hints but no definitive clarification. Just before the passage quoted above from 'The immanence of the world beyond', he frames the vectorial subject in terms of the coming existence of God:

we have not as yet obtained a full clarification of the meaning which we ascribe to the word 'God' in the statement: 'God does not as yet exist', but we have begun to understand an essential aspect of it. The deification of humanity can in fact be understood as a trajectory which in the present world enables the vectoral subject to overcome the double experience of dilemma and of nihilism in order to turn himself into a 'bridge' between the third and the fourth world. (IWB 477–8)

The vectorial subject is an 'essential aspect' of the coming existence of God. That could be read in two ways which are not mutually exclusive. According to the first reading, the anticipatory living of the vectorial subject serves somehow to summon forth the arrival of God. This seems to be the sense of the passage from 'The Divine Inexistence' in which Meillassoux evokes 'the inexistent God of whom humans are the possible ancestor' (ExID 232). When Meillassoux evokes a 'link' between the human and the divine and explains that '[t]he practice of this link in the course of our lives I call the divinization or immortalization of humans' (ExID 232), it begins to sound as if divinisation is a becoming-divine of the human, but Meillassoux firmly closes that door in the sentences that follow:

This divinization is not a deification of humans, because it is not a Promethean identification of humans with God. The divine is the affirmation of an uncrossable ontological divide between humans and the omnipotence of the Master, a worthless omnipotence of the revealed God whose happy abandonment inaugurates the philosophical God as justice and as gesture. (ExID 232)

The 'justice and gesture' which Meillassoux evokes here are the two actions of the God to come, whom he calls the Child of Man. This God will bring about universal justice, even for the dead, and then perform 'the unique gesture of abandoning the power of this advent, once the justice is accomplished for which the advent was (only) the condition' (ExID 224) in order to foreclose the possibility of becoming a subject of Promethean force or an object of religious worship. In this gesture of laying aside its power, the Child of Man (whom Meillassoux also calls the *infans*) affirms to all humans 'the unequalled value of their own humanity',[10] thus reinstating humanity as ultimate value. Nevertheless, the *infans* is the only human ever to have had the opportunity to lay down such unimaginable power in this way, and so it is difficult to see how even the disempowered *infans* does not bask in a greater degree of glory than the average Joe Human on the street,[11] and how it is possible for the Child, absolute and universal justice having been accomplished at their hand, simply to melt away again into the crowd. If this were possible, Clark Kent would not need to keep his true identity a secret.

The second reading is that, in the above passage, Meillassoux is redefining the word 'God' such that the anticipatory living of the vectorial community is itself revealed to be the arrival of God through its enactment of justice in the present. According to this latter sense, the divinisation of humanity is the human anticipatory enactment of justice in the present. God is defined as being the one who brings universal justice, and if human anticipatory living foreshadows and enacts that coming justice, however imperfectly, then those responsible for this adumbration can legitimately be considered to fulfil the requirements attaching to the signifier 'God'. The identification of the human with the divine is made more complicated when Meillassoux reaches for metaphors (though is he speaking literally?) of procreation: 'We are the possible ancestors of God rather than his creatures' for 'we bear God in our wombs, and our essential disquietude is nothing other than the convulsions of a child yet to come' (ExID 231). This clarification could be understood as substantiating either reading of the passage we are presently considering, but seems to fit snugly with neither: if God is a human child then Prometheanism and deification would seem, after all, to be the order of the day, at least for the child in question, but if we are merely the wombs and incubators of a nonhuman progeny then, once more, it seems unclear how our actions are commensurate with the ultimate value of humanity. Even a God who existed only for a brief span and subsequently divested itself of its power, as Meillassoux seems to suggest, would challenge the ultimate value of humanity and tickle once more the inexorable desire to worship something superhuman.

If only the former thesis is true (vectorial living serves to summon the deity) then we in turn must be patient and await, in the fullness of time, a fuller explanation from Meillassoux as to how the actions of a small number of human beings on one planet orbiting an insignificant sun in an obscure corner of the universe can bring about, through their attempts to act in line with the value of universal equality,[12] the consummation of the destiny of the universe in the resurrection of the dead. If only the second thesis is true (vectorial living is itself divine to the extent that it brings about universal justice) then (1) the belief in the coming of God in the terms that Meillassoux presents it (including the resurrection of the dead) is reduced to being the opiate of the egalitarian, a noble lie intended to control behaviour in the present; (2) justice is no longer universal because it excludes the dead; and (3) the door would seem to be open again for the glorification of humanity which Meillassoux vehemently resists in the case of Promethean humanism. It is for these reasons that some combination of the two theses about the divinisation of the human seems likely eventually to emerge as Meillassoux's settled position. Until and unless some as yet undefined combination of the two readings is offered, the question remains a structural weakness of his thought, like Badiou's account of the relation between the human animal and the immortal.

Human thought and human value

As already indicated in the section above, Meillassoux rests the value of humanity on its capacity to think the absolute. This places the capacity for rational thought at the heart of his anthropology in the same way that the capacity to hold oneself to a truth is at the heart of Badiou's. Furthermore, and in what is now a familiar pattern, thought proves a problem for Meillassoux's anthropology in the same way as we saw it did for Badiou's. In this section I will first show how thought functions in relation to the human for Meillassoux, and then I will argue that it cannot do the job he requires it to fulfil.

The capacity to think the principle of factiality is identified by Meillassoux as the locus of human value and dignity, the jewel in the human crown. In an interesting twist on Badiou's capacity, Meillassoux draws human value and dignity out of what in the first instance presents itself as an incapacity, namely the incapacity to think the absolute. According to the Meillassouxian 'intellectual intuition of the absolute' (*AF* 111/*AfF* 82), our own epistemological lack of sufficient reason is not seen as a humbling impasse of knowledge but is 'projected into' the thing itself. We 'put back into the thing itself what we mistakenly took to be an incapacity in thought' (*AF* 72/*AfF* 53), taking 'the absence of reason inherent in everything' not as a limit to our thought but as 'the ultimate property of the entity' (*AF* 73/*AfF* 53); an epistemological incapacity to know that anything exists necessarily is turned into a capacity to know the ultimate lack of necessity in all that exists. Nevertheless, such a moment of intuition itself relies on the positive exercise of the capacity for rational thought, and so it is still correct to say that value and dignity for Meillassoux rely not, in the final analysis, on an incapacity but on a capacity to intuit the true nature of what initially appears to us as our own incapacity.

Humans, for Meillassoux, do not hold their value in a way that is independent of their capacities, but rather 'humans acquire value because they know the eternal' (ExID 211). For Meillassoux it is not, as Graham Harman rightly points out, that the eternal commutes its own value to the human, for the eternal is only 'the blind, stupid, and anonymous contingency of each thing' (ExID 211). Furthermore, Meillassoux reasons that if humanity derived its value from the eternal, then that value could never be ultimate because it would rest on something outside the human. Meillassoux is seeking to prove that humanity is not just very valuable but of ultimate value, and therefore this value cannot rest on anything outside the human. His solution is that human value is not in the eternal that is thought, but in the thinking of the eternal: 'humans have value not because of *what* they know but *because* they know' (ExID 211). In this, Meillassoux's human-as-knower-of-the-eternal is significantly different to Badiou's human-as-faithful-to-the-inhuman. For Badiou, the value is in the immortal Idea and humans share in its nobility; for Meillassoux the value is not in the principle of factiality but in gaining knowledge of it: to seek somewhat imperfectly for a common vocabulary, we might say that for Badiou human value is in the object of human knowledge (knowledge's *what*) and for Meillassoux human value is in the fact of human knowledge (knowledge's *that*). We might also say, recalling the threefold schema of the substantial, functional and relational human from the Introduction,[13] that for Badiou, human value is at bottom relational or externalist (it obtains only in, and only because of, a relation of fidelity to the inhuman), whereas for Meillassoux human value is functional or internalist (the value is in the function performed by the human – namely rational thought – and not in any object of that thought).

But if value is functional in this way for Meillassoux, then why is it that being able to think the absolute means that humans have value? Beavers know how to build dams. If value rests on nothing to do with what is known but merely on the fact of knowing, why do beavers not have equal value with human beings? After all, both know something of ultimate value for their existence. And if 'knowledge' is being used in a restricted sense of knowing the eternal contingency of all things (and therefore knowledge is only ever the knowledge of one thing), then what sense can it make to assert that 'humans have value not because of *what* they know but *because* they know' (ExID 211)?

Let us begin trying to answer this question with an easy observation, and then move to harder territory. What Meillassoux does not mean is that humans have a value because they are clever (and therefore if a new species or machine came along that was smarter than human beings by some relevant measure or other, it would have more value and dignity than they). Meillassoux does not grade intelligence on the curve and he does not run a league table of smarts; he has a binary distinction which affirms 'the *necessary superiority* [. . .] of the thinking being over all other beings' (ExID 209). Secondly, it is potentially misleading to claim that what is important is not *what* humans know but *that* they know, because what matters for Meillassoux is knowledge of the eternal absolute, knowledge of the principle of factiality. Human value comes 'from the *thought* of the eternal of which it is the mortal stakeholder' (ExID 210). Value is intimately bound together not with the fact *that* humans know *tout court*, but that humans know the eternal, which may come as a disappointment to the aspirant beaver.

The question still remains: why should thinking the absolute be the host capacity of value, any more than building dams or having the largest (or smallest) incisors? Meillassoux does not lay out an unambiguous answer to this question. He is clear that the capacity for rational thought defines human beings,[14] and he is also clear that the world of thought is the last world to have emerged, after matter and life. Michael O'Neill Burns makes the helpful argument that the ultimate value of humanity does not stem from the fact that thought is hierarchically superior to life and matter for Meillassoux, because each of the three Worlds emerged *ex nihilo*, without reason. He concludes that 'humanity is extraordinarily unique for no good reason whatsoever', and that 'for Meillassoux the thinking being is the ultimate precisely because this being "knows his own contingency"'.[15] One of these two statements may be true, but they cannot both be. Either humans are superior for no good reason whatsoever, or they are ultimate because they know their own contingency. Burns may be confusing two senses of 'reason': there is no reason (metaphysical justification) for why thought emerged, but there is a very good reason (an explanation in terms of a host capacity) for why humans are of extraordinary value. Perhaps rationally thinking beings are more valuable than other beings because they may play a role in the emergence of the fourth world of justice? But surely the same *ex nihilo* argument should obtain for this hypothesis as well. Perhaps in the end (we may need to await further clarification from Meillassoux on this question) it comes down to the fact that Meillassoux just thinks that it is obvious that human beings are more valuable than other animals. Obvious to whom? To (some) human beings of course.

Human beings happen, by fluke of hyperchaos, to be the temporary carriers of a particular self-identified capacity. Even if we admit that thinking the eternal in itself is of value, this does not make human beings valuable simply because they think the eternal, in the same way that if I have a gold filling it does not necessarily render me, as a person, more valuable than someone with no fillings, or in the same way the possession of an ivory tusk does not make an elephant as such more valuable than an animal with no tusks in anything but the most mercenary terms. This sort of argument becomes important when we consider that not all human beings have the capacity to think the eternal. In the same way that we saw neonates, the senile and those with severe mental disabilities pose as yet unanswered problems for Badiou's anthropology of the human animal and the immortal, so also it is by no means clear that human beings with a temporary or permanent incapacity to think the eternal would necessarily be valued in Meillassoux's system, however horrified he might personally be at such a situation.

Another similarity with Badiou's negotiation of the question of the human is that Meillassoux also establishes rational thought as the host capacity of human equality:

> this knowledge gives us access to the strict *equality* between all humans qua human. The eternal truths to which our condition grants access are in fact *indifferent to differences*, to the innumerable and necessary differences between individual <u>thinkers</u>. The differences are necessary because humans, as simple existents, are contingent and particular beings indefinitely differentiable from other humans. Yet these differences are undifferentiated by the impersonal reason that marks <u>all bearers of truth</u>. This is why humans, *as long as they think, are affected* by injustice whenever it strikes them, since nothing permits us to found an inegalitarian difference of humans from themselves. (ExID 191; original italics; my underlining)

When, in this passage, Meillassoux evokes 'the strict *equality* between all humans qua human', it is clear from the context that he does not mean 'all those who are genetically human' or 'all those whom a certain community considers to be human', but rather 'all humans qua rational thinkers'. The following idea, that the eternal truths are 'indifferent to differences', carries therefore the implicit qualification 'indifferent to differences among rationally thinking beings', which means that eternal truths are anything but indifferent to the differences between rationally thinking beings and everything else. Where does this leave the categories of people mentioned above, those who do not fit the criterion of 'humans, *as long as they think*'? Graham Harman seems to have this concern with Meillassoux's thought in mind when he insists, following Badiou almost word for word, that 'every human is capable of grasping' the universal,[16] and Meillassoux himself claims that 'we know that humans have access to the eternal truth of the world' (ExID 190). No we do not. Unless 'grasping the truth' and 'having access to the eternal truth of the world' mean something different to what Meillassoux seems to mean by those phrases, the only way that this assertion could be true is if some who are genetically human are defined out of humanity through a temporary or permanent incapacity for rational thought.[17] All humans have access to eternal truths because those who do not are not human. Some human beings have temporary, others permanent, mental incapacities which by every available test leaves them with less capacity for rational thought than some nonhuman animals. So if equality is to obtain for all humans and for no nonhumans then it cannot be on the basis of the capacity to think the eternal, either *in potentia* or *in actualis*. For Badiou and Meillassoux alike, a host capacity approach to equality raises more questions than it answers.

One area in which Meillassoux's account of the host property of rational thought differs from Badiou's is in his willingness to open the possibility of rational thinking beyond the human species to include all 'rational beings capable of grasping the absolute truth of contingency, and not simply the bipedal species in which such a reality now happens to be encountered' (ExID 190). This raises yet more questions, particularly as to how this possibility of nonhuman rationality relates to Meillassoux's assertion that 'The fact that the value of the human is ultimate seems to be such an insupportably banal assertion' (ExID 210). It seems that the tent of equality has room for more than humanity alone, and this is confirmed when Meillassoux asserts 'the superiority in principle of the human, its eternally unsurpassable unparalleled worth (except for the worth of other thinking beings)' (ExID 210).

Where does this leave other thinking beings at the resurrection, including those beings that, for want of a longer history, would have existed but did not yet exist? Will the resurrection give them the birth they never received? When Meillassoux talks of rebirth, he talks of the rebirth of humans and not of animals. Imagine that, in the future, artificial intelligence is capable of thinking the eternal. Will those computers of sufficient processing power be reborn along with all the humans who have the same capacity? Would such artificial intelligence de facto come under the definition of 'human' because 'Humans are in fact defined by their access to truth, understood as the eternal contingency of that which is' (ExID 190)? Furthermore, if humans are valued because they are the 'mortal stakeholder' (ExID 210) of the thinking of the eternal, and if nonhuman animals or machines could eventually think the eternal, then surely it would change the value of human beings if the thinking of the eternal no longer rested entirely upon their shoulders.

There is one further problem that lingers around Meillassoux's account of the host capacity of thought. Meillassoux's thought is a materialism, which he defines in the following way: 'for me, materialism holds in two key statements: 1. Being is separate and independent of thought (understood in the broad sense of subjectivity), 2. Thought can think Being' (IntDT 79). Furthermore Meillassoux considers the paradigm of all materialisms to be the Epicureanism according to which:

> thought can access the absolute nature of all things through the notions of atoms and void, and which asserts that this nature is not necessarily correlated with an act of thought, since thought exists only in an aleatory manner, being immanent to contingent atomic compounds (for the gods themselves are decomposable), which are in-essential for the existence of elementary natures. (AF 50/AfF 36)

If thought is immanent to atomic compounds as Meillassoux describes it here, and if those atomic compounds (otherwise known as the human brain) are subject to hyperchaotic change in the same way that everything else that in/exists is, then how can human thought be exempt from the hyperchaotic change which is the absolute and universal condition of everything?[18] In other words, Meillassoux owes us an account of the relation between thought and the brain, in the absence of which we must assume that material human thinking – including the capacity to think the eternal – is subject to hyperchaotic change just as much as anything else that exists, and therefore that the thoughts produced by that material reasoning, whether they be thoughts about the principle of factiality, the ultimate value of human beings or anything else, cannot be taken as an absolute guide to the eternal nature of the universe because, like everything else, they can change. And, if they can be taken as such a guide, and if the atomic compounds of the human brain are just as subject to hyperchaotic change as everything else, then in what way can Meillassoux coherently claim to be a materialist? What is thought if, even in its immanence to contingent atomic compounds, it is not subject to the hyperchaotic changes that those compounds can undergo? And what is materialism, if it denies the equation of thought with (material) brain activity? Peter Gratton concludes that 'it's unclear if Meillassoux considers thought to be extra-material, that is, non-reductive to physical processes in the brain'.[19] My own conclusion is slightly different: it seems that Meillassoux considers thought to be material and yet not reducible to physical processes in the brain, and I do not see how he can have his cerebral cake and eat it in this way. We have now arrived at a point where we cannot advance in our investigation of materialism without addressing the question of the relation between the brain and thought. It is to that question that we shall turn in the next chapter, after finishing our investigation of Meillassoux by considering his treatment of the theme of anthropocentrism.

Escaping anthropocentrism

Meillassoux's Cartesian (anti-)anthropocentrism

It is one of the most thoroughly discussed aspects of Meillassoux's thought that the argument of *After Finitude* seeks to identify and to move away from the pervasive 'correlationism' that characterises post-Kantian philosophy. Correlationism is a double thesis, with implications for both thought and reality: it 'consists in disqualifying the claim that it is possible to consider the realms of subjectivity and objectivity independently of one another' (*AF* 18–19/*AfF* 5). The weak (Kantian) correlationist holds that we can know *that* there is an in-itself independent of our thought and that this in-itself is non-contradictory, even if we cannot know it directly; the strong correlationist denies that we can even know whether there is an in-itself independent of our thought at all, much less whether any such in-itself may or may not be non-contradictory (*AF* 48/*AfF* 35).

The problem with correlationism for Meillassoux is that it is an irreducibly anthropocentric and anthropomorphic paradigm: anthropomorphic because I can know nothing as it is 'in itself', only ever as it is 'for me'; and anthropocentric because it becomes unintelligible to conceive any reality not always already correlated to human consciousness. In contradistinction to this correlationist anthropocentrism, Meillassoux insists upon the anti-anthropocentric nature of his own speculative materialism. Both speculation and materialism are intended to strike a blow at the dependence of truth on human cognition. Meillassoux defines 'speculative' as a resistance to anthropocentrism: 'By "speculative" I mean every pretension of thought to arrive at an absolute: that is, an eternal truth independent, on this account, of the contingencies (psychological, historical, linguistic) of our relationship to the world' (IWB 445). As for 'materialism', it is intended as a bulwark against anthropomorphising the nonhuman:

> for me, materialism holds in two key statements: 1. Being is separate and independent of thought (understood in the broad sense of subjectivity), 2. Thought can think Being. Thesis number 1 is opposed to any anthropomorphism which seeks to extend subjective attributes to Being: materialism is not a form of animism, spiritualism, vitalism, etcetera. (IntDT 79; see also *AF* 50/*AfF* 36)

Speculative materialism seeks to overcome the anthropocentric bias of post-Kantian correlationism by thinking a world independent of human thought, summed up in the motif of the 'Great Outdoors' or the 'Great Outside' (*le Grand Dehors*), which Meillassoux defines as 'the eternal in-itself, whose being is indifferent to whether or not it is thought' (*AF* 86/ *AfF* 63). Figured in temporal terms, the Great Outdoors designates 'a past where both humanity and life are absent' (*AF* 37/*AfF* 26) and, in the future, a 'world in-itself' that 'would subsist despite the abolition of every relation-to-the-world' (*AF* 97/*AfF* 71). Meillassoux's Great Outdoors as presented in *After Finitude* has two main traits, both of which underline its non-anthropocentric nature. First, it is independent of us, 'existing in itself regardless of whether we are thinking about it or not', and secondly, it is indifferent to us and to its own givenness, a 'glacial world [. . .] in which there is no longer any up or down, centre or periphery, nor anything else that might make of it a world designed for humans' (*AF* 159/ *AfF* 115; see also CEA 6–7/CAA 6).

Meillassoux's claim to access the Great Outdoors rests on a Cartesian thesis. In 'Contingency and Absolutisation of the One' he sums up his project as 'a reactivation of the Cartesian spirit against the Kantian spirit – namely, the ability to establish by reason the absolute value of mathematical reconstructions of reality as certifiable, revisable hypotheses, whose meaning is ultimately realist rather than transcendental' (CEA 4/CAA 4). What is important for Meillassoux is Descartes' insistence that the mathematisable is the absolutisable. Lest the idea of a mathematisation of the absolute conjure in our minds images from *The Matrix* that cloud our understanding of what Meillassoux is claiming, it is important to be clear on both the nature of the knowledge that this mathematised absolute yields for Meillassoux and how it is that mathematics yields it. Answers to both queries can be found in the phrase that concludes the paragraph from *After Finitude* already quoted: 'It is a question of absolutizing the mathematical [. . .] by grasping in the fundamental criterion for every mathematical statement a necessary condition for the contingency of every entity' (*AF* 175/*AfF* 126). This brief quotation raises two questions: (1) what is 'the fundamental criterion for every mathematical statement'?, and (2) what does it mean to grasp 'the contingency of every entity'?

Meillassoux elaborates a response to the first question at length in the third section of 'Iteration, reiteration, repetition', in the course of his discussion of the meaningless sign. He identifies the meaningless sign as 'a basic quality, common enough so as to characterize all symbolic language, and yet precise enough to remain foreign to all natural language' (CEA 19/CAA 19).[20] All formal languages, both logical and mathematical, rely on meaningless signs, Meillassoux notes, and he illustrates what he means with reference to set theory. In addition to 'operator-signs' (such as ⊂ (includes), ∈ (belongs to), or = (is equal to)), set theory wields 'signs with which these operators ultimately work', which Meillassoux calls 'base-signs' (CEA 19/CAA 19). It is the base-signs that are meaningless, as Meillassoux explains:

> The standard axioms of Set theory, to put it crudely, begin with signs – 'a', 'b', 'c', etc. – which are commonly called 'sets'. But Set theory never actually defines what a set is. And of course in and of themselves the signs signify nothing whatsoever – and necessarily so – precisely because they're tasked with providing a foundation devoid of all meaning on which the operator-signs can function. (CEA 19/CAA 19)

What is significant about these non-signifying signs for Meillassoux is that their non-signification itself signifies their utter and irreducible contingency: they could signify anything at all. Therefore 'the condition of possibility for the very thinkability of the SDM [sign devoid of meaning]' (CEA 20/CAA 20) is our grasp of eternal contingency, namely the principle of factiality. To understand the non-signification of the meaningless sign is to have understood 'the eternal contingency of everything'. It is for this reason that 'there is an essential link between this sort of sign and absolutized contingency' (IRR 18).

Meillassoux presses the meaningless sign into service with a move reminiscent of the moment of the 'intellectual intuition of the absolute' (*AF* 111/*AfF* 82) in *After Finitude*. In a similar way, the non-referentiality of formalised mathematical signs is usually 'a way of neutralizing any ontological question or aim' (IRR 23), but Meillassoux makes it the very basis of mathematical ontology. Mathematics is not to be equated with reality itself, nor does it describe reality in every detail. Rather it foregrounds the radical and eternal contingency of all reality, which is precisely what constitutes Meillassoux's absolute knowledge.[21] So the fundamental criterion for every mathematical statement is that it instantiates the necessary contingency of the meaningless sign, and in so doing that it demonstrates the principle of factiality. This is not Meillassoux looking down on the sciences of biology and physics as inferior or unworthy of study. He chooses formalised mathematics not out of some snooty disdain for practicality but because it is the meaningless sign of formalised languages that alone instantiates the factiality which is our only knowledge of the absolute. That is why 'mathematics and mathematized physics give us the means to identify the properties of a world that is radically independent of thought' (IRR 18).

It is this absolute quality of the meaningless sign that drives forward Meillassoux's mathematisation, and not some latter-day Pythagoreanism or a conviction that 'all is number'. His purpose is not 'to assert that Being is inherently mathematical: it is rather to explain how it is that a formal language manages to capture, from contingent-Being, properties that a vernacular language fails to restitute'. He continues: 'My thesis on mathematics is a thesis on the scope of formal languages, not a thesis on Being' (IntDT 80). When Meillassoux claims that reality is exhaustively mathematisable he means that all of reality in/exists in a way that is demonstrated by the infinite contingency of the mathematical meaningless sign, not that everything can be exhaustively expressed in terms of numbers.

In response to the second question raised by Meillassoux's summary of the absolute knowledge gained through mathematics – namely 'what does it mean to grasp the contingency of every entity?' – mathematical reasoning affords access not to the *what* of the Great Outdoors but to its *how*. As a speculative philosopher Meillassoux is not interested in what is, but in what is necessary, not what happens to be or can be, but what must be.[22] The principle of factiality yields no insights about the treeness of a tree (whether fossilised or contemporary), for example, and in 'Iteration, reiteration, repetition' Meillassoux insists on the importance of empirical science for investigating what happens to exist. What it does yield is access to the tree's facticity, its in/existence: I know absolutely that it could not exist, in the same way that I know absolutely of anything that inexists (in other words, that does not currently exist) that it could exist. What I know absolutely is how ('how' in the sense of 'in what manner') everything that is is, and how everything that is not is not: everything that exists could not exist, and everything that does not exist could exist. So through the principle of factiality I know precisely as much about unicorns as I do about horses (I know that the former could exist, and the latter could not exist), which is also exactly the same that I know about flying spaghetti monsters. I access the Great Outdoors not in terms of a *what* but a *how*.

It is now time to highlight two important problems or ironies in Meillassoux's Cartesian anti-anthropocentrism.[23] The first irony is that the anti-anthropocentrism of the Great Outdoors leaves open a back door through which the anthropocentric can sneak back in. This back door anthropocentrism is hinted at but not decisively exposed by Peter Hallward when he argues that 'the idea that the meaning of the statement "the universe was formed 13.5 billion years ago" might be independent of the mind that thinks it only makes sense if you disregard the quaintly parochial unit of measurement involved'.[24] The point Hallward is seeking to make, of course, is that the year as a unit of measurement belongs to earth-bound human experience; without humans and without the solar system, time would not be measured in 'years'. The Meillassouxian can easily brush off Hallward's argument in the terms it is stated by pointing out that Meillassoux's point is not about any particular unit of measurement but about the status of the meaningless sign in formalised language. As Nathan Brown argues, Hallward's point has force only insofar as it stretches Meillassoux's arguments 'beyond the proper domain of their application – to which Meillassoux himself is careful to restrict them'.[25] Meillassoux does not argue that units of measurement or mathematical descriptions of objects 'might be independent of the mind'.[26] He argues that 'what is mathematizable cannot be reduced to a correlate of thought' (*AF* 162/*AfF* 117). For Meillassoux (after Descartes) the mathematical descriptions of physics or cosmology index primary qualities.[27] Hallward's critique would only hold if Meillassoux were a naïve realist, claiming that the world is absolutely transparent to human language, but Meillassoux's realism is speculative and not naïve, and he leaves everything but the principle of factiality to empirical science.[28] What is more, the observation quickly becomes a ubiquitous platitude. If the unit of measurement is quaint, so also are the notions of 'quaintness' and 'the parochial', so is the notion of the Great Outdoors, which is only 'great' from our point of view, and so on ad infinitum and ad nauseam. All that this in principle unending string of observations demonstrates is the tautology that human *language* is *human* language, which is precisely why Meillassoux turns to the meaningless sign of mathematics.

Hallward's argument does, however, tangentially indicate an irony in speculative realist thought that cannot so easily be dismissed. There is a sense in which anti-anthropocentrism can only be expressed in terms that are themselves irremediably anthropocentric, for every assertion that the universe is indifferent to human concerns is concerned not to be indifferent to the misguided anthropocentrism of correlationism. Meillassoux's concern to clarify that we live in a 'glacial world [. . .] in which there is no longer any up or down, centre or periphery, nor anything else that might make of it a world designed for humans' (*AF* 159/*AfF* 115), along with his concern to show the ill-foundedness of correlationism, are just as anthropocentric as the concern of some in past centuries to demonstrate that the earth was at the centre of the universe, or that all truth is relative to human consciousness. The universe, it will be remembered, is not anti-anthropocentric but indifferent. A true break with anthropocentrism would therefore not be an equal and opposite insistence on the peripheral or unimportant nature of humanity, but an immoveable and deep indifference as to whether the universe is judged (by humans no less!) to be anthropocentric or not, and Meillassoux (along with the other speculative realists) is anything but indifferent on this matter. Contrasted with this supreme indifference of the universe to whether humans have anthropocentric or anti-anthropocentric thoughts, it is hard to fit a cigarette paper between the anthropocentrism of the correlationists and the anti-anthropocentrism of the speculative realists. Why should the non-anthropocentrist care if some people think the universe is anthropocentric? After all, the universe doesn't. To care (either way) is to be anthropocentric. The irony is illustrated even more acutely by Graham Harman in *The Quadruple Object*:

> However interesting we humans may be to ourselves, we are apparently in no way central to the cosmic drama, marooned as we are on an average-sized planet near a mediocre sun, and confined to a tiny portion of the history of the universe.[29]

The quaint parochialism here is not in a unit of measurement but, first, in the assumption that it matters either way, and secondly in the implicit equation of size and longevity with importance. This latter assumption is a very human (perhaps a very modern Western, even capitalist) move to make: bigger and longer must be better and more important. Whether human beings are tiny (relative to the size of the universe) and short-lived (relative to its duration) should not in itself lead either to the conclusion that they are central or peripheral, important or unimportant. Or at least, it only leads to those conclusions on anthropocentric grounds. The antidote to self-aggrandisement is not self-abasement but self-forgetfulness.

Furthermore, to want to *know* our place (as significant or insignificant, as central or peripheral, little matter) is a very anthropocentric desire, one which Meillassoux and others[30] foreground, and one which once again departs markedly from the indifference of the universe. To recognise myself as peripheral to the universe is still, by dint of my own powers, to have found my (very small) place in the universe, and the size of the place in this context is not as significant as the feat of having reasoned my way to it. In other words, the very moment that would appear to be a triumph of anti-anthropocentrism can only be construed as such in the first place because of a great human achievement: I am the only animal who can demonstrate how insignificant I am. If that makes me frustrated that I am not larger or longer-lasting, then I need only remember the famous line of Mill's *Utilitarianism*: 'It is better to be a human being dissatisfied than a pig satisfied; better to be Socrates dissatisfied than a fool satisfied.'[31] It takes greatness to recognise and not shy away from one's insignificance and peripheral place in the universe, and a rigorous anti-anthropocentrism is a jewel in the crown of human knowledge and achievement. To know that one is not central is still to know, and it is to know more – and better – than those who falsely assume they are central or those who have no thoughts on the matter at all. This is a dynamic acknowledged and embraced in the nihilism of Ray Brassier, who argues that 'I think that it is possible to understand the meaninglessness of existence, and that this capacity to understand meaning as a regional or bounded phenomenon marks a fundamental progress in cognition.'[32] At the very least, it is always possible for a recognition of ontological insignificance to be sublated into an aggrandising moment of significant epistemological recognition, and for anti-anthropocentrism to be revealed as an anthropocentric triumph. Loser wins.

The second irony in Meillassoux's anti-anthropocentrism is that correlationism is only a problem in the first place if he assumes (as he does) a Cartesian dualism of the for-me and the in-itself, of the subject and the object. Ray Brassier acknowledges that Meillassoux's thought remains entangled with 'the Cartesian dualism of thought and extension',[33] and Robert S. Gall points out that Meillassoux's approach 'starts with assumptions about the distinctions between subject and object, thought and extension, primary and secondary qualities', and that 'it is only within such an epistemological framework that the problem of the existence of the external world is a problem'.[34] Though it is dangerous to set too much store by illustrations and explanatory devices, it is nevertheless the case that the term 'Great Outdoors' minimally presupposes an 'inside' (a reworked Cartesian *cogito*) and an 'outside' (a variant of the *res existensa*), along with a means of accessing the latter from the former. The very existence of the 'Great Outdoors' relies on a concomitant 'Cramped Interior'. Why assume the radical dichotomy of inside and outside to begin with, only then to labour to overcome it? Meillassoux's reasons are no doubt in part polemical: he is seeking to destabilise correlationism from inside, to come up with a demonstration which the correlationist, on her own terms, must be forced to accept, and so he works within her assumptions as a fifth column.

Nevertheless, Meillassoux's distinct lack of interest to overcome the in-itself/for-me distinction (and the reliance of his own cornerstone principle of factiality on the same distinction) strikes a further blow to his attempt to reject anthropocentrism and anthropomorphism, for it partitions off the human thinking-self from the rest of the universe with a dualism of thought and non-thought. Rather than seeking to overcome anthropocentrism by arguing that (human) thought has access to the factiality of the in-itself (which, once more, exalts the achievements of human knowledge in a way that walks straight into the jaws of anthropocentrism), a more effective strategy would be to labour to overcome the dualism in the first place. In Chapters 3–6 of the present book it is this alternative strategy of undermining the dichotomy of inside and outside that will come to the fore, in Catherine Malabou's recent work on epigenesis, Michel Serres's invagination of the 'inside' and the 'outside' in his image of the Klein bottle, and Bruno Latour's rejection of the 'modern constitution'. In these chapters we shall see that the important point is not that there is a mind-independent reality, but that there is no reality-independent mind.

From within a Meillassouxian frame of reference, a similar result could be achieved through a strategy which would seek to think correlation not as a specifically human problem but rather as a principle according to which everything in reality is co-related, and nothing is in-itself. The strategy could make use of Meillassoux's three existing *ex nihilo* Worlds of matter, life and thought.[35] It would look something like this: let us imagine that what Meillassoux calls 'correlationism' is but one instance of a wider phenomenon that obtains in each of these Worlds. Two stones are co-related in terms of matter (they are non-porous to each other; they can sit one on top of the other, and so on). A stone and an animal are co-related in terms of matter and life on the side of the animal (the stone can be a bed, a tool, an object under which grubs can be found, and so on), and in terms of matter alone on the side of the stone. The world is co-related to me according to my capacity for thought, according to my nature as a living being and according to my materiality. Such a re-thinking of correlation would make it trivial and ubiquitous, and the correlation of the world to human thought would be only one instance of a wider phenomenon that obtains in each of Meillassoux's three Worlds, with the result that we would flatter ourselves and make too much of our own importance if we were to think of co-relation as a uniquely human issue. The problem is not that things correlate to us, but that we anthropocentrically assume that they correlate *only* to us. In the absence of such a strategy, Meillassoux is committed to anthropocentrism from the moment he identifies correlation as a problem.

Vitalism, subjectialism and anthropocentrism

We can see some of the complexities of Meillassoux's rejection of anthropocentrism in the essay 'Iteration, reiteration, repetition', in which he develops and refines some of the main arguments of *After Finitude*. In the essay he identifies – on his own account more clearly than in the previous book (IRR 4) – two separate antagonists whose positions he is seeking to disrupt: the subjectialist[36] and the correlationist. Both positions are anthropocentric because they both fail to do justice to a reality independent of human thought, and they are both anthropomorphic in that they ascribe to the whole of reality traits only properly found in human experience.

Correlationism and subjectialism both belong to the 'era of the Correlation' which runs from Berkeley to the present day, and they compose 'two opposite movements regarding the absolute' (IRR 3). Correlationism 'in the form of skepticism, the transcendental, phenomenology or postmodernism, denied thought all access to the absolute' (IRR 3). The correlationist knows along with Kant that there is an absolute, but has no access to that absolute in itself, only to its correlation with the categories of our thought. Subjectialism, on the other hand, is not a scepticism but an absolutism; it does not de-absolutise thought like correlationism but it absolutises (human) thought itself, in one of two ways. The first variant form of subjectialism is idealism, which claims that we can have access to the absolute because the absolute is nothing other than the correlate itself. This is the position of Bishop Berkeley who, though he was the 'inventor of the argument of the correlationist circle, was not a correlationist, but a subjectialist' (IRR 6). For Berkeley, all that exists are (human or divine) minds and ideas. The second variant is vitalism, which like idealism also 'absolutises various features of subjectivity' (IntDT 72). Contemporary Nietzschean or Deleuzian vitalisms absolutise or hypostatise 'will, perception, affect, et cetera' (IntDT 73), understanding the whole of reality to be shot through with these features of agency and consciousness previously reserved for human beings alone, and understanding these human features to be 'radically independent of our human and individual relationship to the world' (IntDT 73). Insofar as it 'claims to accede to an absolute reality', subjectialism is also a realism of ideas (IRR 6).[37] Our interest in subjectialism and correlationism in this chapter lies in the question of their respective relation to anthropomorphism and anthropocentrism, and what light those relations shed on Meillassoux's own argument. I will work through each position in turn, beginning with a discussion of idealist subjectialism, followed by vitalist subjectialism and, finally, correlationism.

Meillassoux does not refute the Berkeleyan idealist form of subjectialism. Peter Gratton finds it odd that 'his [Meillassoux's] method has nothing to say about idealisms that simply deny any correlation at all', and that as a result 'since he [Berkeley] doesn't posit any correlation of thinking and being, anything Meillassoux has to do to critique correlationism will not, strangely, affect realism's most avowed enemy, idealism'.[38] Berkeleyan idealism is, in Adrian Johnston's neat summation of Meillassoux's position, 'presumed without argument to be prima facie untenable in its ridiculous absurdity'.[39] Rather than merely accepting this position and quickly moving on to Meillassoux's engagement with vitalist subjectivism, I would like (in the spirit of Meillassoux's own constructive contrarianism) to tarry awhile on this ridiculous absurdity which both he and his commentators deem barely worthy of engagement.

Johnston dismisses the correlationist's insistence that every 'ancestral utterance' of the scientist referring to a moment before the appearance of sentient life on earth be completed with the addendum 'for humans (or even for the human scientist)' as a 'superficial tactic' and an 'irrefutable, cheap-and-easy trick (reminiscent of the un-falsifiable idealist assertions of Bishop Berkeley)',[40] and Gratton similarly dismisses Berkeley's idealism as a 'tiresome conundrum'.[41] However, if the prerequisite of depth, non-trickery and difficulty is falsifiability, then it is far from clear that Meillassoux fares any better than his idealist antagonist. How would we falsify the principle of factiality? By, *per impossibile*, allowing an infinite span of time to pass and observing no hyperchaotic change? Even if that were possible it would not provide a satisfactory refutation of hyperchaos, because of what I have previously called a 'split rationality critique' of Meillassoux.[42] Meillassoux's whole philosophy turns not on a falsifiable demonstration, in the final analysis, but on a moment variously called 'intellectual intuition' (*AF* 111/*AfF* 82), a 'jolt' (*saccade*) (ID 342–5), the 'transmutation of reason' (CEA 12/CAA 12) and 'a switching of our mode of apprehension' (IRR 37). It is the intuition by virtue of which a failure (for example: I cannot think any necessary being) is transformed into a breakthrough (for example: there are no necessary beings), and it is at the root of the principle of factiality.[43]

In 'Contingency and Absolutisation of the One' Meillassoux describes intuition in the following terms:

> I propose that facticity *ought to no longer mark* the index of a limitation on the inability of thought to discover the reason of things; now, rather, facticity *should be regarded as* an index of thought's ability to discover absolute unreason – the absolute absence of all reason for everything. (CEA 12/CAA 12; my emphasis)

Why ought it no longer? Why should it? In response to these questions Meillassoux can furnish a phalanx of more or less convincing pragmatic and ethical reasons, but he can give no demonstration of the necessity of this intuition for the very good reason that it is not necessary at all, no more nor less necessary in fact than Berkeley's own move (we could equally call it an 'intuition') which takes him from being unable to assert the non-ideal existence of the world to asserting his idealism. Neither Berkeley's position nor Meillassoux's is rightly characterised, in my opinion, as either superficial or cheap merely by virtue of being unfalsifiable. Berkeley's 'conundrum' is only 'tiresome' if, with anthropocentric flourish, we consider that the universe owes us absolute knowledge. It is only tiresome in the way that a lofty and unscalable mountain is tiresome. Positions like Berkeley's and Meillassoux's could well be held for cheap or superficial reasons – and in this I am quite in agreement with Johnston –

but the positions themselves are neither inherently cheap nor superficial, apart from on anthropocentric grounds.

Let us turn now from idealist to vitalist subjectialism. Meillassoux considers the vitalist subjectivist to be hoist by her own anthropological petard. In the first section of 'Iteration, reiteration, repetition' he reconstructs the vitalist critique of idealist subjectialism, a critique anti-anthropological in its intent:

> it claimed to be antihumanist, or counter-anthropological: It is a question [. . .] of breaking (so we are told) with the derisory anthropocentrism in which man believes himself the sole depository of the subjective faculty that one intends to absolutize; of showing that man is but one particular representative, misguided by the prejudices of his consciousness, of a sensibility, of a life, that overflows him in every direction. He must, so it was insisted, go back down within himself to the infra-conscious level, to participate fully in this a-human subjectivity whose flux conveys him and transpierces him. (IRR 5)

However, this attempt to debunk the anthropomorphism (of holding that only thought exists) backfires, according to Meillassoux, because what it substitutes is a further anthropomorphism, this time projecting qualities of human subjectivity onto the nonhuman world:

> But this refusal of anthropocentrism in fact leads only to an anthropomorphism that consists in the illusion of seeing in every reality (even inorganic reality) subjective traits the experience of which is in fact entirely human, merely varying their degree (an equally human act of imagination) [. . .]. To free oneself of man, in this strange humanism-in-denial, was simply to disseminate oneself everywhere, even into rocks and particles, and according to a whole scale of intensities. (IRR 5)

All vitalism succeeds in doing is replacing anthropocentrism with anthropo-inflationism, hypostatising facets of human subjectivity (Meillassoux names a number of examples in IRR 4: 'will to power' and 'the inorganic life of things', sensation, perception, creation) throughout the nonhuman world.

I have two points to make about the way in which Meillassoux reads the failure of the vitalist critique of idealist subjectialism. First, on what basis can we decide between the two claims that these hypostatised traits of human subjectivity either (1) belong properly only to the human and are falsely ascribed to the nonhuman world, or (2) are properly general features of the world, and their appearance in human subjectivity is but one instantiation of this wider phenomenon? As far as I can see, there is no way to decide this question other than in terms of a *parti pris* for one position or the other (vitalism or factiality). Meillassoux offers no evidence accessible to anyone not yet already in agreement with him that these traits are exclusively human. Consider again the following quotation from an interview published in 2012:

> for me, materialism holds in two key statements: 1. Being is separate and independent of thought (understood in the broad sense of subjectivity), 2. Thought can think Being. Thesis number 1 is opposed to any anthropomorphism which seeks to extend subjective attributes to Being: materialism is not a form of animism, spiritualism, vitalism, etcetera. (IntDT 79)

Meillassoux simply assumes here that the 'subjective attributes' in question are not originally in 'Being' but have to be 'extended'. This is by no means an uncontroversial position to take, and indeed it seems to run athwart the biological and natural sciences that would precisely see human capacities to be on a continuum with features found in the nonhuman natural world, rather than of a different (*ex nihilo*) origin or nature. Meillassoux is taking the rather anthropocentric position that whatever traits characterise human subjectivity are properly and exclusively human, and are only ever falsely attributed to nonhuman existence. Neither here nor elsewhere does he defend this position in its own terms, rather he merely assumes that all the traits which characterise humanity (will to power, sensation . . .) are primordially and proprietorially human: human beings own the copyright on everything they possess. Meillassoux finds himself, rather awkwardly to my mind, defending the twin positions that (1) humans are not natural (a rather anthropocentric view!), and that (2) any trait shared by humans and the nonhuman world must be a human trait (a rather anthropomorphic view!) Why must we assume that everything in the nonhuman world that looks similar to something in the human world must necessarily be first and foremost a human trait that is only ascribed to the nonhuman through a surfeit of anthropocentrism? Is it not at least equally valid to argue that the anthropocentrism here is the very assumption that those traits belong to humanity alone in the first place? It is this Meillassouxian assumption that ring-fences a robust human exceptionalism, not the vitalist's hypostatisation. While Meillassoux labours to argue that the 'natural' world is not human, we shall see Michel Serres in the fifth chapter argue that the 'human' world is quite natural.

My second point in relation to Meillassoux's dismissal of the vitalist critique of idealist subjectialism is that there is a sense in which he falls into exactly the same trap in which he sees the vitalist ensnared. He too hypostatises one feature that previously described humanity alone, making it pervade the whole universe. That feature is not subjectivity or the will to power as in the case of the vitalists, but exemption from law-governed determinism. Whereas the natural world has for centuries been considered by scientists and philosophers alike to be fundamentally constrained by laws which make its movements and changes predictable and deter-mined, exemption from such law-governed determinism has been seen as the province of human existence alone. To take but one of the most prominent examples, for the Sartre of *Being and Nothingness* the nonhu-man world is in-itself, identical with itself: it 'is what it is'. It is nihilating human consciousness alone which is for-itself, which 'is not what it is and is what it is not'; in Meillassoux's terms it 'inexists' in the sense that it could become what it is not and could cease to be what it is. Human consciousness alone is not condemned to law-governed predictability but can become what it is not. What Meillassoux does is to take this peculiarly anthropological possibility for change and hypostatise it so that it is writ large across the whole universe: the only absolute is that everything can be different; everything 'from trees to stars, from stars to laws, from physical laws to logical laws' (*AF* 73/*AfF* 53) can be what it is not, and can cease to be what it is. Furthermore, in the same way that Meillassoux has no way of demonstrating his position over against that of the vitalist, so also the decision is undecidable between Meillassoux's own hypostatisation of the human exemption from deterministic laws and his own account accord-ing to which the principle of factiality is a feature of the universe and not a projected anthropological trait. What we can say is that the structure of his critique of the vitalist ineradicably puts his own position into question in the very same terms.

We turn now, and finally for this section, to Meillassoux's engagement with correlationism. The correlationist, it will be remembered, is forced – on pain of becoming a subjectialist – to hold that, even though we do not know *what* the absolute is, we do know *that* it exists: we have no direct access to the noumenon but we do not doubt its existence. Meillassoux considers this position to be anthropocentric, but I want to suggest that his refutation of correlationism betrays a deeper anthropocentrism than the one he dispatches. In order to show how this is the case we will focus on that section of 'Iteration, reiteration, repetition' in which Meillassoux clarifies the relation of empirical science to the absolute.

Meillassoux distinguishes two senses of the word 'absolute': in the first sense, he explains, '"absolute" refers to a property that is necessary for every being – such a property is absolute in the speculative sense. Thus facticity, and the logical consistency derived from it, are absolutely neces-sary and infrangible properties of every being' (IRR 18). This first sense he calls 'primo-absolutizing properties'. The second sense of the word 'abso-lute' concerns the natural sciences and 'designates properties of the world that I do not posit as absolutely necessary, but as facts which, as to their existence, are *radically independent of thought*' (IRR 18; original emphasis). These, for Meillassoux, are 'deutero-absolutizing properties'.[44]

He explains:

> To say it more clearly: the laws and constants described by the natural sciences are not, for me, necessary – like every thing, they are subject to that superior regime of Time that I call Hyperchaos. But I would like to show that these laws and constants are not, for all that, mere correlates of thought; that they are absolute in the primary sense of *absolutus* – separate from us, independent of the thought that we have of them. (IRR 18)

Scientific naturalism, then, deals only with deutero-absolutising properties, with laws and constants that are independent of our thought about them, and it chooses not to concern itself with speculative primo-absolutising properties to which its methodology can give it no access.

We must, I submit, make a similar distinction between two forms of anthropocentrism. There is, to be sure, a naïve anthropocentrism – let us call it the 'deutero-anthropocentrism' – of a correlationism for which I only ever have access to objects, laws and constants as correlates of my thought. But there is also a second anthropocentrism, a 'primo-anthropocentrism' that is just as inescapable as a Meillassouxian primo-absolutising property. To see the nature of this primo-anthropocentrism, consider Meillassoux's critique of correlationism in terms of two steps, to which it will in time prove necessary to add a third. Step one: as a correlationist I am forced to argue (lest I have no way to differentiate myself from the subjectialist) for the necessary contingency of the way things appear to me (in other words: they could always be different to how I perceive them). I am forever doomed to be a prisoner to my own apprehension. This is the position of the correlationist sceptic in *After Finitude*, and it is what I am calling a deutero-anthropocentrism. Step two: Meillassoux disabuses the anguished correlationist of her deutero-anthropocentrism by pointing out that her realisation of the necessary contingency of every correlation is not an epistemological defeat but an ontological breakthrough to the bedrock of an absolute, namely the absolute of factiality. It is not just that everything is necessarily *contingent*, but that everything is *necessarily* contingent. This is Meillassoux's principle of factiality, in chapter 3 of *After Finitude*.

Meillassoux stops at the second step, but we must go further and add a third. Because Meillassoux has no mechanism to ensure that the hyperchaos which makes the laws of nature and the laws of logic contingent along with everything else (*AF* 73/*AfF* 53), and that therefore guarantees the epistemological breakthrough of factiality, obediently turns back when it reaches the shores of 'necessity' and 'contingency' themselves. Meillassoux assumes that, through any hyperchaotic change, the concepts of 'necessity' and 'contingency' as I currently understand them (along with my current grasp of hyperchaos) will remain constant and will continue to give me an absolute hold on the way things are, in just the same way that the naturalist whom he critiques thinks that the present state of our science gives us an absolute hold on the way things are. And it will not do to retort that any change in such fundamental notions and the laws of logic on which they rely is strictly unthinkable, because if we limited ourselves only to what is currently thinkable we would not have much of a hyper-chaos. It is the *mise en jeu* of Meillassoux's own thinking (and yours, and mine) that is at stake here. He cannot, Canute-like, halt the rising tide of hyperchaos at the shores of his own reasoning, any more than the naturalist can halt it at the laboratory door.

So just as Meillassoux invites the scientist to renounce her deutero-anthropocentrism, we must counsel Meillassoux to abandon the anthropo-exceptionalism of refusing to admit that his own thinking is part of the situation he describes. In Meillassoux's account of primo-absolutising properties, only contingency is absolute; in order for that assertion to make sense he also has to hold to the primo-anthropocentrism according to which only human reasoning is exempt from hyperchaotic changes in the laws of logic. There is an ineliminable primo-anthropocentric moment in Meillassoux's thought.

Conclusion

What is at stake for Meillassoux's figure of the human is the possibility of marrying the supreme and ultimate value of humanity to an anti-anthropocentrism. He seeks to achieve this by understanding humans as the bearers of value by virtue of their capacity to think the eternal absolute. But in the course of this chapter we have seen that there are problems both with his account of the value of humanity and the way in which he develops the anti-anthropocentrism of his speculative materialism. His account of human value relies upon the effective exercise of the capacity for rational thought in a way that repeats the dangers we identified in Badiou's philosophy, namely that the value of some of the most vulnerable groups of human beings (neonates, the senile, those with severe mental disabilities) is insufficiently accounted for.

However, because of his account of the Great Outdoors and his attempt to escape anthropocentrism, he also comes up more acutely than Badiou against the subtle tentacles of anthropocentrism and anthropo-morphism. He is able to overcome what we have called the 'deutero-anthropocentrism' of correlationism only through a more fundamental 'primo-anthropocentrism' which enshrines one's understanding of certain truths as the only constant in the whole universe which is not subject to hyperchaotic change. The anti-anthropocentrism of Meillassoux and other 'speculative realists' cohabits quite peacefully with a deeper anthropocentrism, all the while living off its borrowed capital. In the case of both of these problems, the issue is related to the way human identity, equality and value, as well as of all eternal and absolute knowledge, are made contingent upon a determinate and positive human capacity, which we have called the 'host capacity' for rational thought. It is in an attempt to search for a materialist account of humanity that does not fall prey to the problems inherent in such a host capacity approach, and to uncouple the human as such from any determinate gatekeeper capacity, that I turn in the third chapter of the book to the thought of Catherine Malabou.

Chapter 3

Catherine Malabou: The Plastic Human

The human is plastic. This means that it gives itself its own form, that it is able to transform itself, to invent and produce itself, and that it is nothing but this very process of self-formation.

Malabou, 'The future of the Humanities'

Je suis la plaie et le couteau!
Je suis le soufflet et la joue!
Je suis les membres et la roue,
Et la victime et le bourreau!

Baudelaire, *L'Héautontimorouménos* [1]

In the first two chapters we saw that Badiou and Meillassoux each make a particular, determinate human capacity the gatekeeper of full-orbed humanity: for Badiou it is the capacity for affirmative thought and for Meillassoux it is the capacity to think the eternal principle of factiality. Such host capacity[2] accounts of the human struggle both with defining humanity so as not to exclude some of those least able to raise their voices in protest and also with the subtleties of an anthropocentrism from which they consider themselves freed. We also saw that, despite their claims to materialism, neither Badiou nor Meillassoux makes efforts to account for the relation between the thought that is so central to their anthropology and the human brain to which (for Meillassoux at least) it is immanent. In the present chapter we turn to the thought of Catherine Malabou in order to explore how contemporary materialist thought might move beyond the problems inherent in a host capacity approach to the human, and how it might fill this lacuna with an account of the relation between thought and brain.

Malabou appropriates the terms 'new materialism' and 'speculative realism' at different times to describe projects with which her own thought is in sympathy. In the early *Plasticité* she interweaves her central notion of plasticity with materialism, arguing that 'it is not possible to conceptualise plasticity without elaborating anew a certain type of *materialism*; that is to say, without bringing to light a determinate relation or ensemble of relations between matter and spirit' (*Pla* 11; my translation). In *Plasticity at the Dusk of Writing* and *Self and Emotional Life* she insists on the need for a 'new materialism' which would signal a serious engagement with neurobiology (*SEL* 71; *PAS* 114/*PDW* 61), adding in the preface to *La Chambre du milieu* that this new materialism will be necessarily dialectic and deconstructive, and yet will eschew the abstract in order to 'think freedom up against [*à même*] matter' (*CDM* 9). Malabou also insists that materialism must be non-reductive (PFPT 27), in other words it will resist dichotomising the material and the ideal, and in *The New Wounded* she makes it clear that central to any contemporary materialism must be a new account of the brain:

> I continue to defend the thesis that the only valid philosophical path today lies in the elaboration of a new materialism that would precisely refuse to envisage the least separation, not only between the brain and thought but also between the brain and the unconscious. It is just such a materialism, as the basis for a new philosophy of spirit, that determined my definition of cerebral reality as an axial logical principle entirely articulated in terms of the formation and de-formation of neuronal connections. (*LNB* 342/*TNW* 211–12)

One of the most constant drumbeats of Malabou's writing is that contemporary philosophy ignores contemporary neuroscience[3] at its peril, and her own turn to neuroscience is driven not by taste but by necessity. She repeatedly laments that philosophy has been blindsided by neuroscience and that it must stop ignoring neuroscientific advances (see *CDM* 229–37; *QF* 36–7/*WSD* 2; EOW 440; *AD* 2). In opposition to Heidegger's assertion that 'science does not think',[4] Malabou seeks to draw on neuroscience as a source not only of examples but also of paradigms for thinking, while at the same time subjecting neuroscientific claims to much-needed philosophical rigour. In short, she seeks to elaborate an account of the materialist self that is neither brainless nor mindless.[5]

In this chapter I shall show how Malabou offers a way to avoid the problems of a host capacity approach to humanity. In her account the human is distinguished not by a determinate capacity but by its self-transformation, or what she will describe as its plasticity. This chapter will introduce Malabou's plastic human in terms of her early engagement with Hegel and her more recent encounters with neuroscience, showing how plasticity does indeed provide a qualitatively different account of the human to a host capacity approach. Along the way, I will indicate two main questions that Malabou must answer.

Plasticity and Hegel

Malabou's first engagement with the paradigm of plasticity is in her doctoral thesis on Hegel, later published as *The Future of Hegel*. The book begins with a reading of the 'Anthropology',[6] a section of twenty-four paragraphs in the third and final volume of Hegel's *Encyclopaedia of the Philosophical Sciences*. The reader beginning to follow the trail set by Malabou through the 'Anthropology' could be forgiven for thinking that these paragraphs provide a quite spectacularly poor basis for elaborating an account of the human that does not rely on determinate host properties. Under the heading 'The knowledge of man's genuine reality – of what is essentially and ultimately true and real'[7] Hegel furnishes his reader with the somewhat underwhelming insight that the essence of man[8] is found in upright posture, the tool-like hand, the mouth, laughing, weeping and speech.[9] Surely Hegel will not insult his reader with the crudest of substantialist accounts of human specificity, showing little advance over the notoriously imprecise 'definition' of man as the featherless biped! Indeed he will not, and what Malabou goes on to describe is a quite brilliant Hegelian attempt to preserve human specificity (the contention that there is a meaningful difference between humans and other animals) without that specificity relying on the possession of any determinate capacities.

The Greek substance-subject is plastic: the becoming-form of accident

This journey to find a specificity independent of determinate capacities begins with a close reading of Hegel's account of habit (*hexis*, ἕξις) in the 'Anthropology'.[10] For both Aristotle and Hegel, Malabou notes, there is a close relation between habit and being human (*ADH* 68/*FOH* 45), but for Hegel it is far from the case that habit substitutes in humans for the role played by instinct in animals. Malabou begins her unfolding of the complex role of habit for Hegel by reading it as an instance of plasticity, a term which she describes as carrying both a positive and a negative sense in the 'Anthropology', referring to both the giving and the receiving of form:

> 'Plastic', as an adjective, means two things: on the one hand, to be 'susceptible to changes of form' or malleable (clay is a 'plastic' material); and on the

other hand, 'having the power to bestow form, the power to mould', as in the expressions, 'plastic surgeon' and 'plastic arts'. (*ADH* 20/*FOH* 8)

In the case of habit, the human being gives form to his or her own behaviour through habit in much the same way that a sculptor gives form to a marble slab, and he or she receives form in the same way that the marble is formed by the sculptor. Thus at the end of the 'Anthropology' Hegel defines man as 'the soul's work of art' (*ADH* 99–100/*FOH* 68) and it is through habit that the body 'is pervaded by soul and has become soul's instrument and means' (*ADH* 56/*FOH* 36). It is this combination of giving and receiving form that Hegel, and Malabou after him, calls 'plastic', not form-giving or form-receiving in isolation but both together.

Malabou highlights two important aspects of habit that make it plastic. First it necessitates, in addition to an intentional self-formation, a necessary 'passivity' or 'slumber' (*ADH* 101/*FOH* 70). The human being becomes what it is only on the condition of being absent to itself. The habit that shapes the human subject is always a self-forgetting (because an action performed deliberately as the result of an express intention is not a habit, only becoming so when it is performed without deliberate intention). Secondly, habit transforms the human inasmuch as it makes an accident into a form or an essence, illustrated in what Hegel calls the 'plastic' or exemplary individuals of ancient Greece:

> 'Plastic individuals' are those who synthesize in their very 'style' the essence of the genus and the accident which has become habitual. What in the beginning was merely an accidental fact – Plato's commitment to philosophy, Pericles' to politics, Phidias' to sculpture – is changed through continual repetition of the same gestures, through practice, achieving the integrity of a 'form' (*eidos*). (*ADH* 106/*FOH* 73–4)

Habit, then, is the process by which the contingent becomes essential (*ADH* 107/*FOH* 74), and the exemplary humans who perfect such habit are 'ideal artists shaping themselves' (*ADH* 105/*FOH* 72), artists who transform their first nature into the 'second nature' of habit (*ADH* 83/*FOH* 57).

It seems at this point in the analysis that habit is fulfilling for Malabou's Hegel a role analogous to that played by thought for Badiou and Meillassoux, namely that it is the capacity which distinguishes the human from the nonhuman: 'Man's potential to duplicate his nature emerges from this as the defining anthropological attribute' (*ADH* 83/*FOH* 57). But Malabou sounds a note of caution: 'Does this mean that the ability to develop habits is sufficient on its own to distinguish a "proper of man" within the element of living things?' (*ADH* 83/*FOH* 57). Hegel answers, she insists, with a resounding 'no'. Taking the Greek definition of ἕξις as 'a way of being which is general and permanent' (*ADH* 84/*FOH* 57), Malabou extends the notion of habit beyond the animal to all organic life which is 'characterized by its effort in maintaining its own unity through the synthesis of differences' (*ADH* 85/*FOH* 58), such that 'second nature is always present in organic nature' (*ADH* 96/*FOH* 66). Far from being the preserve of *Homo sapiens* alone, such adaptation and auto-differenti-ation can be seen throughout the vegetable and animal kingdoms (*ADH* 85/*FOH* 58–9). Habit may be more immediately discernible in animals than in plants, but it is certainly not the exclusive preserve of humanity. The formation of habits does not adequately distinguish human from nonhuman life, and habit itself is 'not essentially a property of man' (*ADH* 93/*FOH* 64). Hegel and Malabou must look elsewhere in the search for something that is 'proper to man'.

In what sense can Hegel claim that habit 'signals the gap between man and animal' (*ADH* 93/*FOH* 64)? The answer lies in considering the distinc-tively human way of relating habit and signification. The 'proper of man' for Hegel does not – contra the host capacity approach – consist in affirm-ing that humanity alone possesses a capacity for expressive signification (*ADH* 94/*FOH* 65), but rather that there is something in human expres-sion 'that does not reduce to a pre-constituted *expressed*' (*ADH* 96/*FOH* 65) or, in other words, to a pre-existing inner nature. For the animal organ-ism, environmental influences are immediately reflected back onto the self, forming a 'simple and ideal unity' (*ADH* 97/*FOH* 66) of signifier and signified, of habit and nature. Animal behaviour thus participates in the 'natural state of signification' according to which 'the outer is merely the expression of the inner', and Malabou characterises this account of signifi-cation as 'the state of nature of a second nature' (*ADH* 97/*FOH* 67). When human beings mistakenly believe that their self-expression makes visible a pre-existing inner reality, they make themselves a prisoner to this state of (second) nature (*ADH* 97/*FOH* 67): when we assume that our words and actions express a pre-existing inner reality we are shackled to the phantom of the inner reality which we are presuming to express.

The claim that 'we are our inner nature' is inadequate. But there is a further false step to be avoided, namely the equal and opposite claim that 'we have no inner nature'. Hegel's account does not see-saw into the apophaticism of denying any inner nature at all, but rather dialectises the outer and the inner. The 'proper of man' is not that we have an originary and immediately signified nature (because we do not), nor that we lack an originary nature (though we do), but to be both, and inseparably, inner nature and outward expression, where the two do not coincide. Malabou insists that for Hegel 'the individual is at once "the inner individuality and not its expression"; and "something external, a reality free from the inner", hence "something quite different from the inner"' (*ADH* 98/*FOH* 67), and for Hegel the body 'is at the same time a sign (*Zeichen*) which has not remained an immediate thing (*Sache*), but something through which the individual only makes known what he really is, when he sets his original nature to work' (*ADH* 98/*FOH* 67).

The situation is summed up in the *Phenomenology of Spirit* with a quotation from Georg Christoph Lichtenberg: 'You certainly act like an honest man, but I see from your face that you are forcing yourself to do so and are a rogue at heart.'[11] The signifier ('you certainly look like an honest man') and the signified ('you are a rogue at heart') fail to coincide, and so what human habit signifies is not the inner self but the fact that it itself signifies nothing (*ADH* 98/*FOH* 67). There is no 'natural man' to signify, and that is precisely what is signified: 'Man appears as the being who must come to experience the non-referentiality of expression, or, in other words, signification's impossible state of nature' (*ADH* 99/*FOH* 68), and therefore it is only when man signifies nothing that he is truly signified. To signify 'man' is not to signify a determinate trait, capacity or host property, but to signify the absence of a determinate inner nature. Once more, it is important to stress that this is not apophaticism. The 'proper of man' is neither that man has an inner nature, nor that man has no inner nature, but rather that man's inner nature qua signified is in a dialectical relationship with the signifiers of behaviour and language, constantly both forming and being formed by those signifiers. The 'plastic individuals' Hegel evokes in the *Aesthetics*[12] are not bereft of all substance or form, but are understood in terms of the 'becoming substance of accident' (or, we might say, 'the becoming signified of the signifier'). Humanity gains a nature (or a form, an *eidos*) through habit, and so a human is what it makes itself to be, but it is also what is made. It gives and receives form. Hegel's account of the human is, for Malabou, neither essentialist nor apophatic, but plastic.

The Christian substance-subject is plastic: the becoming-accident of form

Despite this attempt to move away from a substantial definition of humanity, however, Malabou notes that Hegel's Greek substance-subject alone is insufficient: 'If Hegel had granted man such a substantive ontological status, there would only remain an anthropological conception of substance. Yet the entire *Anthropology* is devoted to destroying such a status' (*ADH* 108/*FOH* 75). Hegel's account of the Greek substance-subject may have moved on from a notion of humanity defined in terms of a determinate substance or quality to humanity as the plastic becoming-substance of accident, but the definition is still, in the end, a substantial one. It is only in the second major section of *The Future of Hegel*, in which Malabou's discussion moves from the Greek notion of the *substance*-subject to the Christian substance-*subject*, that we witness the consummate breakdown of the substantial view of the human, along with the dismantling of a host capacity account. The discussion once more turns around the central notion of plasticity.

With the advent of Christianity the Greek understanding of the subject as the becoming form of accident finds its antithesis in the Christian notion of the becoming accident of form, the paradigm of which is the incarnation. The great innovation brought to the Western notion of the subject by Christianity is, according to Hegel, the moment of negativity or alienation introduced into the divine by the self-emptying kenosis[13] of incarnation. The idea that the incarnation is a moment of self-emptying is drawn from the early hymn fragment reproduced in the second chapter of the apostle Paul's letter to the church in Philippi, which serves as the source of Hegel's discussion:

> Have this mind among yourselves, which is yours in Christ Jesus, who, though he was in the form of God, did not count equality with God a thing to be grasped, *but emptied himself* [ἀλλὰ ἑαυτὸν ἐκένωσεν], by taking the form of a servant, being born in the likeness of men. And being found in human form, he humbled himself by becoming obedient to the point of death, even death on a cross.[14]

Rendered in German by Martin Luther as *Entäußerung* and usually translated into French as *aliénation*, kenosis is a moment absent in Greek thought. Hegel never uses the term when discussing the Greeks, Malabou notes, and the idea of an alienated Greek God 'would be something unimaginable' (*ADH* 158/*FOH* 113). For his part, Hegel understands kenosis as a becoming-other: the incarnation is 'the alienation of the divine'.[15] For Hegel kenosis is a becoming accident of form or substance inasmuch as '[t]he universal substance is actualized out of its abstraction into an individual [singular] self-consciousness; [. . .] in the eternal sphere he is called the Son, and is transplanted into the world of time (*in die Zeitlichkeit versetzt*)'.[16] Hegel also follows Luther's lead in understanding the Philippians 2 passage to be saying that God himself died, for whatever is true of Christ's human nature is taken to be true also of his divine nature (in accordance with the doctrine known as *communicatio idiomatum*). According to Luther and Hegel, both Christ's divine and human natures are emptied (*ADH* 133/*FOH* 93) in the incarnation. This stands in contrast to the Catholic doctrine according to which it is not God himself who is emptied and dies on the cross, but a pre-existing *Logos*, and it is Christ in his human nature who is emptied, but not Christ in his divine nature (*ADH* 133/*FOH* 93).

This Hegelian account of the incarnation causes theological discomfort for many, Malabou notes, because it is thought to introduce a moment of lack into the plenitude of the godhead (*ADH* 130/*FOH* 91). Nevertheless, she asks, is kenosis really best interpreted as a moment of negativity? According to the Philippians passage Christ, after all, emptied *himself* (ἑαυτὸν ἐκένωσεν; my emphasis). He is not merely the passive object of emptying but also its active agent. Rather than negativity and passivity, is this not better described, Malabou persuasively argues, as a moment of divine plasticity, where plasticity 'is a name for the originary unity of acting and being acted upon, of spontaneity and receptivity' (*ADH* 247/*FOH* 186)? Malabou argues that this double movement of the kenotic giving and receiving a form is not lost on Hegel:

> The concept of 'alienation', carefully dissected, shows us that if God does accept the form of subjectivity, if He does submit himself to being a subject, it is He who gives subjectivity the very form He receives from it. In alienating himself, God imprints subjectivity with a special type of self-extension, an 'exteriorization'. He gives himself this same form, the form of development. Thus alienation must be seen from both sides, as a receptivity and a spontaneity in God. (*ADH* 119/*FOH* 84)

The argument is not a denial that Christ is passive in kenosis, but an affirmation that passivity is only half the story. This reflects the point made in relation to the Greek subject discussed above, that plastic subjectivity is neither straightforwardly substantial nor apophatic. While it is true that 'Christ *empties* himself', it is also and equally true that 'Christ *himself* empties'. It follows that divine negation no longer manifests a lack of passivity in God, but rather a divine plasticity (*ADH* 146/*FOH* 104).

This negation is itself negated in the resurrection, understood by Hegel (once more following Luther) as 'the death of death (*der Tod des Todes*)' (*ADH* 151/*FOH* 107).[17] This double negative is captured in Malabou's framing of the 'plasticity, or, to put it another way, the "*non-impassivity*" of the subject' (*ADH* 179/*FOH* 129; my emphasis). Passivity and impassivity are not denied or suppressed, rather they are sublated in a plastic movement of self-formation. So a full account of kenosis will go beyond self-emptying in order to assert that '[k]enosis is the movement through which God, by positing Himself in exteriority and becoming alien to Himself, achieves the fulfilment of His being and becomes at once predicate and accident' (*ADH* 166/*FOH* 119).

It is this dialectic movement of negation and sublation, Hegel argues, that shapes the modern philosophical concept of subjectivity. Kenosis finds itself transposed into modern philosophical subjectivity by the Kant who must 'deny knowledge in order to make room for faith'.[18] This 'continues and completes the significance of kenosis' because what was previously understood as a plastic act of the divine (namely the self-emptying incarnation and death of Christ) now becomes a philosophical process in which '[t]he truth of kenosis is philosophically realized by subjectivity's self-dispossession when it confronts the limits it cannot cross', forging 'an essential and indissoluble rapport between the kenosis of the divine and the emptiness of the transcendental' in a philosophical movement which 'brings to light the essence of modern subjectivity as kenosis' (*ADH* 155/*FOH* 111). In the same way that, in Hegel's reading of divine self-emptying, God becomes alien to himself and thereby achieves the fulfilment of his being in becoming both predicate and accident, so also the modern meaning of subjectivity is 'characterized by the relation the subject forms with itself through the mediation of its other' (*ADH* 167/*FOH* 119).

At this point in the analysis we need to circle back to our main question, and recognise that it has not yet been adequately answered. We are seeking to explore to what extent Malabou offers an account of the human that does not rest on the possession of a determinate capacity or capacities. We have shown from her reading of Hegel that the wagon of humanity is not hitched to a particular host property or capacity, but that in both its Greek and Christian moments it is characterised in terms of plasticity. As Malabou notes in her lecture on the future of the humanities, '[t]he human is plastic. This means that it gives itself its own form, that it is able to transform itself, to invent and produce itself, and that it is nothing but this very process of self-formation' (Hum 3). But the objection might well be raised at this point: surely the definition of the human as plastic simply brings us back to the 'host' account of humanity after all. If, for Badiou and Meillassoux, the host property of humanity is a capacity for thought or the ability to reason, surely Malabou retains the structure of a host property perfectly intact, merely substituting plasticity for thought, *Homo plasticus* for *Homo sapiens*. Even Hegel's insistence in the 'Anthropology' on the distribution of plasticity throughout the organic world, it could be argued, does not sufficiently guard against a host property account of the human, because it is still the uniquely human ignorance of its own lack of a determinate and constant nature, rather than anything else, which emerges as the determinate and constant mark of humanity. Malabou, however, has a further Hegelian card up her sleeve, one that challenges the idea of a determinate human nature at a deeper level still: plasticity is itself plastic.

Plasticity is itself plastic

From *The Future of Hegel* onwards Malabou makes it abundantly clear that she does not consider plasticity to be simply a descriptive term detailing a particular mode of transformation or self-forming. At the beginning of *The Future of Hegel* she declares her purpose to 'form a concept' of plasticity:

> To 'form a concept' in the sense intended here means first of all to take up a concept (plasticity), which has a defined and delimited role in the philosophy of Hegel, only in order to transform it into the sort of comprehensive concept that can 'grasp' (*saisir*) the whole. (*ADH* 16/*FOH* 5)

There are two observations to make from this brief description. First, Malabou clearly intends the concept of plasticity to be both active (it '*grasps*') and global (it 'grasps *the whole*'). Plasticity is not simply something that Malabou describes; it is how she describes everything. Secondly, the way in which Malabou is thinking about plasticity here is itself plastic. Plasticity, as we have seen, is the receiving and giving of form. In her avowed intention to 'transform' the plasticity that she finds in Hegel, Malabou is receiving the form of Hegelian plasticity and giving it a new form. In short, the concept of plasticity for Malabou is itself plastic or (to put it another way) should be treated plastically. Nor does Malabou intend this re-casting of Hegelian plasticity to be the concept's final transformation. In the essay 'Les Enjeux idéologiques de la plasticité neuronale' ('The ideological stakes of neuronal plasticity') she insists that 'its definition constantly evolves. As I have said elsewhere, plasticity is what it is, plastic. It is itself supple, itself adaptable, formed by and forming itself' (*CDM* 226; my translation).[19]

A little later in the introduction to *The Future of Hegel* Malabou draws on Georges Canguilhem's notion of elaborating a concept:

> To elaborate (*travailler*) a concept is to vary both its extension and its intelligibility. It is to generalize it by incorporating its exceptions. It is to export it outside its original domain, to use it as a model or conversely to find it a model, in short it is to give to it, bit by bit, through ordered transformations, the function of a form.[20]

This builds on the previous observation about the plasticity of plasticity by developing the notion of form: in becoming 'a comprehensive concept that can grasp the whole' plasticity is itself becoming a form (εἶδος, *forma*) in the same way that it describes the becoming form of accident in the Greek *substance*-subject. Malabou's project in *The Future of Hegel*, she explains, is 'giving the function of a form to a term which itself, in its first sense, describes or designates the act of giving form' (*ADH* 19/

FOH 7). Another way to describe and understand what it means to claim that plasticity itself is plastic is to say that '[t]he meaning of the notion of plasticity is the same as its way of being' (*ADH* 248/*FOH* 186) or, rather too schematically and with a nod to *Forrest Gump*, 'plastic is what plastic does'. We are mistaken, Malabou insists, to understand the operation of receiving and giving form as a rigid and unchanging structure, as a form in the Platonic sense; we must understand it as 'an instance which can evolve, which means that it can give itself new forms' (*ADH* 248/*FOH* 186).

Although Malabou transforms Hegel's notion of plasticity, she derives the notion that plasticity itself is plastic from her reading of Hegel. She notes that in the preface to the *Science of Logic* Hegel insists that the subject of plasticity demands 'a plastic receptivity and understanding':

> A plastic discourse (*ein plastischer Vortrag*) demands, too, a plastic sense of receptivity and understanding on the part of the listener (*einen plastischen Sinn des Aufnehmens und Verstehens*); but youths and men of such a temper who would calmly suppress their own reflections and opinions in which 'the need to think for oneself' is so impatient to manifest itself, listeners such as Plato imagined, who would attend only to the matter at hand (*nur der Sache folgender Zuhörer*), could have no place in a modern dialogue; still less could one count on readers of such a disposition.[21]

Plasticity in Hegel's preface has three meanings: (1) the mode of being of philosophical content, (2) the mode of being of this content's exposition, and (3) the mode of being of the reader who must let her grip loosen around (*se laisser dessaisir de*) the philosophy's initial form in order to receive the form of its 'matter at hand',[22] of that with which it has to do (German *Sache*, which Malabou translates into French as the capitalised *Chose*), in order then, in return, to give it a new form (*CDM* 94). Let us look a little more closely at (1) and (2) (we have already sketched an instance of the third meaning in describing above how Malabou transforms Hegel's concept of plasticity in her reading of it). The 'plastic discourse' to which Hegel refers in the preface is a plastic way of understanding the relation between the subject and the predicate of a proposition, or between a substance and its accidents. Usually, Malabou explains, we think that the subject simply receives its predicates from outside itself, so to speak, and cannot produce them internally. This relation of exteriority is what Hegel calls the 'predicative proposition'. In plastic discourse however, the relation between subject and predicate, as well as between substance and accident, is 'understood as a process of substance's "self-determination"' (*ADH* 25/*FOH* 11) that 'develops in a temporal fashion' and 'contains self-differentiation in its very concept' (*ADH* 165/*FOH* 118). This is what Hegel calls the 'speculative proposition'.

Plasticity as the description of the mode of being of the exposition of philosophical content (the second of Hegel's three meanings of plasticity in the preface) describes, Malabou admits, the experience of reading Hegel himself, and it parallels the attempt to signify the 'inner self' we sketched above in relation to Hegel's account of the Greek substance-subject. Such a reading begins in frustration: 'What seems obvious at the first grasp of the proposition is in reality its fundamental unreadability' (*ADH* 239/ *FOH* 179). This sets the reader off on a quest for the origin or substratum of the proposition in just the same way that, in Malabou's discussion of Greek subjectivity, she describes how we naïvely assume that our speech, bodies and behaviour must signify a hidden but pristine determinate 'inner self'. As in the case of the inner self, however, what the reader discovers is that there is no constant and stable substrate. What happens then is that, '[p]lunged into the void of the proposition, the reader is brought to formulate new propositions in return' (*ADH* 240/*FOH* 179), in order to seek to transform (and, in so doing, to make sense of) the original unreadable propositions. Once more, this parallels the transformation that leads from seeking to signify the truth of the inner self to seeking to signify the absence of any substantial nature subtending the self. In sum, statements written in the speculative mode of exposition 'cannot be read without being rewritten' (*ADH* 240/*FOH* 180), and yet this rewriting is not an arbitrary or subjective invention, for that would be to reduce plasticity to a unilateral giving of form. The reader, to be sure, 'rewrites what he or she reads' such that he or she has 'become the author of the enunciation' (*ADH* 240/*FOH* 181), but that which is rewritten is 'what he or she reads' and nothing else, and that of which he or she is the author is 'the enunciation' and not any arbitrarily or subjectively chosen proposition. What this requires of the reader is an attitude neither of passivity nor of *ex nihilo* creativity but of plasticity, just as what is required of the Christian God in Malabou's reading of kenosis in Hegel is neither divine passivity nor pure divine activity, but divine plasticity. In what Malabou calls her 'radical application of plasticity' (*ADH* 165/*FOH* 118), 'plastic' denotes not just the 'what' of philosophy, but also its 'how'; it is not just adjectival but also adverbial.

The importance of what, in *The Future of Hegel*, Malabou calls the plasticity of plasticity is only strengthened in her subsequent writing, emerging more clearly in *The Heidegger Change* and *Counterpath*,[23] whereas the evocation of the plasticity of plasticity is only a passing thought in *The Future of Hegel*. Indeed, in *Plasticity at the Dusk of Writing* Malabou says that the capacity of plasticity to transform itself and become other 'lies in wait' (*reste en attente*) in the Hegel book (*PAS* 53/*PDW* 24). It is in *The Heidegger Change* and *Plasticity at the Dusk of Writing* that this folding over of plasticity onto itself is made more explicit and treated at greater length. Furthermore, it is this greater development in later writing that allows us to read the plasticity of plasticity as a bridge between Malabou's engagements with Hegel and Heidegger, as she indicates herself:

> *The Future of Hegel* had already tested the plasticity of the concept of plasticity, because speculative Hegelian philosophy rips the concept away from its strict aesthetic ties (or sculptural ties, to be precise), definitively conferring the metaphysical dignity of an essential characteristic of subjectivity upon it. Since then, I have ceaselessly sought to interrogate this mutability. (*PAS* 32/*PDW* 13)

The first observation to make from Malabou's reading of her own work here is that her treatment of Heidegger is not adequately described as a break from the work on Hegel, but is better thought of as a plastic transformation of Hegelian plasticity to a point where it is profoundly altered but not unrecognisable. In the move from Hegel to Heidegger, plasticity is itself ever more plastic. The way in which it becomes more plastic is that, in the Heidegger book, the interrogation of mutability focuses on thinking change as ontological in a way that closely mirrors the folding back on itself of plasticity in the notion of the 'plasticity of plasticity'.

In *The Heidegger Change* this plasticity as ontological mutability goes under the name 'metamorphosis' (German: *Verwandlung*), and forms part of 'triad of change' in Heidegger, namely change, transformation and metamorphosis (*Wandel*, *Wandlung* and *Verwandlung*). *Verwandlung* is a 'transformative rupture' (*PAS* 43/*PDW* 19), or what Heidegger calls 'an adoption and transformation of what has been handed down to us' and which he also identifies with the term 'destruction'.[24] In the concept of *Verwandlung* itself as it is described here we can perceive strong echoes of the Hegelian notion of plasticity as a receiving and giving of form.

For Malabou's reading of Heidegger, '"ontology" is only the name given to an originary migratory and metamorphic tendency' (*LCH* 344/ *THC* 270). This insistence on the metamorphosis of ontology itself is a recasting of the motif of the plasticity of plasticity from *The Future of Hegel*, a recasting in which 'metamorphosis inscribes the motive of plasticity right at the heart of the thought of being' (*PAS* 59/*PDW* 28). Or, more precisely, in *The Heidegger Change* the terms 'plasticity' and 'metamorphosis' are no longer considered synonymous, as Malabou admits they were in *The Future of Hegel*. Plasticity now names 'an immanent movement in the dialectical process' and 'metamorphosis' names 'a tendency that supersedes the process' (*PAS* 54/*PDW* 24–5). Malabou calls metamorphosis a 'new orientation to the motif of plasticity' (*PAS* 57/*PDW* 26), one which questions destruction and deconstruction genetically, interrogating not the transformations they perform but how they themselves are transformed, which – once more – is what is hinted at in *The Future of Hegel* with the term 'plasticity of plasticity'. Indeed, Malabou's own characterisation of the Heidegger book frames it as nothing other than an exploration of the plasticity of plasticity:

> By engaging in the process of self-differentiation to the point where it momentarily lost its name – Heidegger hardly ever uses the term Plaztizität – plasticity became distanced from itself, it spaced itself out to form or refigure itself elsewhere, differently. (*PAS* 58/*PDW* 27)

Even more explicitly, Malabou herself frames her engagement with Heidegger as an endeavour to 'test the plasticity of the concept of plasticity even further, examining its metabolic power, its capacity to order transformation' (*PAS* 47/*PDW* 21). This 'metabolic power' which tests the plasticity of plasticity accounts for the metamorphosis that occurs between different terms for Heidegger: 'between man and Dasein, God and god, being (*Sein*) and be-ing (*Seyn*), and essence, and essencing or swaying (*Wesung*)' (*LCH* 37/*THC* 24). The becoming ontological of the plasticity of plasticity crystallises most clearly in Malabou's insistence on 'the originary possibility of being and beings changing into each other' (*LCH* 29/ *THC* 17). Retranslated into the terms of the Hegel book, this means that plasticity does not simply describe the transformations of (determinate) beings, but it describes the structure – the metabolism – of the becoming of being itself.

This self-reflexivity of plasticity is further explored in *Counterpaths*, Malabou's book on Derrida, and what emerges from the three books taken together is that the movement which, in *The Future of Hegel*, carries the name 'plasticity of plasticity', is not a movement confined to a Hegelian register alone, although Malabou admits that, in *The Future of Hegel* itself, this remains unclear (*PAS* 49/*PDW* 22). So the 'plasticity of plasticity' in *The Future of Hegel* is one name for a 'metamorphic structure' that 'did not belong entirely to the dialectic, destruction, or deconstruction, although it articulates all three of them' (*PAS* 57/*PDW* 26). Indeed, '[p]lasticity could thus lose its name *for a moment* to become metamorphosis in Heidegger', for 'in *Le Change Heidegger* it was able to abandon the heavy burden of its etymon for a while, *without ceasing to be itself*' (*PAS* 73/*PDW* 37; my emphasis). In other words, what the plasticity of plasticity names is not a local feature of Hegelian thought but a mutability that Malabou finds beyond Hegel: a feature not of one isolated era of thought but of the very articulation between different eras of thought. It is a fundamental structure of her thinking, not just of her reading of Hegel. Furthermore, insofar as plasticity remains itself by transforming itself and being transformed, the motif of metamorphosis in *The Heidegger Change* can be read as the same plasticity that we find in *The Future of Hegel*, the same on the level of the movement or structure of transformation, though of course different on the level of its content: the same *because* it has changed.

With this broader canvas in view, we can affirm that it is not the notion of plasticity *simpliciter* which is the genius of Malabou's contribution to contemporary materialist accounts of the human, but the plasticity of plasticity, and it is in insisting on the plasticity of plasticity that she distinguishes her own approach both from a deconstruction of subjectivity and from Badiou's and Meillassoux's stable and enduring host capacity accounts. In an essay on deconstruction and plasticity entitled 'La Lecture: pierre d'angle défectueuse ou blessure qui se referme. Dialectique et déconstruction' ('Reading: defective cornerstone or self-healing wound. Dialectic and deconstruction', *CDM* 89–101) Malabou explains that, while she began writing about plasticity in Hegel as if it were a deconstructive gesture, she found that the concept led her increasingly away from deconstruction (*CDM* 98). She pinpoints the difference between the notion of plasticity and Derridean deconstruction when, in an essay on Félix Ravaisson's theory of habit, she insists that the propensity of philosophers to reject habit as passive and unthinking can, just like the propensity for deconstructing presence, become a tic, something we do just as unthinkingly as the habit it is intended to disrupt (*CDM* 287). The point that Malabou is making, quite simply, is that there is no plasticity in deconstruction. The metaphysics of presence is always but always to be deconstructed; the symmetry of the cogito, the adequation of self to self, the metaphysics of subjectivity is always but always to be shown to be other to itself, already outside itself.[25]

'Wait a minute,' the proponent of deconstruction might objurgate, 'does Derrida not resist precisely the sort of mindlessly repetitious gesture of which Malabou seems to be accusing him here?' Does he not refuse to employ the same terms across different texts for the express reason of avoiding this very problem, moving through deconstruction, dissemination, supplementarity, spectrality and a host of other terms, seeking to reinvent 'deconstruction' afresh in each encounter with a new text?[26] In other words, is not deconstruction always-already plastic? The answer is negative, not because Derrida never varies the terms he deploys in his encounters with texts, and not because of any vain attempt to argue that the Derrida of *Of Grammatology* and the Derrida of *Spectres of Marx*, for example, are at all points in every way exactly the same. No, the difference between Malabou and Derrida here is that, while plasticity is itself necessarily plastic, deconstruction (if there is such a thing) cannot itself be deconstructed. This non-redoubling is signalled in Derrida's writing by the motif of the 's'il y en a', 'if there is such a thing'. Justice, 'if such a thing exists, outside or beyond law, is not deconstructible, no more than deconstruction itself, if such a thing exists'.[27]

What sets plasticity apart from Derridean deconstruction is not the way in which it brings about its transformation, but the formal self-reflexivity of Malabou's central notion. Plasticity can transform itself so that it no longer works in the way it did previously, and Malabou's adoption and transformation of the term from Hegel is a prime example. Plasticity plasticises itself. Deconstruction does not deconstruct itself. This means that, while Derrida's deconstruction of the self or subjectivity will always resemble itself insofar as it is, precisely, deconstructed and not, for example, sublated, negated or simply affirmed, the transformations which plastic notions of selfhood can undergo are radically unpredictable and therefore resolvable neither to a determinate substance or quality (as is the case for Badiou and Meillassoux) nor to a determinate gesture (as is the case for Derrida's deconstruction of subjectivity). In this way, Malabou's plasticity undermines the possibility of defining humanity in terms of a host capacity more radically than Derrida's deconstruction.

It is also the self-referentiality of plasticity that sets Malabou's account apart from that of Meillassoux. For Meillassoux the contingency of being leads to the necessity of non-contradiction for the very good reason that if a being were contradictory it would be its own negation and therefore it could not be otherwise than it is, that is it would be necessary, and no being is necessary (ID 49). In his as yet unpublished doctoral thesis 'The Divine inexistence' Meillassoux elaborates on this fundamental element of his thought by developing what he calls the 'problem of participation' (ID 165) and the related philosophical gesture of non-redoubling (*non-redoublement*) (ID 175). He illustrates the principle of non-redoubling with a series of examples: for Plato, what makes a phenomenon such and such a phenomenon cannot itself be a phenomenon; in the Cartesian cogito, I doubt everything apart from doubt itself; in terms of Leibniz's logical truths, nothing is in the mind that was not in experience, apart from the mind itself; and in Kant's a priori forms of perception, the form of phenomenal data in experience cannot itself be given as a phenomenon in experience (see ID 175). In each of these cases the structure of non-redoubling is 'only X is not X', expressed in Meillassoux's own case by the principle 'only contingency is not contingent'.

Malabou's plasticity stands as a notable exception to this general principle. Far from subscribing to non-redoubling with an awkward 'only plasticity is not plastic', Malabou actively and enthusiastically embraces the plasticity of plasticity as one of its most important features, with the result that she does not have to justify or explain how it can be an exception to itself. Derrida's unease with deconstruction being undeconstructible can be discerned in his cautious 's'il y en a', and Meillassoux's insistence that factiality is not itself factial rests on the shaky foundation of the 'intellectual intuition of the absolute' (*AF* 111/*AfF* 82) by which one comes to turn the epistemological despair of realising the contingency of necessity into the ontological foundation of recognising the necessity of contingency. Compared with these pirouettes, Malabou's plasticity is universal, material, monist and immanent to itself: everything is plastic, including plasticity.

So far I have presented a maximally sympathetic reading of Malabou's plasticity, but the moment has now come to be a little more critical. It is quite possible to read Malabou's plasticity against the grain of her own account, and to argue that rather than having sketched out a novel response to the question of the relation between humanity and host properties, she has simply reproduced an even more radical and entrenched version of the problem which besets Badiou and Meillassoux on the level of substance and Derrida on the level of operation or gesture. This negative reading of Malabou's plasticity follows Meillassoux's reasons for affirming the necessity of non-contradiction discussed above. It is this: Malabou has simply changed the host property of humanity from one determinate capacity to the capacity to transform and destroy capacities. Badiou's and Meillassoux's accounts of humanity are predictably and stably characterised by a host capacity; Derrida's account is predictably and stably characterised by the deconstruction of any such host property; Malabou's account is predictably and stably characterised by a self-transforming plasticity that is unpredictable and unstable, even to the point of incorporating stasis within its possible transformations. In the same way that a contradictory being for Meillassoux would be a necessary being, the notion of plasticity as a host property, incorporating into itself any possible change (including the plastic transformation of plasticity itself) swallows all its rivals and regurgitates them as instances of its own plastic transformation, asserting itself as absolute and necessary. Does the human remain the same? That is plastic. Does the human change? That is plastic too. Is it deconstructed? That could be a moment of plasticity. If plasticity is itself plastic then it becomes rigorously impossible to conceive of an alternative to or interruption of plasticity, incorporating as it does its own negation.

It also follows from this that, if plasticity is truly universal and if even stasis can be the result of a plastic transformation, then plasticity itself is, after all, no longer plastic because there is nothing other than itself that it can become. Like Meillassoux's contradictory being, it cannot be other than what it is (because there is nothing other than what it is, given that unlike the capacity for rational thought or the gesture of deconstruction it can transform itself into what it is not) and therefore it cannot change on the level of its own gesture or operation. It becomes determinate, predictable, necessary, in fact the only necessity, which is precisely what Meillassoux sees as pernicious in the existence of a contradictory and therefore necessary being. If everything is plastic, including plasticity itself, then plasticity itself is unchanging and necessary, and therefore not plastic qua plasticity, and although the way in which everything is plastic can change, the way in which plasticity is plastic cannot. There can be no resistance to plasticity, no Bartleby-inspired 'I would prefer not to', because resistance itself is a moment of plasticity:

> The dialectical process is 'plastic' because, as it unfolds, it makes links between the opposing moments of total immobility (the 'fixed') and vacuity ('dissolution'), and then links both in the vitality of the whole, a whole which, reconciling these two extremes, is itself the union of resistance (*Widerstand*) and fluidity (*Flüssigkeit*). (*ADH* 26/*FOH* 12; see also *QF* 168–9/*WSD* 71–2)

Perhaps the only way to resist the plasticity of plasticity (rather than to perform the moment of resistance within plasticity) is to destroy or burn it, but in the second half of this chapter we shall see that Malabou understands plasticity to incorporate even deflagration and destruction. Human beings may transform their capacities, but their plasticity itself remains constant. My conclusion is this: in introducing and insisting on the plasticity of plasticity, Malabou does not solve the question of the definition of humanity in relation to its host properties, instead she raises its stakes. If we follow her own reading of the plasticity of plasticity then we can conclude that she has indeed brilliantly succeeded in liberating the human from the problems attendant upon the appeal to determinate capacities, for which we can all thank her. The alternative, however, is that she has elaborated a determinate definition of the human more radical and more incontestable than ever before, in terms of a meta-capacity that brooks no rivals because – like Hegel's God – it has already incorporated its negation as a moment in its own self-realisation: Badiou's and Meillassoux's host capacities have become sublated, under Malabou's pen, into a host potency which incorporates even its own passivity and destruction.

Plasticity and neuroscience

After Hegel, the second great influence on Malabou's notion of the plastic are twentieth- and twenty-first-century theories of neuroplasticity. Malabou is a vociferous advocate of the plastic transformation of philosophy in an encounter with neuroscience, condemning the inertia exhibited by fellow thinkers when faced with paradigm-changing neurological discoveries and their stubborn refusal to part from the cherished but quaint idea that, when it comes to the mind, nothing can be predicted and nothing is biologically determined (PLR). In a quotation from Jean-Pierre Changeux's *Neuronal Man* to which Malabou returns time and again, the eminent French neuroscientist insists that 'the impact of the discovery of the synapse and its functions is comparable to that of the atom or DNA'.[28] Recent neurobiological discoveries render it simply unacceptable, Malabou argues in *Avant demain*, to suppose an unbridgeable gulf between the logical and biological origins of thought (*AD* 2).

Malabou situates her own attempt to initiate a new plastic encounter between philosophy and neuroscience in terms of what she sees as the failed exchange between Changeux and Paul Ricœur in the 1998 *What Makes Us Think?*, a series of five conversations between the materialist neuroscientist and the hermeneutic phenomenologist which, for Malabou, bear baleful testimony to a wider dialogue of the deaf that has, until now, reigned in the relation between neuroscience and French philosophy. Changeux's position is emblematic of the reductive 'cognitivists' who 'seek to elaborate a natural philosophy of mind by exposing the neuronal substrates of our mental activities', and Ricœur exemplifies the 'Continentals', for whom contemporary neuroscience is quite simply a crude determinist threat to freedom of thought and action (*CDM* 230). Malabou, for her part, wishes a plague on both their houses and takes both sides of the discussion to task for their inadequate views of the relation between brain and mind. Changeux is chided for perpetuating what she takes to be 'the chief affirmation of the neurosciences in general, and of the cognitive sciences in particular' (*QF* 136/*WSD* 54), namely that the mental is absolutely transparent in, and in linear continuity with, the neuronal allowing an easy back and forth from one to the other. Any assertion of an unproblematic continuity between the neuronal and the mental is in fact not a scientific position at all, Malabou argues, but necessarily philosophical or epistemological in a way not always clearly articulated by the science in which it is embedded (*QF* 137/*WSD* 56). In fact, contemporary neuroscience suffers from the lack of any strong theoretical discourse, without which it resorts to ad hoc metaphors to describe epigenesis (*AD* 263), such as the claim that RNA can 'read' genes or the suggestion that the transition from genotype to phenotype is like the 'musical performance' of genetic code. For Malabou, the neurosciences today are heavily loaded with an ideology that should elicit a healthy scepticism in the philosophical reader (PLR).

Malabou characterises Ricœur as holding that 'neither the knowledge we accumulate about brain functioning nor even our certainty that our mental states are conditioned by neuronal organization teaches us the slightest thing about either ourselves or the way we think' (*QF* 185/*WSD* 82).[29] This 'metaphysical anti-reductionism' (*CDM* 214) maintains that 'the brain is the substrate of thought [. . .] and thought is the indication of an underlying neuronal structure',[30] a position Malabou considers to be 'clearly untenable' (*QF* 185/*WSD* 81; see also *CDM* 214). For Malabou, Ricœur's position demonstrates a disregard for the sciences that pervades twentieth-century French thought, shared by Foucault and Derrida who consider science as an 'enterprise of normalisation, regulation and control' (Hum 2). The speculative realists themselves (Meillassoux alone is named) are little better, for they ignore biology and therefore have nothing to say about the question of life (PLR) which recent advances in neuroscience place at the heart of philosophical inquiry.

For Changeux and the cognitivists, the mind is transparently determined by the brain and there is an uninterrupted linear continuity between the two; for Ricœur and the Continentals, the mind floats free of the brain and is unaffected even by severe brain trauma. Malabou characterises the exchange in *What Makes Us Think?* as a 'good example' of shoehorning the question of the mind–brain relation into the alternatives of reductionism and antireductionism:

> On one side – that of the cognitive sciences, in particular – we find massive affirmation of the possibility of an absolute naturalization of cognition and mental processes. On the other, we find the affirmation of the perfectly transcendental character of thought, irreducible to biological determinations. (*QF* 185/*WSD* 81)

It is this dead-end alternative between reductionism and antireductionism that Malabou seeks to overcome by trying to find a way neither to resist nor simply to accept the reduction of the mental to the neuronal (*CDM* 230) but to dialectise the relation in what she calls a 'reasonable materialism' (*QF* 186/*WSD* 81) in which philosophy echoes and interprets the new questions raised by neuroscience, and scientific advances benefit from a philosophical rigour that problematises some of their reductive assumptions (*CDM* 9). What Malabou is aiming for in this thinking of the relation between mind and brain according to a 'neuronal materialism' (*QF* 162/*WSD* 69) is not just one more dialogue or exchange between philosophy and science, but a hybridisation (PLR). It is a position with which we are already familiar from her engagement with Hegel. In the same way that, for Malabou's Hegel, humanity cannot be understood simply as the giving of form or simply as the receiving of form but must comprehend them together in their resistance to each other, so also here it is in the very antagonism between cognitivism and antireductionism that

Malabou seeks to unfold the unique contribution of her own thinking. A reasonable materialism is one that takes account of 'the dialectical tension that at once binds and opposes naturalness and intentionality' (*CDM* 216), a tension which Malabou expresses and explores in her elaboration of 'a supple and – so to speak – plastic materialism' (*CDM* 215). We shall now examine Malabou's reasonable or plastic materialism as it shapes her account of the human being.

What is neuroplasticity?

Malabou's interest in neuroplasticity begins as far back as *The Future of Hegel* itself. In a long footnote detailing different senses of 'plasticity' (*ADH* 255–6 n2/*FOH* 229 n15) she draws the reader's attention to Donald Hebb's hypothesis in *The Organization of Behavior* that the passing of signals across neural synapses strengthens those connections and that, concomitantly, connections that are not used become weaker, an observation encapsulated in the summary that 'cells that fire together, wire together'[31] or, in terms of Malabou's own concept of plasticity, 'synapses are not simple transmitters of nervous information, but themselves act to form and inform that information' (*ADH* 255–6 n2/*FOH* 229 n15).

In the same way that Malabou situated Hegelian plasticity between a passive reception of form and an *ex nihilo* and unconditioned self-formation, she also elaborates the notion of neuroplasticity in contradistinction to, on the one hand, rigidity or elasticity and, on the other hand, polymorphism or flexibility. This dialectic pattern of situating a concept as a sublation of the difference between two opposite and equally undesirable alternatives is characteristic of Malabou's thought, and we have already encountered it twice, once in relation to the giving and receiving of form and once in her account of the mind–body problem that seeks to hybridise Changeux's cognitivism and Ricœur's Continental antireductionism. If plasticity is Malabou's signature motif, then this sublation of unappealing dichotomies is her signature philosophical gesture. The way in which neuroplasticity sublates the difference between elasticity and flexibility is captured in the following short passage from *What Should We Do With Our Brain?*:[32]

> In mechanics, a material is called plastic if it cannot return to its initial form after undergoing a deformation. 'Plastic' in this sense is opposed to 'elastic.' Plastic material retains an imprint and thereby resists endless polymorphism. This is the case, for instance, with sculpted marble. Once the statue is finished, there is no possible return to the indeterminacy of the starting point. So plasticity designates solidity as much as suppleness, designates the

definitive character of the imprint, of configuration, or of modification (*QF* 61/*WSD* 15)

Plasticity is different to elasticity in that the latter, retaining a 'memory' of an original state to which it can always return, exhibits a fetishism of the origin. This notion of return to a prior state is allied for Malabou to religious concepts of redemption or salvation (*SEL* 57), and it has no place in her reasonable, plastic materialism.

Whereas elasticity retains an ineliminable memory of, and propensity to return to, an original state, flexibility mounts no resistance whatsoever to change. The term is frequently used by Malabou in an economic context, describing the 'efficacy, adaptability – unfailing flexibility' (*QF* 92/*WSD* 31) of the neoliberal market as it moves smoothly and unproblematically from expansion to downsizing, from efficiency to efficiency. Flexibility is passive with relation to change, offering no resistance to transformation:

> A flexible material is a material which can be bent in all directions, without resistance. Whereas a material is called plastic if it can be formed but never returns to its initial form. You can bend it, but it always resists being deformed. (PLR; my translation)

In fact, passivity is a quality shared by elasticity and flexibility alike, for the elastic will always passively return to its original state, in the same way that the flexible is passive in offering no resistance to endless transformation. Plasticity, however, refuses both the stubborn passivity of elasticity and the pliant passivity of flexibility, in favour of a notion of change that incorporates both creative activity and resistance. This complex notion of change is described by the three different senses Malabou gives to the term 'plasticity'. The first sense, that plasticity is a receiving of form, is the most established of the three notions, captured in Francesco Varela's idea of autopoietic or self-regulating systems maintaining a homeostatic equilibrium with their environment (*CDM* 226). The second, positive sense of plasticity is the meaning that predominates in the neurosciences, where it denotes 'a sort of natural sculpting that forms our identity, an identity modelled by experience and that makes us subjects of a history, a singular, recognizable, identifiable history, with all its events, gaps, and future' (*OdA* 10/*OoA* 2). The third[33] sense is plasticity as destruction or explosion, and it is the sense that will be central to our discussion for the rest of this chapter and the next.

It is upon this third, destructive sense of plasticity that Malabou repeatedly insists, drawing on the meaning of the masculine French noun *plastic* (plastic explosive) and the verb *plastiquer* (to blow up). The notion of destructive plasticity is introduced in *The Future of Hegel*, where Malabou discerns it in a passage from the preface to the *Phenomenology of Spirit*: 'The process of plasticity is dialectical because the operations which constitute it, the seizure of form and the annihilation of all form, emergence and explosion, are contradictory' (*ADH* 26/*FOH* 12). This explosion is different to receiving form because of its violence and destruction. It is not merely an imprinting but a non-reversible annihilation; it is not that something is transformed, but that something is transformed by being wholly or partially destroyed. In the conclusion to *The Future of Hegel* Malabou describes this dialectic of emergence and explosion in terms of birth:

> Birth combines blossoming (*éclosion*) and explosion. A process of formation and of the dissolution of form, plasticity, where all birth takes place, should be imagined fundamentally as an ontological combustion (*déflagration*) which liberates the twofold possibility of the appearance and the annihilation of presence. (*ADH* 249/*FOH* 187)

In *What Should We Do With Our Brain?* Malabou returns to the notion of destructive plasticity and supplies her reader with a metaphor for understanding its explosive transition: the burning of glycogen stored in muscle tissue to produce muscle movement. In this process 'force simultaneously loses itself and forms itself differently, just as the metamorphic crisis frees a butterfly from its chrysalis' (*QF* 170/*WSD* 73–4). Malabou elaborates further upon the notion of destructive plasticity in *Ontology of the Accident* (the subtitle of which is *An Essay on Destructive Plasticity*), where she introduces another metaphor:

> In the usual order of things, lives run their course like rivers. Sometimes they jump their bed, without geological cause, without any subterranean pathway to explain the spate or flood. The suddenly deviant, deviating form of these lives is explosive plasticity. (*OdA* 9/*OoA* 2)

Finally, she discusses destructive plasticity at length in *The New Wounded* where she frames it as 'the dark double of the positive and constructive plasticity that moulds neuronal connections' which can 'make form through the annihilation of form' (*LNB* 15/*TNW* xv) and 'create an identity through loss of past identity' (*LNB* 113/*TNW* 60). It is in terms of this destructive plasticity that Malabou brilliantly reworks the mind–body problem and offers a materialist account of the human being: body, mind and spirit.

A plastic reading of 'you are your synapses'

In order to explore the implications of destructive neuroplasticity for the figure of the human that emerges in Malabou's work, I propose to focus the following investigation around one short phrase to which she returns on a number of occasions and that opens onto the problematic of the self more broadly. The phrase is taken from Joseph LeDoux's 2003 *Synaptic Self*:[34] 'you are your synapses'. What is at stake in this exploration is how Malabou's reading of the phrase in terms of destructive plasticity allows her to make a powerful and unprecedented intervention towards a non-reductive materialist conception of the mind–body problem, but not, I will argue, in the sense in which she originally intends.

In the literature popularising recent discoveries in neuroscience there is no shortage of variations on the phrase 'you are your brain'.[35] The proposition is often offered as part of an overtly reductive agenda which insists that the mind and the brain are in a relation of uninterrupted linear continuity. One classic expression of this position is Francis Crick's famous line from *The Astonishing Hypothesis*: 'You, your joys and your sorrows, your memories and your ambitions, your sense of personal identity and free will, are in fact no more than the behaviour of a vast assembly of nerve cells and their associated molecules.'[36] In the secondary literature, variations on this position carry the labels 'brainhood', 'cerebral subjectivity', 'neuro-chemical selfhood' and 'neuro-essentialism',[37] and many criticisms of the position have been forthcoming. Alain Ehrenberg considers that accounts of cerebral subjectivity slip unthinkingly from a methodological focus on the brain to an ontological exclusivity of the brain; in 'a step that jumps from the necessary methodological neutralisation of the social to conceptual blindness, the entity broached in terms of its body is often assimilated, implicitly or explicitly, to the entity considered as a whole'.[38] Or, in the words of François Vidal, '[t]he idea that "we are our brains" is not a corollary of neuroscientific advances, but a prerequisite of neuroscientific investigation'.[39] In addition, Ehrenberg notes, the claim that 'you are your brain' confuses individuation with individuality. The brain is indeed sufficient to individuate someone (in other words, no two brains are structurally identical), but it does not follow that the brain provides a sufficient account of that same person's individuality, in the same way that although we can sufficiently individuate people through their fingerprints, we could not hope to gain a sufficient understanding of their individuality by looking at those unique digital patterns.[40]

In sum, a reductive understanding of the relation between brain and mind as linear and continuous raises significant philosophical and semantic problems. The tantalising contribution which Malabou offers to this tangled debate is an account which does not reduce the mind to the brain while at the same time remaining within a materialist frame. Malabou displays a caution sorely lacking in the proponents of 'brainhood' about the translatability of brain activity into cognitive states, wisely warning that 'no one today is in a position to prove that all cognitive, emotional, or practical activities are the reformulated and re-systematized equivalents of neuronal configurations' (*QF* 149/*WSD* 62). However, in Malabou's case this rejection of the reductionist position does not lead to a 'Continental' antireductionism but to a third, plastic way of thinking the relation between brain and mind.

The key that unlocks Malabou's novel and productive account of the mind–brain relation is the meaning of the verb 'are' in the phrase 'you are your synapses'. In other words, what can it mean to identify synapses, an object properly described in an analytic, scientific discourse, with the phenomenological 'you'? The phrase 'you are your synapses' stands as the title of the final chapter of Malabou's *What Should We Do With Our Brain?*, in which she discusses the relation between the neural and the mental. In this chapter, Malabou wants to subject LeDoux's phrase, and particularly its verb, to critique: '"You are your synapses": I have nothing against this sentence. I simply want to understand the meaning of "being" here' (*QF* 162/*WSD* 69). The meaning of being which Malabou seeks to understand is a plastic meaning, and she argues that the phrase could equally be expressed 'you are your plasticity' insofar as plasticity 'forms your brain by coding all the information that impresses your lifestyle into your cerebral construction' (LNBc 2; my translation). Malabou's own gloss on the phrase is to understand the verb as a moment of destructive or explosive plasticity, which in this context she also calls a 'plasticity of transition', 'intermediate plasticity' or 'plasticity-link' (*QF* 162/*WSD* 69) between the neuronal and the mental, which allows her in turn to avoid the difficulties inherent in considering the mind–body problem in terms of linear continuity.[41] Her promise is that destructive plasticity acts as an 'intermediate plasticity' between the proto-self (which she takes to be a synonym for the synaptic self[42]) and the conscious self (*QF* 162/*WSD* 69), a function which 'would enable and qualify the formation of the singular person on the basis of the neuronal matrix' (*QF* 161/*WSD* 69), in other words which would solve the problem of the relation between brain and personhood.

Malabou deploys the notion of plasticity in this context not simply as a way to describe how neurons behave, but as a paradigm to provide a theory of how we might understand the transition from the brain to the mind neither as a simple continuity (Changeux's reductionist position) nor as two incommensurable discourses bearing no necessary relation to each other (Ricœur's position), but as a transition from the neuronal to the mental that 'supposes negation and resistance':

> There is no simple and limpid continuity from the one to the other, but rather transformation of the one into the other out of their mutual conflict. We must suppose that mental formation draws its being or identity from the disappearance of the neuronal, born of a sort of blank space that is the highly contradictory meeting point of nature and history. Only an ontological explosion could permit the transition from one to the other, from one organisation to another, from one given to another. (*QF* 167/*WSD* 72)

The biological matrix 'cancels itself' in the sculpture of the self, and the transition from nature to thought takes place in the struggle between them such that 'thought is therefore nothing but nature, but a negated nature, marked by its own difference from itself' (*QF* 184/*WSD* 81). Denying a linear continuity or a commonality between the neuronal and the mental, she argues that they are related in a 'complex continuity' (*QF* 137/*WSD* 56) which we understand, from her engagement with Hegel, as dialectical.[43]

This plastic understanding means that, in the phrase 'you are your synapses', plasticity informs our understanding not only of the predicate but also of the verb. In other words, it is the relation between 'you' and 'your synapses' that is described by the idea of plasticity, not just the capacity of the synapses themselves to undergo plastic transformation. The relation between brain and mind is plastic insofar as 'you are your synapses' is understood to describe an agonistic, explosive, non-linear relationship[44] that we might venture to render 'you are-and-are-not your synapses' or 'you are the plastic negation or transition of your synapses'. It is only with the full destructive as well as creative sense of the Hegelian *Aufhebung* that we can characterise the theory of 'neuronal personality' of which 'you are your synapses' is one expression, as 'the idea that the self is a synthesis of all the plastic processes of synaptic formation at work in the brain'.[45] Any 'synthesis' of the transition from brain to mind is not simply a gathering together; it is a destructive resistance as much as it is a summation.

Malabou's reading of 'you are your synapses' in terms of destructive plasticity is powerful in providing responses to some of the persistent 'Continental' objections to neuroscience, such as the claim that the mind is not made of matter any more than poetry is made of ink and paper.[46] Malabou's rejection of a linear continuity between brain and mind puts her account in a very strong position to answer a whole range of objections accusing materialism of a 'reductionist' approach to the mind–body problem. It is, however, vulnerable at least on a first reading to another accusation, namely that conceiving the relation between brain and mind in terms of destructive plasticity is little more than a convenient metaphor with only poetic, rather than scientific, explanatory power. It is to the question of plasticity as metaphor that we now turn, for rather than undermining Malabou's account of the relation between mind and brain, the trope of metaphor allows us to develop a bridge between Malabou's Hegelian and neurobiological readings of materialist selfhood.

Is 'plastic self' a metaphor?

Metaphors of the brain, it seems, have a short shelf life, prone as they are to fall into desuetude with advances in neurological research. None is more famous than the computer-brain, which has now 'become absolutely obsolete' (*SEL* 27) and 'has had its day' (*SEL* 34), as has the related metaphor of the brain as a central telephone exchange, a figure which 'completely fails to capture plasticity and does not take into account synaptic and neuronal vitality' (*QF* 97/*WSD* 34). Freud's metaphor of the psyche as the city of Rome, 'always capable of exhibiting its memory and overcoming wounds and loss' (*SEL* 61) has likewise been shown to be inadequate by incontrovertible demonstrations of the link between brain lesions and psychic trauma, and his metaphor of the brain as an 'electrical centre' (*SEL* 213) has fared little better.

In *What Should We Do With Our Brain?* Malabou is particularly sceptical of neuroscientist Antonio Damasio's metaphor of narration to explain the relation between brain and mind in his book *The Feeling of What Happens.*[47] Throughout the book Damasio insists upon a distinction between three selves by virtue of which, he argues, he is able to demonstrate a continuous and linear transition from brain to mind: (1) protoself or primordial self, (2) core consciousness (the self that, in the present tense, can say 'I'), and (3) extended consciousness or autobiographical self (the 'invariant aspects of an individual's biography').[48] For Damasio, the protoself is an unconscious representation of the organism to itself and consists in 'the ensemble of brain devices which continuously and nonconsciously maintain the body state within the narrow range and relative stability required for survival',[49] which Malabou glosses as 'a form of organic representation of the organism itself that maintains its coherence' (*QF* 142/*WSD* 59). For Damasio the proto-self is the 'nonconscious forerunner' or 'preconscious biological precedent'[50] of the core and autobiographical selves, and is constituted as a process of 'cerebral auto-affection' in which the brain maintains a dialogue with itself. Malabou characterises this dialogue as a continuous exchange – 'How are you doing?' 'I'm alright;' 'How are you doing?' 'I'm alright;' (CCM 9) – and it is out of the fabric of this minimal dialogue that the conscious self is woven:

the core you is only born as the story is told, within the story itself. You exist as a mental being when primordial stories are being told, and only then; as long as primordial stories are being told, and only then. You are the music while the music lasts.[51]

Damasio seeks to describe the transition between the neuronal and the mental in terms of the proto-self's 'narration' or 'account'. In the proto-self, the brain 'somehow recounts its own becoming' in 'something like a poetic activity or wordless recitative function' (*QF* 146/ *WSD* 60). Damasio readily acknowledges that the idea of the proto-self giving an 'account' or a 'narration' is but a metaphor, and Malabou notes that his 'metaphorics of transformation' allows us to 'formulate the hypothesis of a metamorphic fluidity assuring the synthesis of the cerebral and the psychical' (*QF* 151/ *WSD* 63). Nevertheless, she critiques this rather too linear presentation of the transition from brain to mind as 'obscure' and 'insufficient on many points' (*QF* 149/ *WSD* 62), concluding that all the different images and metaphors offered by neurologists – 'change', 'translation', 'account' and 'narrative' – are 'too vague and, without further analysis, do not let us grasp [. . .] the transition from one level of organisation to another (from the neuronal to the mental)' (*QF* 152/ *WSD* 63). I will now use this judgement as the yardstick against which to measure Malabou's own account of the relation between brain and mind in terms of destructive or explosive plasticity.

In a conference address entitled 'Les Nouveaux Blessés' ('The New Wounded'), Malabou insists explicitly and directly that 'in neurology, to speak of the plasticity of the brain is not metaphor, but an objective biological process. To say that the brain is plastic is to say that it simultaneously gives and receives form, and is therefore not rigid' (LNBc; my translation). However, this claim is not as straightforward as it may appear. Before considering whether plasticity itself is a metaphor, let us recall the other metaphors that Malabou offers: destructive plasticity is 'the metamorphic crisis that frees a butterfly from its chrysalis' (*QF* 170/ *WSD* 73–4), the glycogen stored in muscle tissue that is converted into muscle movement, an explosion, and a river jumping its bed (*OdA* 9/ *OoA* 2). How are we then to understand a 'transition between the neuronal and the mental' (*QF* 167/ *WSD* 72) in these metaphors? The neuronal does not cease to be in order that the mental may come forth, as combustible material is consumed or as the caterpillar or chrysalis are destroyed to make way for the butterfly. It seems inexact to speak of a transition *from* the neuronal *to* the mental, and if we are to insist on retaining the metaphor of transit then it would perhaps be more accurate to speak of a transition from the neuronal to the neuronal-mental.

In addition, Malabou's metaphors do not figure a transition from one level of organisation to the other. A river which jumps bed is still the same dynamic three-dimensional body of flowing water, not the idea of a river; although combustion may transform fuel and atmospheric oxygen into heat and smoke, the whole process can be described from beginning to end on the same physico-chemical level; and a butterfly is still a three-dimensional material organism, just like the caterpillar which built its chrysalis. However, in the case of the brain and the mind Malabou is seeking to describe the 'transition' from a very complex three-dimensional material structure to something which is not, or at least not without further explanation on her part, obviously three-dimensional and material. Finally, what is destroyed in the destructive transition from brain to mind? In *What Should We Do With Our Brain?* Malabou seems to suggest that it is the biological matrix of the brain that is destroyed: 'Sculpture of the self is born from the deflagration of an original biological matrix, which does not mean that this matrix is disowned or forgotten [*reniée ou oubliée*] but that it cancels itself [*se résilie*]' (*QF* 170/ *WSD* 74). But the 'original biological matrix' does not undergo destructive or explosive plastic transition in the sculpture of the self; it is plastically transformed in the sense that it receives form by virtue of the electro-chemical signals passing through it which effect the selective stabilisation of its synapses. The appropriate plasticity to describe the brain here is the receiving of form, not an explosive deflagration. Synaptic de-potentialisation can only in the loosest (the most metaphorical) way be called an explosion or a deflagration.

The image that seems most fit to measure up to Malabou's own yardstick is that

> one must think the transition from the neuronal to the mental, on the model of the transition from the action of storing glycogen in the muscles to the voluntary action effected through these muscles. Energetic explosion is the idea of nature. (*QF* 170/ *WSD* 73–4)

Here we have combustion (the glycogen is burned), transition (there is no glycogen at the end of the process) and a change of levels (from a chemical to a movement). To fold this back onto Malabou's attempt to account for brain–mind transition, it is not the 'original biological matrix' of the brain which is subject to combustion but the electro-chemical 'signals' that fire across the synapses, expending and transforming their energy in the process. It is energy which is the object of an explosive plastic transformation, not the physical structure of the brain itself. Malabou rallies to this position when, towards the end of *What Should We Do With Our Brain?*, she insists that 'the explosions in question are clearly understood as energetic discharges' (*QF* 171/ *WSD* 74). The glycogen example only gets us so far, however, because it still assumes the very 'voluntary action' that an explanation of the mind–brain relation should describe. It may be the best of Malabou's metaphors, but in the final analysis it does not dispel the obfuscation of the relation between brain and mind any better than Damasio's narrator.

The evidence is mounting to suggest that the problem is not with this or that metaphor of the relation between mind and brain; the problem is with describing the relation between mind and brain in terms of a metaphor *tout court*. Any chosen metaphor constrains and renders determinate an organ that is understood by Malabou precisely in terms of its indeterminate and transformative plasticity, in addition to being a hostage to scientific fortune as the paradigm of the computer-brain has painfully shown. At this stage of our investigation of the relation between brain and mind we have arrived at the same point we reached at the end of the second chapter of this book: just as no determinate host capacity is adequate to account for the specificity of humanity, so no metaphor can adequately articulate the relation between brain and mind.

Thus far in this investigation metaphor has been the enemy of clarity: ad hoc metaphors to describe epigenesis, outdated metaphors of the brain, Damasio's obfuscatory metaphor of the proto-self as narrator and Malabou's own problematic metaphors of destructive plasticity. But what if we folded Malabou's reading of plasticity in Hegel back onto the thorny problem of mind–brain metaphors? What if we took the genius of her account of plasticity, namely that plasticity is itself plastic, and used it to elaborate not a determinate metaphor of the self but an account of the self as a metaphor? As this chapter draws to a close I want to argue that Malabou's great contribution to a materialist theory of selfhood is not that she offers us (yet another) new metaphor for the self but that she allows us to figure the self as a movement of metaphoricity. In turning to the resources of metaphor we are going beyond the letter of Malabou's text, but I hope to show that we are doing so in a way that is in keeping with the spirit of her reading of Hegel.

It will be remembered that for Malabou the self is not the result or the product of an explosive transformation from brain to mind, but emerges from within their mutual antagonism and tension: 'The neuronal and the mental resist each other and themselves, and it is because of this that they can be linked to one another' (QF 168/WSD 76). Brain does not cease to be in order that mind may begin to exist, but rather the self arises from the mutual refusal of brain and mind to yield to each other. This mutual resistance presents itself as the structure of a metaphor, namely the 'tensive' metaphor described by Paul Ricœur.[52] Metaphor, for Ricœur, is the possibility of incompossibility, 'a work on language consisting in the attribution to logical subjects of predicates that are incompossible with them'.[53] For Ricœur's metaphor, as for Malabou's self, there is no easy linear continuity between the elements held in tension, no smooth transition from one to the other, and Ricœur's notion of metaphor as impertinent predication cuts with the grain of Malabou's non-linear reading of the verb in 'you are your synapses'. Ricœur also mirrors Malabou's insistence that the neuronal and the mental are in a relation of mutual resistance when he asserts that 'before being a deviant naming, metaphor is a peculiar predication, an attribution that *destroys* the consistency or, as has been said, the semantic relevance of the sentence as it is established by the ordinary, that is the lexical, meanings of the terms employed'[54] and 'in the most radical terms possible, tension must be introduced into metaphorically affirmed being'.[55] For both Ricœur and Malabou, this tension or resistance is not a problem to be reduced but the very agonistic precondition of the emergence of metaphorical sense (for Ricœur) and the self (for Malabou), avoiding what Ricœur calls the 'ontological naivety'[56] of assuming a linear and continuous relation between the two terms and of trying to reduce the 'is and is not' of metaphor to an 'as if'.

Ricœur employs language remarkably similar to Malabou's negation, explosion and destruction when he describes how metaphorical sense arises from the 'ruin' and 'destruction' of the literal:

> Just as the metaphorical statement captures its sense as metaphorical midst the ruins of the literal sense, it also achieves its reference upon the ruins of what might be called (in symmetrical fashion) its literal reference.[57]

> [T]he meaning of the metaphorical statement rises up from the blockage [*l'échec*] of any literal interpretation of the statement. In a literal interpretation, the meaning abolishes itself [*se détruit*]. Next, because of the self-destruction [*auto-destruction*] of the meaning, the primary reference founders. The entire strategy of poetic discourse plays on this point: it seeks the abolition of the reference by means of self-destruction of the meaning of metaphorical statements.[58]

What is destroyed is the fetishism for an uninterrupted, linear account of the relation between (for Ricœur) literal and figurative sense or (for Malabou) mind and brain, and what emerges is a self that resolves to neither of the two poles of 'semantic impertinence' – you are neither straightforwardly your brain nor your mind – but a self held in the tension and resistance between the two. This metaphorical approach is a dialectising – or as Malabou puts it a 'hybridisation' (PLR) – of the 'Continental' and 'cognitivist' positions. Cognitivism figures the relationship between brain and mind in terms of an 'an absolute naturalization of cognition and mental processes' (*QF* 185/*WSD* 81): the brain is the mind. Continental antireductionism figures the relationship in terms of the 'perfectly transcendental character of thought' (*QF* 185/*WSD* 81): the brain is not the mind. Metaphor, on the Ricœurian model we are currently elaborating, is the hybridisation of these two positions: the brain 'is and is not' the mind, and the self emerges in this deep and irreducible tension within the metaphorical 'is'.[59]

This is not a metaphor of the self but the self as metaphoricity, allowing us to rehabilitate the notion of metaphor this time not as a threat to or an obfuscation of Malabou's material account of the self but as its only faithful description. If a determinate metaphor of the self is a Hegelian bad infinite (because it forms part of an in principle endless sequence of such metaphors, each of which in turn needs to be replaced in response to fresh advances in neurological research) then the self as metaphoricity is a good infinite, not a determinate figure but a gesture or movement of figuring entire unto itself which, like the plasticity of plasticity, has the potential to change and respond to scientific advances. In the same way that we saw how Malabou's decisive contribution to a contemporary philosophical understanding of the self is not plasticity per se but the plasticity of plasticity, here we see that her intervention into the mind–body problem is best construed not as the introduction of yet one more metaphor of plastic selfhood to the increasingly large string of such metaphors, but as the invitation to think of selfhood in terms of a metaphorical structure. If Malabou's plasticity of the self is itself plastic, then her metaphor of the self is itself metaphorical, a metaphor not *of* anything other than of metaphoricity itself: the irreducible tension of metaphoricity. To determine the self in terms of a particular metaphor is the equivalent, in terms of the mind–brain relation, to the host capacity approach to the definition of the human in terms of particular determinate capacities, and in the same way that Malabou destabilises the host capacity approach by insisting upon the plasticity of plasticity, so also we can find in her thought the resources to interrupt the interminable, reductive and constraining series of metaphors of the self by the introduction of plasticity not as a determinate metaphor but as a metaphor of the self's metaphoric structure. To affirm that 'the self is plastic' is not a metaphor of the self; it is the self as a metaphor.

Conclusion

Does Malabou, then, succeed in avoiding a 'host capacity' account of the human? No and yes. No, in the sense that her reading of Hegel's 'Anthropology' in the light of the threefold plasticity he introduces in the preface to the *Phenomenology of Spirit* still understands humanness as such in terms of one particular property of humanity, namely plasticity, but 'yes' in the sense that plasticity is not a property unique to humanity, and it is not the possession of plasticity per se that differentiates the human but rather the human's unique ignorance of its own plasticity. Plasticity, therefore, does not act as the gatekeeper of a unique human status and cannot be said to be that which is 'proper to man'. Nevertheless, the price that Malabou must pay for escaping the problems attendant on a host capacity approach to humanity is the absolutising of plasticity in a way that makes it undermine itself. If plasticity can transform itself to include even stasis and constancy, then everything is plastic and, as a consequence, plasticity itself cannot be anything other than it is because there is nothing which it is not already and which it could therefore become. Plasticity emerges, despite everything, as a determinate and static concept describing not merely human but all organic life.

Turning to Malabou's sustained engagement with neuroscience, we are able to apprehend with greater clarity that human plasticity for Malabou is not adequately articulated merely in terms of the receiving and giving of form, but must also comprehend a destructive plasticity which accounts for the relation between the brain and the mind. It does not do so by simply throwing one more figure of the self – namely the plastic self – onto the growing heap of metaphorical obsolescence, but figures the self as a movement of plastic metaphoricity. This provides a powerful new tool for articulating a non-reductive materialist conception of the self that resolves neither to a cognitivism for which the brain and mind are in a linear and continuous relation, nor what Malabou calls a 'Continental anti-reductionism' which allows the brain no substantial influence on psychic experience.

There is a further problem with Malabou's account of 'you are your synapses', however, not this time in terms of the response that it gives to the mind–body problem but in the fact that it should be a response to the mind–body problem that she offers in the context of a discussion of 'you are your synapses' at all. The chapter of *What Should We Do With Our Brain?* entitled 'You are your synapses' deals with the relation between the neuronal and the mental, and it is clear that Malabou understands the problem raised by LeDoux's phrase to be the problem of the relation between the 'mind' and the 'body'. But this is not precise, or at least we should say that it assumes without justification that the 'you' is equivalent to the 'mind'. In the current chapter I have been turning a blind eye to Malabou's carefree slippage from 'mind' to 'self' and back again, but the time has now come to focus on the relation not between brain and mind but between brain and self, for the two relations are by no means identical.

Chapter 4

Catherine Malabou: The Epigenetic Human

> Si l'Ame d'un Huron eût pu hériter du Cerveau de Montesquieu, Montesquieu créeroit encore.
>
> Bonnet, 'Essai analytique sur les facultés de l'âme'[1]

> Nier la continuité du biologique au culturel – si l'on fait de la plasticité un fil directeur – est impossible et philosophiquement intenable.
>
> *CDM* 236[2]

This second of two chapters on neurological transformations of the human will focus on epigenesis, a particularly fruitful notion for the elaboration of a non-reductive materialist account of the self. At the end of the previous chapter I drew a distinction between the mind–brain problem and the self–brain problem; in the present chapter I will take up that distinction in order to pursue the question of the identity of self (rather than the mind or brain) over time. In the previous chapter I considered how Malabou can overcome the tethering of the question of humanity as such to the possession of determinate capacities or qualities; in this chapter I move with Malabou beyond the question of narrow host capacities and towards an ecological account of the self as neither merely neuronal nor conceived apart from the neuronal.

In her 2014 *Avant demain* Malabou continues to elaborate a non-reductive account of the human being. Whereas previously she was happy to own the label of materialism, she now distances herself from the term altogether, preferring rather to stress the affinities between her own thought and the concerns of speculative realism: 'Realism is a way out of the dilemma between materialism and idealism. Sartre said it already: "I am neither an idealist nor a materialist, I am a realist"' (PLR).[3] In contrast to both idealism and materialism, she insists, realism does not depend on the subject/object dichotomy which it is part of the purpose of *Avant demain* to move beyond. Malabou considers the importance of speculative realism (which she seems to equate with the philosophy of Quentin Meillassoux) to lie in the fact that it is currently re-evaluating the place of Immanuel Kant in contemporary thought for the first time since the publication of the first edition of the *Critique of Pure Reason* in 1781 (*AD* 2), questioning four postulates which have passed broadly without challenge from that time until now, namely:

> the finitude of knowledge, the phenomenal given, *a priori* synthesis as the originary relation between subject and object, and finally the whole structural apparatus intended to guarantee the universality and necessity of laws, both the laws of nature and the laws of thought: the 'transcendental'. (*AD* ix)[4]

Malabou situates her own intervention as a rejection both of the correlationism[5] that Meillassoux's speculative realism identifies in Kantian and post-Kantian philosophy, and also of his own principle of factiality. She does so by returning to Kant, specifically to paragraph 27 of the *Critique of Pure Reason*, in which Kant evokes an epigenesis of the transcendental. It is this motif of epigenesis that Malabou elaborates at length in *Avant demain*. It allows her to distinguish her own position from Meillassoux's brand of speculative realism and it opens the way for her to elaborate an account of the human which moves on significantly from her previous work.

If, as Malabou notes, Meillassoux's *After Finitude* can be read as an 'after Kant' (*AD* 2), then *Avant demain* is an exercise in returning to Kant after Kant. The stakes of this return are triple. First, insofar as Kant is 'the guarantor of the identity of continental or "European" philosophy' (*AD* 222), Malabou's return to Kant is an intervention intended to chart the recent past and shape the future of that tradition. Secondly, insofar as an adhesion to the transcendental marks 'better than any other criterion' the line of demarcation between the Continental and Analytic philosophical traditions (*AD* 223), *Avant demain* is an attempt to think beyond that division. Thirdly, given that Malabou's return to Kant foregrounds the relation between the categories of our understanding and the world, what is at stake are the possibilities for a new, epigenetic understanding of the human.

This chapter will begin by laying out some of the implications of epigenesis for the development of Malabou's thought in *Avant demain*, before reflecting on her treatment of the transformation of identity over time in her previous work. After highlighting some fundamental concerns with Malabou's approach to identity prior to *Avant demain*, in the final section I will develop some of the insights contained *in nuce* in that text and fold them back onto Malabou's previous discussions of selfhood in order to yield what I will argue is a more adequate and satisfying materialist account of the transformation of human identity over time than Malabou has given us to date.

Epigenesis and epigenetics

From the prefix ἐπί (upon, over) and the noun γένεσις (generation), epigenesis carries the meanings 'to be born after', 'to eventuate' or 'to be added to'. It is a term that straddles philosophical and neurobiological discourse, and in *Avant demain* Malabou explores and interweaves its meanings in both of these fields. In coming to terms with how the notion of epigenesis functions in Malabou's account of the human, it will help to begin with a thumbnail sketch of 'epigenetics' in neurobiology. The word was coined in 1940 by the English biologist Conrad Waddington in order to designate that branch of molecular biology which studies the relationship between genotype (the genetic constitution of an organism, as opposed to its observable characteristics) and phenotype ('the sum total of the observable characteristics of an individual, regarded as the consequence of the interaction of the individual's genotype with the environment'[6]). Epigenesis can be both prenatal and postnatal. Prenatal epigenesis refers to the way in which a genotype is 'interpreted' by epigenetic actors[7] in order to produce the phenotype. Malabou helps her reader to grasp this first meaning by reproducing a line from Thomas Morgan's acceptance speech upon reception of the Nobel Prize in Physiology or Medicine in 1935: 'if the characteristics of the individual are determined by their genes, why are not all the cells of an organism identical?' (quoted on *AD* 132). The answer to Morgan's question is that it is epigenetic actors which ensure that, whereas all cells in the body start with an identical or near-identical genetic patrimony, the phenotype contains many different cell types. Thanks to the selective epigenetic activation of certain genes, the organism creates different types of cells from the same genetic nucleus (*AD* 133). The second meaning of epigenetics is broader, and relates to human neoteny, that feature more pronounced in humans than in other species according to which 'we evolved by retaining the youthful features of our ancestors',[8] one aspect of which is that, in humans, a greater proportion of brain development occurs outside the womb and as a result of epigenetic factors:[9] 'the organization of the brain is affected by experience, and therefore, it has to be exercised, experimented, and because of this nature of our brain, we are constantly rewired and reorganized' (Hum 5–6). This means that 'humans are biosocial creatures':[10]

our brains are formed to a marked extent by epigenetic factors in our pre- and postnatal environments.

Epigenesis between preformation and equivocal generation

Malabou develops her philosophical understanding of epigenesis in *Avant demain* in the context of a tight and sinuous dialogue with Kant's *Critique of Pure Reason*. She begins her exploration of Kant with a lengthy assessment of the brief section 27 of the first *Critique* (a mere two pages in the Cambridge edition), in which Kant explores the nature of the agreement (*Übereinstimmung*) of experience with the 'pure concepts of the understanding'.[11] There are only two ways in which this agreement can be thought as necessary, Kant insists: 'either the experience makes these concepts possible or these concepts make the experience possible'.[12] He quickly dismisses the possibility that it is our experience that makes possible the categories of our understanding, on the basis that it 'would be a sort of *generatio aequivoca*' or equivocal generation, a notion which describes the process, thought in the eighteenth century to occur in the natural world, whereby a thing of one nature arises out of something of a different nature, such as the generation of life from non-living matter or of flies from rotting meat.[13] When Kant returns to epigenesis in section 81 of the *Critique of Judgment*, equivocal generation is now viewed as an instance of occasionalism, according to which 'the supreme world-cause, in accordance with its idea, would immediately provide the organic formation to the matter commingling in every impregnation'.[14] Kant's dismissal of such occasionalism is categorical:

> If one assumes the occasionalism of the production of organic beings, then everything that is natural is entirely lost, and with that is also lost all use of reason for judging the possibility of such a product; hence it can be presupposed that no one who cares anything for philosophy will assume this system.[15]

Malabou concurs with Kant's judgement, adding that equivocal generation requires a generative vital principle which, if admitted, would make the a priori into the equivalent of an inorganic origin from which the categories of the understanding would miraculously spring (*AD* 36–7), but Kant makes it clear that the categories are categories *of* the understanding, not of some immaterial vital principle. Equivocal generation, Malabou concludes, contradicts the very idea of generation itself.

Kant continues in section 27 by introducing a second possible way of accounting for the genesis of the categories of our understanding:

'Consequently only the second way remains (as it were a system of the epigenesis of pure reason): namely that the categories contain the grounds of the possibility of all experience in general from the side of the understanding.'[16] The eighteenth-century concept of epigenesis to which Kant is surely referring here is the belief that 'the germ cells of the two parents give rise to the embryo as a new product, rather than as the evolution of something preformed',[17] and later in section 27 Kant glosses this second position as holding 'that the categories were neither self-thought a priori first principles of our cognition nor drawn from experience'.[18]

In the second half of section 27 Kant adds a third option, a 'middle way' between equivocal generation and epigenesis, which consists in 'a kind of preformation-system of pure reason'[19] according to which the categories of the understanding are 'subjective predispositions for thinking, implanted in us along with our existence by our author[20] in such a way that their use would agree exactly with the laws of nature along which experience runs'.[21] For Malabou as for Kant, such preformation smacks too much of a theological loading of the dice: 'to follow down the preformationist "route" amounts to considering that the pure elements of knowledge are innate logical tendencies, planted in us by God and arranged such that their use is in perfect harmony with objects' (AD 37). Furthermore, if preformation is correct then all that would remain for the individual would be meekly and passively to receive the implanted categories in the absence of any spontaneity of understanding (AD 41). The principle of preformation is also unhelpful when it comes to describing the development of the human phenotype, Malabou insists, for it would imply that the entire phenotypic complexity of the individual organism is contained in nuce within the genotype, merely requiring linear elaboration. The simple fact that the complexity of the brain is many orders of magnitude greater than the complexity of the genome is enough to dismiss this position (AD 143). Preformation is a hyper-normative vision of the genesis of the categories of understanding (AD 223), a version for which 'the transcendental represents a sort of censorship that absolutely forbids any intermixing [of the transcendental] with experience or, as a consequence, any becoming or any transformation of logical forms' (AD 223). Malabou characterises this hyper-normativity as a stern policeman enforcing conformity at all times to the unchanging categories.

We can profitably think of the relation between preformation, equivocal generation and epigenesis along lines now familiar to us from our consideration of rigidity/elasticity, flexibility/polymorphism and plasticity in the previous chapter.[22] Like rigidity and elasticity, preformation adheres and always returns to an originary and foundational given (AD 52). Like flexibility or polymorphism, equivocal generation issues in an unconstrained and chaotic transformation. Like plasticity (a term to which it is closely related in the neuroscientific literature), epigenesis describes a transition or transformation which is neither fully conditioned by its original state nor only arbitrarily related to that state. Once again, just as we saw in the previous chapter that both elasticity and flexibility are passive and only plasticity is active,[23] so also for Kant and Malabou both preformation and equivocal generation open wide the door to scepticism (*AD* 38) and only epigenesis resists it. Equivocal generation leads to scepticism because it is a hypo-normative position (*AD* 223) which allows for no way of understanding or predicting what wild transformations may occur, paving the way for a chaos in which, in principle if not in fact, anything can happen. Preformation opens the door to scepticism because if, for example, I observed what I understood to be a relationship of cause and effect, 'I would not be able to say that the effect is combined with the cause in the object (i.e., necessarily), but only that I am so constituted that I cannot think of this representation otherwise than as so connected'.[24] There can be no objective necessity of the pure concepts of the understanding if there is a preformed agreement between concepts and phenomena, for under such a regime it is impossible that the concepts could be otherwise than they are and therefore they derive their necessity merely from arbitrary divine fiat and not from any necessary relation with the objects of experience: they are purely contingent and must be accepted as a fait accompli. In short, 'pre-established harmony undermines the necessity of the categories' (*AD* 41).

Of the three options, only epigenesis provides the categories with 'the necessity that is essential to their concept'.[25] According to the epigenetic paradigm, the relation between the pure concepts of the understanding and the phenomena of experience develops over time by a principle of auto-differentiation, just like the embryo in utero (*AD* 29), in a way that is neither arbitrary nor preformed. It is important to understand that this development or transformation of the relation is not, for Malabou, an asymptotic approximation to a pre-given standard. She warns her reader that, although the prefix 'epi-' means 'above' or 'beyond', the term 'epigenesis' is often taken to signify that which is both logically and ontologically 'below' or 'under' a first genesis, subordinated to it and always following along behind it (*AD* 59) in a way that would yield not a plasticity of identity but an elasticity. She rejects this subordination of the epigenetic to the genetic and insists that we understand epigenetic development to be above and beyond the genetic, not under it.

These Kantian peregrinations are of first importance for our purposes in this chapter because section 27 is addressing nothing other than the correlation (*Übereinstimmung*) between the categories and the objects of experience (*AD* 27), a relation which we have already seen is central to Meillassoux's forging of a new understanding of the human. In elaborating the principle of epigenesis as a rejection both of theological preformation and occasionalist equivocal generation, Malabou is splitting the horns of Meillassoux's dilemma between (what he takes to be Kantian) correlationism and an access to the 'Great Outdoors' secured by a transcendental, preformed mathematics. Rejecting both of these positions, Malabou introduces an epigenesis of the categories that, as we shall see in the rest of this chapter, yields a very different picture of the human from Meillassoux's own. According to Malabou, Meillassoux performs the remarkable feat of falling off the donkey on both sides at once. On the one hand, the 'brutality' of his turn to and reliance upon a transcendental and unchanging structure in the laws of logic smacks of a divinely ordained preformation, and far from his turn to mathematics interrupting the religiosity of post-deconstructive thought 'it rather seems that it is its twin [*son pendant*]' (*AD* 241). On the other hand, his hyperchaos and principle of insufficient reason resolve to the occasionalism of equivocal generation because 'the transcendental structures appear in the final analysis as facts and therefore cannot account for their own formation' (*AD* 19). If 'the thesis of speculative realism' (by which Malabou means Meillassoux's principle of factiality) is correct, then we must either adopt the reactionary position of denying any speculative realist threat to the a priori, or else adopt the 'position of post-critical absolutization' which holds 'that rationality has had done with finitude and the question of the harmony [*accord*] between our thought and objects, whether epigenetic or not, can no longer be a rational question' (*AD* 267). What this abandonment of the transcendental betrays in speculative realism, Malabou argues, is a confusion between genesis and epigenesis (*AD* 63). In other words, Meillassoux falsely sees his own principle of factiality as the only alternative to the metaphysics of a necessary being.

What we need, Malabou insists, is a third position, an alternative to Meillassoux's mathematical thinking of the human, and a 'new interpretative paradigm' which will 'open a new perspective on rationality' (*AD* 267–8). Epigenesis furnishes Malabou with the paradigm for which she is looking because it allows the agreement between the pure concepts of the understanding and the objects of the understanding to be thought not mathematically or mechanically, but organically (*AD* 54). This in turn transforms the nature of the transcendental, because 'if it is true that an organism forms itself in transforming itself and not in elaborating a pre-established pattern [*en se déroulant*], we must admit that the transcendental itself is equipped with a certain transformability' (*AD* 54). What epigenesis introduces into the first *Critique*, and also into Malabou's own thought, is the element of 'life', which can reconcile the biological and the transcendental 'without according to either one the supremacy of being taken literally [*la suprématie d'un sens propre*]' (*AD* 276), in other words without either the biological or the transcendental establishing itself as the literal and primary discourse of meaning in relation to which all other discourses are considered metaphorical or derivative. 'Life' and 'the living' are neither ideas nor concepts nor forms: they have 'no transcendental status' (*AD* 276) but they nevertheless provide the philosopher with a totality which generates order and stability (*AD* 316), just like Meillassoux's appeal to reason.

To understand the epigenetic development of life as a paradigm is not merely to see in it a set of principles and methods but to see it as 'an instrument of reading and interpretation that, at a particular moment, establishes itself in diverse theoretical and disciplinary areas' (*AD* 269). To think of epigenesis as a paradigm in this way mirrors what Malabou argues in *The Future of Hegel* about understanding plasticity as a concept (*ADH* 16/*FOH* 5). What is at stake in establishing the epigenetic paradigm is brought out with great clarity in an interview given shortly after the publication of *Avant demain*: 'my project consists in precisely this: to make life an essential dimension of the real' (PLR). It is the question of what Malabou means by 'making life an essential dimension of the real', and its implications for a transformed notion of humanity, that will occupy us in the second half of this chapter. Before we are in a position to address this issue directly, however, we need to understand how Malabou relates the Kantian critical notion of epigenesis to neuroscience, and how this shapes her understanding of the human.

Neural Darwinism between genetics and epigenetics

The astute reader of the previous section may well have raised an eyebrow upon noting that I offered no clarification of how, in the epigenetic paradigm, the pure concepts of understanding can develop or be transformed. This omission was for the very good reason that Kant himself offers no account of such a transformation, as Malabou readily acknowledges (*AD* 150–1). For this piece of the puzzle Malabou needs to turn from epigenesis to epigenetics, and specifically to the 'neural Darwinism' of Jean-Pierre Changeux. The complex relation between genetics and epigenetics in contemporary biology closely shadows the debate between preformation and epigenesis (*AD* 135) in Kant. To hold that the development of the phenotype is influenced predominantly by genetic factors approximates to a contemporary preformationism, whereas to insist on the primary importance of epigenetic factors is the neurological equivalent of Kant's own epigenesis.

When seeking to understand the place of epigenetics in contemporary neuroscience, Malabou turns to the neural Darwinism of Jean-Pierre Changeux. Changeux did not originate the theory of neural Darwinism[26] but his account of how such a process might operate is one of his two great contributions to contemporary neuroscience.[27] According to Gerald Edelman, neural Darwinism takes Charles Darwin's 'population thinking', according to which 'variation in individuals of the species provides the basis for the natural selection that eventually leads to the origin of other species',[28] and elaborates a theory of the mind along the same lines. Edelman's theory has three main tenets: (1) *developmental selection* ('connectivity at the level of synapses is established by somatic selection during an individual's ongoing development'), (2) *experiential selection* ('extending throughout life, a process of synaptic selection occurs within the diverse repertoires of neuronal groups'), and (3) *re-entry*, or a higher-order selection that binds together disparate parallel neural circuits processing diverse features of an object (speed, size, colour, friendliness . . .) to create a coherent output.[29] Edelman's innovation is to understand the development of the brain not as a teleological and guided trajectory but along the lines of a-teleological Darwinian natural selection. Parallel to Edelman's development of neural Darwinism, Changeux elaborated in the 1970s a model of 'the selective stabilisation of synapses by neuronal activity'.[30] According to this theory, the development of the brain can be understood in three stages: growth (the brain produces an overabundance of neurons and synapses), 'transient redundancy' (over time, those neural connections which are not strengthened by repeated use wither away), and 'selective stabilisation' (those neurons and synapses which are more frequently stimulated are thereby strengthened and stabilised). Just as in the case of the large-scale evolution of species, this 'analogous Darwinian scheme'[31] adopts an appearance of teleology: the brain appears to be proactively adapting itself to its epigenetic environment as the systematic coincidence between cognitive structures and mental objects is accounted for by a 'natural dynamic' which is 'biologically determined' (*AD* 131).

Malabou notes the similarities between Changeux's theory of selective stabilisation and Kantian epigenesis: 'it is striking that it is once more a case, with this theory, of the process elaborating the agreement between cognitive categories and objects of experience', although the crucial difference is that with Changeux's theory epigenesis 'loses its status of being an analogy in order to appear as a physiological reality' (*AD* 131). In a move now familiar to us from the discussion of plasticity in Chapter 3, Malabou insists, in the light of Changeux's theory of selective stabilisation, that transcendental epigenesis must also be understood as epigenesis of the transcendental itself (*AD* 271). The transcendental rests upon no foundation, either in experience or in metaphysics, but is the result of a non-foundational epigenesis. This renders vain all speculation as to whether it is innate or constructed (*AD* 271). The categories of our understanding develop epigenetically in a recursive and circular interaction with first the prenatal and then the postnatal environment. Malabou carefully distinguishes this position from denying the transcendental altogether. One may well hold, along with Changeux (in conversation with the mathematician Alain Connes) that mathematical objects exist only in and as mental processes,[32] but that is not to deny the transcendental. It is simply to maintain, along with the Kant of the *Critique of Pure Reason*, that there are realities that cannot exist 'elsewhere than in thought', and Malabou insists that 'if one shares this opinion, as I do, one maintains the validity of the transcendental' (*AD* 319). There is nothing inherent in the notion of the transcendental, Malabou is arguing, that means it must be original and unchanging: the transcendental itself develops epigenetically.

For Malabou, Changeux finally brings to a satisfactory conclusion the line of thought initiated by Kant in section 27 of the first *Critique*. Changeux's epigenesis reduces neither to genetic determinism nor to the 'selective imprint of the environment' on the individual (*AD* 19), and the origin of thought is to be found in the relation (we might almost say the synapse) between the two, not in either genetic determination or epigenetic development alone (*AD* 19). It is this epigenetic model which facilitates a break with the theory of innateness, and it is through this turn to contemporary epigenetics that Malabou 'will push the Kantian thesis to its limit' (*AD* 57). The limit to which Malabou is referring is the limit of the biological, for epigenesis provides not only a theory of synaptic formation but also, Malabou hints in *Avant demain*, a naturalised account of meaning, an extension of epigenesis which allows her to begin to elaborate an epigenetic hermeneutics of the self.

An epigenetic hermeneutics of the self

Malabou's epigenetic paradigm paves the way for a non-reductive materialist understanding of the self. In *Avant demain* she draws Changeux's neural Darwinism back into philosophy by elaborating an account of the self which is both epigenetic and hermeneutic. This move begins with the recognition of just how often epigenetic development is described by scientists with the metaphor of improvisation or artistic elaboration 'as if, over against genetic determinism, it referred to the register of interpretative freedom [*la liberté interprétative*]' (*AD* 151). In both French and English, the notion of 'interpretation' can be used to describe both an artistic performance and a hermeneutic encounter with a text, a double meaning which leads Malabou to argue that 'the recourse to this image seems to indicate the opening of a hermeneutic dimension at the heart of biology' (*AD* 151). Let us be clear: Malabou is not here smuggling a molecular-level homuncular hermeneut into her account of the human, and to claim that epigenetic actors 'interpret' DNA is not to ascribe to them human-like powers of inspiration, deliberation or speculation. For a full account of what it can mean to deploy concepts like interpretation non-metaphorically at the molecular level, we shall have to wait for the next chapter and our discussion of Michel Serres's biosemiotics; pending that detailed justification I will merely affirm here that the language of interpretation is being used neither metaphorically nor in a way that smuggles a homunculus into Malabou's account.

The insistence that biology has a hermeneutic dimension yields for Malabou a new definition of the transcendental, not as a predisposition to certain logical categories but as a hermeneutic latitude, a 'power of meaning opened at the heart of biology' (*AD* 153). This affirmation becomes one arm of a chiasmic movement in Malabou's thought: biology is hermeneutic and meaning is epigenetic, the two arms of which allow her to elaborate an account of the self that is neither reductively biological nor dualistic. I will examine these two affirmations one at a time. First, biology is hermeneutic because epigenesis so intertwines the influences of genetics and environment that it becomes a fool's errand to seek to separate their respective roles in the phenotypic development of an organism. Epigenetic and genetic transformations find themselves in a plastic relation in which each one both forms and is formed by the other, in which both genetic and epigenetic modifications are heritable (*AD* 138), and in which each 'interprets' the other.

What does it mean, secondly, that meaning is epigenetic? In order to explore this question, Malabou takes a detour via the work of Paul Ricœur, whom she notes is the only philosopher to thematise the difference between genesis and epigenesis in relation to meaning (*AD* 269–70). It is through this detour that Malabou clarifies the way in which she uses the word 'meaning' (*sens*) in a biological context. In the essay 'Psychoanalysis and the movement of contemporary culture'[33] Ricœur notes how 'Freud explains genetically whatever does not possess positive truth'[34]: behaviour is to be understood in terms of originary trauma, which accounts for 'Freud's utter lack of interest for whatever is not a simple repetition of an archaic or infantile form'.[35] However, in the case of religion Ricœur questions Freud's fetishism of the origin: 'is meaning in genesis or in epigenesis? In the return of the repressed or in the rectification of the old by the new?'[36] For Malabou, the notion of the 'rectification of the old by the new' nicely captures the meaning of epigenesis (*AD* 270) because it contains a double sense of relation and transformation, a relation to the old (rather than an occasionalist innovation utterly dislocated from anything previously existing) in order that it be transformed by the new (rather than being elastically reaffirmed or merely developed along existing trajectories). This is precisely the sense of epigenesis 'because the embryo gradually grows in complexity by adding new parts which complete [*achèvent*] pre-existing parts' (*AD* 273), rather than transforming itself arbitrarily beyond all recognition. The result of this, and the point which is crucial both for Malabou and for the argument of this chapter, is that 'the epigenetic economy and the hermeneutic economy coincide' because they both bring together 'repetition and exploration, recapitulation and invention' (*AD* 273).

Malabou pursues the central importance of meaning for her account of epigenesis by considering a thought experiment introduced by Leibniz in the *Theodicy* and taken up by Gérard Lebrun in his *Kant et la fin de la métaphysique*:[37] a traveller happens upon a land empty of all inhabitants and finds it full of books and clocks. He would certainly have lost his mind, Leibniz affirms, if he were to conclude that he had arrived in a country where books write themselves. For Leibniz the point is clear: either the books wrote themselves or their writing was superintended by a deity, and faced with this choice 'there is a moral certainty that it is Providence which governs matters'.[38] Lebrun notes that Kantian epigenesis refuses 'this alternative of madness and piety: life is this country where doubtless books do not write themselves, but where they are not written by dictation either'.[39] Malabou elaborates on Lebrun's third option in the following way: this country in which books neither write themselves nor are verbatim copies of some archi-original Scripture is the only possible way of thinking about interpretation at all, namely as 'preliminarily orientated without being programmed' (*AD* 169). A self-written book would mimic the flexibility of chaotic transformation and a dictated book would be shackled to the rigidity of an original archetype. Neither would be an interpretation, and neither would be plastic.

It is Lebrun who cuts a path for Malabou from epigenesis to hermeneutics when he 'dispenses with the strictly biological and epistemological limits in order to open the problem of *meaning (sens)*, or rather of meaning as an absence of preformed meaning' (*AD* 169). This idea of 'meaning as an absence of preformed meaning' can be understood in relation to the insistent motif of indifference in Malabou's work since *Ontology of the Accident*. The world is indifferent to meaning in the same way that life, for Malabou, is indifferent to the pure concepts of the understanding. In a statement very reminiscent of Meillassoux's ancestrality, Malabou affirms that things are indifferent to being thought, indifferent to the subject–object relation (*AD* 206), and that the world could well be perfectly indifferent to '"our" structures of knowledge and thought' (*AD* 3). It is into this privation of meaning that the epigenesis of the transcendental can develop just as, for the Kant of the third *Critique*, it is an encounter with life that reveals 'a modifiability of the categorical structure' that opens a third option beyond preformation and occasionalism (*AD* 25).

The way in which Malabou understands the relation between indifference and the epigenesis of meaning is heavily dialectic. Indifference to meaning incorporates its own negation because 'that which is indifferent makes sense (*fait sens*) all by itself' (*AD* 292–3). How so? Because the indifferent natural world is sufficient to itself, is its own law, its own category, its own judge, and by that token it both makes thought useless by its independence and solicits it at the same time 'to the highest degree' (*AD* 292) because it is not already replete with meaning but rather a blank canvas ready for the eager brush of interpretation. All too ready to oblige, rationality invents its forms and categories in response to this necessary privation (*AD* 169). In the same way that it is the indifference of the world to our categories that allows for their epigenetic development, so it is the indifference of the world to meaning that calls forth our hermeneutic encounter with it. In fact, these are not two different ideas but two ways of expressing the same truth: epigenesis is not an analogy or a metaphor of hermeneutics (or vice versa); it is its synonym.

This hermeneutic excursus climaxes in a claim that will be central to my reading of Malabou in the rest of this book: the epigenetic nature of meaning and the continuity between biology and culture that is thereby established 'is a game changer' (*AD* 170)[40] not only for Malabou's attempts to think neuroscience alongside transcendental philosophy but also for other new materialist accounts of the human. It bursts the frontiers of the cranium and opens up the prospect of a selfhood and humanity that are much more ecologically situated, much less trapped within the nervous system, than has proved possible thus far in our engagement with Malabou. In order to begin to demonstrate the full potential of this game-changing move (a potential which Malabou herself has not thus far explored at length), I want to show how it can turn her previous problematic accounts of identity on their head by taking them outside their skull.

Epigenesis beyond cognitivism

Malabou's account of epigenesis in *Avant demain* provides us with a powerful way to re-read some of her earlier work, ironing out the problems raised by previous texts in relation to the question of the persistence of human identity over time. These problems arise from a combination of Malabou's notion of plasticity and her engagement with neuroscience which, necessarily, focuses narrowly on the brain in its account of identity. This combination leads to internal tensions in how Malabou can conceive changes in human identity over time, and after laying bare those problems I will show, in the final section of the chapter, how they can be overcome through an appeal to the paradigm of epigenesis as elaborated in *Avant demain*.

Brain trauma and the question of identity over time

Malabou works through the question of human identity over time in relation to two notable examples: the brain trauma of the nineteenth-century railroad worker Phineas Gage and her own observation of the effects of Alzheimer's disease in her late grandmother. The story of Phineas Gage is perhaps the most famous and certainly one of the most frequently cited cases in the history of neurology. Malabou explains the Gage case as follows:

> A railroad construction foreman in Vermont at the end of the nineteenth century, Phineas Gage was directing a rock-blasting operation when the accident happened. He triggered an explosion as he was compacting a charge in a rock formation with a long iron rod. The force of the blast drove the rod all the way through his skull. Miraculously, he survived the accident, but his frontal lobe was gravely damaged. Gage became both irritable and indifferent to everything. Having lost any feelings for his friends and family, he seemed utterly disaffected. (*LNB* 46/ *TNW* 15)

The neuroscientific interest in the case is not in Gage's unlikely survival but in the indication it provides – or so it is argued – of the causal relation between lesions in specific areas of the brain and particular personality changes. Antonio Damasio, upon whom Malabou heavily leans in her discussion of Gage, sums up the significance of the case by saying that:

> Phineas Gage will be pronounced cured in less than two months. Yet this astonishing outcome pales in comparison with the extraordinary turn that Gage's personality is about to undergo. Gage's disposition, his likes and dislikes, his dreams and aspirations are all to change. Gage's body may be alive and well, but there is a new spirit animating it.[41]

The phrase from the case history that attracts both Malabou's and Damasio's attention originally formed part of the medical report of the case written by J. M. Harlow, one of Gage's physicians, who faithfully cared for him over the twelve-year period from the injury to his patient's death. In his account, written some years after the unfortunate event, Harlow states that:

> Previous to his injury, though untrained in the schools, he [Gage] possessed a well-balanced mind, and was looked upon by those who knew him as a shrewd, sharp businessman, very energetic and persistent in executing all his plans of operation. In this regard his mind was radically changed, so decidedly that his friends and acquaintances said he was 'no longer Gage'.[42]

The case provides the inspiration for Damasio's book *Descartes' Error*, and it is Damasio who extrapolates Harlow's report into the sentence 'Gage was no longer Gage.'[43] Malabou echoes Damasio's emphasis on the radical change in Gage's personality attested by Harlow, citing it as an instance of 'the discontinuity produced by the traumatizing event and of its destructive power to transform identity' (*LNB* 254/*TNW* 153). For Malabou, the irreversibility of the change produced by the trauma, along with the emphatic change in Gage's personality, provides an example of a non-elastic destructive plasticity: 'the sort of transformation that occurs in such cases is not a partial modification but a complete metamorphosis of the personality. [. . .] The previous personality is totally lost and there is no remainder' (*SEL* 57).

However, the reading Malabou offers of the Gage case is unstable because the phrase 'Gage was no longer Gage' repeats the ambiguities of 'you are your synapses'. In the same way that the relation between the 'you' and the 'your' ostensibly identifies a phenomenological whole ('you') with an analytic element of that whole ('your synapses') so also the symmetrical construction of 'Gage was no longer Gage' creates an ambiguity not between parts and wholes but between continuity and change. First, '*Gage* was no longer Gage': it is clear that there must be a minimal continuity between the 'Gage' before the lesion and the 'Gage' after, such that we can say that it was Gage, and no one else, who was 'no longer Gage'. In order for there to be any change at all (rather than two different and utterly unrelated people) some element of the individual's identity has to remain constant through the transformation. Without this continuity there could be no rupture. Secondly, 'Gage *was no longer* Gage': there must also be a fundamental rupture in identity, such that we can say that the former Gage had not just changed somewhat but 'was no longer'. This is the element of the phrase that sits most comfortably with Malabou's notion of plastic transformation. Thirdly, 'Gage was no longer *Gage*': there were certain traits indicative of the 'former' Gage which, now being absent, give us cause to claim that the old Gage is no longer. So what is being claimed in the phrase 'Gage was no longer Gage'? A minimal reading would be: 'the human being called Gage no longer has the same personality as before the lesion of his frontal lobe' much the same way as we frequently make observations like 'he is not himself today' or 'that's quite unlike her'. But as we shall see, this is most emphatically not Malabou's reading. Instead, she identifies personhood with personality in a way that provides a problematic substantialist account of being human that reveals itself, despite its materialist pretensions, to be strangely disembodied.

Malabou insists on the radical nature of the transformation brought about by brain lesions. For too long, she argues, we have maintained in the West that, however form may change, substance remains the same (*OdA* 15/*OoA* 7). Daphne may transform from a woman into a tree, but her substantial identity remains constant throughout the transformation. This sort of secondary change which assumes the subsistence of some underlying metaphysical constant is of no interest to Malabou, and she dismisses it as 'a trick, a strategy or a mask always ready to be lifted to reveal the authentic features of the face' (*OdA* 17/*OoA* 9). Thinking beyond a mere change of appearance, Malabou insists on plastic transformation as a change in nature, a change deeper than which nothing is. This also entails that the sort of destructive transformation Malabou sets out to conceptualise in the Gage case cannot be a moment in any economy of salvation or redemption: there can be no prospect of Gage being able to return to a previous 'normal' state. Rejecting the psychoanalytic elasticity that would seek to understand any present self in relation to an original trauma which no amount of cerebral damage can erase (PT 226–7), and equally rejecting an elastic religious messianism which always holds out the possibility of a final return to a lost original state (PFPT 24, 29–30), Malabou sets out to think the Gage case in terms of utter and fundamental transformation, in line with her understanding of plasticity. But this begs one important question that Malabou does not conclusively answer: transformation of what? What has changed for Gage and what, if anything, remains the same?

Malabou presents a spectrum of possible views on the object of change in Gage's brain lesion. On the least radical end of the spectrum the change is said to take place on the level of personality: 'the patient's personality is transformed to such a degree that it might never regain its lost form' (*LNB* 92/*TNW* 47). The personality can undergo a 'complete metamorphosis' (*SEL* 57) or a 'lasting modification' (*LNB* 253/*TNW* 152) such that, in Gage's case, 'the previous personality is totally lost and there is no remainder' (*SEL* 57). Elsewhere, however, Malabou evokes not a change of personality but a change of person: 'When a psyche is shredded, it corresponds to the birth of a new, unrecognizable person' (*LNB* 94/ *TNW* 48). The former 'person, properly speaking, no longer exists' (*LNB* 95/ *TNW* 49) and 'we witness [. . .] the birth of a new person' (LNBc 6). Closely allied to the language of personhood is that of 'one' or 'someone'. Everyone who has suffered a cerebral lesion 'has become someone else' (LNBc 6).

The same insistence upon the radical nature of transformation is evident in Malabou's poignant description of Alzheimer's disease in her grandmother:

> Indeed, this was not a diminished person in front of me, the same woman weaker than she used to be, lessened, spoiled. No, this was a stranger who didn't recognize me, who didn't recognize herself because she had undoubtedly never met her before. Behind the familiar halo of hair, the tone of her voice, the blue of her eyes: the absolutely incontestable presence of someone else. (*LNB* 10/ *TNW* xi)

In a passage in which she distances herself from Freud's elastic notion of the psyche, Malabou maintains that 'a person with Alzheimer's disease, for example, is not – or not only – someone who has "changed" or been "modified," but rather a subject who has become someone else' (*LNB* 45/ *TNW* 15). In still other passages Malabou chooses different terms, evoking a loss of past 'identity' (*LNB* 113/ *TNW* 60) and a 'new identity with loss as its premise' (*LNB* 94/ *TNW* 48), or a new 'individual' (LNBc 7), new 'form of life' (LNBc 12) or new 'self' (*SEL* 57).

One notable characteristic of Malabou's discussion of both brain lesions and Alzheimer's is that there is a lack of clarity in the distinction between terms like 'person' and 'personality', 'psyche' and 'identity', with terms emphasising an underlying continuity like 'change', 'metamorphosis' and 'transformation' sitting alongside terms emphasising discontinuity and rupture like 'destruction' and 'disappearance'. An easy gliding between different concepts can be seen in the following paragraph from *Self and Emotional Life*, in which Malabou ranges over 'you', 'self', 'subjectivity', 'inner life' and 'psyche':

> In *The Brain and the Inner World*, Mark Solms affirms: 'There is a predictable relationship between specific brain events and specific aspects of who we are. *If any of us were to suffer a lesion in a specific area, we would be changed and we would no longer be our former selves.* This is the basis of our view that anyone with a serious interest in the inner life of the mind should also be interested in the brain, and vice versa.'[44]

One important reason for this easy transition between self, person, identity and so forth is that Malabou's reliance upon and deep engagement with neuroscience have caused her to reduce notions of identity and selfhood to questions of an individual's personal memory and capacity for cognitive functioning. 'Person' is interwoven with 'personality' and 'psyche' with 'identity' because, for Malabou, the personality is the person and the psyche is the identity. In fact, Malabou consistently identifies the brain with the entirety of the self or the person:

> 'Brain events' are intimately linked with our identity. We may even say that they constitute them. That is why there is a profound correspondence between the brain and subjectivity, between the brain and the 'inner life.' We have to understand today the way in which the brain 'produces' our subjective mental life. This subjective mental life appears to be a new name for the psyche. (*SEL* 28)

In a case of brain damage it is 'our whole "self," our subjectivity itself', which is altered (*SEL* 28). Identity for Malabou is inscribed in the brain of the individual who has undergone the trauma, and nowhere else. Indeed, Malabou insists that, from a neurological point of view, should an individual undergo such a trauma then 'the hypothesis of absolute danger designates the risk of brutal and sudden disappearance of the trace resulting in the formation of an identity without origin and without memory' (*LNB* 254/*TNW* 152–3). But such a person's identity is only without memory if the only memory we count as significant is the person's own, and only if we understand the 'neurological point of view' to be restricted to the neurology of the individual who has suffered the trauma. In other words, it only works on the basis of assuming an atomised individualism. Malabou's explicit focus on neurology is doubled by an unspoken atomisation and isolation of the individual who has undergone the trauma such that, if they have no memory of 'their' former identity, that identity is said not to exist. Identity is intra-cranial, or it is not at all. Having worked hard to circumvent a host capacity approach to thinking the human, what we see here is that Malabou is working in terms of a 'host substance'. The cerebral matter is the 'host substance' of human identity and personhood, and just as rational thought acted as a gatekeeper of humanity for Badiou and Meillassoux, so here we see personal memory in the individual's brain as the gatekeeper of personhood and identity for Malabou.

Malabou does open a possible second source of identity, only to shut it again. In the course of a discussion of the uniqueness of each brain she alludes to an identity richer than individual memories:

> the brain of a pianist is not strictly identical to that of a mathematician, a mechanic, or a graphic artist. But it is obviously not just a person's 'trade' or 'specialty' that matters here. The entire identity of the individual is in play: her past, her surroundings, her encounters, her activities; in a word,

the ability that our brain – that every brain – has to adapt itself, to include modifications, to receive shocks, and to create anew on the basis of this very reception. (*QF* 47/*WSD* 7)

Here, environmental factors are only deemed to be significant for identity to the extent that they leave a neurological trace or what Changeux calls an 'epigenetic signature'.[45] What the brain encodes are certain of the 'surroundings', 'encounters' and 'activities' which form the individual's identity. And yet, it is not these extra-neuronal factors as such that are significant for identity but the brain that has been structured in a particular way by them. Even in acknowledging the influence of these factors on the brain, Malabou does not allow that they can be thought directly constitutive of identity. If the brain should lose all memory of such activities, for example, they no longer hold any significance for personhood or identity: my identity and personhood are still wholly cloistered within my brain, whatever the epigenetic influences upon the brain may or may not have been. The limits of Malabou's position are starkly exposed when, for example, she asserts that, in the case of Gage, '[e]ven if some capacities remain untouched, the patient is unrecognizable' (*SEL* 57). It may well be that the patient's personality has changed, but the patient as such is by no means unrecognisable: if nothing else, a minimum continuity is required in order that he be identified as 'the unrecognisable patient' at all.

The dogmatism of Malabou's position is belied not least by the testimony of Phineas Gage himself. Malabou claims that '[t]he accident appears to be the plastic explosion that erases any trace and every memory, and that destroys any archive' (*SEL* 58). This may well be the testimony of Harlow, but it is not the testimony, it appears, of Gage. Commenting on the extant documents surrounding the Gage case, David Evans notes that

> It was never Gage who complained of feeling so thoroughly different that he must be considered as another, stranger kind of person than he had been used to being. It was third parties, work colleagues as reported by a physician, who commented that he could no longer be considered to be Gage.[46]

Here is the irony at the heart of Malabou's position: the claim being made is that identity and personhood are adequately understood through and in terms of the brain, and yet the very judgement which seeks to ground that position – illustrated in the claim that 'Gage was no longer Gage' – is a third-party judgement, an identity conferred within a community of discourse on the basis of medical expertise, in a way that at least prima facie invalidates the position that personhood is personality and identity is psyche. Malabou is mistaken when she asserts that the event of a lesion 'cannot be woven into the thread of an individual's history' (*LNB* 101/ *TNW* 53). It is quite possible that it cannot be woven in by the one who suffers the lesion herself (as, for example, in many cases of Alzheimer's), but it cannot but be woven in by others, as Malabou emphatically and poignantly demonstrates when she weaves her grandmother's Alzheimer's into her history in the opening chapter of *The New Wounded*. That is also precisely what we see happening in the case of Phineas Gage, and indeed it is what makes 'Gage' into a case. Unless the event of his accident is woven into his story by his family and surgeons then there is (if we follow Harlow's disputed account) nothing but a new man bearing no relation to any past, and being embedded in no relationships. The thread of the story may be cut for the individual in question but not for the stories of which he is part: the stories narrated by Harlow, Damasio and Malabou herself.

Malabou's agenda in her writing on brain lesions is to counter psychoanalytic elasticity by emphasising the radical and irreversible change undergone by people with brain lesions, but her own language betrays a more complex situation. Take this short passage from *The New Wounded* as an example:

> Rehabilitating the event is thus a matter of taking into account the discontinuity produced by the traumatizing event and of [sic] its destructive power to transform identity ('Gage was no longer Gage'). If we ask patients about their experiences of these changes of personality, we observe that this is no metaphor. The patients find themselves really changed; they no longer recognize themselves as they were before. (*LNB* 254/ *TNW* 153)

Malabou quite correctly emphasises that the patients do not recognise themselves. What she does not comment on is that at least Malabou, and possibly the patients as well, still recognise that it is the patients themselves, and not another, whom they do not recognise. In other words, in order for the very transformation and misrecognition on which Malabou insists to obtain, there needs to be a continuity of some sort from the person before the transformation to the person after. If psychological continuity of the atomised individual were really the only factor in identity, there would simply be a new person without any relation to any previously existing person, but this is not what Malabou claims.

At the very heart of Malabou's and Damasio's neuro-discourse are notions of identity and personhood that, while it would be incorrect to suggest that they have nothing to do with the neuronal, cannot be exhaustively understood and explained in neuronal terms alone.[47] Malabou has sought to overcome the Cartesian dualism of subject and object but has replaced it, despite herself, with an equally unwarranted dualism of the intra- and extra-neuronal. In *Ontology of the Accident, The New Wounded* and *Self and Emotional Life*, Malabou's understanding of personhood and identity labours under this tension: she can explain why Gage was no longer Gage, but cannot offer an adequate account of why it was Gage whom Gage no longer was.

The model of selfhood for which Malabou is arguing here is bound up with the modernity from which she is elsewhere careful to distance herself. It was John Locke who, in the second edition of his *Essay Concerning Human Understanding*, introduced the idea that 'person' should be defined as a continuity of memory and consciousness, establishing 'each individual's absolutely inalienable self-ownership'.[48] Paragraph 9 in chapter 27 of the second book of the *Essay* describes unerringly, *avant la lettre*, the notion of personhood that emerges in Malabou's writing:

> to find wherein *personal Identity* consists, we must consider what *Person* stands for; which, I think, is a thinking intelligent Being, that has reason and reflection, and can consider itself as itself, the same thinking thing, in different times and places; which it does only by that consciousness which is inseparable from thinking, and, as it seems to me, essential to it [. . .] since consciousness always accompanies thinking, and 'tis that, that makes every one to be, what he calls *self*, and thereby distinguishes himself from all other thinking things, *in this alone consists personal identity*, i.e. the sameness of a Rational Being: And as far as this consciousness can be extended backwards to any past Action or Thought, so far reaches the identity of that *Person*; it is the same *self* now it was then; and 'tis by the same *self* with this present one that now reflects on it, that that Action was done.[49]

Locke's position atomises the individual and makes him or her the sole owner and possessor of their personhood and identity such that in his *Second Treatise on Government* he can say that 'every Man has a Property in his own Person'.[50] This reduction of selfhood and identity to a proprietary continuity of consciousness not only raises the problem already identified – namely that such a notion is always implicitly dependent upon the judgements of third parties in a way which it cannot explain or justify – but it is also a 'host substance' account of personhood, returning us to the problems we identified in Badiou and Meillassoux. Personhood is extended to those who have a memory they can express, and only for as long as that expressible memory persists.

Malabou's work on epigenesis in *Avant demain* provides a powerful and compelling set of tools to understand identity and selfhood in a way that breaks decisively with the modern, Lockean model that haunts her earlier work. It allows her to transgress the artificial barrier between the nervous system and the rest of the world in order to think the self and the person as ecological, not just as neuronal. I propose to call this theory, incipiently present in Malabou's latest work, 'eco-synaptic' personhood, where the prefix denotes the situation of the self or the person in terms of both neuronal synapses and also the myriad of other social, cultural and political synapses which it interprets and which interpret it, without recognising a qualitative difference between neuronal and non-neuronal synapses.

Rethinking identity as eco-synaptic epigenesis

For the most part, contemporary theories of the self fall into two mutually exclusive and mutually antagonistic categories:[51] cognitivism and social or symbolic interactionism. Cognitivism locates the self within the brain, 'inside' the body or mind (it is the position of Descartes, Locke and Hume), and social interactionism understands self and identity as products of social and symbolic interaction, irreducible to the individual in isolation. In this final section of the chapter I want to show how *Avant demain* moves beyond the opposition between cognitivism (which accurately describes Malabou's reading of the Gage case and of her grandmother's Alzheimer's) and social interactionism, with a view to elaborating a situated ecological and synaptic selfhood. Drawing upon hints and lines of inquiry opened in *Avant demain* I will argue that a self-consistent materialist notion of selfhood, personhood and identity should be considered as properly neither 'internal' not 'external' to the mind or brain, as properly neither 'biological' nor 'cultural', but as arising at the synaptic limit of the internal and the external, of biology and culture, as a product of the tension or resistance between them.

The seeds of an ecological self beyond the nervous system are present in Malabou's work before *Avant demain*. In What *Should We Do With Our Brain?* she already provides some hints about how the brain might be extended beyond the nervous system:

> the functional plasticity of the brain deconstructs its function as the central organ and generates the image of a fluid process, somehow present everywhere and nowhere, which places the outside and the inside in contact by developing an internal principle of cooperation, assistance, and repair, and an external principle of adaptation and evolution (*QF* 99/*WSD* 35)

Malabou is referring here to contemporary theories of cognition (such as Changeux's Global Workspace Theory) that consider the brain to be a decentralised conglomeration of diverse and loosely associated units, rather than one central and coherent homunculus. Commenting on this passage, Hugh Silverman suggests that, according to Malabou, 'there is no centrality even for the brain and its functioning, but rather [. . .] the "brain" is distributed (plastically) throughout the body'.[52] In other words, the reception, processing and omitting of signals is by no means the sole preserve of the cerebral matter contained within the cranium; the whole body participates in the processing and transmission of signals, of which system the brain is but one part.

Silverman takes this line of thinking further than Malabou herself when he suggests that the notion of the synapse can be extended beyond the nervous system: 'self-reflection increasingly means the expanding awareness of ourselves as just such a multiplicity of synapses, of interconnections. These interconnections are within us but they are also interpersonal and socio-political.'[53] Silverman's instinct to redraw synaptic selfhood more broadly than the limits of the physical body cuts with the grain of much neurological research over the past decades, not least with Richard Dawkins's and Daniel Dennett's 'extended phenotype', which 'not only extends beyond the "natural" boundary of individuals to include external equipment such as shells [and internal equipment such as resident bacteria]; it often includes other individuals of the same species',[54] and also with Joseph LeDoux's insistence on the importance of the 'mind' being distributed across the regions of the brain in a non-localisable, non-totalisable network.[55] In *What Should We Do With Our Brain?* Malabou herself draws tantalising links between the synaptic and decentralised structure of the brain and modern democratic society (*QF* 109–12/*WSD* 40–6) but the nature of the relation between brain and politico-economic order remains ambiguous in her work. It is unclear whether we are to understand the brain on the model of society, or society on the model of the brain, and it is further unclear by virtue of what the similarity between the two should be considered normative. If it is a good thing to organise society like a brain Malabou does not give us any reason why, other than an implicit and as yet unjustified assumption that structural congruence between the two should itself be considered desirable.

What *Avant demain* allows us to do is fill in the missing links in these earlier suggestions and elaborate a robust notion of the synapse that transgresses the boundary between the inter- and extra-neuronal and allows us to think the self not just as a neuronal self but as an ecological self. At the end of the first section to this chapter I began to show how Malabou insists that epigenesis and meaning (*sens*) are synonymous, and that neither one is the original model for the other but they are both instances of the same process. I now pick up that line of investigation with a question: if there is no difference in kind between epigenesis and meaning then why should we assume a difference in kind between the synapses within the nervous system and the interactions and interpretations that are passed across social, cultural or other avenues of communication outside the nervous system? Drawing a boundary at the limit of the skull or the skin is just as artificial as drawing a limit between epigenesis and meaning, between nature and culture, an idea we shall see only reinforced in Chapters 5 and 6 of this book.

In fact, the paradigm of epigenesis invalidates any attempt to isolate the nervous system as the unique locus of identity and personhood.
Hermeneutics/epigenesis is not confined, for Malabou, to the nervous
system, rather in its epigenesis the nervous system partakes of a general
process of becoming that structures transformations on both a micro and
a macro scale. This is what Malabou means when, in *Avant demain*, she
evokes an epigenesis not just of the brain but of the real:

> Cerebral activity is a natural and material grasping [*saisie*] of nature and
> material, the contingency of its epigenesis thus also concretely engages that
> of the world. The brain is no more a subject than the world is an object.
> The epigenetic development of the brain affects the totality of the real. (*AD*
> 259–60)

The epigenesis of the brain, then, is not a process particular to that organ
but one instance of the natural and material development of 'the totality
of the real'. We must now think in terms of 'the epigenetic structure of the
real' (*AD* 261), or in other words 'the adaptive pliability of the world and
the metamorphic power of traces [*empreintes*]' (*AD* 261). There is nothing
unique about the brain in this respect; like the rest of the natural material
world it develops by epigenetic/hermeneutic transformation. The brain is
not the only locus of epigenesis; it participates in the epigenetic structure
of the real. Malabou is following here Changeux's theory of nested levels
of epigenesis: the paleo-ontological evolution of species, the epigenetic
evolution of neuronal connections in the individual's brain, extra-cerebral
cultural evolution, and finally the evolution of personal thought, including personal and cultural memories (see *AD* 260) are analogous with
each other. The epigenesis of the real will only mark a historic moment,
Malabou insists, 'if we stop taking history to be the absolute other of
nature and meaning to be the result of their difference' (*AD* 321). If we are
fully to enter the age of the epigenetic paradigm, she continues, we must
understand meaning (*sens*) no longer as the mutual irreducibility of the
symbolic and the biological, but as an exchange between them (*AD* 321).
It is when we stop making hard and fast distinctions between neuronal
epigenesis and the hermeneutic development of cultures and symbols that
we can begin fully to comprehend the epochal potential of the epigenesis
of the real.

Malabou is categorical: 'to deny the continuity of the biological and the
cultural – if we take plasticity as a guiding principle – is impossible and
philosophically untenable' (*CDM* 236). An adequate account of epigenesis
can never describe simply the development of the nervous system, because
in reality the 'nervous system' is only a contingent subsystem itself part of
a much broader epigenetic trajectory: 'it is the system constituted by the

organism and its environment that really develops'.[56] The epigenesis and development of every living thing must be thought henceforth to take place 'in the interval or gap [*l'entre-deux*] between biology and history' (*AD* 153).

It is not the case here that the epigenetic is primary and the hermeneutic secondary; epigenesis and hermeneutics must be understood in a relationship of mutual plasticity, a mutual giving and receiving of form. Malabou repeatedly insists upon the fact that, with recent advances in brain imaging technology, the brain is for the first time becoming not only the means of consciousness but an object of consciousness in itself. In an essay entitled 'For a critique of neurobiological reason' (*CDM* 229–37), she underlines the importance of the fact that, with the introduction of various brain-scanning technologies, we have now become conscious of our brains in a way never before envisaged: 'how should we be conscious of our brains and what happens when the brain becomes the consciousness of an epoch?' (*CDM* 237). Malabou describes the brain becoming conscious of itself as 'a dialectic adventure' fraught with conflicts and contradictions, and not necessarily leading to happiness or to truth (*CDM* 237). The conflict which it creates is one between hermeneutics and epigenesis, and it is consonant with the phenomenon of 'biolooping',[57] a term that comes from Ian Hacking and describes how hermeneutics and epigenetics are mutually formative, such that 'medical diagnoses – such as one of depression – interact not only with the self-understanding of the patient, but also with the biological processes related to the condition diagnosed'.[58] Rather than a linear model where the epigenetic phenotype serves as a foundation for epiphenomenal hermeneutic interpretation, the relationship is one of a continuous loop between the biological and the hermeneutic. The mutually informative relation is evident within the field of neuroscience itself. Paul Martin and Richard Ashcroft give one representative example:

> A potentially significant social impact of the new neurosciences is the formation of new forms of personal and social identities. Nikolas Rose has analysed the rise of psychopharmacology and the way this particular solution to mental health problems is being promoted by the pharmaceutical industry. One result of this is the creation of new forms of identity and 'selfhood' in which 'It seems that individuals themselves are beginning to recode their moods and their ills in terms of the functioning of their brain chemicals, and to act upon themselves in the light of this belief.'[59]

A similar looping, in which a self arises from the tension and interaction between biological and hermeneutic epigenetics, is the phenomenon of brain scans as an active constituent of selfhood. This phenomenon has been observed in patients with brain illnesses who have been shown images of their own CT, MRI or fMRI scans. The results are reported by Simon

Cohn in his essay 'Disrupting images: neuroscientific representations in the lives of psychiatric patients':

> By investing the scan with the qualities of a revealing portrait, people see in them a new sense of who they can be. What is taken as 'biological' by the patients is consequently not the possible causal base beneath their outward behaviour that the scientists seek within the interior of the brain, but rather a definitive, overarching explanation of their diffuse experiences and intangible suffering that can be transposed as part of their experience of the condition [. . .] for the patients the notion of a biological representation of their illness is invested with a hope for discontinuity that is embraced as a means to interrupt the patterns and routines that constitute their living experience. [60]

It is in the light of this epigenetic 'looping' paradigm that Malabou's own previous understanding of the self must be rethought. Faced with the continuity between epigenetics and hermeneutics it is no longer good enough simply to claim that environmental factors are encoded in the brain (as is the case in Malabou's example of the musician) and that therefore the brain alone is a sufficient criterion of identity and personhood (as she implies in her discussions of Phineas Gage and her grandmother's Alzheimer's). My brain is not the only place where my surroundings, encounters and activities are encoded; they are also inscribed in the brains of others and the symbols and stories that are passed between us. In the same way that Malabou, LeDoux and others insist that the brain is a distributed phenomenon, we must push further and affirm that the self and the person do not reside as hermits in the homuncular stronghold of the brain but are similarly distributed phenomena, transgressing the artificial boundary between biological epigenesis and cultural hermeneutics. We should not restrict the notion of selfhood merely to one dimension of a hermeneutico-epigenetic existence, namely synaptic epigenesis, and if there is really no hard and fast division between epigenesis and meaning then we must also consider the self to be encoded not only in the epigenesis of its nervous system but also within the hermeneutics of the symbols and stories which it tells and are told about it. Such symbols and stories are not mere epiphenomena of an identity that is fundamentally forged elsewhere (namely in the brain), but they are indispensable epigenetic actors in the process and substance of self-formation. Malabou shows an awareness of this entanglement of stories in an epigenetic concept of selfhood when she contrasts flexibility to plasticity in terms of 'the difference between continuous change, without limits, without adventure, without negativity, and a formative change that tells an effective story and proceeds by ruptures, conflicts, dilemmas' (*QF* 181/*WSD* 79). To assert that epigenesis tells a story is not a metaphor, any more than to assert that narrative is epigenetic.

This relentless collapsing of the dichotomy between the biological and the hermeneutic opens up new responses to the questions of personhood and identity that Malabou raises in relation to brain lesions and Alzheimer's. The self that emerges from the epigenetic/hermeneutic paradigm is a self which is inextricably formed by, and forms in turn, its (biological and cultural) environment, a synaptic self in the sense that it emerges where the 'inside' meets the 'outside'. It is not a cerebral self (sufficiently contained within narrow limits of its cranium), and it is not a social interactionist self (consisting of nothing but its relationships), but an eco-synaptic self which comprehends, seamlessly, both cerebral and interactionist, both biological and cultural epigenetics.

One important consequence of this is that it ceases to be the case that, if my memory is lost, then my identity or my personhood are also lost. My self and my identity develop with an extra-corporeal hermeneutic plasticity at the same time that my prenatal brain forms itself epigenetically; in other words, as my brain starts to form according to the interpretative paradigms of epigenetics, so also my existence begins to be interpreted in the stories and symbols used about me in utero by others. It is just as true to the paradigm of epigenetics to claim that 'I am my stories' as it is to claim that 'I am my neuronal synapses', and just as partial to make either claim in a way that excludes the other.[61]

In order to illustrate how the epigenetic paradigm can supplement the cerebral self with a narrative self in such a way that the two are not in conflict with each other but expressions of the same undivided epigenetic process, I want to turn once more to Paul Ricœur. Although Malabou praises Ricœur as the only thinker to thematise the difference between the genetics and the epigenetics of meaning, she is dismissive of his use of epigenetics on the basis that it does not allow us to advance 'in our understanding of the link between this underlying epigenetic development and the individual story [histoire] of the human subject' (AD 321–2). It is true that Ricœur underestimates the potential of the paradigm of epigenetics at this point, but it is also true that, without evoking epigenetics directly, he elsewhere offers an account of narrative selfhood that conforms remarkably well to the epigenetic paradigm and that helps us to address some of the problems raised by Malabou's understanding of the self in her earlier texts.

Ricœur's account of narrative selfhood is epigenetic because it is (1) non-originary, (2) collaborative, (3) tensive, and (4) never definitive. First, in the same way that there is no archi-originary genetic deposit to act as a foundation for epigenesis, but rather a plastic looping of genetics and epigenetics stretching back into the mists of prehistory, so also for Ricœur there is no original moment in the stories which form and are informed by my identity:

> Now there is nothing in real life that serves as a narrative beginning; memory is lost in the haze of early childhood; my birth and, with greater reason, the act through which I was conceived belong more to the history of others – in any case, to my parents – than to me. As for my death, it will finally be recounted only in the stories of those who survive me. I am always moving toward my death, and this prevents me from ever grasping it as a narrative end.[62]

Secondly, this passage from *Oneself as Another* also highlights the necessarily collaborative nature of the narrative self. In the same way that epigenetic development does not create itself *ex nihilo* but transforms what it first receives, so also the first words of my story are never written by me, and later I only ever transform what is already extant. One very important implication of this is that I do not own my hermeneutic development as my exclusive property and possession, but I am welcomed into a narrative rhythm already sketched for me by others, and I never write the final word of the narratives which shape me. A self is never the product of any one single author,[63] and my story can never be considered in isolation from those of others. In fact 'life stories are so intertwined with each other that the narrative anyone tells or hears of his own life becomes a segment of those other stories that are the narratives of others' lives'.[64] This militates against the atomisation of the self which is common in cognitivism and which, as we have seen, Malabou does not always avoid.

Thirdly, both Ricœur's narrative identity and Malabou's epigenetics are tensive; in both cases transformation takes place not as a smooth linear flow but out of dynamics of mutual resistance. Just as there is no single unproblematic linear epigenetic development that can account for my personhood and identity (but rather a series of mutually forming tensions and resistances), so also narrative identity is unstable and contains flaws or fault lines, and 'it is always possible to write several plots about the same incidents (which by virtue of these facts no longer deserve to be called the same events)' just as there are always 'different, even opposed, plots about our lives'.[65] The self emerges in the tension and resistance within and between different and competing narratives, between the stories I tell about myself and those told about me 'by my progenitors, continuing with those of my friends and, why not, of my enemies'.[66] Fourthly, in the same way that plastic transformation never reaches a definitive and stable endpoint, so also Ricœur stresses that his notion of narrative identity never arrives at a final version, even after death, but always maintains a tension of concordance and discordance that imperils identity. Jean Greisch describes this tension as 'not a "synthesis of the heterogeneous" free from doubt and suspicion – a self-possession [*une possession de soi*] secured once and for all – but the fragile balance between the possession and the dispossession of self'.[67] It is always possible, Ricœur insists, to tell the story otherwise[68] and narrative identity brings diversity, not unity, to a life.[69]

In this extension of epigenetic selfhood to the hermeneutics of narrative, the self is distributed more radically than even LeDoux and Malabou allow, not merely throughout the body but throughout a web of epigenetic and hermeneutic synapses, resistances and tensions, both biological and cultural. Therefore, if the brain is partially destroyed it does not follow that a new person or a new identity emerges, because the brain is only one locus of the hermeneutico-epigenetic coding of my identity and personhood. Identity is not contained within the brain; it is not synaptic but eco-synaptic. This extension of the self also means that my personhood and identity are no longer reliant upon the possession of one or more host capacities, because personhood and identity are (also) given to me in the stories told about me. Those with a severe mental disability or with dementia, as well as neonates who do not yet possess such and such a host capacity, are carried along in the tensions between different stories that are told about them, regardless of their capacities. It is important to recognise that this does not lead to two classes of people: those who are carried and those who write their own stories. Both narrative and biological epigenetic identities are in each and every case given before they are reworked, and each of us is carried in a web of stories before we can epigenetically collaborate in the narratives in which we figure. Before I tell any stories about myself, from my earliest days, I am woven into stories that others tell about me, and my stories are not and never were mine alone, any more than I can claim the sole authorship of my genetic patrimony.

My hermeneutic selfhood is not simply given to me by others (that would be the hermeneutic equivalent of Kant's preformation), nor do I invent it *ex nihilo* (that would be the equivalent of equivocal generation), but I receive, interpret and transform a non-totalisable set of stories and meanings that are given to me along with my genes: that is epigenesis. To evoke narrative identity within a materialist frame – if we are to follow Malabou's own understanding of the term – is no alien metaphysical imposition upon pure materiality but a rigorously irreducible aspect of the inextricable weaving of sense into the material world, and part of the epigenetic paradigm that spans biology and culture. What emerges from Ricœur's account of narrative selfhood accords very closely with Malabou's epigenetic paradigm: there is neither preformation nor equivocal generation, but rather meaning emerges in the tension and mutual resistance between narratives, not in any single narrative; the self is not a centralised instance but a distributed network of relationships. In other words, Ricœur provides for us one possible sketch of the hermeneutic side of Malabou's seamless hermeneutico-epigenetic paradigm of the self.

Conclusion

As we draw on Ricœur's epigenetic theory of narrative identity to sketch in a missing aspect of Malabou's general epigenetics, a new picture of the self emerges. I would like to highlight what I consider to be three of its most important features: tension, process and dispossession. First, tension. The eco-synaptic self is different to a relational or interactionist model of the self because it does not reify or ontologise the synapse as a thing in itself that can be abstracted from that which it is a gap between. Both neuronally and culturally, identity is formed in relations of mutual resistance, in the tension between concordance and discordance, and also in the tension between the biological and the cultural themselves. This means that selfhood is never a *fait accompli*, never a given, but always a process of transformation that is irreducible to its product. Secondly, at the end of the previous chapter the crucial importance emerged of the difference between the self as a metaphor and the self as metaphoricity. In the same way, it would run quite athwart Malabou's epigenetic paradigm to suggest that the self is contained in the synaptic structure of the brain or equally in stories that are told about it by itself and others. The self is not the product of epigenesis, not an object standing at the static endpoint of a process of interpretation, nor again a particular configuration of neuronal synapses that encodes such and such a set of memories. To be consistent with Malabou's incisive reading of Hegel we must hold that the self is not a particular configuration of meanings or synapses but rather the process of tension, resistance and plasticity that transforms those epigenetic and hermeneutic connections. The self is epigenetic and hermeneutic, rather than simply an encoded product of epigenesis or a hermeneutic interpretation. Thirdly, an important advance towards an ecological notion of the self beyond the subject/object dichotomy is that, as radically distributed, the eco-synaptic self is a possession neither of the individual – such that I have autonomous and unimpeded sovereignty over my own identity, as in the modern concept of the self found in Locke and Descartes – nor of the wider society or community – such that my identity can be defined for me, against my will and my personhood circumscribed or taken away by an instance outside of me – but rather the self eludes the proprietorial claims of both radical autonomy and radical heteronomy. The self is in an irresolvable tension between possession and dispossession, not an appropriable substance but a changing series of synapses both biological and cultural, a bio-cultural epigenetic efflorescence that cannot be atomised and therefore owned, either by itself or by another. One benefit of understanding the self as a self-transforming series of synapses, as Malabou fully understands in her discussions of the relation between brain and mind, is that no single influence can arrogate to itself the responsibility of forming the self or the person in a linear and direct way. The person and the self are not 'made' according to a premeditated pattern, but arise precisely in the gaps between the different influences, constraints and intentionalities which are both biological and cultural, both within and outside the brain.

This elaboration of the eco-synaptic self is in the spirit of Malabou's *Avant demain*, though it goes beyond its letter. It brings us closer than ever to a naturalised, non-reductive self that moves beyond the subject/object dichotomy and opens onto an ecological understanding of identity. The ideas of narrative, metaphoricity and the breakdown of the dichotomy between the biological and the cultural are at the heart of Michel Serres's powerful account of the self in what he calls his 'new humanism', and it is to Serres that we now turn in order to develop further the notion of the ecological self that has begun to emerge in this chapter.

Chapter 5

Michel Serres: Universal Humanism

La demeure de l'homme est l'horizon.[1]

From the background noise, nothing follows. Or sometimes. But that's another story.

EH 14

In Chapter 4 we saw how Malabou in *Avant demain* opens the door to the possibility of an eco-synaptic account of personhood and selfhood which moves beyond the problematic way in which her earlier work tethers the human to the 'host substance' of the brain. Furthermore, *Avant demain* moves towards a more situated, complex figure of the human being taking into account the various co-written narratives in which each human being is entangled, as well as (and on equal terms with) the synaptic encoding of memories and the allied capacity for recall. This move towards a more situated, ecological notion of the self has the benefit of being able to 'carry' human beings who, for one reason or another, fail to measure up to this or that host capacity, and it allows for a more sophisticated notion of identity over time, taking into account factors external as well as internal to the individual psyche. In the present chapter I want to show how Michel Serres offers a more detailed account of the continuity of nature and culture, and a more developed understanding of the role of narrative in building a figure of the human.

Serres has sustained for over three decades a detailed reflection on the nature of humanity, culminating in a tetralogy of as yet untranslated books published between 2001 and 2009 which outline what he calls his new universal humanism and the 'Great Story' of the universe.[2] The question 'what is the human?' stands at the centre of his work and, he claims, at the centre of twentieth-century thought in general (TH 71). I want to explore his own response to this question in two parts. First, we shall see how he elaborates a fresh approach to the question of determinate capacities that we have been tracing through the previous four chapters of this book. We shall then turn in the second part of the chapter to see how he supplements this reworking of capacities with a narrative identity which, unlike the figures of the human in Badiou, Meillassoux and Malabou, explicitly broadens the scope of his account beyond the human as such to include nonhuman life and, indeed, the whole universe. Without denying all meaningful differences between the human and the nonhuman, Serres offers a radically situated, ecological notion of the self. Before we are through we shall see that there are problems with Serres's approach, but he nevertheless provides us with a landscape of paths that take us beyond the host capacity of Badiou and Meillassoux and further beyond the host substance of the early Malabou than she herself achieves in *Avant demain*.

Perhaps the inclusion of Michel Serres in a book on philosophical anthropology alongside the likes of Badiou, Meillassoux and Malabou still requires a word of explanation today. The chronic under-reception of Serres's writing in anglophone philosophical circles owes a lot to his style. He eschews (like Meillassoux) the footnotes that customarily serve as philosophical epilates guaranteeing a certain rank of rigour and erudition such that, as Alan Murray observes, 'for many first-time readers, it is not immediately obvious that what they are dealing with is, in fact, philosophy at all'.[3] The omnicultural competence of Serres's thought reflects the circuitous route through which he arrived at his philosophical vocation. After passing out from France's prestigious Naval College in 1949 he entered the ENS in 1952 to receive a training in mathematics and logic, passing his *agrégation* in philosophy in 1955. From 1956–8 he served as an officer in the French navy, before completing his doctorate on Leibniz in 1968. Like his own life trajectory, Serres's thought moves through a series of diverse discourses, including physics, literature, philosophy, myth, theology and everyday observation. His style is disarming and sometimes playful, coming across as almost flippant at times and turning many an earnest but impatient philosophical reader away at the door of his oeuvre. But make no mistake, behind the badinage and bonhomie is a nuanced and precise reflection – and what a tonic it is to read a French thinker who says what he means with simplicity, flair and lightness of touch. 'To start by being familiar with everything, then to start forgetting everything' (*Ec* 38/*Conv* 22) is Serres's definition of a good philosophical training, and he admirably embodies the principle in his own work. To bob along the surface of Serres's prose as if he has read nothing is to take the easy way out;

to dive beneath its tossings and lappings is to find an ocean of reflection and erudition, and requires the courage of the explorer.

Capacity and de-differentiation

In his assessment of possible host capacities for humanity, from the outset Serres strikes a sceptical note. Through whatever capacity we humans may choose to define ourselves, 'ethology almost always finds an animal, a plant, even a bacterium, possessing the characteristic supposedly specific to our species' (TH 90–1). The Western philosophical tradition never tires, with great fanfare, of launching one 'definition' of humanity after another, but sooner or later the theory is scuppered as we unearth a rival naked ape or a second featherless biped (Diogenes of Sinope needed only the time it took to pluck a chicken).[4] Animals laugh, make tools (TH 87), and make love face to face (RH 37); ants, beavers and chimpanzees are political animals (RH 38). Are we foolhardy enough to define humanity as the thinking animal? With his characteristically playful lightness of touch Serres wonders how we presume to know that the cow, finding itself in its little corner of a hayfield, is not ruminating, along with its mouthful of grass, on its own existential dereliction (RH 38). Who, he adds more seriously, has ever entered into coenaesthesia with a bat, to be able to conclude that no thought takes place in the pteropine cranium?[5] Only old Aristotle and a handful of recent historians and biologists, Serres comments wryly, have tried to define the human in the way one defines an oak or a marsupial (Inc 270–1).

Having arrived at this impasse, Serres neither admits defeat nor keeps on looking for the elusive host property of humanity. In a move with echoes of Meillassoux's jolt (though in a very different context) he embraces the 'failure' and turns it into the very point of his whole anthropological project. There is no unique human capacity? Well then perhaps humans are not unique! Animals make tools? Well then perhaps there is a continuity, not an ontological break, between humans and animals! It is hard to overestimate the importance of this pivot for Serres; we can read it as the fulcrum of his whole anthropology and as that by virtue of which he brings something genuinely new to the themes discussed in this book. The inability to define the human in contradistinction to the animal is not a stumbling block for Serres but a springboard, lifting us out of anthropology per se and into ecological thought that is neither anthropocentric nor anti-anthropocentric but otherwise than anthropocentric.

It is easy to mistake Serres's pivot to ecology for something less radical than it is. If Serres were merely arguing that the capacity for rational thought – to take one example – should be extended a little beyond the limit of the human to include, say, the higher primates, then nothing, fundamentally, would be resolved in the problematic of host capacities. We would still be faced with the problem of drawing the line between language users and non-language users. Do the lower primates have language? Do worms? Do vegetables? But Serres does not merely nudge the dividing line between language users and non-language users further out into the animal kingdom; he erases it altogether and warns that seeking to trace a definitive source of language is as fruitless as trying to localise the source of a great river to one single point (*Ge* 37–8/*Gen* 17; cf. *Dis* 271). Indeed, just like that fluvial origin, language is everywhere in the landscape.

For Serres, language is shared not simply with animals but with all matter. Understood in terms of information theory, which Serres reminds us is itself a subdiscipline of thermodynamics (*Dis* 261), language can be understood as the receiving, storing, processing and emitting of information, and these are capacities we see throughout the natural world (TU 212): in the great howls of wolf-packs, the plumage of the bird of paradise, in poison pollens, in the colours of orchids, in the cracking and screeching of thawing ice, in the modulating music of the breeze, in the numberless glinting smiles of the ocean and the rock face criss-crossed with holds and pegs (TU 212). Serres is emphatic that we do not simply project these capacities for communication onto the nonhuman world in a binge of anthropocentric vanity:

> We perceive and understand the world in the same way that it perceives and understands itself. The background noise of my body hears and understands [*entend*] the background noise of the world: harmonic, anharmonic,[6] disharmonic? Our conversations imitate those that the stubborn crystals, molecules, clouds, rock faces and rivers incessantly entertain between themselves. We live as slices of the world [*parts du monde*]. Brains like planets resting on feet of clay. Objective and subjective flowing together confusedly. We see a certain animism return, that of Proust or Woolf, in the company of my own humble brand. Perception receives, treats and stocks information. In so doing it functions in a universal way. (TU 212)

Far from imposing an alien order on the meaningless flux of nature (an idea for which we have to thank a Cartesian dualism of subject and object which Serres and, in his wake, Bruno Latour have done so much to pick apart),[7] our languages take up and echo the rhythms of the natural world (*Ge* 118/*Gen* 69–70) or what Serres calls the 'proto-language' of cells and molecules (*Dis* 267; cf. BPP 102). Nothing, in short, distinguishes me ontologically from a crystal or from a plant (*Dis* 271), and we find that in a world no longer sundered from the human by the epistemological gulf of subjectivity and objectivity, 'many operations of knowledge are already at work within the objects of the world' (SR 231). We can discern here a full blossoming of what Malabou begins to develop in *Avant demain*: a seamless account of epigenesis and hermeneutics which admits no qualitative distinction between the information processing of, say, a quartz crystal, and a sentence uttered in a human language. Genetics, as Serres reminds us, is a story progressing slowly 'from the production of animals to the production of texts' (*H3* 20). In Basarab Nicolescu's neat summary, 'we live in the semiosphere, as much as we live in the atmosphere, hydrosphere, and biosphere'.[8] All we might want to add, from a Serresian point of view, is that these four spheres have significant overlaps and cannot be separated from each other.

This is no new idea. In fact, the notion that the natural world does not speak is, like Foucault's man at the end of *The Order of Things*, an invention of recent date, and one perhaps nearing its end.[9] Lest anyone attempt to say that Serres is equating a human with a crystal, he is ready to acknowledge a great difference between mammal and mineral, but it is a great quantitative difference, not a great qualitative difference. There is of course a distinction between crystalline communication and human communication, but it is a distinction of degree and not of kind. In fact, amid this ubiquity of language one lone uniqueness remains to us: although we humans are not the only ones to use signs, we are still the only ones to think we are the only ones to do so (TU 212). Serres here is providing a different path to that traced by Meillassoux's refutation of correlationism. Whereas Meillassoux begins by sharing the correlationist's assumption that there is an uncrossable gulf between the interiority of the subject and a putative inaccessible Great Outdoors, Serres renders redundant the subject/object dichotomy by establishing a biosemiotic continuity across the nature/culture divide. Whereas Meillassoux labours to accede to the Great Outdoors through the principle of factiality, Serres refuses to confine human thought to the Cramped Interior in the first place.

It may come as something of a surprise, in the face of Serres's pivot to a ubiquity of language and his undoing of the human claim to qualitative uniqueness, that he should nevertheless maintain that there is something distinctively human that is shared by no other animal, vegetable or mineral. It is not a determinate capacity but quite the opposite: the human uniquely lacks fixed determinations. Whereas other animals evolve specialisations over time – a beak for winkling nuts or grubs, front-set eyes for predatory hunting – it is the peculiarity of the human species to become gradually de-specialised, de-programmed and un-differentiated over evolutionary time, as if it retreated from its perch on one branch of the evolutionary tree to return to its pluripotent trunk (*Inc* 80). In an example to which Serres frequently returns he argues that the human hand, in losing its usefulness for walking and swinging, becomes not a supernumerary appendage but an unprecedentedly versatile and extensible tool (*Inc* 81; TH 86; *Hom* 100, 263; SR 231). In addition, humans are omnivorous and our survival depends on no particular climate or ecology (*Inc* 271–2). It is this versatility that Serres has in mind with his notion of humanity as 'the incandescent' in the book of that name: a glowing pluripotency that contains within it all colours *in potentia*, though no single colour in a fixed way (*Inc* 81). This idea also underpins Serres's characterisation of humanity as *blanc* (meaning both white and blank), both everything in potential and nothing in particular. So in the human we find a strange confluence of uselessness (we are specialised for nothing) and universality (we have a potential to do almost anything), of zero and infinity (*Inc* 112–13); we are 'suited to nothing and good for everything' (*Inc* 82) and 'we have no niche but the world' (SR 231).

Serres's incandescence is reminiscent of Malabou's indeterminate definition of the human as plastic: the animal with the capacity to change its capacities. Humanity for Serres, then, is less analogous to Badiou's or Meillassoux's 'animal+' (animal plus language, or animal plus thought), and resonates more with what we could call Malabou's 'animal–' (minus determinate identifying qualities, minus specialisation, minus a differentiated place in the ecosystem): the potential animal. While every other animal has its territory, humanity is the totipotential wanderer (*Hom* 181), an anti-species among species, an animal which evolves in reverse from greater to lesser specialisation (*Inc* 81–2), which Serres christens 'stem cell species' (*Inc* 132). Humanity is an *animal viator*, perpetually on the point of leaving: we left animality not long ago, Africa some time ago, the caves at some point, Antiquity just recently; we left dry land to navigate by sea, we left gathering and hunting the day before yesterday, agriculture yesterday, and we are leaving evolution itself little by little (*Ram* 147–8): 'Our species leaves. There you have its destiny without a definition, its end without finality, its project without a goal, its voyage, no, its wandering, the "*escence*" of its *hominescence*' (*Ram* 148).

Serres sets a second sort of abandonment alongside the geographical peregrinations of the *animal viator*, namely that humans leave their family environment. In fact, Serres argues in *The Birth of Physics* that the most revolutionary moment in the history of humanity is not the accession to abstraction in and through language, but being pulled away from the relations we entertain with our kinship group in order to recognise something exterior to this gathering, something that is not 'I', 'you', 'it' or 'us', but 'that', *ecce* (*NP* 163–4/*BP* 132). In this we are greatly aided by a Christianity which has at its core a Holy Family consisting of a mother who is not the mother, a father who is not the father, and a child who is not their child: blood relations are replaced by the paradigm of adoption for a new universal belonging in a Christian community whose members nevertheless address each other as 'father', 'brother' and 'sister', opposing to the biological necessity of birth the free choice of adoptive new birth (*Hom* 199–200; see also *Ram* 86–7, *Inc* 260).

Problems with Serres's human de-differentiation

Just as we saw in the case of Malabou's meta-capacity of plasticity, however, there are a number of problems with this Serresian characterisation of humanity. The identification of human distinctiveness with de-specialisation, rather than being an exception to the logic of determinate capacities, leaves itself open to the same problems inherent in the identification of the human with the host capacity for language or thought that it treats so dismissively. The question that brings us to the heart of the matter is this: is Serres suggesting that there is no nonhuman de-specialisation? No pluripotent (if not totipotent) animal or mineral function? Does not the igneous stone de-specialise from its super-heated origins to become a guide for a river, a home for mosses and lichens, a hunting ground for insects and a welcome stool for weary ramblers? We could, to take one of Serres's examples from a passage about language, say the same about the breeze: from its thermodynamic origin it fulfils a functionally endless series of roles. Serres, it seems, is far from having demonstrated that de-differentiation is an exclusively human trait. Humans, to be sure, may be quantitatively much more de-differentiated than anything else, but this is just the same as the quantitative difference we have already encountered in relation to the questions of human language and thought.

The second problem with Serres's account of de-specialisation as the basis of a figure of the human is that it is far from clear that the 'blankness' of humanity does not after all present us with just one more capacity, but this time a meta-capacity more imperialistic than any we have encountered so far. Is not de-differentiation the capacity to have capacities, a second-order capacity or what Russell Disilvestro in his treatment of human capacity and dignity calls a higher-order capacity?[10] Why not just say that the lion is specialised for hunting, the flower for blooming, and the human for being unspecialised? The lack of immediate specialisation becomes reified as just one more capacity among others, and rather than circumventing the need for recourse to determinate capacities to account for the specificity of the human being, Serres can be read as having reinstated a super-capacity more potent than any he has dismissed. There are hints in Serres's writing that he is wise to this danger and seeks to forestall it. In *Hominescence* he argues that, while we are now finally in a position to answer humanism's question 'what is man?', we must give the response 'this animal that refuses to know who it is, because its whole wealth [*fortune*] consists in not knowing it' (*Hom* 78) and that, if we were to define ourselves, we would find ourselves on a level with the brute animals and unmoving plants that *are* something. However, hints like this are rare and are outweighed in frequency by Serres's unguarded assertions that de-differentiation is the human speciality. This is a danger analogous to that pointed out by Jacques Derrida in relation to Nancy's deconstruction of Christianity: the deconstruction risks revealing itself to have been, all along, a hyperbole of what it has sought to resist.[11] Similarly, Serres's rejection of any definition of the human resting on determinate capacities risks being recuperated as a more complete 'host property'[12] account of humanity than ever.

The structure of this second problem is doubled in Serres's differentiation between affiliation (*appartenance*) and identity (*identité*) (see HN; *Hom* 224; *Ram* 69; *RH* 40–1; *Inc* 138), a difference fundamental to his account of the human. We shall first describe the difference and then explain why it is problematic. Using himself as an example, by 'affiliation' Serres intends all the general categories which describe him – old, male, writer . . . – and where he comes from – locale, family, tribe, nation, religion – but none of these categories or provenances designates him in his singularity; none of them gives his identity (*Hom* 224). To confuse identity and affiliation is to commit a grave logical error that Serres labels as racism and a crime against humanity (*Hom* 224; *Inc* 138): the reduction of a person to one or more of his or her affiliations. To reduce a person to a set of affiliations can be equated to reducing a person to a host capacity or a host substance: all singularity is lost in the attempt to institute a universal criterion of humanity.

Serres argues that the distinction between affiliation and identity can be traced back to the apostle Paul, 'both in theory, because he proclaimed it, and in his life, because the good news he announces breaks with the old formats' (*Ram* 69), the 'formats' in question being Hebrew, Greek and Roman structures of society (*Ram* 70). These societies, Serres claims, knew only affiliation and no identity, as illustrated in the anecdote about Diogenes of Sinope taking a lamp and wandering the streets in the daytime unable to find any human [*anthropos*]. Serres glosses the anecdote in the following way:

> He was seeking in vain to meet an individual person or universal man, as a species or kind. Why? Because neither the one nor the other existed in his age and in the city all he could find was citizens or strangers, slaves or free men, men or women, sailors or farmers . . ., all of them members of a politi-

cal, social, religious, sexual or artisanal community . . ., in short, pairs of terms having to do with affiliation. No *ego*, no humans. (*RH* 104)

In describing the Pauline innovation of identity Serres concentrates on two passages in particular. The first is Galatians 3: 28, in which Paul proclaims to the Galatian Christians that 'There is neither Jew nor Greek, there is neither slave nor free, there is no male and female, for you are all one in Christ Jesus.' In this verse Serres discerns the decisive epochal break with the old formats and collectivities. The second verse to which he turns for an explanation of the Pauline distinction between affiliation and identity is 1 Corinthians 15: 9–10: 'For I am the least of the apostles, unworthy to be called an apostle, because I persecuted the church of God. But by the grace of God I am what I am.' If the Galatians verse sounds the end of the format of affiliation, the 1 Corinthians passage for Serres points the way to the new regime of identity:

> What remains is the 'new creature': I, adoptive son of God, by faith in Jesus Christ, I with faith and without the works by which I have no business to glorify myself; I, empty, poor and nothing: universal. Who am I? I am I, that is all. (HN)

This new regime of identity avoids the snares of Greek essence, logic and concepts with its 'I = I' that functions outside any society (*Ram* 41). But it is at this point that we can begin to see a problem with Serres's account of the difference between affiliation and identity. Let us look closely again at the Galatians passage: 'There is neither Jew nor Greek, there is neither slave nor free, there is no male and female, for you are all one in Christ Jesus.' Here, the arrayed affiliations of religion, social standing and gender are not replaced by a unique rigid designator but by a new meta-belonging, the affiliation of being 'in Christ'. Elsewhere in the two letters from which Serres quotes, Paul is comfortable with using the language of belonging to Christ (1 Corinthians 15: 23; Galatians 5: 24), and in the 1 Corinthians passage Paul's affirmation that 'I am who I am' is only a closed and circular 'I = I' if we elide the preceding 'by the grace of God . . .'. Both passages can easily be read as suggesting that one set of affiliations is superseded by a greater, overriding affiliation, rather than that affiliation is superseded by identity. Once more, what Serres presents as a conclusive trajectory from affiliation to identity is in fact much more of a tightrope of undecidability between the overcoming of affiliation and its dialectically hyperbolic re-emergence stronger than ever.

A third problem with Serres's account arises not, this time, in relation to de-specialisation but in that, despite all his warnings against giving a positive definition of humanity, he still risks relapsing into a physical sub-stantialist determination of the human reminiscent of the early Malabou's insistence on routing all personhood and selfhood through the cerebral tissue. This problem is that, despite his general refusal to make any determinate quality or capacity the gatekeeper of humanity, Serres does seem to make one worrying exception. Having denied that my name or affiliations can give me a rigid designation, he goes on to suggest that I do have one singular name, namely my genetic sequence: 'for the first time it is my real name, the code which corresponds so well to my body that it made it and to which no other body corresponds' (*Hom* 104). The question we need to ask of Serres at this point is this: my genetic code may well individuate me (and there are problems even with that hypothesis, as I discuss below), just like my fingerprints or any unique number might, but does it bespeak my identity? At this point Serres seems close to affirming that 'I am my genes' in the same way that Malabou is happy to say 'you are your synapses'. Is he making the human genome the original expression of humanness *as such*, in a way analogous to Changeux's 'neuronal man'? Before critiquing Serres's recourse to the genetic here – and there is certainly much in it to critique – we need to be clear about what he is not saying. It is clear from elsewhere in his work that he is not a proponent of a crude genetic determinism or (to use Malabou's language) preformationism for which 'nurture' counts for nothing in identity formation. He insists that we can work out a future trajectory from initial conditions in the case of cannon balls, but not in the case of human beings (*Inc* 346). Despite this qualification, however, the equation of my name with my DNA is still problematic. For a start there is the fact that identical twins share the same genetic code but not the same identity. Even if we chalk this indiscretion up to Serres painting a general word picture and not intending to propound a scientific theory with mathematical precision, however, other difficulties still remain.

Assume for the sake of argument that Serres is correct in claiming that my genetic code is unique to me (with apologies to all identical twins). What implications does this genotypic rigid designation have for my phenotypic self? It says nothing about 'me', or at least nothing to which I would be happy for my self to be reduced. 'I' (phenomenologically encountered first-person) am not the sum of my genetic predispositions (analytic, third-person), any more than 'I' am my synapses. The slippage by which Serres here collapses identity into coded genotype can be seen in the passage from *Hominescence* in which he discusses DNA: 'Yes, everything is number. The real originates from this exact coding' (*Hom* 104). There is a slippage here from 'is' to 'originates from' that smacks of material reductionism and the anthropological equivalent of the etymological fallacy. Surely it cannot follow, from the uncontested fact that DNA is coded and that, through a complex process involving RNA, proteins and epistatic interaction, this 'code' informs the phenotype, that 'everything is number'. Let us be precise here: the problem is not with number but with the copula 'is'. The claim that 'nothing is without number' or 'everything can be numbered' is uncontroversial enough, amounting to the claim that everything is amenable to the discourse of number. But to claim that everything 'is' number is to give this discourse a primacy and originality over all other discourses that amounts to an unwarranted imperialism and is structurally analogous to what, in relation to the confusion of identity with affiliation, Serres calls racism and a crime against humanity (*Hom* 224; *Inc* 138).

As when Changeux tethers the phenomenological 'man' to the analytical 'neuronal', or when Malabou endorses LeDoux's 'you are your synapses', the error being committed is a confusion which we can seek to clarify by distinguishing between 'extensive' and 'exhaustive' discourses. There is nothing that cannot be numbered, one way or another: in this sense number is extensive, by which I mean that there is nowhere it cannot reach, nothing it cannot describe in its own terms. But there is nothing (not even mathematics) which can be exhausted by the discourse of number in a way that leaves nothing unsaid for any other discourse (biological, political, theological . . .) to say. In this sense number is not exhaustive, and any non-reductive account of the human or of human identity requires a polysemy of discourses. If, when he says that 'everything is number', Serres intends the first, extensive sense, then it is an innocuous pronouncement and can be set alongside the parallel claims that everything is material, sexual, economic, political, theological and so forth. If, however, 'everything is number' is meant to give number a primacy over other discourses – everything is first of all number before it is anything else; everything is number in a way that cannot be said of other discourses – then Serres has reintroduced the imperialism that elsewhere he works so hard to expunge.

Finally, even if I grant that my genetic code is unique, that acknowledgement can do no ethical or political work for me. Think of it like this: even if we allow that humans are the only animal that thinks, it does not follow *eo ipso* that thinking animals should be treated any differently to non-thinking animals. The missing premises in this syllogism are that ontology is normative and that ontological sophistication is better than simplicity. But neither of these premises has been shown in the argument to be true. My genetic makeup carries no coding for normative politics. There is no correlation between the complexity of a genome and the complexity of an organism: humans have only around one fifth the number of chromosomal base pairs of the marbled lungfish *Protopterus aethiopicus* (*Inc* 79) but are not, for that reason alone, of one fifth the value of their ichthyic relatives.

A new approach to capacities? Harlequin and Pierrot

Despite these three problems, however, Serres's account of identity and affiliation does strike a genuinely fresh note in the composition of concerns I have been addressing throughout this book. The freshness comes in the way in which Serres seeks to think the human both in terms of a blank universalism stripped of all qualities and a rich set of determinate specifications at the same time. In certain passages it appears as if he is seeking to arrive at a universal humanity by systematically abstracting all determinate qualities whatsoever. When he urges us, once a day, to 'forget your culture, your language, your nation, the place where you live, your village football team, even your sex and religion, in short the narrowness of your enclosures' (*Inc* 141) he goes both too far and not far enough. He goes too far because these affiliations, even though they are not essential, are not utterly trivial or inconsequential to human identity either, and their systematic bracketing does not leave behind 'me' in any recognisable sense but an undifferentiated, inhuman abstraction. He does not go far enough, however, because his own logic of forgetting has no business drawing the line at football teams and gender. Why not also forget our humanity, our existence, our materiality, our being? We find ourselves here in the double bind evoked in Pascal's famous passage on love and qualities:

> And if someone loves me for my judgement, for my memory, is it me they love? No, because I can lose these qualities without losing myself. Where is self then, if it is neither in the body nor in the soul? And how can you love the body or the soul except for its qualities, which do not make up the self, since they are perishable? For would we love the substance of a person's soul in the abstract, whatever qualities it contained? This is impossible, and would be unjust. Therefore we never love a person, only qualities. Let us, then, jeer no more at those who are honoured for their rank and office. For we love a person only on account of borrowed qualities.[13]

Identity cannot be reduced to a set of affiliations but neither can it, to follow Pascal's lead, be thought to be utterly independent of affiliations. To seek a pure humanity stripped of all affiliations is akin to the early Malabou's attempt to make the brain a host substance, a sufficient repository of personal identity. This is also the problem with humanity thought in terms of a host capacity. It is inadequate, even dangerous, to allow determinate capacities to be the gatekeepers of humanity, but it is equally inadequate to dispense with them altogether.

Serres, for his part, seeks neither an empty apophaticism of blank identity nor a smorgasbord of accumulated affiliations. Or rather, his solution to the dilemma just sketched is to seek to hold both of these at the same time: the human is nothing *and* everything, white/blank [*blanc*] *and* multi-coloured: 'So universal humanity becomes this virginity received at birth, realised at death, the plastic becoming which we recognise in ourselves. Thus we give it two identity cards, one white/blank [*blanche*] and the other multi-coloured' (*Inc* 154).

A passage from *L'Incandescent* (pp. 137–8) illustrates how Serres seeks to have his cake and eat it when it comes to identity and affiliation. Imagine that a person's identity can be expressed as the complete sum of all their affiliations (this is the 'multi-coloured' pole of the tension). At this point the following question arises: 'At the limits of this series or this sum, does there exist an accumulation point outside of their development?' (*Inc* 137). In other words, is the sum of the elements exhaustively contained in the elements themselves? If so I can never hope to gain a sense of the whole but only ever a partial and vanishing apprehension. If there is nothing outside the elements in the sum then I am nothing but my untotalisable affiliations. If, however, there is some 'exterior accumulation point' then how am I to articulate my identity between the kataphatic elements and their apophatic sum? In what could stand as a paraphrase of Pascal's conclusion quoted above, Serres states that 'only the tautology "me identical to me" rigorously closes this proliferating immanence or this inaccessible transcendence. But with the blank transparency, the incandescence of this repetition, we learn nothing' (*Inc* 138). We are left having to navigate between the Scylla of an unwieldy list of overlapping affiliations and the Charybdis of a blank, silent and featureless identity.

Serres's response to this seemingly un-squareable circle is to seek a way to cross affiliation with identity. He takes his lead from the immune system. On the one hand, the system ferociously guards the difference between me and non-me (*Inc* 143), rejecting anything that does not belong to the body. However, the uterus stands as a notable exception to this high-security policing of the self's borders: 'the uterus is like the self [*le moi*], not defined by some affiliation but by the transparent principle of identity' (*Inc* 144). The uterus does not require that any 'foreign body' entering it produce its genetic identity papers. Both the affiliations of the immune system and the identity principle of the womb are necessary for human life. If we only had the immune system then we would live only one generation and would 'pass away like the grass of the field' (*Inc* 144–5). With the principles of affiliation and identity cohabiting in our bodies, it is for Serres as if we were living two lives: the life of the individual and the life of the species, as if we were living in two times: one brief and the other multi-generational, and as if we were living with two bodies: one with open doors of blank identity and the other with crenelated ramparts of affiliation (*Inc* 145).

Thus far I have been referring to the relation between the 'blank/white' identity and 'multi-coloured' affiliation as a tension, as if they were inversely proportional to each other and as if one needed to be switched off for the other to be switched on. Indeed, there is a sense in which, as we have seen, they are in a productive but nevertheless strict opposition, and this is the sense of Serres's analogy of the immune system and the womb. But there is also an important sense in which they stand in direct proportion to each other. Another of Serres's chosen metaphors – white and multi-coloured light – illustrates the point well. The greater the number of colours combined together, the more blank/white the light becomes. As the light is refracted, say through a series of prisms, it will by turns appear multi-coloured and white, all the while remaining the 'same' light. This oscillation between the perception of multi-coloured and white light is what Serres describes as the peculiarity of humanity: incandescent like Pierrot, blended and mixed like Harlequin:

> the more you impress others onto the self the more it is affirmed as singular, because no other possesses this same remarkable hue, but also the more it approaches a sum just as white as the wax it began with. This whiteness can look like a colour or like the integration of all colours. Pierrot tends towards Harlequin, Harlequin tends towards Pierrot; this double incandescence is what makes human time. (*Inc* 154)

Rather than opposing identity to affiliation it would better reflect Serres's position here to oppose, on the one hand, little identity and a modest breath of affiliation to, on the other hand, a more developed identity and a richer panoply of affiliations. Harlequin and Pierrot, far from being enemies, prosper under the same roof.

So far my reading of Serres has been cautious at best: his account of the human takes two steps forward and one and a half steps back in relation to the Pascalian dilemma of qualities and the problem of seeking an account of capacities in a way that does not leave the human as such contingent on the possession of any particular host capacity or substance. However, Serres does offer us a supplement to his account of identity and affiliation, a supplement which takes us further than the Harlequin–Pierrot partnership in marrying universalism with specificity. That supplement is Serres's incorporation of his figure of the human into the 'Great Story' of the universe, a story that yields a human being not abstracted from its 'nonhuman' milieu.

Humanity and econarratology

In addition to bringing identity together with affiliation, Serres seeks to develop a robust universalism in terms of an all-enveloping narrative of the universe that he calls the Great Story (*le Grand Récit*). Serres is not shy about his claims for the Great Story. Today, he asserts, we are living through the tumult of a Renaissance compared with which the renaissance of the fifteenth- and sixteenth-century humanists seems like nothing more than a gentle ripple on the surface of time's river (*Hom* 371). Now, for the first time in history, we have the opportunity to do justice to the universalism of the term 'humanism' because 'for the first time in the millennial process of hominization we have the scientific, technical and cognitive means [. . .] to give it a federating and non-exclusive content worthy of its name' (*Hom* 371–2). What Serres has in mind are the discoveries, older than any recorded and culturally specific history, of our earliest human ancestors, the 'Lucys'[14] of the east African savannah whose descendants would spread throughout the globe. This prehistory is universal because it is owned by no culture – Lucy predates Homer, Confucius and Abraham – and because it is 'written in the encyclopaedic language of all the sciences and [. . .] can be translated into each vernacular language, without partiality or imperialism' (*Inc* 32).

For Serres, narrative introduces a powerful temporal dimension into the Harlequin–Pierrot doublet. In the same way that Malabou incipiently acknowledges a narrative component to identity in *Avant demain*, so also Serres's Great Story allows him to add complexity and nuance to his account of the human. The narrative of a life 'plunges deeper than abstractions and quintessences' (*Ram* 42), and whereas the empty verb 'to be' in the questions 'who am I?, who are you?, who is he?' bores a hole through any question and empties its answer of any content, 'the story of a life, however tiny, that of another life I have chosen, or of my own timid life, weaves a sort of tracery that closes that hole' (*Ram* 42–3). Moreover, narrative can capture that which escapes every logical concept: the tendencies, the colours, the contradictions of every life as it is lived (*Ram* 43). In short, the question 'who am I?' is best answered with a story:

> Who am I? My life, this original time that unfolds here and there, yesterday and today, is told in the company of associates and in a varied landscape. Who am I, then? That story, the detail of its resting points, its spectacular turns of events and its sudden developments [. . .] who am I? This fleshly narration, its space and its time, this story and its landscape. (*RH* 43)

If this were all that Serres had to say in relation to identity and narrative then he would go no further than Ricœur's account of narrative identity and not as far as Malabou's continuity of epigenesis and hermeneutics. But it is not all he has to say because for Serres this narrative of human identity is nested inside, and inseparable from, a much longer and larger story.

The Great Story

The lineaments of Serres's account of narrative in general will be familiar to readers of his earlier work on Lucretius and the clinamen. In his account of the Roman atomist in *The Birth of Physics* he argues, in information-theoretical terms, that meaning emerges as an aleatory, local deviation in the 'window' between two modes of chaos: monotony and white noise (*NP* 181/*BP* 146). In the same way, in his later work he understands narrative in terms of the interplay between two elements: a relatively constant line (which in *Rameaux* he calls the 'format') and unexpected deviations in that line which he pictures as the kinks and twists of an arboreal branch. Like the information-carrying signal that sits on the spectrum between the chaos of a monotone and the chaos of white noise, so also the growth of a story takes place under a double tension: the necessity of using pre-established forms in order to communicate in a way that can be understood, and an obligation to rupture, to deviate from and to remake these forms because simply repeating them would hold no message at all (*RH* 154). It is in this information-theoretical tension between format and variation that stories emerge, tracing a continuity, branch-like, through haphazard, contingent and chaotic points (*RH* 153).[15]

Like a growing branch, a developing story need have no final end point, predetermined or otherwise (we are a long way here from the Aristotelian *mythos*, and also from any deconstructive weak messianism), and though its eventual form may seem to have a certain retrospectively apprehended teleological balance, its growth is a series of contingencies. We must, Serres insists, quell the prophetic instinct to project the end of the story onto its beginning as if a single intention held together its disparate parts, and instead force ourselves to think a repetition or rule without finality and without anthropomorphism (*RH* 188).

Though stories are lived prospectively as contingent they are recounted retrospectively as what Serres calls a quasi-necessity, and it is as such a retrospective, necessary-seeming narration that he introduces the reader of *Rameaux* to his fullest explanation of the Great Story. The Story is told by Serres retrospectively as a series of four major bifurcations in the branch that leads to human beings, four events each more ancient than the last. The first event already takes us back millions of years to the appearance on the planet of *Homo sapiens*, and gives us a representative sense of Serres's staccato narration as he introduces us to:

> the quadruman who invented bipedal walking, made fire, left Africa, arrived in Australia and then Alaska via the Aleutian Islands, who cut and polished stone, hunted mammoth, boldly sailed the Atlantic, with its floating and fractured ice-floes, from South-West France to the Americas, domesti-

cated the dog, reared sheep and cattle, cultivated corn and barley, interbred pigeons and apple trees, ferociously stoned the bodies of kings to build multiple pyramids, forbade human sacrifice, discovered universal attraction and noncommutative geometry, wrote *The Divine Comedy, Don Quichotte* and *The Essays* . . ., composed *Le Tombeau de Couperin*. (*Ram* 113–14)

Humanity derives its identity from its place in the Great Story, not by virtue of a biological or psychological particularity – such as rationality or bipedalism – that may or may not mark the 'difference' between the human and the nonhuman. The move from his earlier biosemiotics to an econarratology here allows Serres's account refreshingly to avoid the interminable and often dangerous debates around what faculty or capacity 'makes humans unique'. Whereas such a capacity-oriented approach advances by drawing more or less unsubstantiated divisions and erecting castles of hierarchy on the shifting sands of our current biological and psychological understanding, Serres's narrative approach identifies the human by drawing it ever more deeply into a story it inextricably shares with the rest of the universe. Rather than asking 'what is proper to humanity?' we would do better to ask at what point a certain activity entered the Great Story (*Inc* 172).

The second event of Serres's Great Story is the emergence of life on earth, beginning with the first RNA with the capability to duplicate itself and moving through the three billion years when bacteria were the planet's dominant life form, to the explosion of multi-cellular organisms recorded in the Burgess shale and the huge proliferation of orders, families, genera and species. 'How should we define life?' Serres asks, answering that it is 'by this story of new, contingent and unpredictable events from the point of view before they happen, but formatted into an almost necessary chain of events when we trace it backwards from ourselves' (*Ram* 114).

The third bifurcation in the Great Story takes us back from biology to astrophysics and to the first formation of material bodies in a young, expanding and cooling universe. When the universe cools to a certain temperature the ionisation that prevented certain particles forming nuclei ceases, and matter begins to become concentrated into galaxies separated by a quasi-void (*Ram* 115). The fourth and most distant event is the birth of the universe itself, the origin of origins.

Properly speaking, these different stages in the story do not form a succession, as if each needed to stop for the next to begin. The universe is still cooling; the earth is still developing and new planets forming; life on earth, and quite possibly elsewhere, is still diversifying and proliferating, and human beings are still evolving. It is better not to think of a succession of chapters (and this is where Serres's image of the branch is potentially misleading) but one harmonic story told by four voices in counterpoint, each successively joining the collective narrative at a given moment. What unites these four voices for Serres is the idea of 'nature', understood etymologically as that which is born, that which marks a temporal distinction, the difference between a 'before' and an 'after'. Nature is 'a story of new-born events, contingent and unpredictable' (*Ram* 115–16).

In an interview with Pierre Léna in the *Cahier de L'Herne* dedicated to his work, Serres draws two immediate consequences from understanding humanity in terms of the Great Story. First, it gives us a new sense of culture. Traditionally, a person would be thought cultured if they had some working knowledge of four thousand years of history, beginning either in Greece or Mesopotamia; when someone discovers fifteen billion years of history behind him he must change his thinking completely or, to translate Serres literally, 'he no longer has the same head' (SP 55). This idea that humanity, when considered as part of the Great Story, no longer has the same head is true literally as well as figuratively. Serres repeats often the now contested scientific commonplace that different areas of the human brain evolved at varying times: the neo-mammalian neocortex, the paleo-mammalian limbic system and the reptilian basal ganglia (TH 90; SR 233; *AP* 29; *Inc* 23). The second immediate consequence of understanding humanity as part of the Great Story is a shift in the notion of narrative itself. What used to be the beginning of 'history' was dated from the dawn of writing some four thousand years ago, but now this is revealed as but a recent chapter in a much more ample narrative which, Serres claims, is recounted by the universe itself. It is to this claim that we now turn.

The 'story of the universe' as double genitive

We saw in the previous section how Serres argues for a fundamental continuity between the capacity of information reception, storage, processing and emission enjoyed by crystals and that same capacity evident in human communication. This is mirrored in the nonhuman origins he accords to narrative. In his definition of story as a sequence of branching bifurcations Serres makes no necessary distinction between natural and cultural stories and storytelling. The succession of branching bifurcations applies just as well to evolution and to my existence as to cultural, scientific or artistic productions, as to the Great Story itself (*Ram* 39). What Lamarck, Darwin and Gould discovered together is nothing other than the realisation that life is recounted: 'O enchanted surprise, natural history stages a meeting between science and literature' (*Inc* 45). The reverse, of course, is also the case: the rules of narrative resemble those of life. So there is for Serres no imperialist imposition of narrative on the recalcitrant, indifferent or meaningless flux of life, no torturing of a helpless nature or a formless 'real' on the rack of merciless syntax. The universe, the earth and life know quite well how to tell the story of their own origin and evolution, and when I write I share in and draw upon the same resources (*RH* 80). We see here a marked difference from Badiou, Meillassoux and Malabou, all of whom (Meillassoux and Malabou explicitly) hold that the universe is indifferent to us and that to impose upon it human categories of meaning is an anthropocentric, even animistic imposition. For Serres, by contrast, it is no more anthropocentric to claim that the universe is meaningful than it is to claim that *Romeo and Juliet* is meaningful: they both participate in the same universal dynamic.

It could be objected that to claim the world tells its own story is more cosmetic than substantial, because (the objection would proceed) however far the Story may stretch back in time it still needs to be told through human investigation and in human language, and is still therefore a story told by humans and for humans which happens to ventriloquise the non-human. However, this objection assumes that human language emerges *ex nihilo* in the Story, which is precisely what Serres contests. For him, the Great Story is not only about nature but also recounted by nature. In the same way that, in *The Birth of Physics*, *Genesis* and *The Parasite* he insists that semiotics is natural, in his elaboration of the Great Story he argues that narrative is an inherent feature of the 'natural' universe, of the universe of natal events. There is no qualitative difference between the story of evolution and the story of the *Odyssey*: they both enact, each in their own mode, the processing, ordering and communication of information in an interplay between format and deviation (*Ram* 178).

In his four books exploring the humanism of the Great Story (*Hominescence*, *L'Incandescent*, *Rameaux* and *Récits d'humanisme*) Serres expands his previous biosemiotic analysis to encompass a new econarratology, describing this expansion with an image drawn from aeronautics:

> A four-stage rocket launches the birth of language, the emergence of the ego and the dawn of narrative which, in telling their story, forms and creates them but forgets their origin: first it bursts forth from heat towards white noise; from this brouhaha to the first signals; then from these to feeble melodies; finally from these to the first vowels . . . Noise, call, song, music voice . . . come before the basic form of enunciation, before the language of story. (*RH* 49–50)

The world does not mutely and indifferently wait for the advent of humanity in order to tell its story; things speak for themselves, write by themselves and write about themselves, performatively communicating their autobiography:

> The universe, the Earth and life know how to tell the story of their origin, of their evolution, the contingent bifurcations of their development and sometimes let us glimpse the time of their disappearance. An immense story emanates from the world. (*RH* 80)

But is Serres here not simply trading on metaphors, embellishing a natural process with the evocative but ultimately philosophically barren romantic notion that the earth is 'telling its own story'? He addresses his own recourse to metaphor a number of times in his published work, and each time he is adamant that his position cannot be dismissed as 'just' a convenient metaphor. In *The Birth of Physics* he insists: 'That atoms are letters is not an arbitrary theory or a decision or a metaphor. It is a necessity of what Lucretius and his predecessors called nature' (*NP* 182/*BP* 147). In 'Temps, usure . . .' he asks 'what does it mean, truthfully, that molecules code? Do they write? That acids answer each other? Do they read? Do they print out?' and he answers with another question: 'What difference separates our way of writing and reading, I mean of engraving traces on material supports, and the stereospecificity of inert or living compounds?' (TU 214). Behind these rhetorical questions, what move is Serres making here? Bruno Latour goes some way towards exculpating the Serresian recourse to metaphor with his artistic analogy that:

> In a position akin to that of Mary Hesse, Serres is not a 'literalist' believing that there is a strong distinction to be made between literal and metaphoric meaning. Like Hesse, he is not for a 'police of metaphors' that would forbid certain uses and turn others into precise, literal ones.[16]

This is no doubt correct, but it does not go far enough in explaining the work that Serres's metaphors are doing. We can get closer to an adequate answer if we describe Serres's move as a sliding from metaphor to synecdoche.

One of Serres's characteristic moves, and we see it here in his defence of metaphorical language, is to alter the structure of our thinking so that elements we previously considered to be in a horizontal, metaphorical relation are now seen to be nested as a synecdoche. In the example we are presently considering, if we object that the rhythms of nature cannot properly be classed as a story in anything other than an anthropomorphising metaphor, Serres might reply that, rather than trying and failing to force the rhythms and events of the world into a mode of storytelling modelled on human syntactic prose, which would merely constrain them to become an uneasy extension of Aristotelian narrative, we should rather realise that the varieties of human storytelling have themselves always already been one local expression of a broader phenomenon:

> Must I find stories or confessions in the inertia of the living? When I write my own stories and confessions, do I realise that, as a fractal fragment of the universe, I am imitating galaxies, the planet, masses of molecules, radioactive particles, the bellowing of a deer or the vain unfurling of a peacock's plumage? (*RH* 80)

In other words, the idea that nature tells its own story is not an unwarranted metaphor; on the contrary, 'storytelling' understood as a human cultural practice is already a synecdoche of a much more widespread natural phenomenon. I write like the light, like a crystal or like a stream; I tell my story like the world. A frequently cited phrase from Serres's *The Birth of Physics* has until now always been translated as 'History is a physics and not the other way round. Language is first in the body' (*NP* 186/*BP* 150). However, this translation collapses the multivalence of the French *histoire*, and the sentence could equally run 'Story is a physics . . .'. In fact, both senses of 'histoire' are at play in Serres's discussion of negentropy in *The Birth of Physics*.[17]

The change of paradigm from the metaphorical to the synecdochic is also a challenge to anthropocentrism. To see eco-narratives as a metaphorical extension of human storytelling is to assume that human storytelling is the non-metaphorical yardstick against which all other putative narratives must be measured, and found wanting. But to see human storytelling as a synecdoche of a much broader phenomenon is, as Serres remarks, to decentre narrative with relation to the human at the moment when nature wrests from us our claim to an exclusivity of language use (*RH* 80). It may be that we can only have access to the Great Story if we translate it into our own language, but in that we are no different from any other information processor.

Serres's econarratology allows us to think the universe not simply as a blank canvas for the quintessentially human practice of storytelling, but as the narrator of its own story. This means that, just as narrative identity allows us to think human identity beyond determinate capacities and beyond the limit of the human and the nonhuman, Serres's ecological narrative identity frees us from having to identify the universe as 'matter' or 'energy', or from dividing it into the animate and the inanimate. This paradigm shift has the power to revitalise and expand the study of narrative identity beyond its customary anthropocentric limits, at a moment when the global issues that face us are irreducible to the human scale. Serres has indeed presented the study of narrative with a valuable gift.

A second important consequence of understanding humanity in terms of its place in the Great Story is that it leaves behind the boundary between the human and the nonhuman. In the first instance it achieves this goal simply by virtue of being a narrative. As we touched on briefly above, defining humanity in terms of a physical, psychological or cultural host property (bipedalism, rationality or language use, for example) necessarily demarcates an opposition to the nonhuman. Simply deconstructing such an opposition will not help, Serres insists, because it begins with the same assumption as that which it seeks to challenge, namely that the problem is to be thought in terms of a division between two values, however complex their interrelation. The Great Story, however, thinks otherwise than in terms of a human/nonhuman boundary, and it does this in two main ways. The first is in relation to the notion of time and Serres explores it through asking the question 'how old am I?':

> So you ask me my age. I can give you the one on my birth certificate, but I can also give the age of the different strata of neurones that make up my brain, some of which appeared with the so-called higher apes, but others of which came from reptiles of previous ages; in the same way, composed of a mixture from my parents, my DNA goes back four billion years in its structure; as for the atoms that make it up, they were formed at the same time as the world, some ten to fifteen billion years ago. But that is the same for all living things. (TH 90)

The dimension of time in the Great Story makes the story of humanity nonhuman or, to put it in a way that leaves the threadbare dichotomy of human and nonhuman behind altogether, the story of humanity is one recent branch of the Great Story. This narrative identity is fundamentally non-anthropocentric precisely because of the length of time it encompasses. How easily we forget not only our car keys, Serres quips, but also that we have a body as old as the rocks of the earth (*Inc* 53). The claim being made here is not simply that the human has nonhuman or inhuman elements within it, which would only give us yet one more deconstructive figure of the Other within the Same, but rather that the Great Story demands of us a new set of concepts and a new way of thinking that no longer force us artificially to parse human and nonhuman, the other and same, at all.

Although Serres does not develop the point, this argument pertains not only to the material of the body but also to aspects of humanity commonly considered psychological. How old, for example, are my thoughts and my language? Not simply as old as the birth of human communication, but as old as the information-storing and -exchanging capacities of the universe itself which, as we have seen, Serres extends back at least as far as the formation of crystals. The Great Story is not only pressed into each one of my cells, but also into every one of my thoughts and mental capacities. It is not a story outside me, but (to adopt a turn of phrase from Merleau-Ponty's *The Visible and the Invisible*) a story 'of which I am'.[18]

There is a second way in which the Great Story makes the human/ nonhuman dichotomy redundant: the stretches of time involved surpass our ability meaningfully to intuit or comprehend them. To reflect on the human in terms of the Great Story is an experience of the dynamical sublime 'which surpasses every standard of sense'.[19] Although I may well have an intuitive measure of the span of my life from birth, and even though I may be able to form some dim sense of the four thousand year period since the beginning of recorded human history, when I seek meaningfully to comprehend myself as a being as old as the emergence of life or as old as the universe 'it's extremely difficult to have any intuitive picture of what is involved in such expanses of time' (SR 233). In both these ways – in the answer to the question 'how old am I?' and in my inability to intuit the response to that question – the human is constituted in terms of an irreducible self-surpassing. Whereas defining humanity in terms of a distinctive trait or capacity tends to reinforce a sense of determinate identity and, with it, of human exceptionalism, Serres's Great Story locates the human only ever as ungraspably beyond itself and as a polyphonic product of all four of the Great Story's harmonising voices.

As well as decentring the human with respect to itself in these two ways, the Great Story also yields a humanity that surpasses itself in terms of landscape (*paysage*). Serres insists that, all too often, our stories – including stories of narrative identity – artificially exclude the landscape in which we dwell. The nature/culture binary reduces the landscape to an object, to 'nature' as 'a place of non-law, a treasury to exhaust without shame and a garbage can to fill without disgrace' (*RH* 137). Such stories treat the world as décor, an incidental and ultimately unreal stage set for the playing out of a human-human story (*RH* 136). But in the Great Story the human is decentred, and this decentring also affords another way of questioning the term 'environment' and its assumption that the human occupies a fixed central point in the world. Serres's econarratology is an undoing of the Copernican Revolution, after which such a central, constituting role for humanity is untenable. Instead of this unwarranted anthropocentrism Christiane Frémont describes Serres's econarrative in terms of an image taken from the twelfth-century theologian Alain de Lille and later reused by Pascal: the landscape is a circle whose centre is everywhere and circumference nowhere.[20]

Such an undoing of Kant's Copernican Revolution recognises that story penetrates landscape and landscape acts upon story. In *Récits d'humanisme* Serres drives the point home with a vivid illustration:

> Surrounded by insects and venomous snakes, marsupials and wild camels,
> does my aboriginal friend from the Australian outback, a nomad who trails

behind him sixty thousand years without agriculture and without stock rearing through a lack of mammals and grasses in his ancestral desert, have the same *me* [*moi*] as his contemporary, a Melbourne doctor settled in his coastal villa who enjoys windsurfing and has been eating animal meat since the Neolithic? My story penetrates into my landscape and the landscape acts in my story. To take up once more the abandoned question 'who am I?', here is my response: the rustling of my story among the leaves of my landscapes, both external and intimate. (*RH* 76)

The Australian aboriginal peoples, Serres notes, are fully aware of the importance of land in their stories; their identity is unthinkable without earth, flora and fauna, whereas the Eurasians, farmers since the Neolithic, are only now waking up to the extent to which the ground, grasses and grubs that surround them are actors in what they persist in calling 'our' story (*RH* 139–40), forgetting that '[t]here is no story without a country, and no Great Story without the universe' (*RH* 139). So fundamental is this situated nature of the human in the land and this move from the paradigm of incidental stage-set décor to landscape (*paysage*) that Paul A. Harris is justified in arguing that Serres's philosophy cannot simply be said to have an ontology or an epistemology; it sets out an ecology with which the ontological and epistemological interact and, we might add, which acts upon them in turn.[21]

Acknowledging the active narrative role played by landscape, air, food, ground and climate (*RH* 139) breaks the spell of what, in *The Visible and the Invisible*, Merleau-Ponty calls the *kosmotheoros*,[22] the detached and self-sufficient observer of the world from outside the world, who can tell the Great Story as an omniscient narrator and who can manipulate the stage-set props of her environment with a puppeteer's transcendent impunity. The *kosmotheoros* is replaced by the familiar Serresian figure of the parasite, not simply meaningfully interacting with her landscape as an agent in her story, but also recognising it as a necessary condition both of her identity and of her survival (*RH* 136). This is a figure of the human with its feet firmly planted on the soily ground.

Before leaving this argument about landscape it is important to note the particular connotations that Serres finds in the term. In the same way that story replaces the two-speed logic of human and nonhuman shared by a host properties approach and its deconstruction alike, and provides a more nuanced and richly textured account than both, so also 'landscape' is the term Serres uses to replace the transparency and regularity of 'system'. Whereas Newton, Lagrange, Laplace, Poincaré and even Einstein follow Plato in elaborating a system, Serres is convinced that the singularities of contemporary astrophysics (such as black holes or gamma-ray bursts: Serres mentions a list of fifty such singularities) compose 'a leafy landscape [*un paysage feuillu*], a sky full of objects that are unexpected, singular, monstrous, sometimes resistant to theories' (SP 48). The universe-as-system is replaced by an extraordinarily diverse and unsystematised (perhaps unsystematisable) landscape of singularities. Whereas in the past the scholar, securely lodged at the heart of a regular system, could systematically unfold its consequences, now a new paradigm of scholarly inquiry is required, for although the singularities cannot all be encompassed within the same system they are nevertheless amenable to being dated and can be woven into the Great Story: 'the complicated landscape inscribed itself into a sort of gigantic evolution which, for me, becomes from now on the background of human culture' (SP 51). Bernadette Bensaude-Vincent imagines this Serresian landscape as a pointillist painting, not reducible to one 'point' but composed of myriad tiny vignettes and little touches.[23] So 'landscape' for Serres carries, along with its customary meaning, a sense of resistance to systematisation. Any definition of humanity in terms of the Great Story must go 'beyond' the human, not in order to inscribe humanity at the centre of a determinate metaphysical system but to reveal it to be decentred in a landscape with which it enjoys a relation of symbiosis.

Given the active symbiosis of humanity and landscape it becomes absurd and artificial to seek to attribute particular actions to one element of the symbiotic partnership, the folly of a latter-day Berlin Conference seeking to scratch static, straight-lined frontiers on a complex and fluid web of relationships. To what or whom should I attribute 'my' actions, Serres asks in *L'Incandescent*? Can I demarcate with a slide rule the contribution of my species, my cultural group, those I have met and know, my mother tongue and learned languages, the objects of my work, the landscape and things of the world? 'Who am I, I who think? You [*tu*], all of you [*vous*], him, them, that, us, these things?' (*Inc* 339). When I write, agriculture and inland water shipping, Christianity and the Second World War, write and think in my place without me noticing (*Inc* 335–6). It makes sense, Serres insists, to say of an object 'it is thinking' with the same force we give to that most slippery of verbs when we say 'it is raining', and given the human influence on global climate it makes just as much sense now to say 'we are raining' or 'we are warm' as 'it is raining' and 'it is warm' (*Inc* 338–9). In *Récits d'humanisme* he captures this mutual permeability in the image of a Klein bottle, a mathematical object that frustrates the distinction between 'inside' and 'outside' in the same way that a Möbius strip frustrates the division between its two sides (*RH* 76).

The problematic universality of the Great Story

Given Serres's insistence on the singularity of a pointillist landscape over the schematised and universal system, it might strike us as discordant for him to insist that the Great Story opens the door to a new humanism, and even more curious that this humanism should be universal. The term 'universal', Serres concedes, 'seems always to hide an imperialism' (*Inc* 162), but he nevertheless exempts particular universals from this pernicious tendency: the non-violent expansion over the globe of fruit and vegetables, agriculture, the spread of mathematics and of the exact sciences which, he claims, 'succeed in principle without imperialism' (*Inc* 163). This figure of universalism without imperialism bleeds beyond the boundaries of the hard sciences, however, to take the form of a new universal culture that will displace existing local cultures. Serres's universal humanism does not sit alongside local cultures but seems to establish itself, at some moments in his writing at least, at their expense:

> Why weep over the relative loss of short stories barely four thousand years old, when we have just gained one that stretches back fifteen billion years? Why deplore the loss of a local culture when the new culture stretches to the community of all people and when we hook the old and singular humanities onto a humanism that is finally close to its universal meaning? (*Inc* 36–7)

We might ask some questions of our own. Why privilege longer-lasting cultures over more recent or extinguished ones? Is this not like privileging the lung fish over the human just because its DNA is five times longer? And why privilege the universal over the local, if indeed that is a meaningful distinction in terms of human cultures to begin with? Further on in the same book Serres seems to deny the term 'human culture' to the local altogether: 'doubtless there is no culture other than that which is growing towards the human universal' (*Inc* 173).

Although he concedes that, historically speaking, it has been the particular which has helped us most towards the universal – he mentions the examples of Homer's *Odyssey* and the Christian religion, *Don Quichotte* and *Cyrano de Bergerac* (*Inc* 175–6) – there is nevertheless the sense that, for Serres, now that we have the Great Story we possess the manifest reality of which all these imperfect local adumbrations were shadows and metaphors. Lucy the *Australopithecus afarensis* trumps Pliny the Elder, the bones scattered across the valleys of Chad predate blind Homer, Noah the vine-dresser, Adam and Eve, and 'all ancestors venerated by all cultures': 'Here it is a question of humanity, and not some evil off-white noise-box [*bavard et méchant blanchâtre*] despising the scarlet barbarian' (*Inc* 196). It seems here that the incandescent Pierrot has the multi-coloured

Harlequin in a stranglehold, the old antagonism between them disappointingly reinstated.

The uneasy cohabitation of 'two voices' in Serres's thinking, a voice of pointillist landscape singularity and a voice of a-cultural universality, has received critical attention in relation to his earlier writing. N. Katherine Hayles criticises what she sees as Serres's attempt 'to extrapolate a general theory from paradigms that imply there are no general theories',[24] diagnosing an equivocation between 'different voices in the channel of Serres' writing', born of 'the conflicting impulses inherent in his interdisciplinary approach'. David Webb evinces a similar discomfort with the Serres who straddles the particular and the universal in his recourse to atomism as 'a model that remains exempt from the endless change and transformation for which it is intended to account, an invariant theory of perpetual variation, a general model of locality'.[25] Webb seeks to square the circle by appealing to Serres's insistence that the Lucretian system is not a series of laws that precede the phenomena they describe but rather that 'physical law only emerges with the combinations and regularities generated by the vortices that follow the breakdown of laminar flow'.[26] Steven D. Brown seeks to let Serres off the hook by arguing that the criticism of the 'apparently freewheeling fashion in which Serres generalizes models' is 'often based on a profound misinterpretation of what Serres is actually seeking to achieve', and that in fact 'the utility of the models he draws upon is that they enable a way of conceiving provisional connections between otherwise disparate phenomena'.[27] But these exculpations do not do justice to Serres's own rhetoric of universalism. He is far from shy of the universal, as we have seen. His resistance to the grand philosophies of history from the likes of Herder, Hegel, Comte and Marx, suggests Marcel Hénaff, is not on account of their universalism but because of their teleology and their circumscription of history to the limits of the human.[28]

A certain discomfort with Serresian universalism in relation to the Great Story is evinced and then overcome by William Paulson. He argues that the Story does not seek to present itself as ethnocentric because 'the recognition of its universalism assumes that the fundamental – but in fact always contentious – fight of the Enlightenment to install science in the place of religion as the sovereign judge of reality has been won'.[29] A story of the world told according to science always runs the risk, however consensually it is recognised as true, of propagating an imposed ethnocentrism in the image of the Darwinian orthodoxy of today's dominant cultures. Serres does maintain, Paulson concedes, that the Great Story resists scientific totalitarianism because its arborescent form gives full weight to contingency: Darwinian 'laws', for example, only entered the story with the emergence of life, less than four billion years ago.[30] Darwinism may be compatible with the processes and patterns of a non-animate world, but not deducible from it. He also underscores that Serres does not impose the Great Story as the basis of his new universal humanism but rather proposes it.[31] Appealing to the contingency of the events in the Great Story, he argues that it is a form that can integrate the whole range of beings and experiences without subsuming them under any finality or law that would fix their meaning in advance. However, as we have already seen, what is lived prospectively as contingency for Serres is recounted retrospectively as a quasi-necessity, and because narrative identity is at least in large part a narrative of the past, this makes for a problematic dogmatism when we might seek to extend its scope, through Serres's work, to a narrative of eco-identity.

Conclusion

Despite all the qualifications marshalled by the phalanx of commentators who rally to Serres's aid, it seems to me that the charge of ethnocentrism is hard to avoid. The Great Story simply is, to take Serres's own example, more the story told by the Melbourne doctor than by the aboriginal outback-dweller. I find it hard to believe that it can seriously be suggested that palaeoanthropology and genetics 'authorise a concept of "human nature" that is finally defined without ideology',[32] as if those two discourses can exhaustively account for 'human nature' (a claim which Serres himself would surely resist) and as if, contrary to the constant burden of Bruno Latour's writing, 'science' can be considered to be an ideologically sterile enterprise restricting itself to pure 'facts' outside any context of institutional or personal concern.

The assumption that needs to be questioned, an assumption common to Serres, Hayles and Paulson, is that the only way to achieve the universal is to have everyone tell the same story, or at least share the same universal and non-ideological scientific trunk from which can sprout all local and particular narrative branches. Serres appears to use the Great Story as a means to retreat to the worst excesses of the two-value logic he was so quick to condemn in his account of landscape when, in an interview with Pierre Léna, he presses it into the service of a 'generic culture', ranging the Great Story on the side of resemblance as opposed to alterity, and seeming to suggest that it negates all rival meaning-giving narratives:

> The old, local culture, different for a German and a Frenchman, for an American and a Russian, was enflamed by the libidinal desire to belong and often threw us into conflict with each other. It caused millions of deaths.

[. . .] if it is true, as biochemists say, that all living things have the same origin, then we are inventing not a general culture, but a generic culture [. . .] there is no longer any need for morality or theology to tell us that we are all brothers, nor for declarations of the rights of man; no, we must simply look at our DNA and read a few fossils. [. . .] Do you see here the change in mentality with respect to everything we used to teach about Difference? Difference was the dogma of yesteryear. Now we are discovering resemblance! What a promise of peace this is! Our old wars only ever pitted twin against twin. (SP 51–2)

This is Serres at his most universal, and this is Serres's universalism at its most worrying and least self-aware. War, we are led to believe, is all on the side of difference and peace all on the side of resemblance. A recognition that we are all twins will quell bloodshed? Serres needs to re-read his own book on the foundation of Rome. The (local, Western) ideology of progress embedded in Serres's idea here of 'old' local cultures and a new generic culture, as well as in 'the dogma of yesteryear' versus today's 'discoveries', is as blinding as his failure to acknowledge it is deafening. The idea that the Great Story displaces the claim of other stories (called 'morality or theology') fosters an unnecessary internecine combat between narratives that need not be rivals but that Serres seems determined to make so. Rather than a host capacity or host substance, we are witnessing here Serres's attempt to install a host narrative of humanity. The host narrative fulfils the same function as its cousins: it is the gatekeeper of humanity, the one narrow opening through which all are required to pass who would claim the name 'human'. It is the literal meaning of humanity that makes all other meanings metaphorical and derivative. In insisting on what, with a nod to Tolkien, we might call this 'one story to rule them all', Serres is confusing extensivity (the Great Story speaks about everything) with exhaustivity (the Great Story is the one narrative that yields up the essence of the human) and rejecting a polysemy that would save his account from its imperialist tendencies. What is most disappointing here is that this is a co-option of the Great Story into the sort of two-speed binarism that he expertly dispatches elsewhere through his appeal to narrative and, what is more, it sits awkwardly with his move from system to landscape. What the system–landscape shift itself teaches us, in contrast to Serres's agonistics of an imperialist Great Story in the Léna interview, is that a landscape is a landscape of micro-systems that resist subsumption into one universal macro- or world-system, not a complete abandonment of systems altogether. He has the tools available in his own thinking to elaborate a polysemic theory of non-rival discourses, but fails to wield them.

We have come a long way from the host capacities of Badiou and Meillassoux and the host substance of Malabou, but with Serres's insistence that the figure of the human inhabit the single, universal, generic Great Story he reintroduces the very sort of narrowness that his marrying of Harlequin and Pierrot sought to leave behind. Figuring the human in terms of an eco-narrative yields, to be sure, a richer account than thinking it only in terms of a gatekeeper capacity, and with Serres we are beginning to see a figure of the human not only encompassing plural capacities like Malabou's plastic human, but plural modes (capacities and narrative). It is the restrictions he places on the narrative mode that are the most troubling aspect of Serres's multi-modal human, and it is this restriction of the universalising Great Story that Bruno Latour avoids in his own multi-modal *anthropos*.

Chapter 6

Bruno Latour: Translating the Human

By stopping being modern, we have become ordinary humans again.

FMOF 8

On revient à l'évidence qu'un humain est attaché et que s'il se détache, il meurt.

MP 58[1]

In the universal humanism of Michel Serres we saw both a development and a change of direction from the accounts of the human elaborated by Badiou, Meillassoux and Malabou. Whereas the figure to emerge in the thought of Badiou and Meillassoux relies on the host capacity of thought, Malabou moves away from determinate capacities but, in her early work at least, seems to favour a host cerebral substance of human personhood. Serres's account of the human, by contrast, is multi-modal: he combines de-differentiation with a recognition of determinate capacities, and also develops a narrative account of humanity as part of the Great Story of the universe. Whereas Badiou, Meillassoux and Malabou each have a predominantly 'internalist' account of the human, locating the host property of humanness within the body or the suite of capacities possessed by the individual, Serres's humanity is neither exclusively internalist nor externalist, understood both as (singular) identity and (group) belonging, and defined in terms of its place in a greater whole. If we were to persist in using these terms we would have to say that it is exo-internalist: humanity is what it is because of what is outside it, not exclusively (or even predominantly) because of its innate capabilities. In Serres's account of humanity the literary and scientific weave together, but there is still a substrate of univocity: the Great Story risks becoming Serres's 'host narrative'.

Bruno Latour develops and proliferates Serres's incipient multi-modal approach, while also taking forward his move away from internalism. This chapter argues that Latour is very careful to offer an account of the human that repeats neither the structure nor the story of what he calls the 'modern parenthesis'. In so doing, he gives us a multi-modal humanity which is not to be understood in terms of any host property or host substance, and which does much to mitigate the partiality of Serres's host narrative. The overall thesis of this final chapter is that we can best understand Latour's successive reworkings of the human in his Modes of Existence project and in his recent lectures on Gaia and the Anthropocene as 'translations', a movement first sketched in his early doctoral work on the theologian Rudolf Bultmann. Latour's figure of the human is related to the modern in complex ways that are often underestimated in the secondary literature.

Humans, actants, relations and modes

Over nearly four decades now, the constant burden of Bruno Latour's diverse work has been to identify and to distance himself from what he calls the 'modern parenthesis' or the 'modern constitution', most famously described in *We Have Never Been Modern*. The modern constitution can be understood in terms of two fundamental elements which are seldom considered in the secondary literature as distinct. Nevertheless, distinguishing clearly between these two elements will help us grasp more adequately the way in which Latour rethinks the figure of the human being. The names I propose to give to the two elements are 'structure' and 'story'.

The 'structure' of the modern constitution requires the combination of three factors: purification, translation and forgetfulness. In *We Have Never Been Modern* Latour describes the first two of these factors as groups of practices which leave the modern human resembling a curious Jekyll and Hyde figure. The first practice, 'purification', produces a series of dichotomies (human and nonhuman, nature and culture, subject and object, faith and reason, fact and value . . .). The second practice, 'translation', produces a series of hybrid networks and hybrid objects, mixing together elements ostensibly purified: human and nonhuman intermingled in industrial manufacturing, the hole in the ozone layer mixing science, politics, economics, law, religion, technology and fiction (*JEM* 9/ *NBM* 2). The third important aspect in modernity's structure is a chronic forgetfulness of the hybrids. Moderns systematically pride themselves on the purity of their dichotomies ('we only deal in facts, not superstition') and seem to remain utterly unaware of the hybridity of their hybrids (the hole in the ozone layer is 'a matter for pure, factual, disinterested science alone'). In order to cease being modern, it is not necessary to deconstruct the dualisms or eradicate the hybrids; all that is needed is to take away the third aspect of forgetfulness, which we do if we merely 'direct our attention simultaneously to the work of purification and the work of hybridization' (*JEM* 21/*NBM* 11).

What are these dualisms and hybrids? We can understand the dualisms of the modern parenthesis (and there are many) in relation to one primary dualism of humans and nonhumans. Modernity goes to extraordinary lengths to create and hermetically to purify 'two entirely distinct ontological zones: that of human beings on the one hand; that of non-humans on the other' (*JEM* 20–1/*NBM* 10–11). Having created these two poles, the moderns proceed to arrogate to the human all initiative, agency, culture, value, subjectivity, language, symbolism, freedom and psyche, calling this human domain the realm of epistemology. This leaves the nonhuman as very much the poor relation: inert, indifferent, meaningless, natural (as opposed to cultural), factual, objective, strictly determined and material: the realm of ontology. Whereas humans strut their stuff as masters and possessors of the world, nonhuman objects are left as lifeless and passive (*EME* 124/*AIME* 117). Finally, everything that does not fit with this inert and mathematisable world of matter is hoovered up into nonexistence in the 'interior' of the human psyche through the 'suction pump' of purification (*EP* 305/*PH* 285): gods, apparitions, ancestors and spirits are all efficiently 'pumped out of existence, emptied of all reality until they are nothing but hollow beliefs' (*EP* 305/*PH* 284), leaving the pristine nonhuman world as purified, mathematised extension.

It is at our peril, Latour warns, that we take modernity to be the age of humanism, for to do so commits just the sort of asymmetrical forgetfulness of which modernity itself is guilty. Modernity is no more nor less the age of the human than it is the age of the nonhuman (*JEM* 23/*NBM* 13). After all, the two poles of the dualism each require the other. 'It is hard to decide which came first' between the inner sanctum of the mind and the exterior wastelands of matter (*EP* 305/*PH* 284). One thing is certain: 'These subjects endowed with an inside are as strange as these objects relegated to an outside' (*EP* 305/*PH* 284).

Purification and hybridisation alone do not adequately account for the modern parenthesis, however, because they do not answer the question of why the moderns apply themselves so assiduously to the task of cultivating and protecting their dualisms. Why do the moderns think that purification is so worthwhile, and why are they so embarrassed by hybridity? The answer is to be found in what Latour calls the Great Narrative of the moderns (IDS 4–5; CP 8; FG 108): the story of emancipation. Emancipation is only mentioned three times in *We Have Never Been Modern* and a reader of that text could be excused for thinking it peripheral to Latour's notion of modernity. But this would be a grave mistake.

According to the glossary on the Modes of Existence project website, the word 'modern'

> refers to a kind of Master Narrative that tells the story of an emancipation based on the distinction between Reason and Illusion and which is to be found in space and time via a modernization front, distinguishing in all collectives an archaic past and an emancipated future. (IMEg: Moderns)

In other words, the Grand Narrative of emancipation sees the past only in terms of superstition, confusion and irrationality, and the future exclusively as a time of increasing clarity, purity and reason (*EME* 20–1/*AIME* 9), with the pickaxe of critique and the hammer of iconoclasm as the tools of historical progress. Thus modernity prides itself on its own increasing capacity to 'separate more accurately what the world is really like from the subjective illusions we used to entertain about it' (IDS 4–5), concocting a purified history for which all the chains, bonds and attachments are in the past and all the freedom in the future (FF 4/FFe 22). In this way modernity hurtles forward on the pure rocket fuel of the emancipation narrative, a fuel to which it has also become lethally addicted: 'this picture of the future is so attractive, especially when put against such a repellent past, that it makes one wish to run forward to break all the shackles of ancient existence. Emancipation is the word' (IDS 5). The case of mistaken identity at the heart of this emancipation narrative is the confusion between living without mastery (which, for Latour, is a good thing) and living without attachments (which is impossible). Modernity thinks that the only freedom is the freedom of the unconditioned, the unconstrained, the un-attached, the freedom only ever enjoyed by an uncaused and serenely inaccessible Prime Mover. As such, the emancipation narrative is a programme of self-deification.

However, emancipation is not the whole story of modernity. In the same way that the modern structure of purification is doubled by a covert hybridity, so also the Grand Narrative of emancipation keeps a twin locked up in its attic: the narrative of attachment. Science, that great lodestar of the modern emancipation narrative, has in fact 'amplified, for at least the last two centuries, not only the scale at which humans and nonhumans are connecting with one another in larger and larger assemblies, but also the intimacy with which such connections are made' (IDS 5). No one is more embroiled with, reliant upon and inseparable from their technologies than the moderns, folded ever more intimately into the nonhuman world like the God of the Bible folding himself into his creation through the incarnation.[2]

Although 'the present historical situation is defined by a complete disconnect between two great alternative narratives' (CP 2) of emancipation and attachment, the two stories are in fact anything but mutually exclusive, providing 'two great narratives for the same history' (IDS 5). Over the same period that the moderns have fancied themselves to be progressively emancipated from all constraints, what they have in fact achieved is an ever deeper and more nuanced set of intimate attachments between the human and the nonhuman. One potent illustration of this double narrative for Latour is the cosmonaut circling the earth, emancipated from all terrestrial ties thanks only to a huge assemblage of human/nonhuman relationships and collaborations: 'the cosmonaut is emancipated from gravity because he or she never lives one fraction of a second outside of his or her life supports. To be emancipated and to be attached are two incarnations of the same event' (CP 8). A given event may be read as proof of one or the other of the narratives, but in fact, like purification and hybridisation, they advance together (IDS 6). The idea of a Great Outside free of all attachment is the great modern myth, for 'we are never outside without having recreated another more artificial, more fragile, more engineered envelope' (CP 8). This frames Meillassoux's account of humanity as a mathematically inflected modernism, hooked on the modern Holy Grail of a pristine and absolute Great Outdoors.

At the end of this survey of modernity, what emerges is that any attempt to elaborate a non-modern account of humanity (or of anything else) must address not only modernism's dualisms but also its emancipation narrative. It must not only find a way of connecting the human and the nonhuman again but it must 'emancipate oneself from the hard drug of emancipation' (FF 3/FFe 22). To accomplish one or the other of these tasks would be relatively simple; to achieve them both is, as we shall see, extremely complex.

In order to begin to understand how Latour seeks to elaborate a non-modern account of the human and fall prey neither to modernity's dualistic structure nor to its emancipation narrative, we need to go right back to the beginning of his intellectual career and briefly consider his doctoral thesis on the theologian Rudolf Bultmann under the supervision of André Malet, Bultmann's French translator.[3] Practitioner of the historical-critical method of biblical interpretation, Bultmann sought to demythologise the synoptic gospels and sift their layers of interpretative and mythological accretion in order to locate their kernel of original historical truth. In Latour's own summary, 'you might end up with no more than three or four "genuine" Aramaic sentences uttered by a certain "Joshua of Nazareth"' (CO 600). In Latour's terms, Bultmann's undertaking is a quintessentially modern exercise of purification, with the suction pumps turned up to full power.

In addition to his thesis, Latour refers to Bultmann's influence in four different accounts of his philosophical itinerary (CO; BoI; AT; WWL). An aggressively demythologising modern textual form critic may seem an unlikely inspiration for Latour's non-modern account of the human, but then again his reading of Bultmann is anything but conventional. Latour does to Bultmann what Meillassoux does to the correlationist: he turns the sceptic's best arguments against him and unmasks his supposed point of maximal strength as his most damning refutation. What the sceptic thought to be his greatest weapon is revealed to have been all along the most cherished tool of the faithful; the discarded husk of mythologisation turns out to be the seed of faith. Whereas Bultmann sees the endless series of interpretations, translations and glosses of the synoptic gospels as an impenetrable barrier to accessing their original, historical truth, Latour sees those same glosses and translations as the very condition of biblical truth: 'the more a layer of texts is interpreted, transformed, taken up anew, stitched back together, replayed, and rewoven, each time in a different way, the more likely it is to manifest the truth it contains' (BoI 289). Latour's own summary of this unlikely turnaround is that 'I had taken the poison out of Bultmann and transformed his critical acid into the best proof we had that it was possible to obtain truth' (CO 600) and that Bultmann emerges from Latour's doctoral thesis 'put back on his Catholic feet' (CO 601).

Now of course this eureka moment needs further explanation, just like Meillassoux's intellectual intuition. How can successive glosses, interpretations and distortions add to the truth of the biblical text rather than obfuscating it? In the case of Meillassoux, our access to the Great Outdoors comes with a reappraisal of what the Great Outdoors is. We accede not to a pre-critical direct and unmediated encounter with objects in the world, but to the absolute inexistence of all objects whatever: of everything that exists we know absolutely that it could not exist, and of everything that does not exist we know absolutely that it could exist. We do not, however, know absolutely what exists. In a similar way, Latour's triumph over the scepticism of higher criticism in the name of the truth of religion comes together with a redefinition of truth. Religious truth is not the *adequatio* of the textual account to any putative extra-textual historical 'facts', and Latour is quite happy to agree with Bultmann that the synoptic gospels contain no (historical) information. The truth of the resurrection narratives is in their capacity to bring about personal transformation, and the pertinent question to ask of them is not whether they correspond to the facts but 'how do such stories manage to resuscitate the person to whom they are addressed?' (BoI 288–9). It is not only the text that has been translated and glossed, but the notion of truth itself.

Latour's response to Bultmann, then, is not 'no', it is 'yes, but'. He does not negate Bultmann (they both reject the claim that the gospel accounts contain significant historical information) but he translates him, transforming and renewing the meaning of his demythologising critique. This notion of the translation that transforms is central to the early Latour's understanding of the biblical texts themselves, to his own reading of Bultmann, and to the rest of his subsequent oeuvre.

According to Latour, translation must be neither an immediate repetition nor a betrayal of the text, and it sits between the two in an uneasy and never completely secure tension. Each transformation, gloss or translation plays out 'the question of fidelity or treason: faithful or falsified invention, impious reworking, or astounding rediscovery' (BoI 288). The same thought is expressed differently when Latour summarises his doctoral thesis as finding a way of 'discriminating between two opposite types of betrayal – betrayal by mere repetition and the absence of innovation, and betrayal by too many innovations and the loss of the initial intent' (CO 600). So instead of Bultmann's two poles of historical fidelity or historical lack of correspondence, Latour understands the truth of translation in terms of three points: the extremes of repetitious betrayal and hyper-innovative betrayal, with the truth that sits between them. This sounds very much like Michel Serres's account of meaning between white noise and monotone that we encountered in Chapter 5, and indeed Latour acknowledges Serres as an important influence on his understanding of translation (BoI 293). A signal for Serres resides between two modes of chaos; religious truth for Latour resides between two forms of betrayal. Latour's notion of translation also bears more than a passing resemblance to Malabou's epigenesis between preformation and equivocal generation. This notion of translation is 'fundamental' for Latour because 'it breaks the apparent logic which considers transportation without deformation as the touchstone [French: *shibboleth*] of any description' (IMEg: Translation). Translation is not a simple relocation but also a transformation, a deviation, a *détournement*.[4]

It is my argument in this chapter that this translation, charting as it does a course between two equally desirable extremes, this notion of translation first worked out in Latour's doctoral studies in biblical exegesis, allows us to see the complexity of the Latourian figure of the human.[5] We can read the whole of Latour's career as a series of exercises in 'putting Bultmanns back on their Catholic feet', one after the other. Indeed, what we shall encounter in the rest of this chapter could well be described as Latour putting the *anthropos* back on its human feet.

Relations and the question of host property

In *We Have Never Been Modern* Latour categorically rejects any essential definition of the human being, for '[i]ts history and its anthropology are too diverse for it to be pinned down once and for all' (*JEM* 186/ *NBM* 136). Nevertheless, if the human has no stable form it does not follow that it is formless (*JEM* 187/*NBM* 137). Giving a new spin to the word 'anthropomorphic', Latour designates the human as a mixer of morphisms, one who takes on multiple forms, and amid the proliferation of these forms 'humanity' itself soon becomes indiscernible:

> The expression 'anthropomorphic' considerably underestimates our human-
> ity. We should be talking about morphism. Morphism is the place where
> technomorphisms, zoomorphisms, phusimorphisms, ideomorphisms, theo-
> morphisms, sociomorphisms, psychomorphisms, all come together. Their
> alliances and their exchanges, taken together, are what define the anthropos.
> (*JEM* 188/*NBM* 137)

Furthermore, trying to isolate the 'human itself' from its morphisms is like trying to isolate the onion itself from its layers: we end up not by finding the human but by losing it (*JEM* 188/*NBM* 137). Conversely, it is in multiplying relations that the human shows itself. If, for Badiou, the human is only what it is in relation to the inhuman Idea, then for Latour's 'relationist' account there is no human without the myriad nonhumans with which it is interwoven.

Latour's relationism gives up the quest for any substantial definition of the human which would seek to isolate and define a uniquely human capacity or property, heading in the diametrically opposite direction of seeking to understand the human as that which cannot be isolated:

> we start from the vinculum [chain] itself, from passages and relations, not
> accepting as a starting point any being that does not emerge from this rela-
> tion that is at once collective, real, and discursive. We do not start from
> human beings, those latecomers, nor from language, a more recent arrival
> still. (*JEM* 176/*NBM* 129)

Whereas modernity began with the absolute distinction of subject and object, Latour's relationism begins with no qualitative distinction between humans and nonhumans; both are understood to be actors (or 'actants'),[6] and 'any entity is defined by an association profile of other entities called actors' (*EP* 165/*PH* 159). Identity is extrinsic to the individual, therefore, not intrinsic: I will not come to an understanding of the human by looking inside, but by looking around. The essence of an actant, whether human or nonhuman, is the sum of its associations (*EP* 165/*PH* 159). Furthermore, each actant is not an irreducible substantial monad but a collective, a set of relations that can be natural and cultural, human and nonhuman.

Latour also radically rethinks the notion of capacity itself. In an early paper on the communal life of baboons he rejects the theory that the fundamental cause of the difference between human culture and primate culture is the complexity and innate superior capacity of the human brain, seeing instead a reciprocal and mutually compounding causality between an increased prevalence of nonhuman actors in human societies and increased human capacities. Baboons have only their own bodies out of which to make a society; their social codes are complex, but not externalised (RTSL 790). The greater stability of human society comes not fundamentally from superior human brain capacity but from exteriorising social codes in 'material resources and symbols' (RTSL 790–1). So whereas baboon society may be complex, human society by contrast is complicated, which means 'made of a succession of simple operations' (RTSL 790–1). In other words humans translate their internal social codes into external material symbols, and it is these 'nonhuman' actors that produce complicated human society as distinct from complex baboon society. The difference between humans and baboons is that humans are more deeply entangled in collectives with nonhumans than baboons are with non-baboons, and the 'capacity' for sustaining such complex societies belongs neither to the human nor to the nonhuman actors in isolation, but to the collectivity which includes them all.

The causality here is two-way: the nonhuman acts causally upon the humanity that has made it, in turn changing and altering the human. Traditional humanism and anthropology have only captured one half of this essentially two-way process: humanity is only *Homo faber* (man the (tool)maker) if it is equally, and at the same time, *Homo fabricatus* (man the artefact). We are made by our tools just as concretely as we make them, for the good reason that it is our tools that elicit from us the sort of behaviours we have come to call 'human'. We are educated (literally: led forth) by 'our' artefacts, which make us perform the actions of subjects and 'teach us who we are' (*EME* 324/*AIME* 230). We do not wield our tools from the outset with a determinate end in mind, rather we are sculpted by them into their end: competence follows performance; we are the sons and daughters of our works, and '[i]f gunshots entail, as they say, a "recoil effect," then humanity is above all the *recoil* of that technological detour' (*EME* 324/*AIME* 230). The point here is not that a recoil is nothing at all; it is that a recoil is utterly incomprehensible without, and inseparable from, the rifle shot.

This mutuality leads Latour to an ahumanism which can be understood as a generalised theory of mediation or translation. Both human and nonhuman actors mediate each other, constructing and altering each other in more or less dramatic ways such that both identity and action are distributed among all the actors of a collective rather than being greedily hogged by the modern human subject. Far from auguring the end of humanity, and true to the dynamic of Latour's thesis on Bultmann, this translation signals its renewal:

> It is true that by redistributing the action among all these mediators, we lose the reduced form of humanity, but we gain another form, which has to be called irreducible. The human is in the delegation itself, in the pass, in the sending, in the continuous exchange of forms. (*JEM* 189/*NBM* 138)

In *Pandora's Hope* and elsewhere Latour uses the term 'mediation' with a meaning similar to the 'translation' that lies between the twin betrayals of hyper-fidelity and hyper-innovation. A mediation is 'an event or an actor that cannot be exactly defined by its input and its output' (*EP* 328–9/*PH* 307) because it alters, translates or transforms what it mediates (see *EP* 82/ *PH* 78–9), never passing it on unchanged.

Humans, for their part, are 'mediating mediators' (OTM 53) but this is not to distinguish them from other actants. Each actant mediates, and is mediated by, all the others in a collective. Mediation and translation do not designate some unique capacity possessed by human beings alone; they are the way in which every actant exists. All actants are 'endowed with the capacity to translate what they transport, to redefine it, redeploy it, and also to betray it' (*JEM* 111/*NBM* 81). It so happens that, in addition to performing such translations through moving or ingesting other actants, for example, human beings can perform translations through language and thought. This amounts to nothing more than the claim that language and thought perform different sorts of translations to those actants who do not think or speak; it is not to claim that they act as the host capacities of any distinctive human nature. This is reminiscent of Serres's point that the crystal receives, stores and transmits information just like the human being and nothing distinguishes them ontologically (TU 212; *Dis* 271): language and thought are not seen as unique human characteristics but as one instance of the universal phenomenon of translation and mediation. For Latour, 'There is nothing special about language that allows it to be distinguished from the rest for any length of time' (*PGP* 279/*PF* 184–5).

Interestingly, Latour's insistence on the irreducible coexistence of human and nonhuman actors in collectives lands him with a problem that is equal and opposite to Malabou's difficulties with Phineas Gage. For Malabou, the problem arose over how to account for persistence of identity over time given the 'internal' cerebral alteration of destructive plasticity. For Latour, by contrast, the problem arises of how to account for the persistence of identity over time given the ever-changing configurations of humans and nonhumans that band together in collectivities. Take the oft-cited example of the gun from *Pandora's Hope*. Latour dismisses the (for him) two equally misguided positions according to which 'guns kill people' and 'guns do not kill people, people kill people' (*EP* 185–6/*PH* 176–8), insisting that 'the prime mover of an action becomes a new, distributed, and nested series of practices whose sum may be possible to add up but only if we respect the mediating role of all the actants mobilized in the series' (*EP* 190/*PH* 181). In other words, techniques (the gun) alter and shape psychological capacity (the human) just as much as psychological capacity develops techniques:

> If I define you by what you have (the gun), and by the series of associations that you enter into when you use what you have (when you fire the gun), then you are modified by the gun – more so or less so, depending on the weight of the other associations that you carry. (*EP* 189/*PH* 179)

Or, in a more lapidary formulation, 'You are a different person with the gun in your hand' (*EP* 189/*PH* 179) because you are the web of relations that you have with actors, which in this case includes your relation with the gun. The question for Latour at this point is: who is the 'you' who becomes a different person? On what basis would it be incorrect to say 'there is now a new person', severing all links from the pre-armed individual? Whereas Malabou's internalism struggles to do justice to the question of the persistence of identity over time, Latour's externalism has more tools at its disposal. The answer is to be found at the end of the quotation above: you are a different person 'more so or less so, depending on the weight of the other associations that you carry'. It is this 'more or less' that Malabou's internalism forecloses. For Latour, the human is not defined simply by her or his relation to the gun (as for early Malabou personhood is defined simply in relation to the brain), but rather by a hugely complex web of thousands of relations to other human and nonhuman actors. When she picks up the gun, most of those associations remain unchanged, but if enough of those relations were to change (either quickly or over time) Latour would have to say that we are dealing with a different person. Relationism's proliferation of variegated associations furnishes Latour with a complex notion of the persistence of personhood over time that allows for parallel similarity and difference on a number of different levels at once. If I undergo a brain lesion, for example, then no doubt many of my relations and associations will change (I will lose, perhaps, my relation to the artefacts of my job, to language, to many of my friends) but there are many other relations that will not change: my family still recognises me as 'me', as attested by the hospital visits and the pictures around the house; for legal purposes the state still identifies me as 'me'; the family dog still bounds up to me, and so forth. No doubt for Latour there would be a tipping point beyond which the number of associations that remained the same would be so outweighed by those that had changed that one would have to say that the former person is no more, but we are now dealing with a much more nuanced account of the persistence of identity over time in Latour's 'externalist' approach than in the case of Malabou's somewhat brutal internalist position (though Serres's exo-internalism allows for a more nuanced account than either Latour or Malabou on this point).

Modes and the host discourse question

In Latour's Modes of Existence project we encounter a figure of the human not only whose capacities are distributed among and shared with the non-human actants with which it is in relation, but whose existence is distributed through a series of mutually irreducible modes. Latour is explicit in underlining the continuity between his previous actor network theory and the Modes of Existence project:

> AIME generalizes the principle of translation that enjoyed great dignity in network theory, and gives it the means of specifying the many ways in which a being can be itself through the intervention of a being other than itself. (IMEg: Translation)

If the relationism of the 'middle' Latour of Actor Network Theory makes a host properties account of the human unthinkable, then the Latour of *AIME* does the same for a host discourse account: the human is not to be found in any one regime of enunciation, for it is gathered together in a series of modes of existence.

To understand how the different modes of existence produce the human being, it is first important to understand what the modes themselves are. Throughout *An Inquiry*, Latour insists that his investigation is not into modes of (human) understanding or modes of comprehension, but modes of existence. If an entity has an effect on another entity, then for Latour's purposes it exists, whether the moderns would chalk the entity in question up to existence (polonium) or nonexistence (poltergeists). Everything that influences anything else exists, whether the entity be material or ideal, collective or individual, 'imagined' or 'real'. Furthermore, although Latour may at times speak of modes of existence as 'regimes of enunciation',[7] he is not elaborating a linguistic philosophy in which everything is reduced to language. He is quite insistent that his investigation is an ontological one. He is also insistent that the project should not be understood to be investigating one mode of existence which can be expressed or interpreted in many different ways, but a true ontological pluralism that cannot be reduced to a superficial plurality of languages or cultures (*EME* 150/*AIME* 142).

Each of Latour's modes of existence has a key and a felicity condition. A felicity condition is a way of judging between the true and the false in the mode in question, between success and failure of the particular mode, and each mode judges truth and falsehood according to its own felicity conditions (*EME* 70/*AIME* 58). The felicity condition of the religious mode of existence, for example, is that it transforms the hearer; the felicity condition of the political mode is that it gathers a constituency, making a fleeting unity out of a multitude. The 'key' (or 'key of interpretation') of a mode of existence is a way of talking about how it translates or mediates.[8] We can draw an analogy here with literary genres. If we open a book and read the incipit 'Once upon a time', we can be justified in making certain prima facie assumptions about the sort of world we are entering, the sort of moves that are allowed and disallowed by this genre, and how we are to judge whether the book in our hands is a successful example of its kind. Now of course Latour is talking about modes of existence and not literary genres, but the principle is the same. Like 'genre', the 'key' is not something that stands above the mode of existence dictating its rules from atop a theoretical Mount Sinai, and nor is it nothing, for without it we would not understand the first thing about the mode in question (*EME* 69/*AIME* 57) and we would be condemned to follow in the footsteps of the moderns in phoning the police when we read that the princess has been taken captive by the troll, and then suing the publishing company for the trauma it caused us when we find out it was all a lie. The story is neither contained in the genre, such that once the genre has been specified nothing further need be said, nor is it independent of the genre, in which case nothing intelligible could be said.

If each mode brings its own key and felicity conditions, it makes no sense to judge all the modes of existence according to one overarching criterion of truth. That is the modern disease, running all existence through the trawler net of scientific verifiability and then proclaiming that whatever cannot be caught by this process is not a fish. Fundamental to the originality of Latour's project is that each mode is to be respected in its own right (*SUL* 5/*Ref* 307). We can say that each mode is 'exhaustive', in other words it says all that there is to say about the sort of entities it produces. However, no mode is 'extensive', in the sense of being able to extend to cover everything that exists, speaking non-reductively about God and gravity, legal fictions and literary fictions, square roots and square rooms.

No mode can be exhaustively reduced to any other; there is for Latour no 'one mode to rule them all'. Nevertheless, Latour notes 'the tendency of each mode to propose a hegemonic metalanguage for speaking about all the others' (*EME* 416/*AIME* 416), a tendency which he calls 'fundamentalism' (*EME* 363/*AIME* 363). If no mode can be reduced to another, then neither can all the modes be viewed from a position where they are considered as a totality, incommensurable as they are. No mode can hold all the other modes together or provide them all with a common language (*EME* 317/*AIME* 315), and no mode can 'fill in the gaps' to make of existence a coherent whole, for each one 'can do no more than add a thread, leaving behind as many empty spaces as full ones' (*EME* 318/*AIME* 316). In a way reminiscent of his earlier argument that 'multiculturalism' be seconded by 'multinaturalism' (*PN* 47/*PNe* 29), Latour insists (borrowing a term from William James) that the modes do not form a universe but a multiverse. The 'world' (to which Latour prefers the term 'multiverse', *EME* 215/*AIME* 211), is not a foundation but a product, a political 'process of composition' (IMEg: Multiverse) of the different modes of existence. There is no more a single and unified 'world' than there is a single and unified 'context' in semiotics, and the multiverse of mutually irreducible modes of existence is 'the only world in which we live' (IMEg: Multiverse; translation altered).[9] This is particularly important when it comes to understanding the way in which the human being emerges among the different modes, because it means that there can never be a single 'host discourse' of humanity.

Where does this leave the human in the Modes of Existence project? Is the human found in the sum of the modes? Is it pre-modal? Does each mode have a different figure of the human? The answer is that the human is a non-totalisable multi-modal 'amalgam' (*EME* 293/*AIME* 291). Each mode contributes to the production of what Latour calls by turns 'humans' and 'quasi-subjects'. The Modes of Existence project in its present state describes fifteen modes, the first nine of which are the most important in building Latour's understanding of the human being.[10] The first group of three modes of existence recognises neither quasi-objects nor quasi-subjects; the second group of three gathers together quasi-objects; and the third gathers together quasi-subjects (*EME* 377–8/*AIME* 378).

The three modes which precede the human and furnish 'the soil in which it grows' are reproduction (abbreviated to [REP]), metamorphosis [MET] and habit [HAB]. The 'key' of [REP] is subsistence over time without the magician's rabbit of an underlying substance. All entities share this mode of existence, 'the mode of existence through which any entity whatsoever crosses through the hiatus of its repetition' (*EME* 101/*AIME* 92): will existence continue from one moment to the next (in which case its felicity condition has been met) or will the existent be no more? [MET] both describes in general terms 'the manner in which existents are transformed or transform in order to subsist' and also, more specifically, 'the mode of existence first detected by psychogenesis' (IMEg: [MET]), such as witches, demons and ghosts. Like beings of [REP], the psychogenic and psychotropic beings of [MET] precede the human and provide now not persistence through time but transformation and changeability. The combination of these first two modes forms 'a sort of matrix or kneading process from which the "human" can later take nourishment, perhaps, can in any case branch out, accelerate, be energized' (*EME* 209/ *AIME* 203). We can think of them as two ways of translating: translating subsistence over the hiatus and the danger of nonexistence, and translating one form into another in metamorphosis. These two modes together are not to be thought of as 'pre-human', Latour insists, but rather they proliferate the reproductions and metamorphoses that the other modes will then take up and translate in different ways: 'rather they form the basso continuo without which no music would be audible' (*EME* 209/ *AIME* 204). They are joined by a third mode, 'habit' [HAB]. If [MET] designates beings which are transformed or transform themselves, [HAB] describes the opposite tendency of beings which 'settle into existence, despite the risk of hiatus and of reprise, as if the trajectory they were on was continuous' (IMEg: [HAB]). This is 'a general property of essences' (IMEg: [HAB]) and includes but is by no means restricted to the habits of humans or other organisms. With this first group of three modes we have built up a picture of beings which exist over time, which can transform and be transformed, and which can generate a continuity of action out of discontinuity.

The second set of three modes, 'technique' [TEC], 'fiction' [FIC], and 'reference' [REF], describes the production of what Latour calls 'quasi-objects'.[11] The prefix 'quasi-' insists on the fact that such an object 'proposes an implied corresponding position for quasi subjects' (IMEg: Quasi-Objects; translation altered). A quasi-object is 'the set of quasi-subjects that are attached to it', and in turn a quasi-subject is the sum of its quasi-objects (*EME* 428/*AIME* 428). Quasi-subjects and quasi-objects are mutually dependent, holding each other in being. The production of techniques [TEC], figures [FIC] and chains of reference [REF] precedes and sculpts the emergence of the human:

> To put it in the shorthand terms of anthropogenesis: humanoids became humans – thinking, speaking humans – by dint of association with the beings of technology, fiction, reference. They became skilful, imaginative, capable of objective knowledge, by dint of grappling with these modes of existence. (*EME* 372/*AIME* 372)

Latour says in relation to technique what is true of all three modes in this second group: it proceeds and creates a space for a quasi-subject such that 'the author learns *from what he is doing* that he is perhaps its author' (*EME* 233–4/*AIME* 230; original emphasis). Once more, it is our tools that educate us and teach us who we are.

What Latour is seeking to avoid at all costs is an analysis that begins with an off-the-peg humanity already speaking, already capable of creating techniques, imagining works and producing objective knowledge, even before any of the objects corresponding to those acts arrive on the scene. Following Greimasian semiotic analysis which, rather than beginning a priori with the empirical figures of an enunciator and an enunciatee, takes them to be structural, abstract (not empirical or anthropomorphic) figures presupposed by any utterance,[12] quasi-objects provide what Latour calls 'offers of subjectivity' (*EME* 372/*AIME* 372), invitations to occupy the positions left open by quasi-objects: the position of the inventor of techniques, the framer of fictions, the pursuer of chains of reference. As in the case of his article on baboons a quarter of a century earlier, this is not the obliteration of the human but the ontological co-implication of the human with what the moderns consider to be artefacts and human products.

Whereas the second group of three modes sketches the existence of quasi-objects, then the third group of 'law' [DRO], 'politics' [POL] and 'religion' [REL] describes the modes of existence of quasi-subjects (*EME* 371/*AIME* 371). The terms do not refer to narrowly 'legal', 'party political' or 'ecclesiastical' contexts, but designate general modes of existence which find particularly acute or clear expression in the domains of society which give them their names. The term 'quasi-subject' is not new to *Inquiry*,[13] but it is given more definition here than in his previous work. Whereas subjects provide a starting point for the ontology of modernity, quasi-subjects are a late-coming product of Latour's modes of existence. Between them, [DRO], [POL] and [REL] produce what we commonly recognise as persons. [DRO] attaches us to our speech and makes us responsible for it, establishing a series of relations between incipient quasi-subjects and 'their' acts and goods. It is in the mode of being of law that people [*les personnages*] become 'responsible, guilty, owners, authors, insured, protected', and it is by virtue of law that 'characters become assigned to their acts and to their goods' (*EME* 370/*AIME* 370). Without law, 'every act of enunciation would disperse possible authors with no chance of ever linking what they say with what they do' (*EME* 373/*AIME* 373). Furthermore, and to return to the question of the persistence of identity, it is law which makes the incipient person capable of continuing through space and over time (*EME* 372/*AIME* 372). [POL] contributes to the production of persons by virtue of the capitalised 'political Circle', a term intended to capture the 'curve' of the political trajectory. Political speech seeks to obtain 'unity from a multitude, a unified will from a sum of recriminations' (*EME* 141/ *AIME* 133), but this unity 'disperses like a flock of sparrows' with the continual transformation of the multitude gathered into a unity (*EME* 141/*AIME* 134). The political Circle is the 'REPRISE of a movement that cannot rely definitively on anything' (*EME* 141/*AIME* 134) of the constantly renewed effort to create unity. [POL] contributes to the creation of persons because, 'while following along the political Circle, humans become capable of opining and of articulating positions in a collective— they become free and autonomous citizens' (*EME* 372/*AIME* 372) who are able to say 'we' and belong to a group (IMEg: Political Circle).

Finally, it is the direct, second person immediate address characteristic of 'religion' [REL] that gives the quasi-subject 'the certainty of existing and being close, of being unified and complete' (*EME* 304/*AIME* 302). Such a word need not be religious in the theological sense, and Latour includes amorous address in this mode of existence: 'What could be more miserable than never being the intended recipient of a loving word: how could anyone who had never received such gifts feel like a person? Who would feel like someone without having been addressed in this way?' (*EME* 304/ *AIME* 302). Without the religious mode there is no wholeness and unity to the second person singular, gathered together and summoned to appear by the words of another. This is the salvific component of religious speech: it saves quasi-subjects by transforming them into people (*EME* 305/*AIME* 303), filling them with 'a new weight of presence' (*EME* 374/*AIME* 374). Having arrived at the end of this third group of three, we now have all the modes necessary to speak of 'persons' who can be 'recognized, loved and sometimes saved' (*EME* 372/*AIME* 372).

We will gain very little by quibbling over Latour's definitions, by objecting that 'surely law gathers the person as the subject of imputation!' or 'surely politics addresses the person who counts for one!' No doubt objections could be made to the way that Latour slices the cake of personhood, and that is in part why the Modes of Existence website exists. What I want to stress here is the general point that quasi-subjectivity and the personhood that develops from it are products of an amalgam of modes of existence, not the condition of possibility or the origin of those modes. The monolithic subject of modernity has been 'completely unmoored, dislocated, distributed, divided up' (*EME* 305/*AIME* 303). It is no longer a point of origin but the fragile intersection of multiple modes of existence; it is drawn forth from its 'outmost being' [*for extérieur*] (*EME* 305/*AIME* 303; translation altered). If we can say that the human subject emerges from 'its' works (and Latour considers the pronoun inelegant), we must equally say that the works summon forth and create 'their' human (*EME* 233–4/*AIME* 230). In passing (we shall return to the point in the following section), we can also note that Latour's quasi-subject circumvents the problems of the mono-directional and all-encompassing emancipation narrative of the modern. The story of the quasi-subject, the person or the human cannot be told as one story for it circulates in at least nine separate and mutually irreducible modes, with identity distributed through these different stories in the different modes of existence.

The publication of the preliminary findings of the Modes of Existence project in 2012 has not succeeded in banishing the charge of anthropocentrism from Latour's door. In *Reassembling the Political* Graham Harman responds to the *Inquiry* with a suspicion about the terms 'quasi-subject' and 'quasi-object':

> When Latour's ontology of actants effaced the difference between nature and culture, it also seemed to eliminate the modern notion that human beings must comprise a full half of any situation. Latour's ontology holds that actants are defined by their relations with other actants, not that they exist only in correlation with a human observer, as in the 'correlationism' attacked by Quentin Meillassoux. Given Latour's global relationism between all actants of every kind, there is no obvious reason why people should be entitled to meddle in half of the modes of existence.[14]

I think that there are two helpful responses to this charge. First, Latour has consistently argued over a long period that human beings are enfolded into more nonhuman actants, and in a greater diversity of ways, than baboons are to non-baboon actants or bacteria to non-bacterial actants. It does not follow, from the fact that half (or even more: I make it twelve out of fifteen) of the modes of existence pertain at least in an incipient way to quasi-subjects, that human beings 'must comprise a full half of any situation'. Human beings are more complicated than other beings (according to the sense of 'complicated' in RTSL), and therefore their modes of existence require more description, but as in the case of our friend the lungfish from the previous chapter, genetic or modal verbosity does not equate *eo ipso* to a privileged status (unless we also unthinkingly adopt the assumption that bigger and more is necessarily better).

The second response to Harman's charge of anthropocentrism is a move reminiscent of Serres's rejection of metaphor in favour of synecdoche. Rather than ascetically seeking to purge the world of all intentionality in order to prevent the charge of anthropocentrism or even panpsychism, Latour embraces the dispersal of intentionality throughout all animate and inanimate objects. To ascribe intentionality to the world 'to be sure [. . .] is somewhat anthropomorphic', he admits in 'Facing Gaia', but what begs for an explanation is not the extension of intentionality to non-humans but rather how it is that some humans have withdrawn intentionality from the living world imagining that they were playing on the planks of an inanimate stage. The enigma is not that there are people [who] still believe in animism, but the persistence of belief in inanimism. (FG 67)

This is not a plea for the recognition of fairies at the bottom of every garden, for the very good reason that the notion of intentionality itself, as Latour fully realises, cannot survive this *détournement* intact: 'The point [. . .] is not about whether to grant intentionality or not, but about what happens to such an intention once every agent has been endowed with one' (FG 68). What happens is that the quintessentially modern notion of intention is rewritten as part of Latour's a-modern account of the modes of existence, in the same way that the notion of truth is rewritten in his response to Bultmann's demythologisation. 'Paradoxically, such an extension quickly erases all traces of anthropomorphism', Latour argues (FG 67). It is not that intention is nowhere present in an indifferent universe, but that intention is everywhere present and no longer a uniquely human trait.

There is a case to be made that Latour's embrace of a generalised anthropomorphism cuts across the modern constitution more effectively than a flat and linear commitment to renounce anthropocentrism and all its works. Flatly to reject anthropocentrism is to walk out of the cave of the modern 'structure' right into the waiting jaws of the modern 'story'. To leave behind the anthropomorphic once and for all is to be emancipated from it, to be able to think (in) its absence, in a radically modern climax to the story of ever-increasing emancipation. To smash down the idol of anthropocentrism in the name of the non-modern is to write a memorable one-liner against soundbites, to denounce the content of modernism in a gesture that precisely and hypertrophically repeats its characteristic story. Latour chooses a different approach to the question of anthropocentrism. Rather than running a mile from the stench of the anthropocentric in a way that leaves the humanist free passage in the Elysian Fields of 'culture', 'society', 'subjectivity' and 'values', his *détournement* of anthropomorphism hijacks and translates (in his Bultmannian sense) the language, gestures and positions that characterise humanistic anthropocentrism.[15] His tactic is to denature, twist and re-purpose (*détourner*) the structure of modernism, but to avoid doing so in a way that reiterates and consummates its story.

In the same way that Meillassoux lays claim to the language of resurrection, God, the Child of Man and perfect justice within a resolutely atheological frame, Latour is here walking unhindered through the humanist garden and plucking all of its most attractive blooms: intentionality, subject and object, anthropomorphism. Whereas an ascetic approach like Harman's risks leaving the modern humanist under attack but with all his or her weapons still functioning, Latour has raided the humanist armoury before mounting his assault on the dichotomies and emancipation narrative of modern humanity. Furthermore, like Meillassoux's intellectual intuition through which the epistemological cul-de-sac of the lack of any necessary reason becomes the ontological highway of the necessary lack of reason, Latour turns the tables in suggesting that what begs explanation is not the extension but the withdrawal of intentionality. Both in Meillassoux's case and in Latour's, it is an intuition that can be pleaded for but not enforced. The whole of the Modes of Existence project, indeed the whole of Latour's anthropo-philosophical reflections from *Irreductions* onwards, can be read as a following through of the implications of this intuition.

It is therefore both correct and misleading to argue that 'Latourian a-humanism reveals itself as a kind of "extended" humanism'[16] or that his 'project is best described in terms of a radically expanded humanism'.[17] It is correct because, as far as it goes, it tells the truth about what Latour is doing: taking notions which in the modern dispensation are reserved for human subjects and dispersing them through a much broader range of entities. It is misleading, however, because it fails to tell the whole truth. Latour is not only extending notions such as intentionality, subjectivity and objectivity, but radically transforming them in the process, wresting them from their modern captivity and setting them back on their human feet. Latour has not extended but translated humanism, picking a fine line between the betrayal of repetition and the betrayal of hyper-innovation. It is the gesture of translation, I submit, that more adequately explains his relation to humanism in particular and the modern in general than either expansion or extension.

For his own part, Latour is doing neither more nor less than what all actants do: he is mediating and resisting the tradition that has been passed down to him, neither obediently repeating it (which would perpetuate modernism's dualistic structure) nor throwing it out and starting again (which would perpetuate modernism's narrative of emancipation). By translating modern anthropocentrism into an anthropology which distributes agency across all beings he does not make modernity (in the guise of emancipation) the victor over modernity (in the guise of dualisms). In the next section of this chapter we shall see how the notions of Gaia and the Anthropocene sharpen and escalate this trajectory of Latour's account of the human, and strike a more decisive blow than ever against modernity's emancipation narrative.

Who faces Gaia?

Latour's Gifford Lectures of 2013, entitled 'Facing Gaia', stand in a complex relationship to his Modes of Existence project. In some ways the lectures amplify and complement the earlier work, particularly in their dismantling of the emancipation narrative. In other ways, however, 'Facing Gaia' seems to retreat from some of the territory occupied by *An Inquiry*, for the *anthropos* takes a more central role. In tracing through the fate of humanity in 'Facing Gaia' we can see that the different moves Latour makes can each be understood as instances – once more – of translating the modern legacy of humanism.

Gaia does not come out of the blue for Latour; it is the (so to speak) natural and almost inevitable development of his relationism and insistence on the distributed agency of humans and nonhumans. Latour's study of Pasteur's microbes had shown how the discovery of bacteria thrusts nonhuman actants into the centre of the 'human' world, showing that 'society is not made up just of men, for everywhere microbes intervene and act' (*PGP* 62/*PF* 35). If Pasteur's microbes form an all-pervasive but imperceptibly thin glaze over everything 'human', then Gaia cascades a veritable tsunami of nonhuman actors into the heart of human concerns. All of Latour's previous work on the complex relations of humans and nonhumans has prepared him to engage with the Anthropocene: he has always been ecological. Given that climate factors are by most measures the most acute instance of 'nonhuman' actors facilitating, constraining and conditioning human action today, it would be bizarre indeed had Latour not come round to this theme.

The Gifford Lectures also bring to boiling point Latour's confrontation with the structure and narrative of the modern constitution. The Anthropocene forces us to leave behind forever the dichotomy of nature and society (*EME* 22/*AIME* 10). In rhetoric reminiscent of a Badiouian 'point' that forces a yes/no decision (*LM* 614–15/*LW* 591), Latour insists that we face a binary choice between 'modernisation' and 'ecologisation' (TME). Just as modernity sets forth its own particular understanding of the human, so also Latour sketches a new, ecologised humanity.

The return of the anthropos

The discussions and analyses of 'Facing Gaia' turn around two central motifs: Gaia itself and the Anthropocene. Gaia, the mother goddess from Hesiod's *Theogony*, is the name used by James Lovelock to describe a 'composite being', a non-unified series of feedback loops between humans and the earth and between the earth and itself, that for Lovelock 'evoke the possibility of a living Earth not in the sense of an organism or even an organization but in the sense of a simple assemblage of loops that achieve equilibrium by chance' (IMEg: Gaia).[18] 'Anthropocene' describes a period of geological history in which the greatest single factor influencing geological, atmospheric and climatic changes is human activity. The question of whether we have 'officially' entered the Anthropocene is still, so to speak, up in the air,[19] but Latour himself is in no doubt that entering the Anthropocene era amplifies and radicalises a number of his previous positions in relation to the human.

Latour has always maintained that the 'objects' of the 'material' world are not innate lumps of Cartesian wax sitting patiently waiting for the free creative inspiration of the subject to make something of them. However, with the advent of the Anthropocene the modern narrative of an inert and pliable 'nonhuman' world becomes more obviously inadequate than ever. The humanity of the modern period is defined in terms of the struggle against the meaninglessness of a cold and indifferent world, epitomised perhaps nowhere more vividly than in Albert Camus's retelling of the myth of Sisyphus. Both Meillassoux and Malabou take up and perpetuate the theme of indifference in their own thought.[20] Latour, in turn, weaves his own myth:

> It is true that a startled blind person can hurl himself fearlessly ahead, unaware of danger (this is the hubris of the Moderns). But if he begins to hesitate, he ends up discouraged (this is postmodernism). If he is truly frightened, the most insignificant terrorist can terrorize him (this is fundamentalism). Three centuries of total freedom up to the irruption of the world in the form of the Earth, of Gaia: a return of unanticipated consequences: the end of the modernist parenthesis. (*EME* 181/*AIME* 175–6; translation altered)

The one who persists in believing the myth of the indifference of the world is characterised by Latour as a self-indulgent dilettante, titillating himself with the terrifying thoughts of the 'death of God' and 'absurdity' of life: 'those who used to enjoy those games remained like epicurean tourists comfortably seated on the shore, safely protected by the ultimate certainty that Nature at least will always be there, offering them a totally indifferent but also a solid, eternal ground' (FG 110).

The late modern and postmodern picture of humanity is summarised and adumbrated in the three hammer blows which Freud, in 'One of the Difficulties of Psychoanalysis',[21] argues have been struck against human pride: humanity is not at the centre of the universe (Copernicus), not at the climax of history (Darwin), and not even master in its own psychological house (Freud himself). A new wound has been inflicted on human pride, Latour argues, but this time it is not through humanity being side-lined or disregarded by an indifferent universe; it is because the world is at war with us, and the world has all the best weapons. Whereas the moderns amuse themselves in thinking that the world's 'primary qualities' were indifference and inertia, and that it was only the fancy of the human imagination that endowed it with agency, Latour notes that the structure has now been reversed: it is now a primary quality of the world that it is in implacable opposition to unlimited human expansion, and it is only our own narcissistic fancy that tells us it may in fact be an inert canvas for the painting of our human emancipatory dreams (FG 128–9).

As Latour rightly points out (FG 55), Freud's so-called hammer blows to human pride were really the seedbed of an ever more expansive moder-nity. Are we not at the centre of the universe? Then we must forge ahead and make our home here on this rocky outcrop. Are we not the climax of history? Then we must tell our own stories and create our own mean-ings, first among them the story of our own emancipation. Are we not the master in our own house? Then so much the better, for without any master insinuating itself into the empty space left by God we are accountable to no one for our actions, not even to ourselves. Though superficially humbling, Freud's hammer blows help clear the ground for an ideology of human autonomy free from exterior constraints. By contrast, the Anthropocene puts us back at the centre of the world (FG 56), but like the unruly child who is made to stand on a chair in the middle of the classroom, occupying the position of centrality is hardly an ennobling experience. If the world were indeed indifferent to us then we could continue merrily along the misguided but harmless path of ever greater expansion and emancipation; the real and lasting hammer blow to human dreams is that the world is most certainly not indifferent to us; it is in fact at war with us.

The substance of this war, for Latour, is that Gaia and humans each want to change the other: humans want to engineer the world to allow for continuous and unrestrained human expansion, to 'push [Gaia] into such a different state that It would become another being altogether' (FG 115), and Gaia for its part sets itself up implacably against the modern expan-sionist picture of the human with its emancipation narrative. Either Gaia will force a change of *anthropos*, or *anthropos* will irrevocably alter Gaia. One thing is certain: they cannot both continue to coexist in their present state. The idea of war and the agency extended to Gaia are merely exten-sions of Latour's former work. In the admirably compact and untranslat-ably elegant French construction 'faire faire' (literally: to 'make make', to make something act), it is the microbes that make Pasteur make their dis-covery, and Pasteur who makes the microbes announce their presence; it is the cigarette that makes the smoker smoke it and the smoker who makes the cigarette be smoked. In the same way, talk of war between Gaia and *anthropos* is not to be understood either as a crude literary personification or as an equally crude New Age panpsychism. Humans make the world make war on them, and the world makes humans make war: the agency is distributed. It is neither people nor planes which fly, but airlines (OTM 45–6); it is neither humans nor Gaia which are alone at war, but the two combined.

Such a generalised state of war calls not for gratuitous platitudes that we are 'all in this together', but a sober and hard-nosed mechanism for accounting for the different human and nonhuman interests at stake in the Anthropocene. It calls for a parliament of things. The idea of the parliament of things can be traced in Latour's work as far back as *We Have Never Been Modern*, and it finds its roots in Michel Serres's *The Natural Contract*. The interest it holds for us in this chapter is the peculiar role that it gives to human beings and the way in which that role, in turn, reflects on some of the concerns I raised in previous chapters. It would be a mistake to understand 'thing' here as a synonym for 'object': 'that the old word for "thing" does not mean what is outside the human realm, but a case, a controversy, a cause to be collectively decided in the "Thing", the ancient word for assembly or forum' (FMOF 5). Latour's parliament of things is not a parliament of objects – with place for a television in government and a microwave in the Cabinet – but a parliament of concerns, in which all the human and nonhuman parties with a stake in a particular concern are gathered together.

Latour's parliament of things rests on the principle of representation. Pace the ancient Athenian experiment in direct democracy, democratic rule has always relied on the principle of representation: representatives of particular constituencies (usually a geographical constituency) or of an entire nation (in the case of the French Republican system) undertake to represent the interests of those whom they represent, although they themselves may not be a member of their own constituency, as we are all quite well aware from the phenomenon of favoured candidates 'parachuted into' winnable seats by the central party hierarchy. All Latour is proposing is an extension of this already tried and tested principle: rather than members of the parliament of things undertaking to represent those living in a different geographical location to their own, its human members would undertake to represent the interests of different quasi-objects. It is a parliament of spokespeople, speaking on behalf of the assembled interests, translating those interests into political discourse. In this way, the mode of representation in the parliament of things is just one more iteration of the translation or mediation that characterises the whole of existence for Latour: the life of the tuna or the existence of CO_2 is already a series of mediations or translations, and the parliament of things merely extends that series of mediations into the political sphere.

If there is a difficulty with this idea it is not to do with the question of which interests to be represented, Latour insists in an interview with Erin Manning and Brian Massumi, but to do with the poverty of our modes of representation: 'our academic organisation is so impoverished and so blocked up that it is hugely difficult simply to represent the beings with whom we make and make up the world' (LB 13–14; my translation). Furthermore, representing the interests of the voiceless is not simply a parliamentary imperative for Latour. It is the job of artists, scientists, politicians and militants together to make ways of making (*faire faire*) the interests of nonhuman actors intelligible and emotionally arresting. It is in the spirit of representation that Latour has co-written the play *Kosmokoloss*, 'An attempt at bringing in on stage the global climate crisis by exploring the disconnect between the dimension of the crisis and the lack of "feel" for it',[22] and it is in the same spirit that he has co-founded the theatre group *Gaia Global Circus* which has performed a play of the same name, written by Pierre Daubigny.[23] In the rather more stark terms of 'Facing Gaia', Latour insists that '[w]ithout making the threat visible artificially, there is no way to make us spring into action', and what we require is a '"prophylactic" use of the Apocalypse' (FG 111). Like Nietzsche's death of God, the war against Gaia is 'still more distant from them than most distant stars – and yet they have done it themselves'.[24] Latour's own evocation of Gaia and the powerful rhetoric of his Gifford Lectures can at least in part be read as an aping of the Nietzschean idiom: we must ecologise with a hammer!

In this sense, there is nothing particularly radical or controversial about the parliament of things; it is the natural evolution of parliamentary representative democracy in the age of the Anthropocene. Furthermore, given that we have never been modern, the parliament of things redresses a deficiency of Western parliamentary representative democracy since its institution. Latour claims to be extending representation, 'naming the extension of speech to nonhuman Civilization, and finally solving the problem of representation that rendered democracy powerless as soon as it was invented, because of the counter-invention of Science' (*PN* 110/*PNe* 71). The parliament of things also reflects and fosters the notion of plural and sometimes conflicting interests and discourses that Latour elaborates in his Modes of Existence project. It is a principle of a parliament that no single representative should arrogate to themselves the claim to 'represent the general will or the common good once and for all' (PNEW 72–3).[25] To extend the notions of host capacities and host discourse, in the parliament of things there is no host party, no one set of interests to which all the others have to genuflect; it 'is no longer possible to appeal outside this political arena, to nature and its laws as if it were a higher court and a higher transcendent authority' (PNEW 73), nor is it possible to appeal to the interests of humanity in the same way.

In the same way that there is no way to express the general will from one position, so also there is no single story that can adequately narrate the history and destiny of *anthropos*. Latour insists on the fragmented, conflictual nature of Gaia not only in the parliament of things but also in the idea of geostory, providing perhaps a fitting narrative pendant to Adrian Johnston's sketch of a riven and agonistic nature in *Prolegomena to Any Future Materialism*.[26] Latour calls for a 'relocalization of the global', warning that 'When we unify it as the terraqueous sphere, we are forcing geostory inside the older format of medieval theology and 19th century epistemology of Nature' (FG 93). In a passage that I think we can read as an explicit rejection of Serres's Great Story, Latour warns of falling back into the smoothness of standard cosmologies:

> deploying the series of atoms, quantas, planets, genes, cells, living organisms, that would always land her on some Master Narrative leading from the Big Bang to human evolution, from Lucy in the Great Rift Valley to the gangs in suburban Los Angeles. (*EME* 107/*AIME* 99)

Instead of this modern story of one single and unified cosmogony, Latour insists on the parallel existences of a splintered and irreconcilable proliferation of different stories, each jostling for position and for representation in the parliament of things. To borrow terms from Régis Debray, Latour's geostory is the 'democratic' recasting of Serres's 'Republican' Great Story.[27]

In the context of this book's discussion of figures of the human, however, I want to highlight one very important principle of the parliament of things, the principle of giving a voice to the voiceless. Throughout this book I have expressed unease with the way in which different accounts of the human tend more or less inadvertently to sideline from humanity those of its members who do not possess particular determinate capacities. These different groups have been abbreviated at various points in the current work to the two categories of neonates and the senile, neither of which has a 'voice' in the usual sense. Latour's parliament of things provides a mechanism for the inclusion of the interests of such groups in public decision-making processes, along indeed with all the other human and nonhuman groups deprived of a voice. He makes explicit mention of such groups in the article 'From Realpolitik to Dingpolitik', arguing that '[t]he inherent limits imposed by speech impairment, cognitive weaknesses and all sorts of handicaps are no longer denied but prostheses are accepted instead' (RPDP 41). It is not a perfect solution – none of us needs much incitement to reel off examples of how representative democracy can represent particular groups or interests very badly – but it is certainly a more sophisticated solution than defining humanity in terms of those who possess a particular host property and then defining politics in terms of that definition of humanity. The dynamics of 'faire faire' mean, in addition, that representation is not reduced to simple ventriloquising. The human representatives would not ventriloquise the inert nonhuman any more than the father in the Mafalda strip reprinted in *On the Modern Cult of the Factish Gods* (*CM* 115/*MC* 55) unilaterally smokes the inert cigarette. The principle is not a complicated one, as Latour explains with the example of chickens: 'the sciences are perfectly capable of making a chicken express its wishes in order to know whether it prefers a wire mesh of one centimetre or three centimetres, because the chicken dies or loses its feathers' (*ŒBL* 146; my translation). Is the scientist able to represent the interests of chickens perfectly? Almost certainly not, but imperfection is not generally seen as a reason to abandon representative democracy. Is she able to represent the interests of the chicken at parliamentary level more adequately than they are currently represented? Almost certainly yes. Can the chickens vote her out if they think she is doing a bad job? No, but this does not mean that representatives of other interested parties cannot call her to account.

It is important to recognise that Latour is not proposing a silver bullet. There are problems with the idea of the parliament of things, some of the principal questions that remain for it to answer being: (1) who gets to decide which interests have a seat?; (2) who gets to decide who represents whom?; (3) according to what principles will rival interests be balanced against each other?; and (4) if, as Latour says, we are in a state of war, what gives us grounds to expect that any decisions of such a parliament would be heeded by those who considered themselves disadvantaged thereby? Despite these outstanding questions, however, it took Western nations centuries to arrive at the current state of parliamentary democracy, and there is still work to be done on the project. If we had waited until we had a perfect proposal, European monarchies would never have fallen.

Emancipated from emancipation?

What about the *anthropos* itself? How is humanity to be figured in the age of the Anthropocene?

The question is phrased by Latour in the following terms: 'what sort of political animals do humans become when their bodies are to be coupled with an animated Gaia?' (FG 58). The answer comes in terms of contrast between two figures introduced by Latour in 'Facing Gaia': the 'human' of modernism and the 'earthbound' of the Anthropocene.

Latour's 'humans' are a modern species. Like Pico della Mirandola's archetypal modern sketch of humanity in his *Oration on the Dignity of Man*, humans are emancipated wanderers, not at home on the earth:

> Either they tell you that they belong to nowhere in particular, defined only by the fact that, thanks to their spiritual and moral quality, they have been able to free themselves from the harsh necessities of Nature; or they tell you that they fully belong to Nature and its realm of material necessity, but what they mean by materiality bears so little relation with the agencies they have previously de-animated, that the realm of necessity looks just as out-of-Earth as the realm of freedom. (FG 118–19)

Humans are of the world but not in it, at least if their own accounts are to be believed. This lack of connection leads to a lack of concern for the consequences of their actions in the world, bolstered by an emancipation narrative that shows them that their technological ingenuity will be able to extricate them from any straits to which their unconstrained ambitions might lead. In a passage that is strikingly reminiscent of Badiou's contrast between the human animal in the immortal subject, Latour characterises the bipolarity of the modern human:

> Either those human characters are understood as neo-Darwinian bodies fused with *Homo oeconomicus* and there is no example of such calculating robots ever being able to take their limited abode into account – they are selfish and irrational for good; or, they are taken as 'subjects' whose entire occupation consists in trying to escape from what they take to be the cold and de-animated domination of objectivity. (FG 127)

The modern human, in short, is more modern than human: a captive animal force-fed the unsustainable diet of an unconstrained emancipation narrative which it believes points the way to its destiny, but whose only sign of progress is the hypertrophied foie gras of an increasingly unliveable world.

In the place of this grotesque caricature, Latour introduces the 'earthbound', the new figure of the *anthropos* meet for the age of the Anthropocene. By contrast with the self-description of the modern emancipated human, the earthbound is a figure of attachments. If the spirit of modernity could be summed up in Ivan Karamazov's perennially misquoted line 'if God is dead, then everything is permitted',[28] Latour characterises the attitude of the earthbound as a lapidary 'if Gaia is against us, then not much is permitted any longer' (*EME* 483/*AIME* 486). If the rallying cry of the modern conquistador was always 'plus ultra', then the earthbound is content with a more modest but more realistic 'plus intra' (FG 141), and '[s]uddenly, as if a brake had been applied to all forward movements, Galileo's expanding universe is interrupted and Koyré's motto should now be read in reverse: "from the infinite universe back to the limited closed cosmos"' (FG 56). The earthbound recognise that they are situated, that despite some vestigial modern dreams of colonising other planets they only have one earth, and in contrast with the modern humans they 'have to explore the question of their limits' (FG 132).

In the same way that the parliament of things puts an end to a restricted sphere of representation but not to the modern institutions of representation, so also Latour intends that his new figure of the earthbound will 'put an end to anthropocentrism' at the same time as 'foregrounding the human agent under another shape' (FG 78). There is a sense in which Latour's 'earthbound', like his parliament of things, is a conservative proposition. It is the modern parenthesis that brings with it a frenzy and extremism of emancipation which distorts our understanding of the relation between human and world, and '[b]y stopping being modern, we have become ordinary humans again' (FMOF 8). In other words, the end of the modern constitution does not spell the end of humanity but rather its return to the stage, now that the hubristic, all-conquering superhero of the moderns has finished its strutting and posing.

Liberty is now defined not as non-attachment but as the right not to be deprived of the links that allow us to live (*CM* 122/*MC* 59; see also FF 14/FFe 29). The figure of the earthbound is a cautious Prometheus, recognising that the narratives of emancipation and attachment advance – and have always advanced – together (CP 8). There is a sense in which this way of proceeding stands in opposition to the emancipation narrative, but also an important sense in which it is a continuation of that same narrative. 'How right the revolutionaries were in calling for emancipation', Latour notes, 'And yet what they could not imagine was that there might be another meaning to being attached to the old soil, this time to the Earth' (FG 108). Latour is not against, and has indeed never been against, emancipation per se; what he is against is the modern narrative that foregrounds emancipation while suppressing and ignoring its necessary twin: the narrative of ever-increasing attachments and ever more enfolding of the human into the nonhuman and the nonhuman into the human. If the motto of the modern human is 'emancipation through the throwing off of attachments', then the motto of Latour's earthbound is 'emancipation through the multiplication of attachments'.

What we see here, once more, is not a rejection of the emancipation narrative but its translation, a mediation of the narrative of the moderns that betrays it neither through blind repetition nor through hyper-innovation. It therefore cannot be right to accuse Latour, as does Tom

Cohen, of an unreconstructed modernism in his evocation of a 'modernist parenthesis' and the period of the Anthropocene which, Cohen argues, must necessarily 'be pronounced in a future past tense which the speaker would inhabit':

> Latour seems unaware to what degree he inscribes himself in this specular construction, both by his use of the retro-organicism of the Gaia metaphor and his premise, a signature of the 'modernist' gameboard, of announcing a temporal break and new beginning, the revolutionary hypothesis of his imagined 'parenthesis.'[29]

Cohen, like the moderns themselves, is half right. We can detect in Latour's conjuring with the motif of emancipation a 'signature of the "modernist" gameboard', but it simplifies Latour's move beyond recognition to characterise it as 'a temporal break and a new beginning'. That is a very fine description of the second betrayal which translation explicitly seeks to avoid: the betrayal of too many innovations and the loss of initial intent. As for the 'retro-organicism of the Gaia metaphor', it goes flatly against Latour's own explanation of the term: 'It is not that Gaia is some "sentient being" but that the concept of "Gaia" captures the distributed intentionality of all the agents that are modifying their surroundings to suit themselves better' (FG 66).

The *anthropos* of the Anthropocene is no longer the modern unified agent of the history of ever-increasing emancipation, but 'many different people with contradictory interests, opposing cosmoses and who are summoned under the auspices of warring entities' (FG 81). If the rhetoric of modernism seeks to usher humanity on the wings of progress to a new Adamitic paradise, the *anthropos* of the Anthropocene is 'Babel after the fall of the giant Tower' (FG 81). In this Latour also takes a marked distance from Serres's Great Story, which despite its many branches is indeed one unified story for the whole of humanity.

Conclusion

Latour's human is neither a repetition nor a rejection of the story and structure of modernity. It neither sits comfortably within the modern structure of dualisms, nor does it reject them out of hand. It neither straightforwardly repeats the modern emancipation narrative, nor with its desire to 'emancipate us from emancipation' does it reject it outright. What it does is to twist, divert, re-appropriate and re-purpose both the structure and story of modernity (would that there were a simple translation of the French 'détourner'!) in a way that, faithful to Latour's reconstruction of

Bultmann in his doctoral thesis, navigates between the twin betrayals of mindless repetition and hyper-innovation. Latour, in a word, translates the modern figure of the human into a new, non-modern humanity. In so doing, he circumvents the problems of a host capacity and host substance approach to the human, and also the Enlightenment dogmatism of Michel Serres's Great Story. His account of the human is multi-modal, and therefore not mortgaged to any one capacity (like Badiou and Meillassoux) or even to any one substance (like Malabou) or narrative (like Serres). The parliament of things provides an imperfect mechanism for hearing the voice of the (human and nonhuman) voiceless, addressing a problem that has haunted the studies in this volume. Of all the figures of the human we have considered, it is the least prone to dangerous exclusions and incorporates the greatest diversity of modes.

Conclusion

Any attempt to draw links between and comparatively evaluate such a diverse range of thinkers as those I have discussed in this volume must necessarily be partial, both in the sense of incomplete and also in the sense of motivated by particular commitments and ideas at the expense of others. The analysis in this book has indeed been partial, although in its defence the main target of its critique has been partiality. The foregoing analysis has sought to expose and remedy the partiality of those accounts of the human which rest, in the final analysis, on a determinate host capacity or host substance. It has been argued that they are too restricted and fail to be able to account adequately for the human, and also fail to address difficult questions which arise in relation to (by these theories' own lights) liminal humans who lack the requisite host property.

This critique of partiality has also dictated the order in which the chapters have been placed. From chapter to chapter there is a gradual increase in the number of ways in which the human is figured. Badiou and Meillassoux figure the human in terms of a central host capacity for thought. For Malabou, the emphasis on determinate capacities is replaced by an insistence on human pluripotential de-differentiation, but in her account of the persistence of identity over time the brain emerges as a host substance of humanity and personhood, limiting her figure of the human to a partial 'internalist' account. Michel Serres, in retaining Malabou's introduction of de-differentiation but splicing it with an external account of the human in terms of the narrative of the Great Story, develops what lies only incipiently in Malabou's latest work: a multi-modal figure of the human which does not rely on partiality either of capacities or of narrative, but seeks to benefit from the different aspects of humanity which these two modes can draw out. Bruno Latour travels further in the same direction by multiplying Serres's Great Story into a plurality of mutually irreducible modes of existence none of which is adequate by itself to capture or deliver the essence of the human.

Any single-aspect account of humanity (either in terms of a single capacity, single substance or single relation alone) will leave aside some of the most vulnerable (neonates, the senile), who remain outside the pale of the human. No host capacity, no host discourse, no host substance and no host story are by themselves sufficient. The partiality of this comparative critique is clear to see: it consistently prefers multiple, layered accounts of the human to simple, unitary gatekeepers of humanity. It considers that each mode of accounting for the human will necessarily be partial, and that therefore the greater the number of modes that can coherently and meaningfully be brought together, the better.

But there's the rub. It is relatively easy blithely to multiply different accounts of the human, quite another thing altogether to do so coherently and meaningfully, without reintroducing precisely the sort of partiality that a multi-modal approach seeks to circumvent. It is by no means clear, for example, that in 'Facing Gaia' Latour escapes such a regression. Can the narrative of climate change, Gaia and the beginning of the age of the Anthropocene be considered Latour's 'host story': the starting point from which any account whatever of the human must begin and without which the human is incomprehensible? It certainly emerges as that with which every other story will have to come to terms. Latour's insistence that the Anthropocene does not bring harmony but a war of all against all risks becoming the narrative equivalent of Malabou's self-reflexive meta-capacity for de-differentiation: a sublated meta-story which always already contains all other stories within it. The problem here is what we might call the 'this changes everything' syndrome.[1] Yes, climate change is real. Yes, climate change changes everything. But my point is that climate change is not the only thing that changes everything, even if it is clearly one of the most important and most pressing, and to single it out at the expense of everything else is to regress to the same sort of gatekeeper-ish simplicity that Latour elsewhere works so hard and so effectively to avoid. The problem of climate change is an epoch-defining issue; it will not be tackled effectively, however, if it is made the controlling issue of everything else. Whether or not the Anthropocene emerges as the 'host narrative' of Latour's account of the human, beyond discussion and beyond questioning, remains to be seen, and its touchstone is the extent to which the parliament of things admits discussion of the story itself.

The most robust and most serviceable accounts of the human are those which are multi-modal, seeking to bring together not just multiple capacities, multiple substances or multiple relations, but a variety of different modes of apprehending the human. The modes explored in this book have included substance, capacity and relation, to be sure, but also narrative, which adds an important dimension of externality to our understanding of the persistence of persons over time and also to the situated position of human beings in the seamless world of nature and culture.

A multi-modal approach challenges the partial hegemony of any single account of the human, but without challenging the integrity of any mode of accounting. This is because, while each mode is 'extensive', none is 'exhaustive'. To claim that each mode is extensive is to argue that there is nothing about which it cannot speak. There is no aspect of human exist-ence, for example, about which cognitive neuroscience has nothing to say, no behaviour about which it must remain silent, no word uttered, book written, war waged which it must leave untouched, and the same is true of physics or chemistry, of set or category theory, of psychoanalysis or Marxism or any number of other theoretical discourses. However, none of these discourses should be considered exhaustive. In other words, none of them says everything that there is to say about anything at all. If we are in the mood for neologisms we could call a claim by any one such theoretical discourse utterly to exhaust its object a 'pantasm', from the Greek *panta* (all, every) and recalling the various pre-Socratic attempts to reduce the complexity of reality to one fundamental element: all is water, all is air, all is undetermined.

The human is best considered as a polyphonic composition, not as a melody played on a single instrument, and as a play rather than as a monologue. The human, like being for Aristotle, can and should be said in a number of different ways or, to put it another way, expressed in a plural-ity of genres. This is one reason why Latour's variegated writing styles are no mere stylistic indulgence of postmodern bravado; they are attempts at 'the adjustment of the apparatus [*du dispositif*] to the object' (ŒBL 125) in order to find the appropriate mode of expression for different aspects of human existence. This requires that we loosen our grip on the idea that any single approach can yield the human as such in a non-metaphorical direct way, and relegate all other modes to the status of metaphors. It does not amount to the claim that there is no such thing as the human, or that the human 'as such' is floating somewhere beyond all discourses and we are condemned to approach it only through a fideistic mysticism. It is not necessary to claim that there is anything 'behind' the different modes in order to insist on the need for a plurality of modes.

It has been my judgement in these pages that, of all thinkers consid-ered, Latour brings us closest to this polyphonic, multi-modal account of humanity, though there remain important problems with his position. Perhaps we need something like a parliament of modes. As Latour's parliament of things demonstrates, to choose the way of plurality rather than univocity is far from a stance of non-commitment and far from a refusal to choose. To acknowledge the need for a plurality of mutually irreducible conceptual schemes is to make things not easier, but more difficult. If accounts of the human can either be understood as fundamentally unimodal or multi-modal, then each set of accounts has difficult questions for the other to answer. For the uni-modal: how is it possible to account for everything without reducing it and excluding, through the privileging of a particular host, some of what the approach in question would seek to include? For the multi-modal: how is it possible to hold the different accounts together and avoid them degenerating into a non-committal pick-and-mix eclecticism? To refuse any single, univocal account of the human is not to refuse to choose but to take the hard road of deliberation and the difficult path of seeking to find ways of interweaving incommensurable modes or at least of holding them in what Ricœur would call a 'concordant discordance'.[2] In my estimation it is that challenge that, above all others, will define the success or the failure of the future French thought as it continues to bring forth new figures of the human.

Notes

Introduction

1. The figures of the 'overman' and the 'last man', both first introduced in the Prologue to *Thus Spoke Zarathustra* and later developed sporadically in *Ecce Homo, Beyond Good and Evil* and notably in the madman parable of *The Gay Science* (fragment 125), are Nietzsche's early attempts to come to terms with the death sentence of the human implicit in the declaration of the death of God. For a detailed examination of the complexities of Nietzsche's position, see Christopher Watkin, 'The death of the author: Rancièrian reflections', *Philosophy and Literature* 39, no. 1 (2015): 32–46.
2. As Nietzsche predicted, the madman's message took time to arrive. For an excellent and thorough account of the progress of the discourse around the 'death of man' in French thought, see Stefanos Geroulanos, *An Atheism That Is Not Humanist Emerges in French Thought* (Stanford: Stanford University Press, 2010).
3. See Thomas Baldwin, 'The humanism debate', in Brian Leiter and Michael Rosen (eds), *The Oxford Handbook of Continental Philosophy* (Oxford: Oxford University Press, 2007) 671–710.
4. See Jean Paul Sartre, *Existentialism Is a Humanism*, trans. Annie Cohen-Solal (New Haven: Yale University Press, 2007), and Martin Heidegger, 'Letter on Humanism', in *Martin Heidegger: Basic Writings from 'Being and Time' (1927) to 'The Task of Thinking' (1964)*, ed. David Farrell Krell (San Francisco: Harper and Row, 1978) 217–65.
5. Jean-Paul Sartre, 'Existentialism and Humanism', in *Jean-Paul Sartre: Basic Writings*, ed. Stephen Priest (London: Routledge, 2001) 45.
6. Heidegger, 'Letter on Humanism' 226.
7. For a more detailed discussion of the problems inherent in this linear account of the relation between the deaths of God and man, see Christopher Watkin, 'The death of the author: Rancièrian reflections'.
8. Michel Foucault, *The Order of Things* (London: Routledge, 2005) 373.
9. A legitimate case for an exception can be made for Deleuze, whose reading of Nietzsche (in *Nietzsche and Philosophy*, trans. Janis Tomlinson (New York: Columbia University Press, 1983)) radically departs from Heidegger's reading of his German predecessor (especially in 'Nietzsche's word: God is dead' in *The Question Concerning Technology and Other Essays*, trans. William Lovitt (New York: Harper Torchbooks, 1977) 53–114) and gives him the status of an outlier in his day and a bridging figure to Michel Serres's account of the human. Nevertheless, Deleuze still situates his thought

in terms of the Nietzschean overman, which for Serres and Latour has become a philosophical museum piece.

10. See Michel Foucault, 'What is Enlightenment?' in *The Foucault Reader*, ed. Paul Rainbow (New York: Pantheon Books, 1984) 32–50.

11. See Jacques Derrida, 'The ends of man', in *Margins of Philosophy*, trans. Alan Bass (Chicago: University of Chicago Press, 1972) 111–36.

12. See Richard Kearney, *Anatheism: Returning to God after God* (New York: Columbia University Press, 2010).

13. The emphasis on enhancement emerges clearly, for example, in Nick Bostrom, 'Transhumanist values', in Frederick Adams (ed.), *Ethical Issues for the Twenty-First Century* (Charlottesville: Philosophical Documentation Center Press, 2003) 3–14.

14. See, as a representative example, the general wave-of-the-hand gesture by Victoria Pitts-Taylor that 'For those pursuing posthumanism at various levels, plasticity renders the world as an infinite source of "wideware" for the brain, and positions the individual brain as inherently connected to others – things, artifacts, other brains' ('The plastic brain: neoliberalism and the neuronal self', *Health* 14, no. 6 (2010): 635–52, 646).

15. Michel Serres, *The Parasite*, trans. Lawrence R. Schehr, ed. Cary Wolfe (Minneapolis: University of Minnesota Press, 2007).

16. I have not found one reference to the terms 'posthumanism' or 'transhumanism' in all the Serres I have read. Whether or not the odd reference exists, it is certainly not his preferred way to describe his own thought.

17. Claire Colebrook, 'Post-Human Humanities', in Bernd Herzogenrath (ed.), *Time and History in Deleuze and Serres* (London: Continuum, 2012) 103–26, 104–5.

18. Colebrook, 'Post-Human Humanities' 106.

19. Colebrook, 'Post-Human Humanities' 110.

20. Colebrook, 'Post-Human Humanities' 107.

21. Latour makes similar arguments on WFG 3, PES 3 and FG 78.

22. Colebrook, 'Post-Human Humanities' 105.

23. It is for this reason that the sort of 'transhumanism' advocated by Nick Bostrom and others is cast, in the light of this volume's thinkers, as a profound misunderstanding of the history of humanity. With its objective of transcending the human condition through biological, cognitive or technological enhancements, it still inscribes itself within the dichotomy of Nietzsche's last man and overman. It is certainly more indebted to the discourse around the death of God and the end of man that the thinkers considered in this book, and almost always more indebted than it realises.

24. See for example the affirmation that 'we must take yet another step, another post-, and realize that the nature of thought itself must change if it is to be posthumanist' (Cary Wolfe, *What Is Posthumanism?* (Minneapolis: University of Minnesota Press, 2010) xvi).

25. Even a whistle-stop tour of the history of the term reveals a number of overlapping and evolving meanings. To date, three broad stages can usefully be discerned in the recent progress of posthumanism. The first is a mechanistic and techno-mechanical posthumanism, exemplified in Donna Haraway's 'A cyborg manifesto: science, technology, and socialist-feminism in the late twentieth century', in *Simians, Cyborgs and Women: The Reinvention of Nature* (New York: Routledge, 1991) 149–81. Secondly, in the twenty-first century the centre of gravity of the posthuman moved to considering the animal, a signal volume in this shift being Cary Wolfe's *Animal Rites: American Culture, The Discourse of Species, and Posthumanist Theory* (Chicago: Chicago University Press, 2003) and, in the French tradition, Jacques Derrida's *The Animal That Therefore I Am*, trans. David Wills (New York: Fordham University Press, 2009) and the two volumes of *The Beast and the Sovereign*, trans. Geoffrey Bennington (Chicago: University of Chicago Press, 2011). In recent years a third focus has begun to emerge, enlarging the sphere of posthumanism's concern from the animal to the ecological,

including a critique of the ideology behind previous posthumanisms. See Timothy Morton, *Ecology Without Nature: Rethinking Environmental Aesthetics* (Cambridge, MA: Harvard University Press, 2007).

26. John Mullarkey, *Post-Continental Philosophy* (London: Continuum, 2006) 1.
27. Mullarkey, *Post-Continental Philosophy* 1.
28. Mullarkey, *Post-Continental Philosophy* 4.
29. Mullarkey, *Post-Continental Philosophy* 3.
30. See Iris van der Tuin, 'Non-reductive continental naturalism in the contemporary humanities: working with Hélène Metzger's philosophical reflections', *History of the Human Sciences* 26, no. 2 (2013): 88–105.
31. John Mullarkey, 'Deleuze and materialism: one or several matters?', in *A Deleuzian Century?*, ed. Ian Buchanan (Durham, NC: Duke University Press, 1999) 59–83.
32. Mullarkey, *Post-Continental Philosophy* 2.
33. Ian James, *The New French Philosophy* (Cambridge: Polity Press, 2012) 9.
34. James, *The New French Philosophy* 3.
35. James, *The New French Philosophy* 4.
36. James, *The New French Philosophy* 83.
37. James, *The New French Philosophy* 5.
38. James, *The New French Philosophy* 5–6.
39. Alexander R. Galloway, *Les Nouveaux Réalistes* (Paris: Editions Léo Scheer, 2012).
40. Galloway, *Les Nouveaux Réalistes* 12.
41. Galloway, *Les Nouveaux Réalistes* 12.
42. Galloway, *Les Nouveaux Réalistes* 11.
43. See Dennis Bruining, 'A somatechnics of moralism: new materialism or material foundationalism', *Somatechnics* 3, no. 1 (2013): 149–68, and also the discussion of Latour's textual paradigm in Chapter 6.
44. Levi Bryant, Nick Srnicek and Graham Harman, 'Towards a speculative philosophy', in Levi Bryant, Nick Srnicek and Graham Harman (eds), *The Speculative Turn: Continental Materialism and Realism* (Melbourne: re.press, 2011) 3.
45. Meillassoux himself is happy to admit this. His attempt is to undermine correlationism from the inside, and he does not hide that he shares the correlationist's assumptions as a strategic incipit and in order to elaborate a critique of correlationism which the correlationist herself cannot possibly avoid.
46. Mullarkey, *Post-Continental Philosophy* 2.
47. James, *The New French Philosophy* 185.
48. Paul Ennis, *Continental Realism* (Winchester: Zero Books, 2011), preface.
49. See Adrian Johnston, *Prolegomena to Any Future Materialism: The Outcome of Contemporary French Philosophy* (Evanston: Northwestern University Press, 2013).
50. James, *The New French Philosophy* 10.
51. In a remarkable volume, Luigi Romeo provides fully 165 pages of *homo* epithets, with an average of around five per page. See Luigi Romeo, *Ecce Homo!: A Lexicon of Man* (Amsterdam: John Benjamins Publishing Company, 1979). *Ecce Homo!* contains not only epithets intended to specify the nature of human uniqueness but also all adjectives appended to the noun *homo* in ancient Roman literature.
52. As will become clear in the following paragraphs, the tripartite schema does not label mutually exclusive categories but rather emphases and tendencies, and the three categories are almost always interdependent.
53. I have no desire to die on the hill of this being the only way of subdividing *homo* epithets, and the argument of this book does not crumble if there are other ways of getting the job done. I am willing to argue, however, that the taxonomy suggested here makes good sense of the range of uses into which *homo* epithets are pressed, and that it arranges the different permutations into a reasonable and heuristically serviceable schema.

54. This taxonomy itself is not an *ex nihilo* invention. It bears affinities with the now classical threefold division of interpretations of the *imago dei* motif of Genesis 1: 27, first elaborated by Millard J. Erickson in *Christian Theology* (Grand Rapids: Baker Academic, 1983). The theological repartition falls into the categories of 'substance', 'function' and 'relation'. I have preferred 'capacity' to 'function' as the latter term suggests a divinely ordained meaning to human life or an Aristotelian final cause of the human that is out of place in a discussion of contemporary French thought. Erickson's schema serves as a tool for analysing theories of artificial intelligence in Noreen Herzfeld, *In Our Image: Artificial Intelligence and the Human Spirit* (Minneapolis: Fortress Press, 2002).

55. A similar distinction between specificity and uniqueness is employed by Warren S. Brown in 'Nonreductive human uniqueness: immaterial, biological, or psychosocial?', in Nancey Murphy (ed.), *Human Identity at the Intersection of Science, Technology and Religion* (Aldershot: Ashgate, 2010) 98.

56. Diogenes Laërtius, *Lives of Eminent Philosophers*, vol. 2, books 6–10, trans. R. D. Hicks (Cambridge, MA: Harvard University Press, 2000) 43.

57. Thomas Aquinas, *Summa Theologiae: Volume 13, Man Made to God's Image: 1a. 90–102*, ed. Edmund Hill (Cambridge: Cambridge University Press, 2006) 71.

58. See Jean-Pierre Changeux, *Neuronal Man: The Biology of Mind*, trans. Laurence Garet (New York: Parthenon Books, 1985).

59. Joseph LeDoux, *Synaptic Self: How Our Brains Become Who We Are* (New York: Penguin Books, 2003) ix, 323–4.

60. The exact phrase is not to be found in Aristotle. At *Politics* 1253a Aristotle argues that 'man alone of the animals possesses *logos*', where it is more reasonable to understand *logos* to refer to the capacity for speech than the capacity for rational thought. In the *Nicomachean Ethics* (1098a) he argues that, while humans share sentience with other animals, they are alone in possessing *logos* and it serves as a means to their happiness. In this instance it seems more reasonable to understand *logos* as the capacity for rational thought. This latter interpretation is even clearer at the beginning of the *Metaphysics* (980b), where he claims that humans alone live by reason. I am indebted for this summary to the analysis in David Mevorach Seidenberg, *Kabbalah and Ecology* (Cambridge: Cambridge University Press, 2015) 62 nn187–8.

61. Anselm of Canterbury, *Basic Writings* (La Salle: Open Court, 1962) 132.

62. J. Wentzel van Huyssteen, *Alone in the World?: Human Uniqueness in Science and Theology* (Grand Rapids: Eerdmans, 2006) 147.

63. See Ernst Cassirer, *An Essay on Man: An Introduction to a Philosophy of Human Culture* (New Haven: Yale University Press, 1972).

64. See Friedrich Schiller, *On the Aesthetic Education of Man in a Series of Letters*, ed. E. M. Wilkinson and L. A. Willoughby (New York: Oxford University Press, 1983).

65. Johan Huizinga, *Homo Ludens* (London: Routledge, 2014).

66. Hans Jonas, '*Homo pictor* and the differentia of man', *Social Research* 29, no. 2 (1962): 201–20.

67. Brown, 'Nonreductive human uniqueness' 98.

68. The *zoon politikon* relies heavily, to be sure, on the capacity for language in the exchange of opinions within the polis, but nevertheless its emphasis if not its foundation is different to the *zoon logon echon*.

69. John Stuart Mill, 'On the definition of political economy; and on the method of investigation proper to it', in *Essays on Some Unsettled Questions of Political Economy* (London: John W. Parker, 1844) 120–64, 137.

70. Peter L. Berger and Thomas Luckmann, *The Social Construction of Reality: A Treatise in the Sociology of Knowledge* (Garden City, NY: Doubleday, 1966).

71. Gabriel Marcel, *Homo Viator: Introduction to a Metaphysic of Hope*, trans. Emma Craufurd (Chicago: Henry Regency Company, 1951).

72. Noreen Herzfeld, 'Creating in our own image: artificial intelligence and the image of

God', *Zygon* 37, no. 2 (2002): 303–16, 308, quoting Karl Barth, *Church Dogmatics III/2: The Doctrine of Creation*, trans. J. W. Edwards, O. Bussey and Harold Knight, ed. G. W. Bromiley and T. F. Torrance (Edinburgh: T&T Clark, 1958) 249.

73. John E. Coons and Patrick M. Brennan, *By Nature Equal: The Anatomy of a Western Insight* (Princeton: Princeton University Press, 1999).

74. Coons and Brennan, *By Nature Equal* 39.

75. See Jean-Pierre Changeux and Alain Connes, *Conversations on Mind, Matter, and Mathematics*, trans. M. B. DeBevoise (Princeton: Princeton University Press, 1995) 7–11.

76. Philip Schaff (ed.), *NPNF2-08. Saint Gregory of Nyssa: Ascetic and Moral Treatises, Philosophical Works, Apologetic Works, Oratorical Works, Letters*. Nicene and Post-Nicene Church Fathers: Series 2, vol. 8 (Edinburgh: T&T Clark, 2015) 90.

77. Giovanni Pico della Mirandola, *Oration on the Dignity of Man: A New Translation and Commentary*, ed. Francesco Borghesi, Michael Papio and Massimo Riva (Cambridge: Cambridge University Press, 2012) 115.

78. Della Mirandola, *Oration on the Dignity of Man* 117.

79. Della Mirandola, *Oration on the Dignity of Man* 117.

80. Della Mirandola, *Oration on the Dignity of Man* 121.

81. Giorgio Agamben, *The Open: Man and Animal*, trans. Kevin Attell (Stanford: Stanford University Press, 2004) 29.

82. Jean-Paul Sartre, *Being and Nothingness: An Essay on Phenomenological Philosophy*, trans. Hazel E. Barnes (London: Routledge, 2003) 58.

83. See Friedrich Nietzsche, *Beyond Good and Evil: Prelude to a Philosophy of the Future*, trans. Walter Kaufmann (New York: Vintage Books, 1966) 62.

84. In offering a transferrable threefold schema of interpretation it does something more valuable than provide such a quickly out-of-date snapshot of an *état présent*: it offers road markers and signposts in order to plot any number of further positions on its map of routes for returning to the human. Jacques Rancière, it will be noted for example, takes a predominantly host capacity approach to the human; moral equality is among 'speaking beings' (see Jacques Rancière, *Disagreement: Politics and Philosophy*, trans. Julie Rose (Minneapolis: University of Minnesota Press, 1999) 16). For a comparative critique of Rancière and Badiou in this respect, see Christopher Watkin, 'Thinking equality today: Badiou, Rancière and Nancy', *French Studies* 67, no. 4 (2013): 522–34)). The humanism that is currently being recovered from Gilbert Simondon's work bears close affinities to a Serresian approach which lifts the boundary between the human and the nonhuman, between nature and culture, without for all that losing sight of human distinctiveness altogether. (For a sketch of Simondon's humanism, see Jean-Hugues Barthélémy, 'What new humanism today?', *Cultural Politics* 6, no. 2 (2010): 237–52).) The interweaving of the technological, cultural, natural and ecological inherent in Serres's *Grand Récit* bears comparison with Simondon's own relational ontology in *On the Mode of Being of Technical Objects*. (See Gilbert Simondon, *Du mode d'existence des objets techniques* (Paris: Aubier Montaigne, 2012)). Bernard Stiegler, for his part, can be read as crossing the qualitative approach with an embrace of technics that shares much in common with the place of technology in Serres's Great Story. The latter similarity is briefly hinted at in the exchange between Serres and Stiegler entitled 'Pourquoi nous n'apprendrons plus comme avant', available at <http://www.philomag.com/les-videos/michel-serres-et-bernard-stiegler-moteurs-de-recherche-3244> (last accessed 2 November 2015). Stiegler's own discussion of humanism takes place in the first two volumes of *La Technique et le temps* (Paris: Galilée, 1994; 1996). Any number of further examples could be approached and analysed using the methodology set out in these pages.

Chapter 1

1. 'Man is an animal enclosed outside his cage. He moves beyond himself.' Paul Valéry, *Œuvres complètes*, vol. 2, Bibliothèque de la Pléiade (Paris: Gallimard, 1960) 525.

2. Alexander Galloway and Ian James both discuss Badiou in their surveys of recent French thought, highlighting his materialism as an important defining characteristic. See Ian James, *The New French Philosophy* (Cambridge: Polity Press, 2012); Alexander R. Galloway, *Les Nouveaux Réalistes* (Paris: Editions Léo Scheer, 2012). In his introduction to *Alain Badiou, une trajectoire polémique* (Paris: La Fabrique, 2009) Bruno Bosteels situates Badiou primarily as a materialist philosopher. Adrian Johnston gives a prominent place to discussions of Badiou in the first volume of his *Prolegomena to Any Future Materialism: The Outcome of Contemporary French Philosophy* (Evanston: Northwestern University Press, 2013), in the main to argue that Badiou is not sufficiently materialist. Geoff Pfeifer puts Badiou at the heart of new materialist thinking in *The New Materialism: Althusser, Badiou, and Žižek* (London: Routledge, 2015).

3. Ed Pluth is a notable exception to this general neglect. See Ed Pluth, *Badiou: A Philosophy of the New* (Cambridge: Polity Press, 2010).

4. For an explanation of the idea and importance of a 'host' capacity, see the Introduction to this volume, p. 13.

5. The phrase comes of course from Jean-Paul Sartre, *Being and Nothingness: An Essay on Phenomenological Philosophy*, trans. Hazel E. Barnes (London: Routledge, 2003). Sartre refers to human consciousness or human reality as 'a being which is what it is not and which is not what it is' (p. 58). In this chapter I am arguing that the human 'is what it is not, and is not what it is' in a way that departs from Sartre's concern with nihilating consciousness. What I mean by the phrase in relation to Badiou is that the human has consistently been conceptualised as requiring an irreducible supplement of the nonhuman or the inhuman in order to be human at all. In the Western tradition, the human is not what it is without either incorporating or being incorporated into that which it is not.

6. My use of the term 'human+' here is not to be confused with the organisation 'Humanity+', which began life as the World Transhumanist Association. Whereas the organisation uses the term 'humanity+' to refer to the project of 'elevating the human condition', driven by 'a new generation of thinkers who dare to envision humanity's next steps' (see <http://humanityplus.org/about/> (last accessed 2 November 2015)), the argument of this chapter is that humanity has always conformed to the grammar of 'human+'. Humanity *simpliciter* is humanity+.

7. Alain Badiou, *Le Siècle* (Paris: Editions du Seuil, 2005) 246; *The Century*, trans. Alberto Toscano (Cambridge: Polity Press, 2007) 168. For more detail, see Badiou's seminar from 2000–1 entitled 'Le Siècle', available at <http://www.entretemps.asso.fr/Badiou/00-01.1.htm> (last accessed 2 November 2015).

8. Jean-Paul Sartre, *The Problem of Method*, trans. Hazel E. Barnes (London: Methuen, 1963).

9. Michel Foucault, *The Order of Things* (London: Routledge, 2005).

10. Foucault, *The Order of Things* 421.

11. Luc Ferry and Alain Renaut (eds), *Why We Are Not Nietzscheans* (Chicago: University of Chicago Press, 1997).

12. Ed Pluth makes this point well. See *Badiou*, 105–6.

13. The transcription of the seminars is freely available online. While not reviewed by Badiou and therefore 'not committing him' as the URL's disclaimer has it, they are nevertheless full prose transcriptions of the seminars, providing valuable further information on ideas sometimes covered more briefly in the published works. See <http://www.entretemps.asso.fr/Badiou/seminaire.htm> (last accessed 2 November 2015).

Fayard are presently publishing the seminars in a series of printed books. All translations from the seminars are my own.

14. *Aristotle: Nicomachean Ethics*, ed. and trans. Roger Crisp (Cambridge: Cambridge University Press, 2000) 196.

15. In the passage from 'The enigmatic relationship between philosophy and politics' quoted above, Badiou says that these victories are won by man 'over his immanent element of inhumanity' (*RE* 48/*PM* 42). Badiou employs the term 'inhumanity' in two senses, one positive and one negative, and it is the negative sense which is intended here, according to which the inhuman is that to which humanity is reduced without the immortality of the idea.

16. Pluth, *Badiou* 204.

17. The equation of human specificity with upright posture is made by Aquinas in the *Summa Theologica* and by Johann Gottfried Herder in the essay 'Organic difference between animals and man'. Appeals to rationality or intelligence are legion, from Aristotle's 'rational animal' in the *Nicomachean Ethics*, through Anselm and Aquinas to many contemporary authors. The idea that humanity is distinguished by an ability to play can be traced to Friedrich Schiller's *On the Aesthetic Education of Man* and Johan Huizinga's *Homo Ludens*.

18. This is one of the ways in which Badiou's account of the human differs from that of Jacques Rancière, for whom language is indeed the determinative capacity. See Christopher Watkin, 'Thinking equality today', *French Studies* 67, no. 4 (2013): 522–34.

19. Pluth, *Badiou* 126.

20. Pluth, *Badiou* 127.

21. 'I think that human beings are animals, animals which have at their disposal a singular ability, a singular, aleatory, and partial ability, which identifies them philosophically as human, within the animal sphere' (*Eth* 132). See also '"the human", or "man" [*l'homme*], are words that designate the capacity to be incorporated into a truth procedure' (*Cont* 120; my translation).

22. Adrian Johnston, Michael Burns and Brian Smith, 'Materialism, subjectivity and the outcome of French philosophy: interview with Adrian Johnston by Michael Burns & Brian Smith', *Cosmos and History: The Journal of Natural and Social Philosophy* 7, no. 1 (2011): 167–81, 175.

23. John Milbank and Slavoj Žižek, *The Monstrosity of Christ* (Cambridge, MA: MIT Press, 2009) 93.

24. Slavoj Žižek, *In Defense of Lost Causes* (London: Verso, 2008) 343.

25. Nina Power, 'Towards an anthropology of infinitude: Badiou and the political subject', *Cosmos and History: The Journal of Natural and Social Philosophy* 2, no. 1–2 (2006): 186–209, 209.

26. Johnston, *Prolegomena* 92.

27. Johnston, *Prolegomena* 97.

28. Bosteels, *Alain Badiou* 122–3.

29. Bosteels, *Alain Badiou* 66.

30. Bosteels, *Alain Badiou* 115.

31. Alberto Toscano, 'A plea for Prometheus', *Critical Horizons* 10, no. 2 (2009) : 241–56, 252.

32. Toscano, 'A plea for Prometheus' 253.

33. Pluth, *Badiou* 129.

34. Pluth, *Badiou* 184.

35. Pluth, *Badiou* 136.

36. Pluth, *Badiou* 136; original emphasis.

37. Pluth, *Badiou* 129.

38. Sartre of course affirms that there is no situation in which a consciousness does not exert some freedom of choice, that 'even the red hot pincers of the torturer do not exempt me from being free' (Sartre, *Being and Nothingness* 506). Sartre later qualifies

the statement, but nevertheless stands as an emblematic (and for some unconscionable) affirmation of his doctrine of freedom.

39. Toscano, 'A plea for Prometheus' 253.
40. See Michael O'Neill Burns, 'Prolegomena to a materialist humanism', *Angelaki* 19, no. 1 (2014): 99–112.
41. Burns, 'Prolegomena to a materialist humanism' 105.
42. *LM* 98/*LW* 87, quoted on Burns, 'Prolegomena to a materialist humanism' 106; my emphasis.
43. *LM* 42/*LW* 33, quoted on Burns, 'Prolegomena to a materialist humanism' 105.
44. Burns, 'Prolegomena to a materialist humanism' 106.
45. Burns, 'Prolegomena to a materialist humanism' 106.
46. Burns, 'Prolegomena to a materialist humanism' 106.
47. Pluth, *Badiou* 129.
48. Pluth, *Badiou* 129.
49. This is not to claim that Badiou is a closet theologian, an accusation which can be all too hastily bandied about. Why, if a particular motif or way of thinking arises in both a theological and an atheistic frame of thinking, should it be assumed that the motif or idea in question is necessarily theological and present in the atheistic thought only as a wolf in sheep's clothing? The latent assumption in this approach is that Christianity has the undisputed copyright on all the forms of thinking it deploys. If a particular motif arises both within Christian theology and in atheistic thought, it makes just as much sense quickly to conclude that Christianity is, after all, atheistic as it does to say that the atheist thought in question is, by virtue of this similarity alone, theologically contaminated. I have written elsewhere about the inclination towards 'ornitheology' among atheistic philosophers, searching out purportedly theological motifs in every bush and thicket. See <http://christopherwatkin.com/2013/12/06/of-ornitheology/> (last accessed 2 November 2015).
50. Pluth, *Badiou* 8.
51. Pluth, *Badiou* 85.
52. Pluth, *Badiou* 105.
53. Pluth, *Badiou* 120.
54. Pluth, *Badiou* 182.
55. Pluth, *Badiou* 182.

Chapter 2

1. David Hume, *Dialogues Concerning Natural Religion*, ed. Dorothy Coleman (Cambridge: Cambridge University Press, 2007) 24.
2. We see an instance of this in 'The immanence of the world beyond' when he says that 'I am interested in the Eternal Return insofar as it is generally scorned by contemporary philosophers and commentators' (IWB 466).
3. Adrian Johnston makes this point when he argues that:

> For Meillassoux, hyper-Chaos testifies to 'the inexistence of the divine' to the extent that positing this absolute contingency correlatively entails denying the existence of the divinity of metaphysical theosophy (as though the signifier 'God' can and does refer exclusively to this sort of divine as its invariant, one-and-only signified). (Adrian Johnston, *Prolegomena to Any Future Materialism: The Outcome of Contemporary French Philosophy* (Evanston: Northwestern University Press, 2013) 168)

In a point that it is not meet to develop in this chapter, there is a certain irony in Johnston's charge here because he himself risks a similar confusion between divine genus and species, particularly in relation to the question of polytheism.

4. I have found Robert S. Gall's work very helpful in clarifying this double definition of religion in Meillassoux. See Robert S. Gall, 'Fideism or faith in doubt? Meillassoux, Heidegger and the end of metaphysics', *Philosophy Today* 57 (2013): 358–68, 360.

5. The sentence is quoted, from page 213 of Quentin Meillassoux's revised version of 'L'Inexistence divine', by Graham Harman. See Harman, *Quentin Meillassoux* 109.

6. In *Difficult Atheism* I discuss at length Meillassoux's superficially paradoxical but fundamentally coherent approach to the religious as a strategy of 'theological integration', seeking to maintain the benefits of religious belief (which, for Meillassoux, are principally related to the hope for universal justice for the dead) while jettisoning its ontological baggage (namely a God who is responsible for the atrocities and suffering of the world). See Christopher Watkin, *Difficult Atheism: Post-Theological Thinking in Alain Badiou, Jean-Luc Nancy and Quentin Meillassoux* (Edinburgh: Edinburgh University Press, 2011) 11–15.

7. Romans 13: 12, New International Version.

8. 1 Thessalonians 5: 4–6, New International Version.

9. On one occasion in IWB, the translation is given as 'vectorial subject' (p. 463), and on all other occasions as 'vectorial subject'. Only 'vectorial' exists in the *OED*, and so in a spirit of lexical parsimony I have chosen in the current chapter to use the recognised English term rather than coining a neologism. I have left quotations from IWB as they stand in the original.

10. The sentence is quoted, from page 225 of Quentin Meillassoux's revised version of 'L'Inexistence divine', by Graham Harman. See Harman, *Quentin Meillassoux* 116.

11. It is just this sort of a laying aside of power that forms one of the earliest hymn or liturgy fragments of the Christian church, quoted by Paul in his letter to the Philippian church:

> Have this mind among yourselves, which is yours in Christ Jesus, who, though he was in the form of God, did not count equality with God a thing to be grasped, but emptied himself, by taking the form of a servant, being born in the likeness of men. And being found in human form, he humbled himself by becoming obedient to the point of death, even death on a cross. Therefore God has highly exalted him and bestowed on him the name that is above every name, so that at the name of Jesus every knee should bow, in heaven and on earth and under the earth, and every tongue confess that Jesus Christ is Lord, to the glory of God the Father. (Philippians 2: 5–11, English Standard Version)

12. The universality of Meillassoux's equality is a limited universality. He gives no indication that he includes nonhuman entities in the coming of universal justice, and to date he has not written an equivalent piece to Bruno Latour's 'Can non-humans be saved?' Given that he holds the ultimate value of the human to be an 'insupportably banal assertion' (ExID 210), we should not hold our breath.

13. See pages 11–12.

14. 'Humans are in fact defined by their access to truth, understood as the eternal contingency of that which is' (ExID 190–1). Meillassoux goes on to develop this definition in terms of the other worlds. First, he affirms that the three Worlds of matter, life and thought 'represent the three constitutive orders of the human. Whatever might be the laws of matter, of forms of life, or of intellectual or artistic inventions – whatever the various intra-Worldly advents might be – the three Worlds remain the definitional invariants of the human as a being of reason' (ExID 191). Finally, he concludes that 'humans are also defined by their relation to a fourth World' of justice (ExID 191).

15. Michael O'Neill Burns, 'Prolegomena to a materialist humanism', *Angelaki* 19, no. 1 (2014): 99–112, 109. Burns is quoting IWB 461.

16. Harman, *Quentin Meillassoux* 109.

17. It would be going too far to attribute this troubling position to Meillassoux without further clarification. For the moment, it suffices to say that it is difficult to see how some liminal cases of humanity could qualify as 'human' under the definition offered by Meillassoux: 'Humans are in fact defined by their access to truth, understood as the eternal contingency of that which is' (ExID 190–1).

18. It is a failure to address the issue of hyperchaos that renders inadequate the discussion of the materiality of thought in Leon Niemoczynski's '21st century speculative philosophy'. He concludes that 'while thought and being are indeed distinct, as Meillassoux states, this is not to say that neither are not material, not natural, or are not conducive to speculative or scientific thinking', but this is only the case if thought is not itself subject to hyperchaotic change. See Leon Niemoczynski, '21st century speculative philosophy: reflections on the "new metaphysics" and its realism and materialism', *Cosmos and History: The Journal of Natural and Social Philosophy* 9, no. 2 (2013): 13–31, 21.

19. Peter Gratton, *Speculative Realism: Problems and Prospects* (London: Bloomsbury, 2014) 74.

20. To be sure, meaningless or nonsense words can occur in natural languages, but such occurrences are a non-necessary feature of such languages. By contrast, the meaningless sign is integral to formal languages (see IRR 22–3).

21. I have found Fabio Gironi's analysis of Meillassoux's meaningless sign insightful, and my own analysis is indebted to it. See Fabio Gironi, 'Science-laden theory: outlines of an unsettled alliance', *Speculations* 1 (2010): 9–46.

22. '[B]ecause I speculate upon the absolute, *I prohibit myself entirely from speaking of that which is*, not to mention that which could be. For that which is, is wholly contingent – and this, indeed, in a vaster sense than that of ordinary or transcendental contingency, which are restrained in various ways by physical laws or by the categories. According to me, anything whatsoever can happen – any world whatsoever can succeed any other' (IRR 12; original emphasis).

23. This is not an attempt at an exhaustive list but a focus on the points most relevant to the current argument. Other objections have been raised to Meillassoux's mathematisation, notably that he discounts the corporeality of mathematical reasoning or that it plays into the hands of capitalism. For corporeality, see Rick Dolphijn, 'The end of (wo)man', in Rick Dolphijn and Iris van der Tuin (eds), *New Materialism: Interviews and Cartographies* (Ann Arbor: Open Humanities Press, 2012) 173–4. For capitalism, see Alexander R. Galloway, 'The poverty of philosophy and post-Fordism', *Critical Inquiry* 39 (2013): 347–66.

24. Peter Hallward, 'Anything is possible: review essay on Quentin Meillassoux, *After Finitude*', *Radical Philosophy*, 152 (2008): 51–7, 56.

25. See Nathan Brown, 'The speculative and the specific: on Hallward and Meillassoux', in Levi Bryant, Nick Srnicek and Graham Harman (eds), *The Speculative Turn: Continental Materialism and Realism* (Melbourne: re.press, 2011) 144–5.

26. Brown, 'The speculative and the specific' 144–5.

27. Brown, 'The speculative and the specific' 145.

28. '[S]peculation assures all other disciplines of thought that they alone have the right to describe and to explain (in a non-necessarist form) the world in which we live. My materialism is so far from being hostile to empiricism, that in fact it aims to found the absolute necessity of the latter' (IRR 12).

29. Graham Harman, *The Quadruple Object* (Winchester: Zero Books, 2011) 63.

30. In addition to Graham Harman, the argument could equally be made in relation to Ray Brassier when he insists, for example, that:

> [N]ihilism is . . . the unavoidable corollary of the realist conviction that there is a mind-independent reality, which, despite the presumptions of human narcissism, is indifferent to our existence and oblivious to the 'values' and 'mean-

ings' which we would drape over it in order to make it more hospitable. (Ray Brassier, *Nihil Unbound* (Basingstoke: Palgrave Macmillan, 2007) xi)

Similarly, Peter Gratton cites from John Nolt a phrase 'which could act as a credo for the disparate speculative realists, who if not anti-humanists, are at least offering an approach beyond humanism: "I have tried to show that we (whoever we are) are not that big a deal"' (John Nolt, 'An argument for metaphysical realism', *Journal for General Philosophy of Science* 35, no. 1 (2004): 71–90, 86; quoted on Gratton, *Speculative Realism* 52). We are the sort of creature who can, with a philosophical tour de force, show to our own satisfaction just how unimportant we are, taking our dignity away at the same moment we restore it through the back door. Demonstrating our unimportance seems to be very important to us.

31. John Stuart Mill, *On Liberty and Other Essays* (Oxford: Oxford University Press, 2008) 140.
32. Ray Brassier and Marcin Rychter, 'I am a nihilist because I still believe in truth: Ray Brassier interviewed by Marcin Rychter', *Kronos* 4 (2011), available at <http://www. kronos.org.pl/index.php?23151,896> (last accessed 2 November 2015).
33. Brassier, *Nihil Unbound* 58.
34. Gall, 'Fideism or faith in doubt?' 360–1.
35. The fourth world of Justice being as yet an inexistent hope, I will leave it aside in this discussion.
36. In *After Finitude* 'subjectialism' was called 'subjectivist metaphysics' (IRR 4).
37. Insofar as Berkeley's philosophy is both speculative and realist, Meillassoux in IRR finds that the designation 'speculative realist' fails to distinguish him from the subjectialist position he is seeking to critique (IRR 6).
38. Gratton, *Speculative Realism* 37.
39. Johnston, *Prolegomena* 155.
40. Johnston, *Prolegomena* 135.
41. Gratton, *Speculative Realism* 17.
42. See Watkin, *Difficult Atheism* 148–53.
43. This principle is the closest Meillassoux gets to a refutation of Berkeleyan idealism: if the principle of factiality is true then idealist subjectialism is false; if speculative materialism is true then speculative idealism is false: 'strong correlationism cannot be refuted by the absolutization of the correlation as believed by the subjectivist, but rather by the absolutization of facticity (wherein resides the meaning of the principle of factiality)' (IntDT 75).
44. Earlier in IRR he introduces a threefold distinction within what are here called deutero-absolutising properties, between (1) that which is 'contingent', namely 'every entity, thing or event that I know is capable of not being, or could have not been, or could have been other'; (2) that which is 'fact', namely 'every type of entity whose being-other I can conceive of, but of which we do not know whether it could, effectively, have been other than it is', including the laws of physics; and (3) 'arche-fact', or 'any fact which I cannot, in any way, conceive of as being other than it is, or as not being, but whose necessity I nevertheless cannot prove – in which regard we must say that it is a fact, in the broad sense' (IRR 9). For the correlationist, correlation is an arche-fact.

Chapter 3

1. 'I am the wound, and rapier! | I am the cheek, I am the slap! | I am the limbs, I am the rack, | The victim and the torturer!' Charles Baudelaire, *L'Héautontimorouménos*, in *Flowers of Evil*, trans. James McGowan (Oxford: Oxford University Press, 1993) 157, translation altered.

2. For an explanation of the term 'host capacity', see the Introduction to this volume, p. 13.

3. Although the differences between the terms 'cognitive science', 'neuroscience' and 'cognitive neuroscience' are not universally stable or observed, the following norms are to be noted. 'Cognitive science' often acts as a broad umbrella term designating 'the study of intelligence and intelligent systems, with particular reference to intelligent behaviour as computation' (H. A. Simon and C. A. Kaplan, 'Foundations of cognitive science', in M. I. Posner (ed.), *Foundations of Cognitive Science* (Cambridge, MA: MIT Press, 1989) 1). The neurological aspect of cognition is not necessarily in the foreground of cognitive science, which can also refer to nonhuman cognition and embraces psychology, artificial intelligence, linguistics, neuroscience, anthropology, and philosophy (*Stanford Encyclopedia of Philosophy*, available at <http://plato.stanford.edu/entries/cognitive-science/> (last accessed 2 November 2015)). 'Neuroscience' is another umbrella term, this time for 'any or all of the sciences, such as neurochemistry and experimental psychology, which deal with the structure or function of the nervous system and brain' (*OED*). It follows that the field of 'cognitive neuroscience' studies the intelligence and cognition in the brain and nervous system of humans and other animals. Throughout the discussion in this chapter I will normally use the term 'neuroscience' to describe the brain research with which Malabou engages, given (1) the central role of the synapse in her account of plasticity, (2) her engagement with the synaptic paradigm beyond an interest in the processes of cognition, and (3) her relative disinterest in non-neural modes of cognition.

4. Martin Heidegger, *What Is Called Thinking?*, trans. J. Glenn Gray (New York: Harper & Row, 1968) 13.

5. This turn of phrase is taken from Michael T. H. Wong, 'Hermeneutics, neuroscience and theological anthropology', in Eric Weislogel (ed.), *Transdisciplinarity in Science and Religion* (Bucharest: Curtea Veche, 2008) 184.

6. Section 1, subsection A of Hegel's *Philosophy of Mind*: §§388–412. See *Hegel's Philosophy of Mind: Being Part Three of the Encyclopaedia of Philosophical Sciences*, trans. William Wallace (Oxford: Clarendon Press, 1971) 1–152.

7. Hegel, *Hegel's Philosophy of Mind* 1.

8. I have retained the gender-specific term 'man' at those points where Malabou employs the cognate French 'homme' and/or where 'humanity' or 'the human' would sound clumsy or give a different nuance to the meaning of a sentence.

9. Hegel, *Hegel's Philosophy of Mind* 146, quoted on *ADH* 39/*FOH* 23.

10. See 'Anthropology', §§409–10. Hegel, *Hegel's Philosophy of Mind* 139–47.

11. Hegel, *Phenomenology of Spirit* 193, quoted on *ADH* 98/*FOH* 67.

12. Georg Wilhelm Friedrich Hegel, *Aesthetics. Lectures on Fine Art, vol. II*, trans. T. M. Knox (Oxford: Clarendon Press, 1998) 27.

13. From the adjective κένωσ (*kenos*, empty).

14. Philippians 2: 5–8, English Standard Version; my emphasis.

15. *FOH* 91, quoting Georg Wilhelm Friedrich Hegel, *Lectures on the Philosophy of Religion*, trans. R. F. Brown, P. C. Hodgson, J. M. Stewart, and H. S. Harris, ed. P. C. Hodgson, vol. 3 (Berkeley: University of California Press, 1984–7) 466.

16. *ADH* 125/*FOH* 87, quoting Hegel, *Hegel's Philosophy of Mind* 300.

17. This movement follows the Philippians 2 passage discussed above (Chapter 2, note 11). The passage reads: 'Therefore God has highly exalted him and bestowed on him the name that is above every name, so that at the name of Jesus every knee should bow, in heaven and on earth and under the earth, and every tongue confess that Jesus Christ is Lord, to the glory of God the Father' (Philippians 2: 9–11).

18. Immanuel Kant, *Critique of Pure Reason*, ed. and trans. Paul Guyer and Allen W. Wood (Cambridge: Cambridge University Press, 1999) 117.

19. Peter Gratton sees in this constancy of the word 'plasticity' across its transformations a denial of radical change: 'Does not Malabou's repeatable formula of plasticity, as

form and reductive eidos, name itself outside of time, since it only ever names itself no matter the site she is investigating?' (Peter Gratton, *Speculative Realism: Problems and Prospects* (London: Bloomsbury, 2014) 191). What this analysis is missing, I think, is that the 'itself' is precisely what is always plastically being transformed through time. The word 'plastic' names an unlimited number of transformations, such that Hegel's plasticity is not Malabou's. Plasticity is only a 'repeatable formula' in the plastic sense, according to which repetition is always a receiving and a giving of form. The question is not whether there is a constant form or eidos, but whether the gesture itself of receiving and giving form acts as a constant meta-capacity for Malabou. That question will be discussed in the rest of this chapter.

20. Georges Canguilhem, 'Dialectique et philosophie du non chez Gaston Bachelard', in *Études d'histoire et de philosophie des sciences*, 2nd edition (Paris: Vrin, 1970) 206, quoted on *ADH* 19/*FOH* 7.

21. Georg Wilhelm Friedrich Hegel, *Science of Logic (Doctrine of Being, Doctrine of Essence, Doctrine of the Notion [Concept])*, trans. A. V. Miller (Atlantic Highlands, NJ: Humanities Press International, 1989) 40. Translation modified by Lisabeth During to reflect the French. Quoted on *ADH* 24/*FOH* 10.

22. This is the translation of *Sache* preferred by Lisabeth During.

23. Catherine Malabou, *The Heidegger Change: On the Fantastic in Philosophy* (Albany: State University of New York Press, 2011), *Counterpath: Travelling With Jacques Derrida* (Stanford: Stanford University Press, 2004).

24. Martin Heidegger, *What Is Philosophy?*, trans. William Kluback and Jean T. White (Woodbridge, CT: Twayne Publishers, 1958) 71, quoted on *PAS* 43–4/*PDW* 19.

25. The instances of this gesture are far too numerous in Derrida's oeuvre to list exhaustively here, and it is not the purpose of this chapter to provide a detailed exposition of Derrida's deconstruction of subjectivity. Some of the most important moments of the deconstruction of the metaphysics of subjectivity can be found in *Of Grammatology* (Baltimore: Johns Hopkins University Press, 1976) 16; *Speech and Phenomena* (Evanston: Northwestern University Press, 1979) 66–8; *Of Spirit: Heidegger and the Question* (Chicago: University of Chicago Press, 1989) 40; *Politics of Friendship* (London: Verso, 1997) 68; and Jacques Derrida and Jean-Luc Nancy '"Eating well" or the calculation of the subject: an interview with Jacques Derrida', in *Who Comes After the Subject?* (Chicago: University of Chicago Press, 1991) 105–9.

26. This point is made by Peter Gratton, who compares Malabou's notion of plasticity unfavourably to Derrida's ever-changing vocabulary. See Gratton, *Speculative Realism* 191.

27. Jacques Derrida, 'Force of law: the mystical foundation of authority', in Drucilla Cornell, Michel Rosenfeld and David Gray Carlson (eds), *Deconstruction and the Possibility of Justice* (New York: Routledge, 1992) 3–67, 35.

28. Jean-Pierre Changeux, *Neuronal Man: The Biology of Mind*, trans. Laurence Garet (New York: Parthenon Books, 1985) xiii, quoted on *QF* 37/*WSD* 2; EOW 440; *PAS* 111/*PDW* 59; PLR).

29. It is not my purpose in this chapter to question Malabou's reading of the Changeux–Ricœur debate. My concern is to set forth the unsatisfactory dichotomy which she intends her own thought to sublate.

30. Ricœur, in Jean-Pierre Changeux and Paul Ricœur, *What Makes Us Think? A Neuroscientist and a Philosopher Argue about Ethics, Human Nature, and the Brain*, trans. M. B. DeBevoise (Princeton: Princeton University Press, 2002) 47. Quoted by Malabou on *AD* 2.

31. The phrase does not appear in *The Organisation of Behaviour*. In the book itself, 'Hebb's law' is expressed in the following terms:

> When an axon of cell A is near enough to excite cell B and repeatedly or persistently takes part in firing it, some growth process or metabolic change takes

place in one or both cells such that A's efficiency, as one of the cells firing B, is increased. (Donald Hebb, *The Organization of Behavior: A Neuropsychological Theory* (New York: Wiley and Sons, 1949) 62)

32. The resonance of the French *Que faire de notre cerveau?* with Lenin's 'what is to be done?' (usually translated into French as 'que faire?') is lost in the English title.

33. In *What Should We Do With Our Brain?* destructive plasticity is introduced as the fourth, and hitherto unheard-of form of neural plasticity, after developmental plasticity, modulational plasticity and reparative plasticity (*QF* 161–4/*WSD* 68–70).

34. Joseph LeDoux, *Synaptic Self: How Our Brains Become Who We Are* (New York: Penguin Books, 2003).

35. The phrase is widespread, appearing notably in Francis Crick, *The Astonishing Hypothesis: The Scientific Search for the Soul* (New York: Simon and Schuster, 1994); Michael S. Gazzaniga, *The Ethical Brain* (New York: Dana Press, 2005); Thomas Metzinger, *Being No One: The Self-Model Theory of Subjectivity* (Cambridge, MA: MIT Press, 2003); Antti Revonsuo, *Inner Presence: Consciousness as a Biological Phenomenon* (Cambridge, MA: MIT Press, 2006).

36. Crick, *The Astonishing Hypothesis* 3.

37. For the 'cerebral subject', see Alain Ehrenberg, 'Le Sujet cérébral', *Esprit*, no. 309 (2004): 130–55. For 'brainhood', see Fernando Vidal, 'Brainhood, anthropological figure of modernity', *History of the Human Sciences* 22, no. 1 (2009): 5–36. For 'neurochemical selfhood', see Joelle M. Abi-Rached and Nikolas Rose, 'The birth of the neuromolecular gaze', *History of the Human Sciences* 23, no. 11 (2010): 11–36, and Nikolas Rose, *The Politics of Life Itself: Biomedicine, Power, and Subjectivity in the Twenty-First Century* (Princeton: Princeton University Press, 2007). For 'neuro-essentialism', see Eric Racine, Sarah Waldman, Jarett Rosenberg and Judy Illes, 'Contemporary neuroscience in the media', *Social Science & Medicine* 71, no. 4 (2010): 725–33.

38. Ehrenberg, 'Le Sujet cérébral' 138; my translation.

39. Vidal, 'Brainhood' 7.

40. Ehrenberg, 'Le Sujet cérébral' 141.

41. In 'Malabou, plasticity, and the sculpturing of the self' Hugh Silverman gives the phrase a slightly different inflection when he argues that it indicates a decentring of the self: 'Inasmuch as our synapses are the "joints" or connecting points between the countless nerve cells in our bodies (most concentrated in brain and spinal cord), this implies, once again, that "we" are de-centered' (Hugh J. Silverman, 'Malabou, plasticity, and the sculpturing of the self', *Concentric: Literary and Cultural Studies* 36, no. 2 (2010) 89–102, 97). However, the fact that the synapse is a gap, and the existence or otherwise of a central self (or homunculus) are two different and unrelated issues.

42. 'So what in fact is this synaptic self, or "proto-self," as Damasio chooses to call it?' (*QF* 140/*WSD* 57).

43. In the light of this account of destructive plasticity it seems odd for Peter Gratton to argue that Malabou fails to 'sharpen just what [she means] by the mental/physical relation, other than it not being dualist. Malabou at points will simply say the mental is the brain, while at others saying there is an ineradicable dialectic between them' (Gratton, *Speculative Realism* 176). Gratton is right to suggest that Malabou does lapse in both of these ways at times, but without evoking the nuanced and Hegel-inspired account of destructive plasticity it gives a false account of the complexity of Malabou's thought.

44. This aspect of Malabou's account is drawn out strongly by Adrian Johnston in *Prolegomena to Any Future Materialism: The Outcome of Contemporary French Philosophy* (Evanston: Northwestern University Press, 2013) 32.

45. Ian James, *The New French Philosophy* (Cambridge: Polity Press, 2012) 97.

46. A number of such objections to materialism are given in M. R. Bennett and P. M.

S. Hacker, *Philosophical Foundations of Neuroscience* (Malden, MA: Blackwell, 2003) 358–9.

47. Antonio Damasio, *The Feeling of What Happens: Body, Emotion and the Making of Consciousness* (London: Random House, 2000).

48. Damasio, *The Feeling of What Happens* 174.

49. Damasio, *The Feeling of What Happens* 22.

50. Damasio, *The Feeling of What Happens* 153.

51. Damasio, *The Feeling of What Happens* 191.

52. See Paul Ricœur, 'On interpretation', in *From Text to Action: Essays in Hermeneutics II*, trans. Kathleen Blamey and John B. Thompson (Evanston: Northwestern University Press, 1991) 1–20, and *The Rule of Metaphor: Multi-disciplinary Studies of the Creation of Meaning in Language*, trans. Robert Czerny (London: Routledge & Kegan Paul, 1986).

53. Ricœur, 'On interpretation' 19.

54. Ricœur, 'On interpretation' 20; my emphasis.

55. Ricœur, *The Rule of Metaphor* 292.

56. Ricœur, *The Rule of Metaphor* 300–1.

57. Ricœur, *The Rule of Metaphor* 26.

58. Ricœur, *The Rule of Metaphor* 271.

59. See Ricœur, *The Rule of Metaphor* 248.

Chapter 4

1. 'If the Huron's soul could have inherited Montesquieu's brain, Montesquieu would create yet.' Charles Bonnet, 'Essai analytique sur les facultés de l'âme', in *Œuvres d'histoire naturelle et de philosophie de Charles Bonnet* (Neuchâtel: de l'imprimerie de Samuel Fauche, Libraire du Roi, 1760) § 771, 370.

2. 'To deny the continuity of the biological and the cultural – if we make plasticity a guiding light – is impossible and philosophically untenable.'

3. All translations from PLR are my own.

4. All translations from *AD* are my own.

5. See Chapter 2.

6. *OED*; see also *AD* 132.

7. Malabou mentions the nucleosome and DNA methylation as epigenetic actors (*AD* 133).

8. Stephen Jay Gould, *Ever Since Darwin: Reflections in Natural History* (New York: W. W. Norton, 1977) 63.

9. 'Although the length of the gestation period is roughly comparable in chimpanzees and humans (224 days and 270 days, respectively), the postnatal development of the brain lasts considerably longer in man. Cranial capacity increases 4.3 times after birth in humans, as against 1.6 times in the chimpanzee. Moreover, cranial capacity reaches 70 percent of the adult volume after three years in humans but after only one year in the chimpanzee. This striking aspect of human cerebral development is of great importance since language learning and acquaintance with social conventions and moral rules take place during the first years following birth. The exceptionally prolonged development of the human brain after birth is one of its most distinctive features, predisposing it to the acquisition and testing of knowledge.' Jean-Pierre Changeux, *The Physiology of Truth: Neuroscience and Human Knowledge*, trans. M. B. DeBevoise (Cambridge, MA: The Bellknap Press, 2004) 189.

10. Suparna Choudhury and Jan Slaby (eds), *Critical Neuroscience: A Handbook of the Social and Cultural Contexts of Neuroscience* (Malden, MA: Wiley-Blackwell, 2012) 59.

11. Immanuel Kant, *Critique of Pure Reason*, ed. and trans. Paul Guyer and Allen W. Wood (Cambridge: Cambridge University Press, 1999) 264. Kant lists twelve such a

priori concepts, divided into four groups of three. There are three categories of quantity (unity, plurality and totality), three of quality (reality, negation and limitation), three of relation (inherence and subsistence, causality and dependence, and community), and three of modality (possibility, existence and necessity).

12. Kant, *Critique of Pure Reason* 264.
13. The latter example is given as an editorial footnote to section 27 in the Cambridge Edition of the *Critique of Pure Reason* (p. 264).
14. Immanuel Kant, *Critique of the Power of Judgment*, ed. Paul Guyer and Eric Matthews, trans. Eric Matthews (Cambridge: Cambridge University Press, 2000) 291.
15. Kant, *Critique of the Power of Judgment* 291.
16. Kant, *Critique of Pure Reason* 264–5.
17. Kant, *Critique of Pure Reason* 727 n48.
18. Kant, *Critique of Pure Reason* 265.
19. Kant, *Critique of Pure Reason* 265.
20. Original: 'von unserm Urheber'. The noun can be translated either as 'author' or 'creator'; Malabou has 'par notre créateur'.
21. Kant, *Critique of Pure Reason* 265.
22. It will be noted that the schema I am offering sets epigenesis between preformation and equivocal generation, whereas in section 27 of the *Critique of Pure Reason* Kant explicitly introduces preformation as a 'middle way' between equivocal generation and epigenesis. It is unclear to me why he should do so. Despite her lengthy treatment of the section Malabou does not remark on the fact either, subtly rearranging the order of in her own presentation.
23. See p. 98.
24. Kant, *Critique of Pure Reason* 265.
25. Kant, *Critique of Pure Reason* 265.
26. The term was originally introduced in Gerald Edelman and Vernon Mountcastle's *The Mindful Brain: Cortical Organisation and the Group-Selective Theory of Higher Brain Function* (Cambridge, MA: MIT Press, 1978) and further developed in Edelman's *Neural Darwinism: The Theory of Neuronal Group Selection* (New York: Basic Books, 1987).
27. The other is Global Workspace Theory (GWT), summarised at Jean-Pierre Changeux, 'Jean-Pierre G. Changeux', in *The History of Neuroscience in Autobiography*, vol. 4, ed. Larry R. Squire (Waltham, MA: Academic Press, 2004) 134–5.
28. Gerald M. Edelman, 'Building a picture of the brain', in Gerald M Edelman and Jean-Pierre Changeux (eds), *The Brain* (New Brunswick, NJ: Transaction Publishers, 2000) 45.
29. Edelman, 'Building a picture of the brain' 45–6.
30. The famous paper is Jean-Pierre Changeux, Philippe Courrege and Antoine Danchin, 'A theory of the epigenesis of neuronal networks by selective stabilisation of synapses', *Proceedings of the National Academy of Sciences U.S.A.* 70 (1973): 2974–8.
31. Jean-Pierre Changeux and Stanislas Dehaene, 'Neuronal models of cognitive functions', *Cognition* 33 (1989): 72.
32. See Jean-Pierre Changeux and Alain Connes, *Conversations on Mind, Matter, and Mathematics*, trans. M. B. DeBevoise (Princeton: Princeton University Press, 1995) 14, 28, 33, 44.
33. In Paul Ricœur, *The Conflict of Interpretations: Essays in Hermeneutics*, trans. Don Ihde (London: Continuum, 2004) 119–56.
34. Ricœur, *The Conflict of Interpretations* 142.
35. Ricœur, *The Conflict of Interpretations* 142. Malabou gives a very similar critique of Freud in *SEL*.
36. Ricœur, *The Conflict of Interpretations* 143.
37. Gérard Lebrun, *Kant et la fin de la métaphysique* (Paris: Le Livre de Poche, 1970).
38. Lebrun, *Kant et la fin de la métaphysique* 706.

39. Lebrun, *Kant et la fin de la métaphysique* 706, quoted on *AD* 168.
40. Original: 'vient changer la donne'.
41. Antonio Damasio, *Descartes' Error: Emotion, Reason and the Human Brain* (New York: Avon Books, 1994) 7, quoted on *LNB* 47/ *TNW* 16. There is some controversy about the reconstructions of the Gage case, meticulously chronicled and critiqued in Malcolm Macmillan's *An Odd Kind of Fame: Stories of Phineas Gage* (Basingstoke: Macmillan, 2002), running to 562 pages. Macmillan concludes that only a few hundred lines by Harlow bear reliable testimony to Gage, leading David Evans to note 'the absence of any of the contradictory or wilful behaviour such as that claimed for the post-injury Gage by Damasio, Changeux and Angier' (see David Cenydd Lloyd Evans, 'Reading neuroscience: ventriloquism as a metaphor for multiple readings of self', PhD Thesis, University of Plymouth, 2006, 172–3). It is not my purpose in treating the Gage case in this context to establish at each point the veracity of the claims being made; my concern is to highlight the tensions and problems which attend Malabou's notion of the self and the person, and these obtain whether or not Damasio's reconstruction of the case, upon which she relies, is accurate.
42. J. M. Harlow, 'Recovery after severe injury to the head', in William G. Van der Kloot, Charles Walcott and Benjamin Dane (eds), *Readings in Behaviour* (New York: Ardent Media, 1974) 302.
43. Damasio, *Descartes' Error* 7–8.
44. *SEL* 28; my emphasis. Quoting Mark Solms and Oliver Turnbull, *Brain and the Inner World: An Introduction to the Neuroscience of Subjective Experience* (New York: Other Press, 2002) 52.
45. Changeux, in Jean-Pierre Changeux and Paul Ricœur, *What Makes Us Think?: A Neuroscientist and a Philosopher Argue about Ethics, Human Nature, and the Brain*, trans. M. B. DeBevoise (Princeton: Princeton University Press, 2002) 18.
46. Evans, 'Reading neuroscience' 177.
47. Adrian Johnston shares this concern in his preface to *Self and Emotional Life*. However, like Malabou, he understands the brain as the sole and exclusive locus of identity and personhood:

> It seems implausible to me that myriad conscious and unconscious elements of his complex ontogenetic life history predating the trauma, elements distributed across many more still-functioning regions of his brain than just the wounded left Frontal lobe, abruptly ceased to play any explicable role whatsoever in his existence in the aftermath of the event. (*SEL* xiv)

For Johnston, the issue is that only a part of Gage's brain has been destroyed and the rest of it, continuing to function, should guarantee the continuity of identity. For the purposes of my argument in this section, Johnston and Malabou are taking the same 'host substance' position.
48. Fernando Vidal, 'Brainhood, anthropological figure of modernity', *History of the Human Sciences* 22, no. 1 (2009): 5–36, 7. The *Essay* is frequently evoked in relation to contemporary neurological discourse, and my treatment of *Locke* in this paragraph is particularly indebted to Vidal's 'Brainhood' and his 'Brains, bodies, selves, and science: anthropologies of identity and the resurrection of the body', *Critical Inquiry* 28, no. 4 (2002): 930–74.
49. John Locke, *An Essay Concerning Human Understanding* (Oxford: Oxford University Pres, 1979) ch. XXVII § 9, 335.
50. John Locke, *Two Treatises of Government*, student edition (Cambridge: Cambridge University Press, 1988) ch. V, § 27, 287.
51. See for example the taxonomy in Alain Ehrenberg, 'Le Sujet cérébral', *Esprit*, no. 309 (2004): 130–55, 131.
52. Hugh J. Silverman, 'Malabou, plasticity, and the sculpturing of the self', *Concentric: Literary and Cultural Studies* 36, no. 2 (2010): 89–102, 94–5.

53. Silverman, 'Malabou' 97.
54. Daniel Dennett, *Consciousness Explained* (New York: Penguin, 1992) 415.
55. See Joseph LeDoux, *Synaptic Self: How Our Brains Become Who We Are* (New York: Penguin Books, 2003) 88, 311–13.
56. Thomas Pradeu, 'Philosophie de la biologie', in Anouk Barberousse, Denis Bonnat and Mikael Cozyk (eds), *Précis de philosophie des sciences* (Paris: Vuibert, 2011) 378–403, 15, quoted on *AD* 139–40.
57. See Ian Hacking, *The Social Construction of What?* (Cambridge, MA: Harvard University Press, 1999) 109–10, 123.
58. Choudhury and Slaby, 'Introduction. Critical neuroscience: between life-world and laboratory', in Choudhury and Slaby (eds), *Critical Neuroscience* 10.
59. Paul Martin and Richard Ashcroft, 'Neuroscience, ethics and society: a review of the field', background paper prepared for the 2005 Wellcome Trust Summer School on 'neuroethics', 2005, 26. Quoting Nikolas Rose, 'Neurochemical selves', *Society* 41, no. 1 (2003): 46–59, 59.
60. Simon Cohn, 'Disrupting images: neuroscientific representations in the lives of psychiatric patients', in Choudhury and Slaby (eds), *Critical Neuroscience* 191.
61. In his review of *The New Wounded*, Raad Fadaak appeals to Adriana Cavarero's argument that the self 'knows itself to be constituted by another' who gives it its story. See Raad Fadaak, 'Catherine Malabou's *The New Wounded: From Neurosis to Brain Damage*' *Somatosphere* (2013), available at <http://somatosphere.net/?p=6289> (last accessed 2 November 2015). Fadaak is drawing on Adrianna Cavarero's *Relating Narratives: Storytelling and Selfhood*, trans. Paul A. Kottman (London: Routledge, 2000) 84. Although he helpfully introduces the notion of narrative he still seems to consider it in opposition to a cognitivist approach to the self.
62. Paul Ricœur, *Oneself as Another*, trans. Kathleen Blamey (Chicago: Chicago University Press, 1995) 160; translation altered.
63. Ricœur, *Oneself as Another* 162.
64. Paul Ricœur, *The Just*, trans. David Pellauer (Chicago: University of Chicago Press, 2003) 7.
65. Paul Ricœur, *Time and Narrative, volume 3*, trans. Kathleen Blamey and David Pellauer (Chicago: University of Chicago Press, 1988) 248.
66. Paul Ricœur, *Lectures 2: la contrée des philosophes* (Paris: Editions du Seuil, 1994) 220; my translation.
67. Jean Greisch, *Paul Ricœur: l'itinérance du sens* (Grenoble: J. Millon, 2001) 386; my translation.
68. Paul Ricœur, *The Course of Recognition* (Cambridge, MA: Harvard University Press, 2007) 104.
69. Ricœur, *The Course of Recognition* 122.

Chapter 5

1. 'The dwelling of man is the horizon.' The phrase is reported as a 'Moorish saying' by Jean, vicomte d'Esme in his *Les Chevaliers sans éperons*. See François Pouillon (ed.), *Dictionnaire des orientalistes de langue française* (Paris: Karthala Editions) 314.
2. The four books in question are *Hominescence* (2001), *L'Incandescent* (2005), *Rameaux* (2007) and *Récits d'humanisme* (2009). In addition to this tetralogy, Serres entertains a direct reflection on the question of humanity throughout his published work, most prominently in the early discussions of the continuity between human and natural language in *La Distribution* (1977), *La Naissance de la physique dans le texte de Lucrèce* (1977) [*The Birth of Physics*, 2000], 'Exact and human' (1979), *Le Parasite* (1980) [*The Parasite*, 1982], *Genèse* (1982) [*Genesis*, 1995], *Le Contrat naturel* (1990) [*The Natural Contract*, 1995], his 1999 contribution to the collected volume *Qu'est-ce que l'homme?*,

and in his two books on the body – *Les Cinq Sens* (1985) [*The Five Senses*, 2008] and *Variations sur le corps* (1999) [*Variations on the Body*, 2011].

3. Alan Murray, 'Rebirth: review of Michel Serres, *The Birth of Physics*', *Radical Philosophy* 105 (2001): 57–8, 57.

4. The famous story of Diogenes' chicken is told by Diogenes Laërtius in his *Lives of Eminent Philosophers*:

> Plato had defined man as an animal, biped and featherless, and was applauded. Diogenes plucked a fowl and brought it into the lecture-room with the words, 'Here is Plato's Man.' In consequence of which there was added to the definition, 'having broad nails'. (Diogenes Laërtius, *Lives of Eminent Philosophers*, vol. 2, books 6–10, trans. R. D. Hicks (Cambridge, MA: Harvard University Press, 2000) 43)

5. The allusion here, characteristic once more of the lightness with which Serres wears his erudition, is to Thomas Nagel's famous paper 'What is it like to be a bat?', *The Philosophical Review* 83 (1974) 435–50.

6. In physics, anharmonicity is 'the extent to which an oscillating physical system deviates from simple harmonic motion' (*OED*).

7. See in particular Latour's seminal *Nous n'avons jamais été modernes: essai d'anthropologie symétrique* (Paris: La Découverte, 1997)/ *We Have Never Been Modern* (Cambridge, MA: Harvard University Press, 1993) and his *Enquêtes sur les modes d'existence: une anthropologie des modernes* (Paris: La Découverte, 2012)/ *An Inquiry into Modes of Existence: An Anthropology of the Moderns*, trans. Catherine Porter (Cambridge, MA: Harvard University Press, 2013), as well as Serres's own discussion of the quasi-object in *LP* 301–14/ *TP* 223–33 (and *Hom* 307–8) and the detailed discussion of objects in *Hom* 205–15.

8. Basarab Nicolescu, 'The idea of levels of reality. Its relevance for non-reduction and personhood', in Eric Weislogel (ed.), *Transdisciplinarity in Science and Religion* (Bucharest: Curtea Veche, 2008) 23.

9. The point is well made by Kate Rigby, who adds the important point that the 'modern' idea of an incommunicative nature has been far from the only position in Western thought since the seventeenth century:

> While animist cultures, such as that of indigenous Australians, assume that all things are capable of communicating in their own right, the premodern Christian view tends to construe nonhuman entities primarily as vehicles for messages hailing from a divine, or potentially demonic, source. From the seventeenth century, with the rise of rationalism and humanism, communicative agency was increasingly restricted to humans, whose command of verbal language was presumed to be a function of the unique mental capacities that raised us above the mute realm of merely material existence. This view was challenged by European writers and philosophers of the Romantic era (c. 1770–1830), such as the German philosopher F. W. J. Schelling (1775–1854), who posited that human language had emerged from, and remained indebted to, the self-organizing, self-transforming, and self-expressive capacity inherent in nature as a whole: Nature, for the Romantics, was the first poet. (Kate Rigby, 'Language', in *Berkshire Encyclopedia of Sustainability*, vol. 1 (Great Barrington, MA: Berkshire Publishing Group, 2009) 263–4)

10. See Russell Disilvestro, *Human Capacities and Moral Status* (Dortrecht: Springer, 2010). For example:

> A hierarchy of capacities is a group of capacities with three interesting features. First, some members of the group are 'lower-order' capacities. Second, some

members of the group are 'higher-order' capacities. Third, the higher-order capacities are just capacities to obtain the lower-order capacities. Examples from chemistry and biology illustrate this. Liquid water has the lower-order capacity to evaporate, while ice has the higher-order capacity to obtain this lower-order capacity. A mature oak tree has the lower-order capacity to support a tree house, while a sapling has the higher-order capacity to obtain this lower-order capacity. (p. 20)

11. In relation to the deconstruction of Christianity, Derrida warns that 'such a difficult, paradoxical, almost impossible task' is 'always in danger of being exposed as mere Christian hyperbole' (Jacques Derrida, *On Touching – Jean-Luc Nancy*, trans. Christine Irizarry (Stanford: Stanford University Press, 2005) 220), as the 'deconstruction of Christianity' is revealed, after all, to have been an objective genitive.

12. For an explanation of the motif of host properties, see the Introduction to this book, p. 13.

13. Blaise Pascal, 'Qu'est-ce que le moi?', in *Pensées*, in *Œuvres complètes*, ed. Michel Le Guren (Paris: Gallimard, Bibliothèque de la Pléiade, 2000) fragment 582/Pascal, *Pensées and Other Writings*, trans. Honor Levi (Oxford: Oxford University Press, 1995) fragment 567; translation altered.

14. 'Lucy' is the name given to the partial skeleton (about 40 per cent complete) of a 3.2 million year old *Australopithecus afarensis* discovered in Ethiopia by palaeontologist Donald C. Johanson in 1974. Until 2009, Lucy was the oldest substantial human ancestor skeleton yet discovered.

15. The structure of Malabou's plasticity and epigenesis is very similar to Serres's here. If, for Serres, the signal finds itself between monotone and white noise, for Malabou plasticity is between flexibility and elasticity, and epigenesis between preformation and equivocal generation. Malabou also adopts this structure when discussing human existence: 'A lifetime always proceeds within the boundaries of a double excess: an excess of reification and an excess of fluidification. [. . .]Plasticity situates itself in the middle of these two excesses' (*PDW* 81. The quotation appears in the 'Afterword' to the English edition of *Plasticity at the Dusk of Writing*, not included in the original French).

16. Bruno Latour, 'The Enlightenment without the critique: a word on Michel Serres' philosophy', *Royal Institute of Philosophy Lecture Series* 21 (1987) 93–4.

17. Serres's account of the Great Story draws our attention to a moment more fundamental than that of Timothy Morton's ecomimesis, and yet a moment upon which ecomimesis relies, and in so doing it challenges the account of the relation between writing and ambiance given in his *Ecology Without Nature: Rethinking Environmental Aesthetics* (Cambridge, MA: Harvard University Press, 2007). Morton sets up the stakes of ecomimesis in terms of overcoming a Cartesian dualism of subject and object, and indeed he cites Serres in order to do so: 'We must . . . change direction and abandon the heading imposed by Descartes' philosophy' (*Ecology Without Nature* 105, quoting *CN* 61/*NC* 34). But Morton cannot escape – he freely admits it – this dualism of an inside (the subject's experience) and an outside (the subjectless world or what Quentin Meillassoux might call the 'Great Outdoors') and it continues to structure his account of ecomimesis. What is more, this dualism must continue to structure Morton's thinking, because mimesis as a figure requires a minimal split between the imitator, the imitation and the imitated, a split which quickly becomes the division between subject, text and object. In contrast to this structurally necessary Cartesian shard in the flesh of Morton's ecomimesis, Serres is beholden to no such ongoing dichotomy, and the shift engendered by the move from metaphor to synecdoche in understanding Serres's work opens the way to placing Morton's ecomimesis in a wider and more radically a-Cartesian context. The subject who is writing is just as much a part of the 'natural' world as is the host of golden daffodils about which she is writing. What is more, for Serres the

language she uses to express this idyllic scene is itself natural, rooted in and dependent on the rhythms and noises of the natural world. Ecomimesis with a Serresian twist is reflexive: ecology imitating itself.

18. See Maurice Merleau-Ponty, *Le Visible et l'invisible: suivi de notes de travail*, ed. Claude Lefort (Paris: Gallimard, 1964) 169/ *The Visible and the Invisible: Followed by Working Notes*, trans. Alphonso Lingis (Evanston: Northwestern University Press, 1968) 127: 'That the presence of the world is precisely the presence of its flesh to my flesh, that I "am of the world" and that I am not it, this is what is no sooner said than forgotten.'

19. Immanuel Kant, *Critique of the Power of Judgment*, ed. Paul Guyer and Eric Matthews, trans. Eric Matthews (Cambridge: Cambridge University Press, 2000) 138.

20. Christiane Frémont, 'Philosophie pour le temps présent', in *Cahier de L'Herne Michel Serres*, ed. François L'Yvonnet and Christiane Frémont (Paris: Editions de L'Herne, 2010) 22.

21. Paul A. Harris, 'The itinerant theorist: nature and knowledge/ecology and topology in Michel Serres', *SubStance* 26, no. 2 (1997): 39.

22. Merleau-Ponty, *Le Visible et l'invisible* 151–2/ *The Visible and the Invisible* 113.

23. Bernadette Bensaude-Vincent, 'Michel Serres, historien des sciences', in *Cahier de L'Herne Michel Serres* 42.

24. N. Katherine Hayles, 'Two voices, one channel: equivocation in Michel Serres', *SubStance* 17, no. 3 (1988): 3.

25. David Webb, 'Michel Serres on Lucretius', *Angelaki* 11, no. 3 (2006): 128.

26. *NP* 152/*BP* 122, quoted on Webb, 'Michel Serres on Lucretius' 128.

27. Steven D. Brown, 'Michel Serres: science, translation and the logic of the parasite', *Theory, Culture & Society* 19, no. 3 (2002): 2.

28. Marcel Hénaff, 'Temps des hommes, temps du monde: Michel Serres et les bifurcations du Grand Récit', in *Cahier de L'Herne Michel Serres* 76.

29. William Paulson, 'Autour du Grand Récit: Michel Serres, philosophe du siècle', in *Cahier de L'Herne Michel Serres* 230.

30. Paulson, 'Autour du Grand Récit' 230, quoting *RH* 185.

31. Paulson, 'Autour du Grand Récit' 231.

32. Frémont, 'Philosophie pour le temps présent' 24.

Chapter 6

1. 'We come back to the obvious point that a human is attached, and if he detaches himself he dies'; my translation.

2. Latour points out that God, at least the Christian God, is diametrically opposed to the picture of emancipation and becomes more and more involved with the world he has created as the bible's narrative progresses, becoming incarnate and dying in order to save his creatures (IDS 12).

3. Bruno Latour, 'Exégèse et ontologie. Essai philosophique sur des textes de résurrection'. PhD Thesis, Université de Tours, France, 1975.

4. The French verb *détourner* would perfectly capture the range of senses at play here. As well as its primary meaning of 'diversion' or 'rerouting', it can carry the sense of a 'hijacking', repurposing or 'embezzlement' (in the phrase 'détournement de fonds'). Its centrality to the events of May 1968, with the Situationist *détournement* of comic books and advertising posters, also lends it a politically subversive hue. This range of meanings makes it a helpful synonym and amplification of Latour's notions of mediation and translation, and also opens an interesting conversation with Malabou's plasticity.

5. The importance of Bultmann for Latour's subsequent methodology has been persuasively argued by Henning Schmidgen in *Bruno Latour in Pieces: An Intellectual Biography*, trans. Gloria Custance (New York: Fordham University Press, 2015).

Schmidgen sees echoes of Latour's PhD thesis throughout his career up to and including the Modes of Existence project (see pp. 4, 46, 56, 100–1 and 128–9, with his main thesis explained on p. 137), and Latour himself acknowledges that 'Bultmann is very, very important, as Henning Schmidgen (2011) showed me in the book he wrote about my work' (AT 305). Schmidgen's emphasis is, however, different to mine, focusing on the way in which Latour approaches his subsequent projects as exercises in exegesis. Godmer and David Smadja also insist that Latour's intellectual trajectory must be understood as a series of exegeses. See Bruno Latour, Laurent Godmer and David Smadja, 'L'Œuvre de Bruno Latour: une pensée politique exégétique. Entretien avec Bruno Latour', *Raisons Politiques* 47 (2012): 115–48, 115.

6. 'Since the word "agent" in the case of nonhumans is uncommon, a better term, as we have seen, is actant' (*EP* 189–90/*PH* 180).

7. The term 'regime of enunciation' appears a number of articles and working papers, as well as in *Rejoicing* (see especially *Jub* 143–4/*Rej* 120 and *FD* 294 n67, 297/*MOL* 273 n68, 276). Latour insists that 'regime of enunciation' and 'mode of existence' are synonyms (SUL 7/Ref 309), and in the online glossary to the Modes of Existence project he insists that he would still use 'regime of enunciation' if it were it not so associated with language and discourse analysis (IMEg: Enunciation).

8. As an alternative to 'key' Latour also uses the term 'preposition': that which conditions the understanding of a proposition.

9. The English version of the site has 'the world where we live', but the French reads 'le seul monde où nous résidions'.

10. This does not imply that the other modes have nothing to do with a human, but by the time Latour arrives at the ninth mode there emerges something like a readily recognisable human being.

11. The term 'quasi-object' is introduced by Michel Serres and most fully described in the chapter of *The Parasite* entitled 'Theory of the quasi-object'. The quasi-object 'marks or designates a subject who, without it, would not be one' (*LP* 302/*TP* 224) and by running 'like a ferret' makes [*fait*] a collective (*LP* 303/*TP* 225). In Serres's now famous example of a ball game, it is the ball that designates the subject – the hero-victim who, as long as she has possession of the ball, is the focus of the game and of all the other players. In its function of arranging the players and dictating the flow of the game, the ball is also a quasi-subject (*LP* 305/*TP* 227).

12. 'When considered as the implicit framework which is logically presupposed by the existence of the utterance, the structure of enunciation involves two domains: those of enunciator and of enunciatee.' See Algirdas Julien Greimas and Joseph Courtés, *Sémiotique. Dictionnaire raisonné de la théorie du langage* (Paris: Hachette Supérieur, 1993) 125/Algirdas Julien Greimas and Joseph Courtés, *Semiotics and Language: An Analytical Dictionary* (Bloomington: Indiana University Press, 1982) 105.

13. Latour mentions the term on OTM 36, published in 1994, and also in *CM*.

14. Graham Harman, *Bruno Latour: Reassembling the Political* (London: Pluto Press, 2014) 146.

15. I am therefore arguing that Latour seeks to deal with humanism in the same way that Meillassoux tackles theology: not by renouncing it in an ascetic gesture that fundamentally leaves the theologian or humanist untouched, nor in seeking to imitate its structures under a suite of pseudonyms, but by leaving no hiding place for the humanist in a new dispensation in which all of her former territory (of subjects and objects, nature and culture, humans and nonhumans) has been occupied and recommissioned by a new set of dispositions, in this case the fifteen modes of existence. For Meillassoux's relation to 'ascetic' and 'imitative' atheism, see Christopher Watkin, *Difficult Atheism: Post-Theological Thinking in Alain Badiou, Jean-Luc Nancy and Quentin Meillassoux* (Edinburgh: Edinburgh University Press, 2011).

16. Anders Blok and Torben Elgaard Jensen, *Bruno Latour: Hybrid Thoughts in a Hybrid World* (London: Routledge, 2011) 142.

17. Blok and Jensen, *Bruno Latour* 146.
18. See in particular James Lovelock, *Gaia: A New Look at Life on Earth* (Oxford: Oxford University Press, 1979) and *Gaia: The Practical Science of Planetary Medicine* (London: Gaia Books, 1991), from which Latour quotes at length in FG.
19. Latour amusingly relates how the question of whether the Anthropocene age has begun is currently being considered by the Anthropocene Working Group of the 'Subcommission on Quaternary Stratigraphy', itself part of the International Union of Geological Sciences (see <http://quaternary.stratigraphy.org/workinggroups/anthro pocene/> (last accessed 2 November 2015)). The group is set to report in 2016.
20. Meillassoux's relation to Latour on the question of indifference is not simple. For Meillassoux, the Great Outdoors is indifferent to being thought (*AF* 86/*AfF* 63). Latour's world is not indifferent to being thought, because what the moderns call thought is just one more mediation in the world, and actors are not indifferent to mediation. However, Meillassoux and Latour are agreed that the world manifests no unified conscious disposition either in benevolence or malevolence towards human beings (Latour rules this out in his definition of Gaia in the Modes of Existence online glossary), and both see the very indifference of the world (in the sense that it is not benevolently or malevolently disposed towards humanity but acts and reacts in feedback loops qualitatively indifferent to human as opposed to nonhuman action) as a threat to humanity (see *AF* 78/*AfF* 57). It is this threat which Latour calls Gaia's lack of indifference. Malabou seems to go further than Meillassoux when she writes 'Isn't it time to acknowledge the existence of an element of indifference in being itself, revealed by this instance to which philosophy usually accords not the slightest onto-logical value: the suffering of the brain?' (*OdA* 24–5/*OoA* 29). This position is more anthropocentric than either Meillassoux's or Latour's.
21. Sigmund Freud, 'One of the difficulties of psychoanalysis', in *Collected Papers*, vol. IV, trans. Joan Riviere (London: The Hogarth Press, 1956 [1917]) 347–56.
22. See <http://www.bruno-latour.fr/node/358> (last accessed 2 November 2015).
23. See <http://www.bruno-latour.fr/node/359> (last accessed 2 November 2015).
24. Friedrich Nietzsche, *The Gay Science*, ed. Walter Kaufmann (New York: Vintage, 1974) 181–2.
25. This is a change from Latour's line in *Un Monde pluriel mais commun*, where Latour does still speak in terms of establishing a general will not by abstracting ourselves from our attachments but by recognising them more and more fully (*MP* 59–60).
26. Latour indeed provides the perfect deity for Johnston's materialism 'split from within', for 'In Theogony, far from being a figure of harmony, Gaia, the mythological char-acter, emerges in great effusions of blood, steam and terror together with Chaos and Eros' (FG 57). Despite this identification of a deity with decentred conflict and strife, however, Latour like Johnston persists in identifying spontaneity and non-linearity with secularity: 'This is what makes Lovelock's Gaia so totally secular: all effects of scale are the result of the expansion of one particular opportunist agent seizing occasions to develop on the fly' (FG 71). I still fail to see why conflict and spontaneity should be any inherently less religious than unity and design; they are less resonant with the Western monotheistic God of the philosophers, to be sure, and that is perhaps all that Johnston and Latour mean, in the final analysis. At least we can say that with Gaia, secularity now has its own patron deity. See Adrian Johnston, 'What matter(s) in ontology: Alain Badiou, the Hebb-event, and materialism split from within', *Angelaki* 13, no. 1 (2008): 27–49.
27. Régis Debray, 'Etes-vous démocrate ou républicain?', *Le Nouvel Observateur*, 30 November–6 December 1995, 115–21.
28. The relevant passage reads:

> Ivan Fyodorovitch added in parenthesis that the whole natural law lies in that faith, and that if you were to destroy in mankind the belief in immortality, not

only love but every living force maintaining the life of the world would at once be dried up. Moreover, nothing then would be immoral, everything would be lawful, even cannibalism. (Fyodor Dostoyevsky, *The Brothers Karamazov* (Oxford: Oxford University Press, 1998) 87)

29. Tom Cohen, 'Introduction', in Tom Cohen (ed.), *Telemorphosis: Theory in the Era of Climate Change*, vol. 1 (Ann Arbor: Open Humanities Press, 2012) 25.

Conclusion

1. See Naomi Klein, *This Changes Everything: Capitalism vs. The Climate* (New York: Simon and Schuster, 2014).
2. See the three volumes of Ricœur's *Time and Narrative*, as well as 'Life in quest of narrative', in *On Paul Ricœur: Narrative and Interpretation*, ed. David Wood (New York: Routledge, 1991) 20–33.

Select Bibliography

Abbas, Niran, ed. *Mapping Michel Serres*. Ann Arbor: University of Michigan Press, 2005.

Abi-Rached, Joelle M., and Nikolas Rose. 'The birth of the neuromolecular gaze'. *History of the Human Sciences* 23, no. 11 (2010): 11–36.

Adamson, Gregory Dale. 'Serres translates Howe'. *SubStance* 26, no. 2 (1997): 110–24.

Ahmed, Sara. 'Open forum imaginary prohibitions: some preliminary remarks on the founding gestures of the "New Materialism"'. *European Journal of Women's Studies* 15, no. 1 (2008): 23–39.

Ahuvia, Aaron C. 'Beyond the extended self: loved objects and consumers' identity narratives'. *Journal of Consumer Research* 32 (2005): 171–84.

Alliez, Eric. 'Badiou: the grace of the universal'. *Polygraph* 17 (2005): 267–73.

Anderson, Pamela Sue. 'Agnosticism and attestation: an aporia concerning the Other in Ricœur's "Oneself as Another"'. *Journal of Religion* 74, no. 1 (1994): 65–76.

Anderson, P. S. 'Ricœur's reclamation of autonomy: unity, plurality, and totality'. In *Paul Ricœur and Contemporary Moral Thought*, ed. J. Wall, W. Schweiker and W. D. Hall. 15–31. London: Routledge, 1999.

Andler, Daniel. 'Cognitive science in France'. In *The Columbia History of Twentieth Century French Thought*, ed. L. Kritzman. 175–81. New York: Columbia University Press, 2006.

Antonello, Pierpaolo. 'Celebrating a master: Michel Serres'. *Configurations* 8, no. 2 (2000): 165–9.

Armezzani, Maria. 'How to understand consciousness: the strength of the phenomenological method'. *World Futures: The Journal of New Paradigm Research* 65, no. 2 (2009): 101–10.

Armstrong, Nancy, and Warren Montag. 'The future of the human: an introduction'. *Differences: A Journal of Feminist Cultural Studies* 20, no. 2 and 5 (2009): 1–8.

Arneson, Richard J. 'What, if anything, renders all humans morally equal?' In *Peter Singer and His Critics*, ed. Dale Jamieson. 103–27. Oxford: Blackwell, 1999.

Ashton, Paul, A. J. Bartlett and Justin Clemens, eds. *The Praxis of Alain Badiou*. Melbourne: re.press, 2006.

Assad, Maria L. 'From order to chaos: Michel Serres's field models'. *SubStance* 20, no. 2 (1991): 33–43.

—. 'Language, nonlinearity, and the problem of evil'. *Configurations* 8, no. 2 (2000): 271–83.

—. 'Portrait of a nonlinear dynamical system: the discourse of Michel Serres'. *SubStance* 22, no. 2/3 (1993): 141–52.

—. *Reading with Michel Serres: An Encounter with Time*. Albany: State University of New York Press, 1999.

Asselt, Willem van, Paul van Geest, Daniela Müller and Theo Salemink, eds. *Iconoclasm and Iconoclash: Struggle for Religious Identity*. Leiden: Brill, 2007.

Badiou, Alain. 'A propos du "et" entre être et événement'. In *Écrits autour de la pensée d'Alain Badiou*. 103–4. Paris: L'Harmattan, 2007.

—. *Abrégé de métapolitique*. Paris: Editions du Seuil, 1998.

—. 'Afterword: some replies to a demanding friend'. In *Think Again*, ed. Peter Hallward. 232–7. London: Continuum, 2004.

—. *Ahmed le philosophe* suivi de *Ahmed se fâche*. Paris: Actes du Sud, 1995.

—. *Alain Badiou: Theoretical Writings*. Trans. Ray Brassier and Alberto Toscano. London: Continuum, 2004.

—. 'Art and Philosophy'. *Lacanian Ink* 17 (Autumn 2000).

—. 'Author's preface'. Trans. Ray Brassier and Alberto Toscano. In *Alain Badiou: Theoretical Writings*. xiii–xv. London: Continuum, 2004.

—. 'Author's preface'. Trans. Oliver Feltham. In *Being and Event*. xi–xv. London: Continuum, 2007.

—. *Beckett: l'increvable désir*. Paris: Hachette, 1995.

—. 'Being by numbers [interview with Lauren Sedofsky]'. *Artforum* 33, no. 2 (October 1994). <https://voidmanufacturing.wordpress.com/2008/09/10/badiou-interview-from-1994-skip-the-intro-secularization-of-infinity-set-theory-truth-philosophy-situ-ations-disaster-love-emancipation%E2%80%A6/> (last accessed 2 November 2015).

—. 'The being of number'. Trans. Ray Brassier and Alberto Toscano. In *Alain Badiou: Theoretical Writings*. 59–66. London: Continuum, 2004.

—. *Briefings on Existence: A Short Treatise on Transitory Ontology*. Trans. Norman Madarasz. Albany: State University of New York Press, 2006.

—. *The Century*. Cambridge: Polity Press, 2007.

—. *Cinq leçons sur le 'cas' Wagner*. Paris: Nous, 2010.

—. *Circonstances 1: Kosovo, 11 septembre, Chirac/Le Pen*. Paris: Editions Léo Sheer, 2003.

—. *Circonstances 2: Irak, foulard, Allemagne/France*. Paris: Editions Léo Sheer, 2004.

—. *Circonstances 3: Portées du mot 'juif'*. Paris: Editions Léo Sheer, 2008.

—. *Circonstances 4: De quoi Sarkozy est-il le nom?* Paris: Paris: Nouvelles éditions Lignes, 2007.

—. *Circonstances 5: L'Hypothèse communiste*. Paris: Nouvelles éditions Lignes, 2009.

—. *Circonstances 6: Le Réveil de l'histoire*. Paris: Nouvelles éditions Lignes, 2011.

—. *Circonstances 7: Sarkozy: pire que prévu. Les autres: prévoir le pire*. Paris: Nouvelles éditions Lignes, 2012.

—. *The Communist Hypothesis*. Trans. David Macey and Steve Corcoran. London: Verso, 2010.

—. 'The communist hypothesis'. In *The Idea of Communism*, ed. Costas Douzinas and Slavoj Žižek. 1–14. London: Verso, 2010.

—. *Court traité d'ontologie transitoire*. Paris: Editions du Seuil, 1998.

—. *Deleuze: la clameur de l'être*. Paris: Hachette, 1997.

—. *Deleuze: The Clamor of Being*. Trans. Louise Burchill. Theory Out of Bounds. Minneapolis: University of Minnesota Press, 2000.

—. 'Dix-neuf réponses à beaucoup plus de questions'. *Cahiers du Collège International de Philosophie* 8 (1989): 247–68.

—. 'Eight theses on the universal'. Trans. Ray Brassier and Alberto Toscano. In *Alain Badiou: Theoretical Writings*. 143–52. London: Continuum, 2004.

—. *Entretiens 1: 1981–1996*. Paris: Nous, 2011.

—. *Ethics: An Essay on the Understanding of Evil*. Wo es war. London; New York: Verso, 2001.

—. 'The event as trans-being'. Trans. Ray Brassier and Alberto Toscano. In *Alain Badiou: Theoretical Writings*. 97–102. London: Continuum, 2004.

—. 'Fifteen theses on contemporary art'. In *Lacanian Ink* (2005). <http://www.lacan.com/frameXXIII7.htm> (last accessed 2 November 2015).

—. 'The formulas of L'Étourdit'. *Lacanian Ink* 27 (2006): 80–95.

—. 'Hegel and the whole'. Trans. Ray Brassier and Alberto Toscano. In *Alain Badiou: Theoretical Writings*. 221–32. London: Continuum, 2004.

—. 'Homage to Jacques Derrida'. In *Adieu Derrida*, ed. Costas Douzinas. 34–46. Basingstoke: Palgrave Macmillan, 2007.

—. *Infinite Thought: Truth and the Return to Philosophy*. Trans. Oliver Feltham and Justin Clemens. London; New York: Continuum, 2003.

—. 'Kant's subtractive ontology'. Trans. Ray Brassier and Alberto Toscano. In *Alain Badiou: Theoretical Writings*. 135–42. London: Continuum, 2004.

—. *L'Être et l'événement*. L'ordre philosophique. Paris: Editions du Seuil, 1988.

—. *L'Hypothèse communiste*. Paris: Nouvelles éditions Lignes, 2009.

—. *La Relation énigmatique entre philosophie et politique*. Meaux: Editions Germina, 2011.

—. *La République de Platon*. Paris: Fayard, 2012.

—. 'La Scène de deux'. In *De l'amour*. 177–90. Paris: Flammarion, 1999.

—. 'Language, thought, poetry'. Trans. Ray Brassier and Alberto Toscano. In *Alain Badiou: Theoretical Writings*. 233–41. London: Continuum, 2004.

—. *L'Antiphilosophie de Wittgenstein*. Paris: Nous, 2009.

—. *Le Concept de modèle*. Paris: Fayard, 2007.

—. *Le Fini et l'infini*. Paris: Bayard, 2010.

—. *Le Nombre et les nombres*. Paris: Editions du Seuil, 1990.

—. *Le Siècle*. Paris: Editions du Seuil, 2005.

—. *Les Années rouges*. Paris: Les Prairies Ordinaires, 2012.

—. *L'Éthique: essai sur la conscience du mal*. Caen: Nous, 2003.

—. 'L'Humiliation ordinaire'. *Le Monde*, 15 November 2005.

—. 'L'Investigation transcendentale'. In *Alain Badiou: penser le multiple*, ed. Charles Ramond. 7–20. Paris: L'Harmattan, 2002.

—. 'L'Offrande réservée'. In *Sens en tout sens: autour des travaux de Jean-Luc Nancy*, ed. François Guibal and Jean-Clet Martin. 13–24. Paris: Galilée, 2004.

—. *Logics of Worlds*. Trans. Alberto Toscano. London: Continuum, 2009.

—. *Logiques des mondes*. Paris: Editions du Seuil, 2006.

—. *Manifeste pour la philosophie*. Paris: Editions du Seuil, 1989.

—. *Manifesto for Philosophy*. Trans. Norman Madarasz. Albany: State University of New York Press, 1999.

—. 'Mathematics and philosophy: the grand style and the little style'. Trans. Ray Brassier and Alberto Toscano. In *Alain Badiou: Theoretical Writings*. 3–20. London: Continuum, 2004.

—. *The Meaning of Sarkozy*. Trans. David Fernbach. London: Verso, 2008.

—. *Monde contemporain et désir de philosophie*. Reims: Noira, 1992.

—. 'Notes sur *Les Séquestrés d'Altona*'. *Revue Internationale de Philosophie*, no. 231 (2005): 51–60.

—. 'Notes toward a thinking of appearance'. Trans. Ray Brassier and Alberto Toscano. In *Alain Badiou: Theoretical Writings*. 177–88. London: Continuum, 2004.

—. 'On evil: an interview with Alain Badiou'. *Cabinet*, no. 5 (2001). <http://www.cabinet-magazine.org/issues/5/alainbadiou.php> (last accessed 2 November 2015).

—. 'On Simon Critchley's infinitely demanding: ethics of commitment, politics of resistance'. *Critical Horizons* 10, no. 2 (2009): 154–62.

—. 'On subtraction'. Trans. Ray Brassier and Alberto Toscano. In *Alain Badiou: Theoretical Writings*. 103–18. London: Continuum, 2004.

—. 'On the truth process'. European Graduate School, 2002. <http://www.lacan.com/badeurope.htm> (last accessed 2 November 2015).

—. 'One divides itself into two'. In *Towards a Politics of Truth: The Retrieval of Lenin*. Essen, Germany, February 2001.

—. 'One, multiple, multiplicities'. Trans. Ray Brassier and Alberto Toscano. In *Alain Badiou: Theoretical Writings*. 67–80. London: Continuum, 2004.

—. *Petit manuel d'inesthétique*. Paris: Editions du Seuil, 1998.

—. *Petit panthéon portatif*. Paris: La Fabrique, 2008.

—. *Peut-on penser la politique?* Paris: Editions du Seuil, 2008.

—. 'Philosophy and mathematics: infinity and the end of romanticism'. Trans. Ray Brassier and Alberto Toscano. In *Alain Badiou: Theoretical Writings*. 21–38. London: Continuum, 2004.

—. 'Philosophy and politics'. *Radical Philosophy* (1999): 29–32.

—. *Philosophy for Militants*. London: Verso, 2012.

—. 'Philosophy, sciences, mathematics (interview)'. *Collapse* I (2006): 11–26.

—. 'Plato, our dear Plato!' Trans. Alberto Toscano. *Angelaki* 11, no. 3 (2006): 39–41.

—. 'Platonism and mathematical ontology'. Trans. Ray Brassier and Alberto Toscano. In *Alain Badiou: Theoretical Writings*. 49–58. London: Continuum, 2004.

—. *Plato's Republic*. New York: Columbia University Press, 2013.

—. *Pocket Pantheon: Figures of Postwar Philosophy*. Trans. David Macey. London: Verso, 2009.

—. 'Politics as truth procedure'. Trans. Ray Brassier and Alberto Toscano. In *Alain Badiou: Theoretical Writings*. 153–60. London: Continuum, 2004.

—. 'Politics: a non-expressive dialectics'. In *Urbanomic* (2005): 1–13. <http://blog.urbanomic.com/sphaleotas/archives/badiou-politics.pdf> (last accessed 2 November 2015).

—. 'Préface: destin des figures'. In Danielle Eleb, *Figures du destin*. 9–11. Ramonville Saint-Ange: Editions Erès, 2004.

—. 'The question of being today'. Trans. Ray Brassier and Alberto Toscano. In *Alain Badiou: Theoretical Writings*. 39–48. London: Continuum, 2004.

—. 'Saint Paul, fondateur du sujet universel'. *Etudes Théologiques et Religieuses* 75, no. 3 (2000): 323–34.

—. *Saint Paul: la fondation de l'universalisme*. Paris: Presses Universitaires de France, 1997.

—. *Saint Paul: The Foundation of Universalism*. Trans. Ray Brassier. Stanford: Stanford University Press, 2003.

—. *Second Manifeste pour la philosophie*. Paris: Fayard, 2009.

—. 'Séminaire: Images du temps présent (1)'. Ecole Normale Supérieure, 2002. <http://www.entretemps.asso.fr/Badiou/01-02.3.htm> (last accessed 2 November 2015).

—. 'Séminaire: Images du temps présent: "Qu-est-ce que vivre?"'. Ecole Normale Supérieure, 2004. <http://www.entretemps.asso.fr/Badiou/03-04.htm> (last accessed 2 November 2015).

—. 'Séminaire: La Politique'. Ecole Normale Supérieure, 1992. <http://www.entretemps.asso.fr/Badiou/91-92.htm> (last accessed 2 November 2015).

—. 'Séminaire: S'orienter dans la pensée, s'orienter dans l'existence'. Ecole Normale Supérieure, 2007. <http://www.entretemps.asso.fr/Badiou/06-07.htm> (last accessed 2 November 2015).

—. 'Séminaire: Théorie axiomatique du sujet'. Ecole Normale Supérieure, 1998. <http://www.entretemps.asso.fr/Badiou/96-98.htm> (last accessed 2 November 2015).

—. 'Spinoza's closed ontology'. Trans. Ray Brassier and Alberto Toscano. In *Alain Badiou: Theoretical Writings*. 81–93. London: Continuum, 2004.

—. 'The subject of art'. *The Symptom* 6 (2005). <http://www.lacan.com/symptom6_articles/badiou.html> (last accessed 2 November 2015).

—. *Théorie de la contradiction*. Paris: Maspero, 1975.

—. 'The transcendental'. Trans. Ray Brassier and Alberto Toscano. In *Alain Badiou: Theoretical Writings*. 189–220. London: Continuum, 2004.

—. 'Truth: forcing the unnameable'. Trans. Ray Brassier and Alberto Toscano. In *Alain Badiou: Theoretical Writings*. 119–34. London: Continuum, 2004.

—. 'Vingt-quatre notes sur les usages du mot "peuple"'. In *Qu'est-ce qu'un peuple?* 9–21. Paris: La Fabrique, 2013.

—. 'Who is Nietzsche?' *Pli* 11 (2001): 1–11.

Badiou, Alain, and Bruno Bosteels. 'Can change be thought? A dialogue with Alain Badiou'. In *Alain Badiou: Philosophy and Its Conditions*. 237–62. New York: State University of New York Press, 2005.

—. 'Peut-on penser le nouveau en situation?' *Failles: Situations de la Philosophie*, no. 2 (2006): 62–93.

Badiou, Alain, Ray Brassier and Alberto Toscano. *Alain Badiou: Theoretical Writings*. London: Continuum, 2004.

Badiou, Alain, and Barbara Cassin. *Heidegger: le nazisme, les femmes, la philosophie*. Paris: Fayard, 2010.

—. *Il n'y a pas de rapport sexuel: deux leçons sur 'L'Etourdit' de Lacan*. Paris: Fayard, 2010.

Badiou, Alain, and Simon Critchley. 'Ours is not a terrible situation'. *Philosophy Today* 51, no. 3 (2007): 357–65.

Badiou, Alain, Alain Finkielkraut and Aude Lancelin. *L'Explication; conversation avec Aude Lancelin*. Paris: Nouvelles éditions Lignes, 2010.

Badiou, Alain, and Peter Hallward. 'Politics and philosophy: an interview with Alain Badiou'. *Angelaki* 3, no. 3 (1998): 113–36.

Badiou, Alain, Peter Hallward and Bruno Bosteels. 'Beyond formalisation: an interview with Peter Hallward and Bruno Bosteels'. Trans. Bruno Bosteels and Alberto Toscano. *Angelaki* 8, no. 2 (2003): 111–36.

Badiou, Alain, and Jean-Claude Milner. *Controverse: dialogue sur la politique et la philosophie de notre temps*. Paris: Editions du Seuil, 2012.

Badiou, Alain, and Elizabeth Roudinesco. *Jacques Lacan, passé présent*. Paris: Editions du Seuil, 2012.

Badiou, Alain, and Fabien Tarby. *La Philosophie et l'événement*. Meaux: Germina, 2010.

Badiou, Alain, and Tzuchien Tho. 'New horizons in mathematics as a philosophical condition: an interview with Alain Badiou'. *Parrhesia* 3 (2007): 1–11.

Bailly, Jean-Christophe. *Le Versant animal*. Paris: Bayard, 2007.

Baldwin, Jon and Nick Haeffner. '"Fault lines": Simon Critchley in discussion on Alain Badiou'. *Polygraph* 17 (2005): 295–307.

Balibar, Étienne. 'Debating with Alain Badiou on universalism'. *Philosophie Française Contemporaine*, 2007. <http://www.cirphles.ens.fr/ciepfc/publications/etienne-balibar/article/debating-with-alain-badiou-on?lang=fr> (last accessed 2 November 2015).

—. '"Histoire de la vérité": Alain Badiou dans la philosophie française'. In *Alain Badiou: penser le multiple*, ed. Charles Ramond. 497–524. Paris: L'Harmattan, 2002.

Bandres, Lenin. 'Badiou et l'atomisme ancien'. In *Ecrits autour de la pensée d'Alain Badiou*, ed. Bruno Bensana and Oliver Feltham. 41–52. Paris: L'Harmattan, 2007.

Barbour, Charles. 'Militants of truth, communities of equality: Badiou and the ignorant schoolmaster'. *Educational Philosophy and Theory* 42, no. 2 (2010): 251–63.

Barker, Jason. *Alain Badiou: A Critical Introduction*. London: Pluto Press, 2002.

Barthélémy, Jean-Hugues. 'What new humanism today?' *Cultural Politics* 6, no. 2 (2010): 237–52.

Bassiri, Nima. 'Material translations in the Cartesian brain'. *Studies in History and Philosophy of Biological and Biomedical Sciences* 43, no. 1 (2011): 244–55.

Battro, Antonio M., Kurt W. Fischer and Pierre J. Léna, eds. *The Educated Brain: Essays in Neuroeducation*. Cambridge: Cambridge University Press, 2008.

Beck, Ulrich, and Patrick Camiller. 'Neither order nor peace: a response to Bruno Latour'. *Common Knowledge* 11, no. 1 (2005): 1–7.

Bell Jr, Daniel M. 'Badiou's faith and Paul's gospel: the politics of indifference and the overcoming of capital'. *Angelaki* 12, no. 1 (2007): 97–111.

Bennett, M. R., and P. M. S. Hacker. *Philosophical Foundations of Neuroscience*. Malden, MA: Blackwell, 2003.

Bensaid, Daniel. 'Alain Badiou et le miracle de l'événement'. In *Essai de taupologie générale*. 143–70. Paris: Fayard, 2001.

Bensaude-Vincent, Bernadette, and Dorothée Benoit-Browaeys. *Fabriquer la vie: où va la biologie de synthèse?* Paris: Editions du Seuil, 2011.

Bergen, Véronique. 'Pensée et Être chez Deleuze et Badiou (Badiou lecteur de Deleuze)'. In *Alain Badiou: penser le multiple*, ed. Charles Ramond. 437–56. Paris: L'Harmattan, 2002.

Besana, Bruno. 'One or several events? The knot between event and subject in the work of Alain Badiou and Gilles Deleuze'. *Polygraph* 17 (2005): 245–66.

—. 'Quel multiple? Les conditions ontologiques du concept d'événement chez Badiou et Deleuze'. In *Écrits autour de la pensée d'Alain Badiou*. 23–40. Paris: L'Harmattan, 2007.

Besana, Bruno, and Oliver Feltham, eds. *Écrits autour de la pensée d'Alain Badiou*. Paris: L'Harmattan, 2007.

Besiner, Jean-Michel. *Demain les posthumains? Le futur a-t-il encore besoin de nous?* Paris: Fayard, 2010.

Bibeau, Gilles. 'Quel humanisme pour un âge post-génomique?' *Anthropologie et Societés* 27, no. 3 (2003): 93–113.

—. 'What is human in humans? Responses from biology, anthropology, and philosophy'. *Journal of Medicine and Philosophy* 36 (2011): 354–63.

Bimbenet, Étienne. '"La Chasse sans prise": Merleau-Ponty et le projet d'une science de l'homme sans l'homme'. *Les Études philosophiques*, no. 2 (2001): 239–59.

Bindé, Jérôme. 'Human, still human!' *Diogenes* 206 (2005): 55–61.

Block, Ned, J. Fodor and H. Putnam. 'Anti-reductionism slaps back'. *Philosophical Perspectives* 11 (1997): 107–33.

Blok, Anders, and Torben Elgaard Jensen. *Bruno Latour: Hybrid Thoughts in a Hybrid World*. London: Routledge, 2011.

Boltanski, Luc. *L'Amour et la justice comme compétences: trois essais de sociologie de l'action*. Paris: Editions Métailié, 1990.

Boltanski, Luc, and Laurent Thévenot. *De la justification: les économies de grandeur*. Paris: Gallimard, 1991.

Bos, René ten. 'Serres's philosophy of science: an introduction for business ethicists'. *Business and Professional Ethics Journal* 30, no. 3–4 (2011): 331–53.

Bosteels, Bruno. *Alain Badiou, une trajectoire polémique*. Paris: La Fabrique, 2009.

Bostrom, Nick. 'Dignity and enhancement'. *Contemporary Readings in Law and Social Justice* 1, no. 2 (2009): 84–115.

—. 'In defence of posthuman dignity'. *Bioethics* 19, no. 3 (2005): 202–14.

—. 'Transhumanist values'. In *Ethical Issues for the Twenty-First Century*, ed. Frederick Adams. 3–14. Charlottesville: Philosophical Documentation Center Press, 2003.

Bould, Mark, and Sherryl Vint. 'Learning from the little engines that couldn't: transported by Gernsback, Wells, and Latour'. *Science Fiction Studies* 33, no. 1, Technoculture and Science Fiction (2006): 129–48.

Braidotti, Rosi. *The Posthuman*. Cambridge: Polity Press, 2013.

—. 'Posthuman, all too human: towards a new process ontology'. *Theory, Culture & Society* 23, no. 7–8 (2006): 197–208.

Brassier, Ray. 'The enigma of realism: on Quentin Meillassoux's *After Finitude*'. *Collapse* II (2007): 15–54.

—. *Nihil Unbound*. Basingstoke: Palgrave Macmillan, 2007.

—. 'Stellar void or cosmic animal? Badiou and Deleuze on the dice-throw'. *Pli*, no. 10 (2000): 200–16.

Brassier, Ray, and Marcin Rychter. 'I am a nihilist because I still believe in truth: Ray

Brassier interviewed by Marcin Rychter'. *Kronos* 4 (2011). <http://www.kronos.org.pl/index.php?23151,896> (last accessed 2 November 2015).

Brenner, Anastasios, and Jean Gayon, eds. *French Studies in the Philosophy of Science.* Dordrecht: Springer, 2009.

Brown, Nathan. 'The speculative and the specific: on Hallward and Meillassoux'. In *The Speculative Turn: Continental Materialism and Realism*, ed. Levi Bryant, Nick Srnicek and Graham Harman. 142–63. Melbourne: re.press, 2011.

Brown, Steven D. 'Michel Serres: science, translation and the logic of the parasite'. *Theory, Culture & Society* 19, no. 3 (2002): 1–27.

—. 'Parasite logic'. *Journal of Organizational Change Management* 17, no. 4 (2004): 383–95.

—. 'The theatre of measurement: Michel Serres'. *The Sociological Review* 53 (2005): 215–27.

—. 'A topology of the sensible: Michel Serres' five senses'. *New Formations* (2011): 162–70.

Bruining, Dennis. 'A somatechnics of moralism: new materialism or material foundationalism'. *Somatechnics* 3, no. 1 (2013): 149–68.

Bryant, Levi. *The Democracy of Objects.* Ann Arbor: Open Humanities Press, 2011.

Bryant, Levi, Nick Srnicek and Graham Harman, eds. *The Speculative Turn: Continental Materialism and Realism.* Melbourne: re.press, 2011.

Burns, Michael, and Brian Smith. 'Materialism, subjectivity and the outcome of French philosophy: interview with Adrian Johnston by Michael Burns & Brian Smith'. *Cosmos and History: The Journal of Natural and Social Philosophy* 7, no. 1 (2011): 167–81.

Burns, Michael O'Neill. 'Prolegomena to a materialist humanism'. *Angelaki* 19, no. 1 (2014): 99–112.

Calarco, Matthew. 'Deconstruction is not vegetarianism: humanism, subjectivity, and animal ethics'. *Continental Philosophy Review* 37 (2004): 175–201.

Calvert-Minor, Chris. 'Epistemological misgivings of Karen Barad's "Posthumanism"'. *Human Studies* 37 (2014): 123–37.

Calvin, William. 'My synapses, myself: do our synaptic connections make us who we are?' *Nature* 417, no. 13 (2002): 691–2.

Canguilhem, Georges. 'The death of man, or, exhaustion of the cogito?' In *The Cambridge Companion to Foucault*, ed. Gary Gutting. 71–89. Cambridge: Cambridge University Press, 2006.

Caporael, Linnda R. '*Homo sapiens, Homo faber, Homo socians*: technology and the social animal'. *Synthese* 190 (1987): 233–44.

Capurro, Rafael. 'Beyond humanisms'. *Journal of New Frontiers in Spatial Concepts* 4 (2012): 1–12.

Cascardi, Anthony J. *The Subject of Modernity.* Cambridge: Cambridge University Press, 1992.

Cepl, Marc. 'La Narrativité comme moralité: pour une lecture "poétique" de l'éthique dans *Soi-même comme un autre*'. *Études de Lettres* 3–4 (1996): 141–58.

Changeux, Jean-Pierre. *Du Vrai, du beau, du bien: une nouvelle approche neuronale.* Paris: Odile Jacob, 2008.

—. 'The Ferrier Lecture 1998: The molecular biology of consciousness investigated with genetically modified mice'. *Philosophical Transactions of the Royal Society of London*, no. 361 (2006): 2239–59.

—. 'Jean-Pierre G. Changeux'. In *The History of Neuroscience in Autobiography*, vol. 4, ed. Larry R. Squire. 116–43. Waltham, MA: Academic Press, 2004.

—. 'La Vie des formes et les formes de la vie: avant-propos'. In *La Vie des formes et les formes de la vie*, ed. Jean-Pierre Changeux. 7–15. Paris: Odile Jacob, 2012.

—. *L'Homme neuronal.* Paris: Fayard, 1983.

—. 'The molecular biology of consciousness'. In *Consciousness Transitions: Phylogenetic, Ontogenetic, and Physiological Aspects*, ed. Hans Liljenström and Peter Århem. 123–60. Amsterdam: Elsevier, 2008.

—. *Neuronal Man: The Biology of Mind*. Trans. Laurence Garet. New York: Parthenon Books, 1985.

—. 'Penser la bioéthique: un débat philosophique'. *Mots*, no. 44 (1995): 123–31.

—. *The Physiology of Truth: Neuroscience and Human Knowledge*. Trans. M. B. DeBevoise. Cambridge, MA: The Bellknap Press, 2004.

—. 'Reflections on the origins of the human brain'. In *The Newborn Brain: Neuroscience and Clinical Applications*, ed. Hugo Lagercrantz, Laura R. Ment, M. A. Hanson and Donald M. Peebles. 1–10. Cambridge: Cambridge University Press, 2010.

—. 'Towards a neuroscience of the capable person: unity, diversity and oneself as another'. In *Symposium of the World Knowledge Dialogue: New Discoveries Defining Complexity*. Crans-Montana (Switzerland), 2006. <http://www.wkdialogue.ch/symposia/2006/videos/friday-15/jean-pierre-changeux/index.html> (last accessed 2 November 2015).

Changeux, Jean-Pierre, and Jean Chavaillon, eds. *Origins of the Human Brain*. Oxford: Clarendon Press, 1995.

Changeux, Jean-Pierre, and Alain Connes. *Conversations on Mind, Matter, and Mathematics*. Trans. M. B. DeBevoise. Princeton: Princeton University Press, 1995.

Changeux, Jean-Pierre, Philippe Courrege and Antoine Danchin. 'A theory of the epigenesis of neuronal networks by selective stabilisation of synapses'. *Proceedings of the National Academy of Sciences U.S.A.* 70 (1973): 2974–8.

Changeux, Jean-Pierre, Antonio Damasio, Wolf Singer and Yves Christen, eds. *Neurobiology of Human Values*. Research and Perspectives in Neurosciences. Dordrecht: Springer, 2005.

Changeux, Jean-Pierre, and Stanislas Dehaene. 'Hierarchical neuronal modeling of cognitive functions: from synaptic transmission to the Tower of London'. *International Journal of Psychophysiology* 35 (2000): 179–87.

—. 'Neuronal models of cognitive functions'. *Cognition* 33 (1989): 63–109.

—. 'The neuronal workspace model: conscious processing and learning'. In *Learning and Memory: A Comprehensive Reference*, ed. R. Menzel. 729–57. Oxford: Elsevier, 2008.

Changeux, Jean-Pierre, and Colin McGinn. 'Neuroscience & philosophy: an exchange'. *The New York Review of Books*, 15 August 2013.

Changeux, Jean-Pierre, and Paul Ricœur. *What Makes Us Think?: A Neuroscientist and a Philosopher Argue about Ethics, Human Nature, and the Brain*. Trans. M. B. DeBevoise. Princeton: Princeton University Press, 2002.

Cherry, Christopher. 'Machines as persons?' *Royal Institute of Philosophy Supplement* 29 (1991): 11–24.

Chiew, Florence. 'Neuroplasticity as an ecology of mind: a conversation with Gregory Bateson and Catherine Malabou'. *Journal of Consciousness Studies* 19, no. 11–12 (2012): 32–54.

Chiong, Winston. 'The self: from philosophy to cognitive neuroscience'. *Neurocase: The Neural Basis of Cognition* 17, no. 3 (2011): 190–200.

Choudhury, Suparna, and Jan Slaby, eds. *Critical Neuroscience: A Handbook of the Social and Cultural Contexts of Neuroscience*. Malden, MA: Wiley-Blackwell, 2012.

Clemens, Justin. 'The age of plastic; or, Catherine Malabou on the Hegelian futures market'. *Cosmos and History: The Journal of Natural and Social Philosophy* 6, no. 1 (2010): 153–62.

Clemens, Justin, and Jon Roffe. 'Philosophy as anti-religion in the work of Alain Badiou'. *Sophia* 47 (2008): 345–58.

Cohen, Richard A., and James L. Marsh. *Ricœur as Another: The Ethics of Subjectivity*. Albany: State University of New York Press, 2002.

Cohen, Tom, ed. *Telemorphosis: Theory in the Era of Climate Change*, vol. 1. Ann Arbor: Open Humanities Press, 2012.

Colebrook, Claire. *The Death of the PostHuman: Essays on Extinction, Volume One*. Ann Arbor: Open Humanities Press, 2014.

—. *Sex After Life: Essays on Extinction, Volume Two*. Ann Arbor: Open Humanities Press, 2014.

Connolly, William E. 'The 'new materialism' and the fragility of things'. *Millennium: Journal of International Studies* 41 (2013): 399–412.

Coole, Diana. 'Agentic capacities and capacious historical materialism: thinking with new materialisms in the political sciences'. *Millennium: Journal of International Studies* 41, no. 3 (2013): 451–69.

Coole, Diana, and Samantha Frost. *New Materialisms: Ontology, Agency, and Politics*. Durham, NC: Duke University Press, 2010.

Coons, John E., and Patrick M. Brennan. *By Nature Equal: The Anatomy of a Western Insight*. Princeton: Princeton University Press, 1999.

Cooper, Simon. 'Regulating hybrid monsters? The limits of Latour and actor network theory'. *Arena* 29/30 (2008): 305–30.

Crépon, Marc. 'Le Malin génie des langues. Note de lecture sur "L'Éloge de la philosophie française" de Michel Serres'. *Rue Descartes*, no. 26 (1999): 143–54.

Critchley, Simon. 'Angel in disguise: Michel Serres' attempt to re-enchant the world'. *Times Literary Supplement*, no. 4842 (1996): 3.

—. 'Comment ne pas céder sur son désir (sur l'éthique de Badiou)'. In *Alain Badiou: penser le multiple*, ed. Charles Ramond. 207–34. Paris: L'Harmattan, 2002.

—. 'Demanding approval: on the ethics of Alain Badiou'. *Radical Philosophy*, no. 100 (2000): 16–27.

—. 'Prolegomena to any post-deconstructive subjectivity'. In *Deconstructive Subjectivities*, ed. Simon Critchley. 13–46. Albany: State University of New York Press, 1996.

Crockett, Clayton, and Catherine Malabou. 'Plasticity and the future of philosophy and theology'. *Political Theology* 11, no. 1 (2010): 15–34.

Crockett, Clayton, and Jeffrey W. Robbins. *Religion, Politics, and the Earth: The New Materialism*. Basingstoke: Palgrave Macmillan, 2013.

Crowley, Martin. *L'Homme sans: politiques de la finitude*. Paris: Nouvelles éditions Lignes, 2009.

D'Allonnes, Myriam Revault, and François Azouvi, eds. *Paul Ricœur: cahiers de L'Herne. Tome 1*. Paris: Editions du Seuil, 2007.

—, eds. *Paul Ricœur: cahiers de L'Herne. Tome 2*. Paris: Editions du Seuil, 2007.

Damasio, Antonio. *Descartes' Error: Emotion, Reason and the Human Brain*. New York: Avon Books, 1994.

—. *The Feeling of What Happens: Body, Emotion and the Making of Consciousness*. London: Random House, 2000.

—. *Looking for Spinoza: Joy, Sorrow, and the Feeling Brain*. London: William Heinemann, 2003.

—. *Self Comes to Mind: Constructing the Conscious Brain*. New York: Pantheon Books, 2010.

—. 'The somatic marker hypothesis and the possible functions of the prefrontal cortex'. *Philosophical Transactions of the Royal Society of London* 351 (1996): 1413–20.

Damlé, Amaleena. 'Posthuman encounters: technology, embodiment and gender in recent feminist thought and in the work of Marie Darrieussecq'. *Comparative Critical Studies* 9, no. 3 (2012): 303–18.

Dauenhauer, Bernard P. 'What makes us think? Two views'. In *Reading Ricœur*, ed. David M. Kaplan. 31–46. Albany: State University of New York Press, 2008.

Dehaene, Stanislas, and Jean-Pierre Changeux. 'Neural mechanisms for access to consciousness'. In *The Cognitive Neurosciences III*, ed. M. Gazzaniga. 1145–57. New York: Norton, 2004.

Dehaene, Stanislas, Jean-Pierre Changeux, Lionel Naccache, Jérôme Sackur and Claire Sergent. 'Conscious, preconscious, and subliminal processing: a testable taxonomy'. *Trends in Cognitive Science* 10 (2006): 204–11.

Dehaene, Stanislas, and Lionel Naccache. 'Towards a cognitive neuroscience of consciousness: basic evidence and a workspace framework'. *Cognition*, no. 79 (2001): 1–37.

Delcò, Alessandro, Matthew Tiews and Trina Marmarelli. 'Michel Serres: philosophy as an indeterminate essence to be invented'. *Configurations* 8, no. 2 (2000): 229–34.

Dennett, Daniel. *Consciousness Explained*. New York: Penguin, 1992.

—. 'The self as a center of narrative gravity'. In *Self and Consciousness: Multiple Perspectives*, ed. F. Kessel, P. Cole and D. Johnson. 275–88. Hillsdale, NJ: Erlbaum, 1992.

Dennett, Daniel, and Marcel Kinsbourne. 'Escape from the Cartesian theater'. *Behavioral and Brain Sciences* 15, no. 2 (1992): 234–48.

Derrida, Jacques. 'Force of law: the mystical foundation of authority'. In *Deconstruction and the Possibility of Justice*, ed. Drucilla Cornell, Michel Rosenfeld and David Gray Carlson. 3–67. New York: Routledge, 1992.

—. 'Le Temps des adieux: Heidegger (lu par) Hegel (lu par) Malabou'. *Revue Philosophique de la France et de l'Étranger* 188, no. 1 (1998): 3–47.

—. *Of Grammatology*. Baltimore: Johns Hopkins University Press, 1976.

—. *Of Spirit: Heidegger and the Question*. Chicago: University of Chicago Press, 1989.

—. *On Touching – Jean-Luc Nancy*. Trans. Christine Irizarry. Stanford: Stanford University Press, 2005.

—. *Politics of Friendship*. London: Verso, 1997.

—. *Speech and Phenomena*. Evanston: Northwestern University Press, 1979.

Derrida, Jacques, and Jean-Luc Nancy. '"Eating well" or the calculation of the subject: an interview with Jacques Derrida'. In *Who Comes After the Subject?* 105–9. Chicago: University of Chicago Press, 1991.

Descola, Philippe. *L'Ecologie des autres: l'anthropologie et la question de la nature*. Paris: Editions Quae, 2011.

Disilvestro, Russell. *Human Capacities and Moral Status*. Dordrecht: Springer, 2010.

Dolphijn, Rick, and Iris van der Tuin. *New Materialism: Interviews and Cartographies*. Ann Arbor: Open Humanities Press, 2012.

—. 'Pushing dualism to an extreme: on the philosophical impetus of a new materialism'. *Continental Philosophy Review* 44 (2011): 383–400.

Doucet, Hubert. 'Anthropological challenges raised by neuroscience: some ethical reflections'. *Cambridge Quarterly of Healthcare Ethics*, no. 16 (2007): 219–26.

Dreyfus, Hubert L. *What Computers Still Can't Do: A Critique of Artificial Reason*. Cambridge, MA: MIT Press, 1993.

Edelman, Gerald M. *Neural Darwinism: The Theory of Neuronal Group Selection*. New York: Basic Books, 1987.

Edelman, Gerald M., and Jean-Pierre Changeux, eds. *The Brain*. Piscataway, NJ: Transaction Publishers, 2000.

Ehrenberg, Alain. 'Le Cerveau "social": chimère épistémologique et vérité sociologique'. *Esprit*, no. 341 (2008): 79–103.

—. 'Le Sujet cérébral'. *Esprit*, no. 309 (2004): 130–55.

Evans, David Cenydd Lloyd. 'Reading neuroscience: ventriloquism as a metaphor for multiple readings of self'. A thesis submitted to the University of Plymouth in partial fulfilment for the degree of Doctor of Philosophy, 2006.

Evers, Kathinka. 'Towards a philosophy for neuroethics'. *Science and Society*, no. 8 (2007): 548–51.

Fadaak, Raad. 'Catherine Malabou's *The New Wounded: From Neurosis to Brain Damage*'. In *Somatosphere* (2013). <http://somatosphere.net/?p=6289> (last accessed 2 November 2015).

Feneuil, Anthony. '"Que le dieu soit là". Le tournant corrélationniste de Quentin Meillassoux'. In *ThéoRèmes*, no. 6: Le Réalisme spéculatif (2014). <http://theoremes.revues.org/651> (last accessed 2 November 2015).

Ferrando, Francesca. 'Posthumanism, transhumanism, antihumanism, metahumanism, and new materialisms: differences and relations'. *Existenz* 8, no. 2 (2013): 26–32.

Gall, Robert S. 'Fideism or faith in doubt? Meillassoux, Heidegger and the end of metaphysics'. *Philosophy Today* 57 (2013): 358–68.

Gallagher, Shaun. 'Philosophical conceptions of the self: implications for cognitive science'. *Trends in Cognitive Sciences* 4, no. 1 (2000): 14–21.

Gallagher, Shaun, and J. Shear. *Models of the Self.* Thorverton: Imprint Academic, 1999.

Galloway, Alexander R. *French Theory Today: An Introduction to Possible Futures.* TPSNY/ Erudio Editions, 2010. <cultureandcommunication.org/galloway/FTT/French-Theory-Today.pdf> (last accessed 2 November 2015).

—. *Les Nouveaux Réalistes.* Paris: Editions Léo Scheer, 2012.

—. 'Plastic reading'. *Novel: A Forum on Fiction* 45, no. 1 (2012): 10–12.

—. 'The poverty of philosophy and post-Fordism'. *Critical Inquiry* 39 (2013): 347–66.

Gazzaniga, Michael S. *The Ethical Brain.* New York: Dana Press, 2005.

Gendron, Pierre-Marc. 'Le Voyage extraordinaire: la méthode et le discours de Michel Serres'. Thèse de doctorat, Université Laval, 2007.

Gerbet, Charles H. 'In the zone, entre Stalker et Meillassoux'. (2012). <http://jeanclet-martin.blog.fr/2012/04/07/in-the-zone-entre-stalker-et-meillassoux-13441542/> (last accessed 2 November 2015).

Geroulanos, Stefanos. *An Atheism That Is Not Humanist Emerges in French Thought.* Stanford: Stanford University Press, 2010.

Gibson, Andrew. *Beckett and Badiou: The Pathos of Intermittency.* Oxford: Oxford University Press, 2006.

—. 'The rarity of the event: on Alain Badiou'. *New Formations* (2004): 136–42.

Gifford, Paul. 'The resonance of Ricœur: *Soi-même comme un autre*'. In *Subject Matters: Subject and Self in French Literature from Descartes to the Present*, ed. Paul Gifford and Johnnie Gratton. Faux Titre, no. 184. 200–25. Amsterdam: Rodopi, 2000.

Gifford, Paul, and Johnnie Gratton, eds. *Subject Matters: Subject and Self in French Literature from Descartes to the Present.* Faux titre, no. 184. Amsterdam: Rodopi, 2000.

Gironi, Fabio. 'Meillassoux's speculative philosophy of science: contingency and mathematics'. *Pli*, no. 22 (2011): 25–60.

Gonzalez-Torres, Miguel Angel. 'Psychoanalysis and neuroscience. Friends or enemies?' *International Forum of Psychoanalysis* 22, no. 1 (2013): 35–42.

Gratton, Peter. *Speculative Realism: Problems and Prospects.* London: Bloomsbury, 2014.

Gullestad, Anders M. 'Literature and the parasite'. *Deleuze Studies* 5, no. 3 (2011): 301–23.

Halberstam, Judith. *Posthuman Bodies.* Bloomington: Indiana University Press, 1995.

Hallward, Peter. 'Anything is possible: review essay on Quentin Meillassoux, *After Finitude*'. *Radical Philosophy*, 152 (2008): 51–7.

—. *Badiou: A Subject to Truth.* Minneapolis; London: University of Minnesota Press, 2003.

—. 'Depending on inconsistency: Badiou's Answer to the "guiding question of all contemporary philosophy"'. *Polygraph* 17 (2005): 7–21.

—. 'Introduction: consequences of abstraction'. In *Think Again: Alain Badiou and the Future of Philosophy*, ed. Peter Hallward. 1–20. London: Continuum, 2004.

—, ed. *Think Again: Alain Badiou and the Future of Philosophy.* London: Continuum, 2004.

Hallward, Peter, and Michel Serres. 'The science of relations: an interview'. *Angelaki* 8, no. 2 (2003): 227–38.

Haraway, Donna. 'A cyborg manifesto: science, technology, and socialist-feminism in the late twentieth century'. In *Simians, Cyborgs and Women: The Reinvention of Nature.* 149–81. New York: Routledge, 1991.

—. *When Species Meet.* Minneapolis: University of Minnesota Press, 2008.

Harlow, J. M. 'Recovery after severe injury to the head'. In *Readings in Behaviour*, ed. William G. Van der Kloot, Charles Walcott and Benjamin Dane. 291–308. New York: Ardent Media, 1974.

Harman, Graham. *Bruno Latour: Reassembling the Political.* London: Pluto Press, 2014.

—. *Prince of Networks: Bruno Latour and Metaphysics.* Melbourne: re.press, 2009.

—. 'Quentin Meillassoux: a new French philosopher'. *Philosophy Today*, no. 51 (2007): 104–17.

—. *Quentin Meillassoux: Philosophy in the Making*. Edinburgh: Edinburgh University Press, 2011.

Harris, Paul A. 'The itinerant theorist: nature and knowledge/ecology and topology in Michel Serres'. *SubStance* 26, no. 2 (1997): 37–58.

Hayles, N. Katherine. *How We Became Posthuman: Virtual Bodies in Cybernetics, Literature and Informatics*. Chicago: University of Chicago Press, 1999.

—. 'Two voices, one channel: equivocation in Michel Serres'. *SubStance* 17, no. 3 (1988): 3–12.

Haynes, Patrice. *Immanent Transcendence: Reconfiguring Materialism in Continental Philosophy*. New York: Bloomsbury, 2012.

Heidegger, Martin. 'Letter on Humanism'. In *Martin Heidegger: Basic Writings from 'Being and Time' (1927) to 'The Task of Thinking' (1964)*, ed. David Farrell Krell. 193. San Francisco: Harper and Row, 1978.

Hénaff, Marcel, and Anne-Marie Feenberg. 'Of stones, angels and humans: Michel Serres and the global city'. *SubStance* 26, no. 2 (1997): 59–80.

Herskovits, Elizabeth. 'Struggling over subjectivity: debates about the 'self' and Alzheimer's disease'. *Medical Anthropology Quarterly* 9, no. 2, Cultural Contexts of Aging and Health (1995): 146–64.

Herzogenrath, Bernd, ed. *Time and History in Deleuze and Serres*. London: Continuum, 2012.

Hewlett, Nick. 'Engagement and transcendence: the militant philosophy of Alain Badiou'. *Modern and Contemporary France* 12, no. 3 (2004): 335–52.

Hinton, Peta. '"Situated knowledges" and new materialism(s): rethinking a politics of location'. *Women: A Cultural Review* 25, no. 1 (2014): 99–113.

Hope, Alexander. 'The future is plastic: refiguring Malabou's plasticity'. *Journal for Cultural Research* 18, no. 4 (2014): 329–49.

Huizinga, Johan. *Homo Ludens*. London: Routledge, 2014.

Huyssteen, J. Wentzel van. *Alone in the World? Human Uniqueness in Science and Theology*. Grand Rapids: Eerdmans, 2006.

Huyssteen, J. Wentzel van, and Erik P. Wiebe, eds. *In Search of Self: Interdisciplinary Perspectives on Personhood*. Grand Rapids: Eerdmans, 2011.

Hyvärinen, Matti. '"Life as narrative" revisited'. *Partial Answers* 6, no. 2 (2008): 261–77.

Isaac, Bonnie J. '"Du fond d'un naufrage": notes on Michel Serres and Mallarmé's "Un Coup de dés"'. *MLN* 96, no. 4 (1981): 824–38.

James, Ian. *The New French Philosophy*. Cambridge: Polity Press, 2012.

Janicaud, Dominique. *Le Tournant théologique de la phénoménologie française*. Combas: Editions de l'Eclat, 1991.

Jeeves, Malcom, ed. *Rethinking Human Nature: A Multidisciplinary Approach*. Grand Rapids: Eerdmans, 2011.

Jeffs, Rory. 'The future of the future: Koyré, Kojève and Malabou speculate on Hegelian time'. *Parrhesia*, no. 15 (2012): 35–53.

Johnston, Adrian. 'Drive between brain and subject: an immanent critique of Lacanian pscychoanalysis'. *The Southern Journal of Philosophy* 51 (2013): 48–84.

—. 'From the spectacular act to the vanishing act: Badiou, Žižek, and the politics of Lacanian theory'. *International Journal of Žižek Studies* 1 (2007): 1–40.

—. 'The misfeeling of what happens: Slavoj Žižek, Antonio Damasio and a materialist account of affects'. *Subjectivity* 3 (2010): 76–100.

—. 'Points of forced freedom: eleven (more) theses on materialism'. *Speculations* IV (2013): 91–8.

—. *Prolegomena to Any Future Materialism: The Outcome of Contemporary French Philosophy*. Evanston: Northwestern University Press, 2013.

—. 'There is Truth, and then there are truths – or, Slavoj Žižek as a reader of Alain Badiou'. *International Journal of Žižek Studies* 1 (2007): 141–85.

—. 'What matter(s) in ontology: Alain Badiou, the Hebb-event, and materialism split from within'. *Angelaki* 13, no. 1 (2008): 27–49.

—. 'The world before worlds: Quentin Meillassoux and Alain Badiou's anti-Kantian transcendentalism'. *Contemporary French Civilization* 33, no. 1 (2009): 73–99.

Jollivet, Servanne. 'Heidegger d'un change à l'autre: Catherine Malabou, Didier Franck, François Raffoul'. *Revue Philosophique de la France et de l'Étranger* 194, no. 4 (2004): 455–68.

Jones, D. Gareth. 'Brain birth and personal identity'. *Journal of Medical Ethics* 15 (1989): 173–85.

Jones, Lisa. 'Oneself as an author (life as narrative, and identity as narrative identity)'. *Theory, Culture & Society* 27, no. 5 (2010): 49–68.

Kearney, Richard. 'The crisis of narrative in contemporary culture'. *Metaphilosophy* 28, no. 3 (1997): 183–95.

Kennedy, Duncan. 'Knowledge and the political: Bruno Latour's political epistemology'. *Cultural Critique*, no. 74 (2010): 83–97.

Kirby, Vicki. 'Initial conditions'. *Differences: A Journal of Feminist Cultural Studies* 23, no. 3 (2012): 197–205.

Lakoff, George, and Mark Johnson. *Philosophy in the Flesh: The Embodied Mind and Its Challenge to Western Thought*. New York: Basic Books, 1999.

Landau, Misia. 'Human evolution as narrative'. *American Scientist* 72 (1984): 262–86.

Latour, Bruno. 'Agency at the time of the Anthropocene'. *New Literary History* 45, no. 1 (2014): 1–18.

—. 'Anthropology at the time of the Anthropocene – a personal view of what is to be studied'. Distinguished lecture, American Association of Anthropologists, Washington DC, December 2014.

—. 'Biography of an inquiry: on a book about modes of existence'. *Social Studies of Science* 43, no. 2 (2013): 287–301.

—. 'Can we get our materialism back, please?' *Isis* 98, no. 1 (2007): 138–42.

—. 'A cautious Prometheus? A few steps toward a philosophy of design (with special attention to Peter Sloterdijk)'. In *Networks of Design Conference – Design History Society*. Falmouth, Cornwall, 3–6 September 2008.

—. *Cogitamus: six lettres sur les humanités scientifiques*. Paris: La Découverte, 2010.

—. 'Coming out as a philosopher'. *Social Studies of Science* 40, no. 4 (2010): 599–608.

—. 'Ein Ding ist Ein Thing. A philosophical platform for a left European party'. *Concepts and Transformation* 3, no. 1/2 (1998): 97–112.

—. 'The Enlightenment without the critique: a word on Michel Serres' philosophy'. *Royal Institute of Philosophy Lecture Series* 21 (1987): 83–97.

—. *Enquête sur les modes d'existence: une anthropologie des modernes*. Paris: La Découverte, 2012.

—. 'Et si l'on parlait un peu politique?' *Politix* 15, no. 58 (2001): 143–66.

—. 'Facing Gaia: six lectures on the political theology of nature'. The Gifford Lectures on Natural Religion. Edinburgh, 2013.

—. 'Factures/fractures. De la notion de réseau à celle d'attachement'. In *Ce qui nous relie*, ed. André Micoud and Michel Peroni. 189–208. La Tour d'Aigues: Editions de l'Aube, 2000.

—. 'Factures/fractures: from the concept of network to the concept of attachment'. *RES: Anthropology and Aesthetics* 36 (1999): 20–31.

—. 'A few steps toward an anthropology of the iconoclastic gesture'. *Science in Context* 10, no. 1 (1997): 63–83.

—. 'Formes élémentaires de la sociologie; formes avancées de la théologie'. Colloque du centenaire Collège de France, Collège de France, Paris, 2012.

—. 'From "matters of facts" to "states of affairs". Which protocol for the new collective experiments?' (2001). <http://www.bruno-latour.fr/sites/default/files/P-95-METHODS-EXPERIMENTS.pdf> (last accessed 2 November 2015).

—. 'From Realpolitik to Dingpolitik, or how to make things public'. In *Making Things Public: Atmospheres of Democracy Catalogue of the Show at ZKM*, ed. Bruno Latour and Peter Weibel. 14–41. Cambridge, MA: MIT Press, 2005.

—. *An Inquiry into Modes of Existence: An Anthropology of the Moderns*. Trans. Catherine Porter. Cambridge, MA: Harvard University Press, 2013.

—. 'An inquiry into modes of existence: glossary'. <http://www.modesofexistence.org/> (last accessed 2 November 2015).

—. '"It's development, stupid!" or: how to modernize modernization'. In *Postenvironmentalism*, ed. J. Proctor. 1–13. Cambridge, MA: MIT Press, 2008.

—. *Jubiler ou Les tourments de la parole religieuse*. Paris: Editions du Seuil, 2002.

—. 'Keynote speech: on recalling ANT'. In *Actor Network Theory and After*, ed. John Law and John Hassard. Chichester: John Wiley & Sons, 1998.

—. 'La Comédie des erreurs'. *La Recherche* Hors série N° 14 – Dieu et les Sciences (2004): 82–5.

—. *La Fabrique du droit*. Paris: Editions la Découverte, 2004.

—. *L'Espoir de Pandore: pour une version réaliste de l'activité scientifique*. Paris: La Découverte, 2007.

—. *The Making of Law: An Ethnography of the Conseil d'Etat*. Trans. Mariana Brilman and Alain Pottage. Cambridge: Polity Press, 2009.

—. 'Morale et technique: la fin des moyens'. *Réseaux*, no. 100 (2000): 39–58.

—. *Nous n'avons jamais été modernes: essai d'anthropologie symétrique*. Paris: La Découverte, 1997.

—. *On the Modern Cult of the Factish Gods*. Trans. Heather MacLean and Cathy Porter. Durham, NC: Duke University Press, 2010.

—. 'On selves, forms, and forces. Comment on Kohn, Eduardo. 2013. *How Forests Think: Toward an Anthropology Beyond the Human*. Berkeley: University of California Press'. *Hau: Journal of Ethnographic Theory* 4, no. 2 (2014): 1–6.

—. 'On technical mediation'. *Common Knowledge* 3, no. 2 (1994): 29–64.

—. *Pandora's Hope: Essays on the Reality of Science Studies*. Cambridge, MA: Harvard University Press, 1999.

—. *Pasteur: guerre et paix des microbes* suivi de *Irréductions*. Paris: La Découverte, 2011.

—. *The Pasteurisation of France*. Trans. Alan Sheridan and John Law. Boston, MA: Harvard University Press, 1993.

—. *Petites leçons de sociologie des sciences*. Paris: La Découverte, 2006.

—. 'A plea for earthly sciences'. Annual Meeting of the British Sociological Association. London, 2007.

—. 'The politics of explanation: an alternative'. In *Knowledge and Reflexivity: New Frontiers in the Sociology of Knowledge*, ed. S. Woolgar. 155–77. London: Sage, 1988.

—. 'Politics of nature: East and West perspectives'. *Ethics & Global Politics* 4, no. 1 (2011): 71–80.

—. *Politics of Nature: How to Bring the Sciences into Democracy*. Trans. Catherine Porter. Boston, MA: Harvard University Press, 2004.

—. *Politiques de la nature: comment faire entrer les sciences en démocratie*. Paris: Editions la Découverte, 2004.

—. 'Pragmatogonies: a mythical account of how humans and nonhumans swap properties'. *American Behavioral Scientist* 37, no. 6 (1994): 791–808.

—. 'Qu'est-ce qu'un style non-moderne? Actes du colloque, 21–22 mai 2004'. In *La Parenthèse du moderne*, ed. Catherine Grenier. 31–46. Paris: Editions du Centre Pompidou, 2005.

—. *Reassembling the Social: An Introduction to Actor-Network-Theory*. Oxford: Oxford University Press, 2007.

—. 'The recall of modernity – anthropological approaches'. *Cultural Studies Review* 13, no. 1 (2007): 11–30.

—. 'Reflections on Etienne Souriau's *Les Différents modes d'existence*'. In *The Speculative Turn: Continental Materialism and Realism*, ed. Levi Bryant, Nick Srnicek and Graham Harman. 304–32. Melbourne: re.press, 2011.

—. *Rejoicing, or the Torments of Religious Speech*. Trans. Julie Rose. Cambridge: Polity Press, 2013.

—. *Sur le culte moderne des dieux faitiches* suivi de *Iconoclash*. Paris: La Découverte, 2009.

—. 'Sur un livre d'Etienne Souriau: *Les Différents modes d'existence*'. 2009. <http://www.bruno-latour.fr/sites/default/files/98-SOURIAU-FR.pdf> (last accessed 2 November 2015).

—. 'To modernize or to ecologize? That's the question'. In *Remaking Reality: Nature at the Millenium*, ed. N. Castree and B. Willems-Braun. 221–42. London and New York: Routledge, 1998.

—. 'Waiting for Gaia. Composing the common world through arts and politics'. Lecture given at the French Institute, London, November 2011. <http://www.bruno-latour.fr/sites/default/files/124-GAIA-LONDON-SPEAP_0.pdf> (last accessed 2 November 2015).

—. *We Have Never Been Modern*. Cambridge, MA: Harvard University Press, 1993.

—. '"What's the story?" Organizing as a mode of existence'. In *Organization and Organizing: Materiality, Agency, and Discourse*, ed. Daniel Robichaud and François Cooren. 163–77. London: Routledge, 2013.

—. 'When things strike back: a possible contribution of "science studies" to the social sciences'. *British Journal of Sociology* 51, no. 1 (1999): 105–23.

—. 'Will non-humans be saved? An argument in ecotheology'. *Journal of the Royal Anthropological Institute* 15, no. 3 (2009): 459–75.

Latour, Bruno, Anders Blok and Torben Elgaard Jensen. '"We would like to do a bit of science studies on you": an interview with Bruno Latour'. In Anders Blok and Torben Elgaard Jensen, *Bruno Latour: Hybrid Thoughts in a Hybrid World*. 151–66. London: Routledge, 2011.

Latour, Bruno, and Michel Callon. '"Thou shall not calculate!" or How to symmetricalize gift and capital'. 1997. Trans. Javier Krauel. <http://www.bruno-latour.fr/sites/default/files/downloads/P-71%20CAPITALISME-MAUSS-GB.pdf> (last accessed 2 November 2015).

Latour, Bruno, and François Ewald. *Un monde pluriel mais commun*. La Tour d'Aigues: Éditions de l'Aube, 2003.

Latour, Bruno, Laurent Godmer and David Smadja. 'L'Œuvre de Bruno Latour: une pensée politique exégétique. Entretien avec Bruno Latour'. *Raisons Politiques*, no. 47 (2012): 115–48.

Latour, Bruno, Graham Harman and Peter Erdélyi. *The Prince and the Wolf: Latour and Harman at the LSE*. Winchester: Zero Books, 2011.

Latour, Bruno, Erin Manning and Brian Massumi. 'Les Baleines et la forêt amazonienne: Gabriel Tarde et la cosmopolitique. Entretien avec Bruno Latour'. *INFLeXions*, no. 3 (2008). <http://www.inflexions.org/n3_latour_frhtml.html> (last accessed 2 November 2015).

Latour, Bruno, and S. S. Strum. 'Redefining the social link: from baboons to humans'. *Social Science Information* 26, no. 4 (1987): 783–802.

Latour, Bruno, and John Tresch. 'Another turn after ANT: an interview with Bruno Latour'. *Social Studies of Science* 43, no. 2 (2013): 302–13.

Lawlor, Leonard. *Thinking Through French Philosophy: The Being of the Question*. Studies in Continental Thought. Bloomington: Indiana University Press, 2003.

Lebrun, Gérard. *Kant et la fin de la métaphysique*. Paris: Le Livre de Poche, 1970.

Lecercle, Jean-Jacques. 'Cantor, Lacan, Mao, Beckett, même combat'. *Radical Philosophy*, no. 93 (1999): 6–13.

LeDoux, Joseph. *Synaptic Self: How Our Brains Become Who We Are*. New York: Penguin Books, 2003.

Leidlmair, Karl, ed. *After Cognitivism: A Reassessment of Cognitive Science and Philosophy*. Dordrecht: Springer, 2009.

Lévy, Sydney. 'Introduction. An ecology of knowledge: Michel Serres'. *SubStance* 26, no. 2 (1997): 3–5.

Locke, John. *An Essay Concerning Human Understanding*. Oxford: Oxford University Pres, 1979.

—. *Two Treatises of Government*. Student edition. Cambridge: Cambridge: Cambridge University Press, 1988.

Lorimer, Jamie. 'Multinatural geographies for the Anthropocene'. *Progress in Human Geography* 36, no. 5 (2012): 593–612.

Lovelock, James. *Gaia: A New Look at Life on Earth*. Oxford: Oxford University Press, 1979.

—. *Gaia: The Practical Science of Planetary Medicine*. London: Gaia Books, 1991.

Lueck, Bryan. 'Toward a Serresian reconceptualization of Kantian respect'. *Philosophy Today* 52, no. 1 (2008): 52–9.

L'Yvonnet, François, and Christiane Frémont, eds. *Cahier de L'Herne Michel Serres*. Paris: Editions de L'Herne, 2010.

Mackenzie, Louisa, and Stephanie Posthumus. 'Reading Latour outside: a response to the Estok–Robisch controversy'. *Interdisciplinary Studies in Literature and Environment* 20, no. 4 (2013): 757–77.

Macmillan, Malcolm. *An Odd Kind of Fame: Stories of Phineas Gage*. Basingstoke: Macmillan, 2002.

Madell, Geoffrey. 'Personal identity and the idea of a human being'. *Royal Institute of Philosophy Supplement* 29 (1991): 127–42.

Malabou, Catherine. 'Again: "the wounds of the Spirit heal, and leave no scars behind"'. *Mosaic* 40, no. 2 (2007): 27–37.

—. 'Another possibility'. *Research in Phenomenology* 36 (2006): 115–29.

—. *Avant demain. Epigenèse et rationalité*. Paris: Presses Universitaires de France, 2014.

—. *Changing Difference: The Feminine and the Question of Philosophy*. Trans. Carolyn Shread. Cambridge: Polity Press, 2011.

—. *Counterpath: Travelling With Jacques Derrida*. Stanford: Stanford University Press, 2004.

—. 'The end of writing? Grammatology and plasticity'. *The European Legacy: Toward New Paradigms* 12, no. 4 (2007): 431–41.

—. 'The eternal return and the phantom of difference'. *Parrhesia*, no. 10 (2010): 21–9.

—. 'An eye at the edge of discourse'. *Communication Theory* 17, no. 1 (2007): 16–25.

—. *The Future of Hegel: Plasticity, Temporality and Dialectic*. Trans. Lisabeth During. London: Routledge, 2005.

—. 'The future of the Humanities'. *Transeuropéennes: Revue internationale de pensée critique* 14 (2014). <http://www.transeuropeennes.eu/en/articles/voir_pdf/281> (last accessed 2 November 2015).

—. *The Heidegger Change: On the Fantastic in Philosophy*. Albany: State University of New York Press, 2011.

—. 'How is subjectivity undergoing deconstruction today? Philosophy, auto-hetero-affection, and neurobiological emotion'. *Qui Parle* 17, no. 2 (2009): 111–22.

—. *La Chambre du milieu: de Hegel aux neurosciences*. Paris: Editions Hermann, 2009.

—. *La Change Heidegger: du fantastique et philosophie*. Paris: Editions Léo Sheer, 2004.

—. *La Plasticité au soir de l'écriture: dialectique, destruction, déconstruction*. Paris: Editions Léo Sheer, 2005.

—. *L'Avenir de Hegel: plasticité, temporalité, dialectique*. Paris: Vrin, 2012.

—. *Les Nouveaux Blessés: de Freud à la neurologie, penser les traumatismes*. Paris: Bayard, 2007.

—. 'Les Nouveaux Blessés. Psychanalyse, neurologie et plasticité'. In *Les Conférences d'AGORA*. D'après les notes prises par Huguette Déchamp et Serge Tziboulsky, 2007.

—. 'Négativité dialectique et douleur transcendantale: la lecture heideggérienne de Hegel dans le tome 68 de la Gesamtausgabe'. *Archives de Philosophie*, no. 66 (2003): 265–78.

—. *The New Wounded: From Neurosis to Brain Damage*. Trans. Steven Miller. New York: Fordham University Press, 2012.

—. *Ontologie de l'accident: essai sur la plasticité destructrice*. Paris: Editions Léo Scheer, 2009.

—. *Ontology of the Accident: An Essay on Destructive Plasticity*. Trans. Carolyn Shread. Cambridge: Polity Press, 2012.

—, ed. *Plasticité*. Paris: Editions Léo Scheer, 2000.

—. *Plasticity at the Dusk of Writing: Dialectic, Destruction, Deconstruction*. New York: Columbia University Press, 2009.

—. 'Polymorphism never will pervert childhood'. Trans. Robert Rose. In *Derrida, Deleuze, Psychoanalysis*, ed. Gabriele Schwab. 61–76. New York: Columbia University Press, 2007.

—. 'Post-trauma: towards a new definition?' In *Telemorphosis: Theory in the Era of Climate Change*, ed. Tom Cohen. 226–38. Ann Arbor: Open Humanities Press, 2012.

—. 'Pour une critique de la raison neurobiologique'. In *La Chambre du milieu: de Hegel aux neurosciences*. Paris: Editions Hermann, 2009.

—. *Que faire de notre cerveau?* Paris: Bayard, 2011.

—. *What Should We Do With Our Brain?* Trans. Sebastian Rand. New York: Fordham University Press, 2008.

—. 'Who's afraid of Hegelian wolves?' In *Deleuze: A Critical Reader*, ed. Paul Patton. 114–38. Oxford: Blackwell, 1996.

Malabou, Catherine, and Judith Butler. *Sois mon corps: une lecture contemporaine de la domination et de la servitude chez Hegel*. Paris: Bayard, 2010.

Malabou, Catherine, and Jacques Derrida. *Counterpath: Travelling with Jacques Derrida*. Trans. David Wills. Stanford: Stanford University Press, 2004.

Malabou, Catherine, and Jean-Marie Durand. 'Catherine Malabou: pour la rencontre entre philosophie et neuro-sciences'. *Les Inrockuptibles*, 20 octobre 2014. <http://www.lesinrocks.com/2014/10/20/livres/catherine-malabou-rencontre-philosophie-neuro-sciences-11530745/> (last accessed 2 November 2015).

Malabou, Catherine, and Adrian Johnston. *Self and Emotional Life: Philosophy, Psychoanalysis and Neuroscience*. New York: Columbia University Press, 2013.

Malabou, Catherine, and Noëlle Vahanian. 'A conversation with Catherine Malabou'. *Journal for Cultural and Religious Theory* 9, no. 1 (2008): 1–13.

Maniglier, Patrice. 'A metaphysical turn? Bruno Latour's *An Inquiry into Modes of Existence*'. *Radical Philosophy*, no. 187 (2014): 37–44.

Mauron, Alex. 'Is the genome the secular equivalent of the soul?' *Science* 291, no. 5505 (2001): 831–2.

—. 'Renovating the house of being: genomes, souls, and selves'. *Annals of the New York Academy of Sciences* 1001 (2003): 240–52.

Meilaender, Gilbert. *Neither Beast nor God: The Dignity of the Human Person*. New York: Encounter Books, 2009.

Meillassoux, Quentin. *After Finitude: An Essay on the Necessity of Contingency*. Trans. Ray Brassier. London: Continuum, 2008.

—. *Après la finitude*. Paris: Editions du Seuil, 2006.

—. 'Contingence et absolutisation de l'un'. *Métaphysique, ontologie, hénologie*. Université de Paris I, 2008.

—. 'Contingency & the absolutization of the One'. Trans. Benjamin James Lozano. Lecture delivered at the Sorbonne, 1 May 2012. <http://speculativeheresy.files.word-press.com/2011/03/contingency-and-absolutization-of-the-one.pdf> (last accessed 2 November 2015).

—. 'The contingency of the laws of nature'. *Environment and Planning D: Society and Space* 30 (2012): 322–34.

—. 'Deuil à venir, dieu à venir'. *Critique* LXII, no. 704–5 (2006): 105–15.

—. 'Histoire et événement chez Alain Badiou'. In *Marx au XXIe siècle: l'esprit & la lettre*. Université de Paris I, 2008.

—. 'The immanence of the world beyond'. In *The Grandeur of Reason*, ed. Conor Cunningham and Peter M. Candler. 444–78. London: SCM Press, 2010.

—. 'Iteration, reiteration, repetition: A Speculative Analysis of the Meaningless Sign'. Lecture delivered in Berlin, 20th April 2012.

—. *Le Nombre et la sirène: un déchiffrage du* Coup de dés *de Mallarmé*. Paris: Fayard, 2011.

—. 'L'Inexistence divine'. Thèse de Doctorat, Paris I, 1997.

—. 'Métaphysique et fiction des mondes hors-science'. In *Le Mois de la science-fiction de l'ENS*. ENS Paris: Diffusion des savoirs de l'École Normale Supérieure – Paris, 2006.

—. *Métaphysique et fiction des mondes hors-science*. Paris: Aux Forges de Vulcain, 2013.

—. 'Nouveauté et événement'. *Alain Badiou: penser le multiple*, ed. Charles Ramond. 39–64. Paris: L'Harmattan, 2002.

—. 'Potentiality and virtuality'. *Collapse* II (2007): 55–82.

—. 'Spectral dilemma'. *Collapse* IV (2008): 261–75.

—. 'Speculative realism: presentation by Quentin Meillassoux'. *Collapse* III (2007): 408–49.

—. 'Subtraction and contraction: Deleuze's remarks on *Matter and Memory*'. *Collapse* III (2007): 63–107.

—. 'Temps et surgissement ex nihilo'. Colloque: Autour de 'Logiques des mondes', ENS Paris, 2006.

—. 'Time without becoming'. CRMEP Research Seminar. Middlesex University, London.

Meillassoux, Quentin, Rick Dolphijn and Iris van der Tuin. 'Interview with Quentin Meillassoux'. Trans. Marie-Pier Boucher. In *New Materialism: Interviews and Cartographies*, ed. Rick Dolphijn and Iris van der Tuin. 71–81. Ann Arbor: Open Humanities Press, 2012.

Meloni, Maurizio. 'Philosophical implications of neuroscience: the space for a critique'. *Subjectivity* 4, no. 3 (2011): 298–322.

Merleau-Ponty, Maurice. *Le Visible et l'invisible: suivi de notes de travail*. Paris: Gallimard, 1964.

—. *The Visible and the Invisible: Followed by Working Notes*. Trans. Alphonso Lingis. Evanston: Northwestern University Press, 1968.

Miller, Adam S. *Speculative Grace: Bruno Latour and Object-Oriented Theology*. New York: Fordham University Press, 2013.

Morton, Timothy. 'Ecologocentrism: unworking animals'. *SubStance* 37, no. 3 (2008): 73–96.

—. 'Here comes everything: the promise of object-oriented ontology'. *Qui Parle* 19, no. 2 (2011): 163–90.

Mullarkey, John. *Post-Continental Philosophy*. London: Continuum, 2006.

Niemoczynski, Leon. '21st century speculative philosophy: reflections on the "new metaphysics" and its realism and materialism'. *Cosmos and History: The Journal of Natural and Social Philosophy* 9, no. 2 (2013): 13–31.

Noys, Benjamin. 'The density and fragility of the world: Latour'. In *The Persistence of the Negative: A Critique of Contemporary Continental Theory*. 80–105. Edinburgh: Edinburgh University Press, 2010.

—. 'The provocations of Alain Badiou'. *Theory Culture Society* 20, no. 1 (2003): 123–32.

O'Hara, Daniel T. 'Neither gods nor monsters: an untimely critique of the "post/human" imagination'. *Boundary 2* 20, no. 3 (2003): 107–22.

O'Mahoney, Paul. 'Hume's correlationism: on Meillassoux, necessity and belief'. *Journal of French and Francophone Philosophy – Revue de la Philosophie Française et de Langue Française* XXI, no. 1 (2013): 132–60.

Ortega, Francisco. 'The cerebral subject and the challenge of neurodiversity'. *BioSocieties* 4 (2009): 425–45.

Ortega, Francisco, and Fernando Vidal. 'Mapping the cerebral subject in contemporary culture'. *RECIIS: Electronic Journal of Communication Information and Innovation in Health* 1, no. 1 (2007): 255–9.

Paulson, William. 'Michel Serres's utopia of language'. *Configurations* 8, no. 2 (2000): 215–28.

Perloff, Marjorie. '"Multiple pleats": some applications of Michel Serres's poetics'. *Configurations* 8, no. 2 (2000): 187–200.

Petit, Jean-Luc. 'Sur la parole de Ricœur: "Le cerveau ne pense pas. Je pense"'. *Revue d'Histoire et de Philosophie Religieuses* 86, no. 1 (2006): 97–109.

Pfeifer, Geoff. *The New Materialism: Althusser, Badiou, and Žižek*. London: Routledge, 2015.

Pitts-Taylor, Victoria. 'The plastic brain: neoliberalism and the neuronal self'. *Health* 14, no. 6 (2010): 635–52.

Posthumus, Stéphanie. 'Translating ecocriticism: dialoguing with Michel Serres'. *Reconstruction* 7, no. 2 (2007). <http://reconstruction.eserver.org/Issues/072/posthumus.shtml> (last accessed 2 November 2015).

—. 'Vers une écocritique française: le contrat naturel de Michel Serres'. *Mosaic* 44, no. 2 (2011): 85–100.

Power, Nina. 'Towards an anthropology of infinitude: Badiou and the political subject'. *Cosmos and History: The Journal of Natural and Social Philosophy* 2, no. 1–2 (2006): 186–209.

Pyyhtinen, Olli, and Sakari Tamminen. 'We have never been only human: Foucault and Latour on the question of the anthropos'. *Anthropological Theory* 11, no. 2 (2011): 135–52.

Racine, Eric, Sarah Waldman, Jarett Rosenberg and Judy Illes. 'Contemporary neuroscience in the media'. *Social Science & Medicine* 71, no. 4 (2010): 725–33.

Ramond, Charles, ed. *Alain Badiou: penser le multiple*, Actes du Colloque de Bordeaux 21–23 octobre 1999. Paris: L'Harmattan, 2002.

Rancière, Jacques. *Disagreement: Politics and Philosophy*. Trans. Julie Rose. Minneapolis: University of Minnesota Press, 1999.

—. *La Mésentente: politique et philosophie*. Paris: Galilée, 1995.

Rasmussen, David M. 'Rethinking subjectivity: narrative identity and the self'. In *Ricœur as Another: The Ethics of Subjectivity*, ed. Richard A. Cohen and James L. Marsh. 57–69. Albany: State University of New York Press, 2002.

Rasmussen, Arne. 'Neuroethics as a brain-based philosophy of life: the case of Michael S. Gazzaniga'. *Neuroethics* 2 (2009): 3–11.

Ricœur, Paul. 'Approaching the human person'. *Ethical Perspectives* 1 (1999): 45–54.

—. *The Course of Recognition*. Cambridge, MA: Harvard University Press, 2007.

—. *Du texte à l'action: essais d'herméneutique II*. Paris: Editions du Seuil, 1986.

—. 'Ethics and human capability: a response'. In *Paul Ricœur and Contemporary Moral Thought*, ed. J. Wall, W. Schweiker and W. D. Hall. 279–90. Chicago: New York, 1999.

—. 'The human being as the subject matter of philosophy'. In *The Narrative Path: The Later Works of Paul Ricœur*, ed. T. Peter Kemp and David Rasmussen. 89–101. Cambridge, MA: MIT Press, 1989.

—. 'La Métaphore et le problème central de l'herméneutique'. *Revue Philosophique de Louvain* 70 (1972): 93–112.

—. *La Métaphore vive*. L'Ordre philosophique. Paris: Editions du Seuil, 1975.

—. *The Conflict of Interpretations: Essays in Hermeneutics*. Trans. Don Ihde. London: Continuum, 2004.

—. *Le Conflit des interprétations; essais d'herméneutique*. Paris: Editions du Seuil, 1969.

—. 'The crisis of the "cogito"'. *Synthese* 106, no. 1 (1996): 57–66.

—. *From Text to Action: Essays in Hermeneutics II*. Trans. Kathleen Blamey and John B. Thompson. Evanston: Northwestern University Press, 1991.

—. *The Just*. Trans. David Pellauer. Chicago: University of Chicago Press, 2003.

—. *Le Juste 1*. Paris: Editions Esprit: Distribution-diffusion Le Seuil, 1995.

—. *Lectures 2: la contrée des philosophes*. La Couleur des idées. Paris: Editions du Seuil, 1994.

—. 'Life in quest of narrative'. In *On Paul Ricœur: Narrative and Interpretation*, ed. David Wood. 20–33. New York: Routledge, 1991.

—. *Oneself as Another*. Trans. Kathleen Blamey. Chicago: Chicago University Press, 1995.

—. *Parcours de la reconnaissance: trois études*. Paris: Stock, 2004.

—. 'Paul Ricœur. "Ce que je suis est foncièrement douteux"'. *Ecriture* 52 (1998): 195–216.

—. 'Que la science s'inscrit dans la culture comme "pratique théorique"'. In *The Cultural Values of Science*. Vatican City: Scripta varia, 2003. <http://www.fondsRicoeur.fr/photo/science(3).pdf> (last accessed 2 November 2015).

—. *The Rule of Metaphor: Multi-disciplinary Studies of the Creation of Meaning in Language*. Trans. Robert Czerny. London: Routledge & Kegan Paul, 1986.

—. *Soi-même comme un autre*. Paris: Editions du Seuil, 1990.

—. *Temps et récit 3: le temps raconté*. L'Ordre philosophique. Paris: Editions du Seuil, 1985.

—. *Time and Narrative, volume 3*. Trans. Kathleen Blamey and David Pellauer. Chicago: University of Chicago Press, 1988.

Ricœur, Paul, and Peter Homans. 'Afterword: conversations on Freud, memory, and loss'. Trans. Peter Homans. In *Mourning Religion*, ed. William B. Parsons, Diane Jonte-Pace and Susan E. Henking. 231–8. Charlottesville: University of Virginia Press, 2008.

Rockmore, Tom. *Heidegger and French Philosophy: Humanism, Antihumanism and Being*. London: Routledge, 1995.

Romele, Alberto. 'Narrative identity and social networking sites'. *Études Ricœuriennes/Ricœur Studies* 4, no. 2 (2013): 108–22.

Rose, Nikolas. 'Neurochemical selves'. *Society* 41, no. 1 (2003): 46–59.

Ryder, Andrew. 'Badiou's materialist reinvention of the Kantian subject'. *The International Journal of Badiou Studies* 2, no. 1 (2013): 14–35.

Salazar, Philippe-Joseph. 'Michel Serres or the turbulence of interpretation'. *Journal of Literary Studies* 5, no. 1 (1989): 46–54.

Saldanha, Arun. 'Back to the Great Outdoors: speculative realism as philosophy of science'. *Cosmos and History: The Journal of Natural and Social Philosophy* 5, no. 2 (2009): 304–21.

Salisbury, Laura. 'Michel Serres: science, fiction, and the shape of relation'. *Science Fiction Studies* 33, no. 1 (2006): 30–52.

Sandoval, Ciro A. 'Michel Serres' philosophy of the "educated third": Hermesian confluences among the humanities, science and technology'. *Philosophy Today* 39, no. 2 (1995): 107–18.

Sankey, Derek. 'The neuronal, synaptic self: having values and making choices'. *Journal of Moral Education* 35, no. 2 (2006): 163–78.

Savulescu, Julian, and Nick Bostrom, eds. *Human Enhancement*. Oxford: Oxford University Press, 2010.

Schaff, Philip, ed. *NPNF2-08. Saint Gregory of Nyssa: Ascetic and Moral Treatises, Philosophical Works, Apologetic Works, Oratorical Works, Letters*. Nicene and Post-Nicene Church Fathers: Series 2, vol. 8. Edinburgh: T & T Clark, 2015.

Schiermer, Bjørn. 'Quasi-objects, cult objects and fashion objects: on two kinds of fetishism on display in modern culture'. *Theory, Culture & Society* 28, no. 1 (2011): 81–102.

Schiølin, Kasper. 'Follow the verbs! A contribution to the study of the Heidegger–Latour connection'. *Social Studies of Science* 42, no. 5 (2012): 775–86.

Schmidgen, Henning. *Bruno Latour in Pieces: An Intellectual Biography*. Trans. Gloria Custance. New York: Fordham University Press, 2015.

—. 'The materiality of things? Bruno Latour, Charles Péguy and the history of science'. *History of the Human Sciences* 26, no. 1 (2012): 3–28.

Schrag, Calvin O. *The Self after Postmodernity*. New Haven: Yale University Press, 1997.

Schrift, Alan D. *Nietzsche's French Legacy: A Genealogy of Poststructuralism*. London: Routledge, 1995.

Schweiker, William. 'Paul Ricœur and the return of humanism'. *Journal of French Philosophy* 16, no. 1 and 2 (2006): 21–41.

Selinger, Evan, ed. *Postphenomenology: A Critical Companion to Ihde*. Albany: State University of New York Press, 2006.

Serres, Michel. *Andromaque, veuve noire*. Paris: L'Herne, 2012.

—. *The Birth of Physics*. Trans. Jack Hawkes. Manchester: Clinamen Press, 2000.

—. 'Differences: chaos in the history of the sciences'. *Environment and Planning D: Society and Space* 30 (2012): 369–80.

—. *Écrivains, savants et philosophes font le tour du monde*. Paris: Editions le Pommier, 2009.

—. 'Ego cogito'. *Contagion: Journal of Violence, Mimesis, and Culture* 12–13 (2006): 1–11.

—, ed. *Éléments d'histoire des sciences*. Paris: Éditions Bordes, 1991.

—. *Éloge de la philosophie en langue française*. Paris: Fayard, 1995.

—. *En amour sommes-nous des bêtes?* Paris: Editions le Pommier, 2002.

—. 'Epilogue: what hearing knows'. In *The Re-Enchantment of the World: Secular Magic in a Rational Age*, ed. Joshua Landy and Michael Saler. 259–73. Stanford: Stanford University Press, 2009.

—. *Esthétiques sur Carpaccio*. Paris: Hermann, 1975.

—. 'Exact and human'. *SubStance* 6, no. 21 (1979): 9–19.

—. *Feux et signaux de brume: Zola*. Paris: Grasset, 1975.

—. *Genèse*. Paris: Grasset, 1982.

—. *Genesis*. Trans. Geneviève James and James Nielson. Ann Arbor: University of Michigan Press, 1995.

—. *Hermes: Literature, Science, Philosophy*. Baltimore: Johns Hopkins University Press, 1982.

—. *Hominescence*. Paris: Editions le Pommier, 2001.

—. 'L'Homme nouveau', Agen, 16 November 2004. <http://catholique-agen.cef.fr/site/im_user/0371_$_conference_michel_serres.pdf> (last accessed 11 November 2015).

—. *L'Incandescent*. Paris: Editions le Pommier, 2003.

—. *Jouvences sur Jules Verne*. Paris: Editions du Minuit, 1975.

—. *Jules Verne, la science et l'homme contemporain: conversations avec Jean-Paul Dekiss*. Paris: Editions le Pommier, 2003.

—. *La Communication: Hermès I*. Paris Editions de Minuit, 1968.

—. *La Distribution: Hermès IV*. Paris: Editions de Minuit, 1977.

—. *La Légende des anges*. Paris: Flammarion, 1993.

—. *La Naissance de la physique dans le texte de Lucrèce: fleuves et turbulences*. Paris: Editions de Minuit, 1977.

—. 'La Plus Précieuse des raretés'. In *Au Tibet avec Tintin*. 7–38. Paris: Casterman, 1994.

—. *La Traduction: Hermès III*. Paris: Editions du Minuit, 1974.

—. *L'Art des ponts: Homo pontifex*. Paris: Editions le Pommier, 2013.

—. 'Le Balancier, la pierre philosophale'. In *Cahier de L'Herne Michel Serres*, ed. François L'Yvonnet and Christiane Frémont. 101–11. Paris: Editions de L'Herne, 2010.

—. *Le Contrat naturel*. Paris: Editions François Bourin, 1990.

—. 'Le Couteau de Jannot'. In *Jules Verne*, ed. Pierre-André Touttain. 213–15. Paris: Editions de l'Herne, 1998.

—. *Le Mal propre: polluer pour s'approprier*. Paris: Editions le Pommier, 2012.

—. *Le Parasite*. Paris: Grasset, 1980.

—. *Le Passage du nord-ouest: Hermès V*. Paris: Editions de Minuit, 1980.

—. 'Le Temps humain: de l'évolution créatrice au créateur d'évolution'. In *Qu'est-ce que l'homme?*, ed. Pascal Picq, Michel Serres and Jean-Didier Vincent. 71–108. Paris: Les Editions le Pommier, 1999.

—. *Le Tiers-instruit*. Paris: Gallimard, 1991.

—. *Les Cinq Sens*. Paris: Grasset, 1985.

—. *Les Messages à distance*. Montréal: Editions Fides, 1995.

—. *Les Origines de la géométrie: tiers livre des fondations*. Paris: Flammarion, 1993.

—. *L'Hermaphrodite: Sarrasine sculpteur*. Paris: Flammarion, 1987.

—. *L'Interférence: Hermès II*. Paris: Editions de Minuit, 1972.

—. 'Literature and the exact sciences'. *SubStance* 18, no. 59 (1989): 3–34.

—. 'Mon temps ou le petit char de ma vie'. In *Cahier de L'Herne Michel Serres*, ed. François L'Yvonnet and Christiane Frémont. 307–8. Paris: Editions de L'Herne, 2010.

—. *The Natural Contract*. Trans. Elizabeth MacArthur and William Paulson. Ann Arbor: University of Michigan Press, 1995.

—. *Nouvelles du monde*. Paris: Flammarion, 1997.

—. 'One God or a trinity?' *Contagion: Journal of Violence, Mimesis, and Culture* 1, no. 1 (1994): 1–17.

—. 'The origin of language: biology, information theory, & thermodynamics'. In *Hermes: Literature, Science, Philosophy*, ed. Josue V. Harari and David F. Bell. 65–83. Baltimore: Johns Hopkins University Press, 1982.

—. *The Parasite*. Trans. Lawrence R. Schehr. Ed. Cary Wolfe. Posthumanities. Minneapolis: University of Minnesota Press, 2007.

—. *Petite poucette*. Paris: Editions le Pommier, 2012.

—. *Rameaux*. Paris: Editions le Pommier, 2004.

—. *Récits d'humanisme*. Paris: Editions le Pommier, 2009.

—. *Rome: The Book of Foundations*. Trans. Felicia McCarren. Stanford: Stanford University Press, 1991.

—. 'Science and the humanities: the case of Turner'. *SubStance* 26, no. 83 (1997): 6–21.

—. 'Tempo: le compositeur'. In *Cahier de L'Herne Michel Serres*, ed. François L'Yvonnet and Christiane Frémont. 56–9. Paris: Editions de L'Herne, 2010.

—. 'Temps, datation: le point à la mer'. In *Cahier de L'Herne Michel Serres*, ed. François L'Yvonnet and Christiane Frémont. 242–7. Paris: Editions de L'Herne, 2010.

—. *Temps des crises*. Paris: Editions le Pommier, 2009.

—. 'Temps, invention: la subtilité des fils'. In *Cahier de L'Herne Michel Serres*, ed. François L'Yvonnet and Christiane Frémont. 152–6. Paris: Editions de L'Herne, 2010.

—. 'Temps: mesure et nature'. In *Cahier de L'Herne Michel Serres*, ed. François L'Yvonnet and Christiane Frémont. 283–8. Paris: Editions de L'Herne, 2010.

—. 'Temps, nouvelles: vices et vertu'. In *Cahier de L'Herne Michel Serres*, ed. François L'Yvonnet and Christiane Frémont. 276–9. Paris: Editions de L'Herne, 2010.

—. 'Temps, usure: feux et signaux de brume'. In *Cahier de L'Herne Michel Serres*, ed. François L'Yvonnet and Christiane Frémont. 203–15. Paris: Editions de L'Herne, 2010.

—. *The Troubadour of Knowledge*. Trans. Sheila Faria Glaser and William Paulson. Ann Arbor: University of Michigan Press, 1997.

—. *Variations on the Body*. Minneapolis: Univocal Publishing, 2012.

—. *Variations sur le corps*. Paris: Editions le Pommier, 1999.

—. '"Voici l'homme"'. In *Cahier de L'Herne Michel Serres*, ed. François L'Yvonnet and Christiane Frémont. 261–3. Paris: Editions de L'Herne, 2010.

—. '['What are the questions that fascinate you?' 'What do you want to know?']: Response'. *SubStance* 32, no. 1 (2003): 56–9.

Serres, Michel, Henri Atlan, Roland Omnes, Georges Charpak, Olivier Mongin, Jean-Pierre Dupuy and Monique Canto-Sperber. *Les Limites de l'humain*. Lausanne: Editions d'Age d'Homme, 2003.

Serres, Michel, and Claude Dagens. *Quoi de neuf chez les cathos?* Bordeaux: Elytis, 2012.

Serres, Michel, and Geneviève James. 'Entretien avec Michel Serres'. *The French Review* 60, no. 6 (1987): 788–96.

Serres, Michel, Luis Join-Lambert and Pierre Klein. 'Knowledge's redemption'. *Revue Quart Monde*, no. 163 (1997).

Serres, Michel, and Bruno Latour. *Conversations on Science, Culture and Time*. Trans. Roxanne Lapidus. Ann Arbor: University of Michigan Press, 1995.

—. *Eclaircissements: cinq entretiens avec Bruno Latour*. Paris: F. Bourin, 1992.

Serres, Michel, and Pierre Léna. 'Sciences et philosophie (entretien)'. In *Cahier de L'Herne Michel Serres*, ed. François L'Yvonnet and Christiane Frémont. 47–55. Paris: Éditions de L'Herne, 2010.

Serres, Michel, and Bertrand Poirot-Delpech. *Discours de réception de Michel Serres à l'Académie française et réponse de Bertrand Poirot-Delpech: suivi de Allocution pour la remise de l'épée de George Duby et réponse de Michel Serres*. Paris: F. Bourin, 1991.

Serres, Michel, and Michel Polacco. *Petites Chroniques du dimanche soir: entretiens avec Michel Polacco*. Paris: Editions le Pommier, 2006.

—. *Petites Chroniques du dimanche soir 2: entretiens avec Michel Polacco*. Paris: Editions le Pommier, 2007.

—. *Petites Chroniques du dimanche soir 3: entretiens avec Michel Polacco*. Paris: Editions le Pommier, 2009.

—. *Petites Chroniques du dimanche soir 4: entretiens avec Michel Polacco*. Paris: Editions le Pommier, 2011.

—. *Petites Chroniques du dimanche soir 5: entretiens avec Michel Polacco*. Paris: Editions le Pommier, 2013.

Serres, Michel, and Bernard Stiegler. 'Pourquoi nous n'apprendrons plus comme avant'. <http://www.philomag.com/les-videos/michel-serres-et-bernard-stiegler-moteurs-de-recherche-3244> (last accessed 2 November 2015).

Silverman, Hugh J. 'Malabou, plasticity, and the sculpturing of the self'. *Concentric: Literary and Cultural Studies* 36, no. 2 (2010): 89–102.

Simondon, Gilbert. *Du mode d'existence des objets techniques*. Paris: Aubier Montaigne, 2012.

Skirbekk, Gunnar. 'Bruno Latour's anthropology of the moderns: a reply to Maniglier'. *Radical Philosophy*, no. 189 (2015): 45–8.

Skúlason, Páll. *Le Cercle du sujet dans la philosophie de Paul Ricœur*. Paris: L'Harmattan, 2001.

Sloterdijk, Peter. '*Rules for the Human Zoo*: a response to the *Letter on Humanism*'. *Environment and Planning D: Society and Space* 27 (2009): 12–28.

Solms, Mark, and Oliver Turnbull. *Brain and the Inner World: An Introduction to the Neuroscience of Subjective Experience*. New York: Other Press, 2002.

Solomon, Robert C. *Continental Philosophy since 1750: The Rise and Fall of the Self*. Oxford: Oxford University Press, 1988.

Somers, Margaret R. 'The narrative constitution of identity: a relational and network approach'. *Theory and Society* 23 (1994): 605–49.

Soper, Kate. 'The humanism in posthumanism'. *Comparative Critical Studies* 9, no. 3 (2012): 365–78.

Sparrow, Tom. *The End of Phenomenology: Metaphysics and the New Realism*. Edinburgh: Edinburgh University Press, 2014.

Spencer, Joseph M. 'Humanism and anti-humanism in the philosophy of Alain Badiou'. *Appraisal* 9, no. 1 (2012): 33–9.

Stiegler, Bernard. *La Technique et le temps 1: la faute d'Epiméthée*. Paris: Galilée, 1994.

—. *La Technique et le temps 2: la désorientation*. Paris: Galilée, 1996.

—. *La Technique et le temps 3: le temps du cinéma et la question du mal-être*. Paris: Galilée, 2001.

Strawson, Galen. 'A fallacy of our age: not every life is a narrative'. *Times Literary Supplement*, no. 5298 (2004): 13–16.

Strum, Shirley, and Bruno Latour. 'Redefining the social link: from baboons to humans'. *Social Science Information* 26, no. 4 (1987): 783–802.

Tallis, Raymond. *Why the Mind Is Not a Computer: A Pocket Lexicon of Neuromythology*. Exeter: Imprint Academic, 2004.

Thomas A. Lewis. 'On the limits of narrative: communities in pluralistic society'. *The Journal of Religion* 86, no. 1 (2006): 55–80.

Toscano, Alberto. 'Against speculation, or, a critique of the critique of critique . . . a remark on Quentin Meillassoux's *After Finitude* (after Colletti)'. Speculative Realism. Centre for the Study of Invention and Social Process: Goldsmiths, University of London, 2007.

—. 'A plea for Prometheus'. *Critical Horizons* 10, no. 2 (2009): 241–56.

Treanor, Brian, and Henry Isaac Venema, eds. *A Passion for the Possible: Thinking with Paul Ricœur*. New York: Fordham University Press, 2010.

Tuin, Iris van der. 'Deflationary logic: response to Sara Ahmed's "Imaginary Prohibitions: Some Preliminary Remarks on the Founding Gestures of the 'New Materialism'"'. *European Journal of Women's Studies* 15, no. 4 (2008): 411–16.

—. 'Non-reductive continental naturalism in the contemporary humanities: working with Hélène Metzger's philosophical reflections'. *History of the Human Sciences* 26, no. 2 (2013): 88–105.

Tuin, Iris van der, and Rick Dolphijn. 'The transversality of new materialism'. *Women: A Cultural Review* 21, no. 1 (2010): 153.

Vainqueur, Bernard. 'De quoi "sujet" est-il le nom pour Alain Badiou?' In *Alain Badiou: penser le multiple*, ed. Charles Ramond. 313–38. Paris: L'Harmattan, 2002.

Vandenberghe, Frédéric. *Complexités du posthumanisme. Trois essais dialectiques sur la sociologie de Bruno Latour*. Paris: L'Harmattan, 2007.

Venema, Henry Isaac. 'Am I the text? A reflection on Paul Ricœur's hermeneutic of selfhood'. *Dialogue* 38, no. 4 (1999): 765–84.

—. *Identifying Selfhood: Imagination, Narrative, and Hermeneutics in the Thought of Paul Ricœur*. McGill Studies in the History of Religions. Albany: State University of New York Press, 2000.

—. 'Oneself as another or another as oneself?' *Literature and Theology* 16, no. 4 (2002): 410–26.

Vidal, Fernando. 'Brainhood, anthropological figure of modernity'. *History of the Human Sciences* 22, no. 1 (2009): 5–36.

—. 'Brains, bodies, selves, and science: anthropologies of identity and the resurrection of the body'. *Critical Inquiry* 28, no. 4 (2002): 930–74.

Wall, J., W. Schweiker and W. D. Hall. 'Introduction: human capability and contemporary moral thought'. In *Paul Ricœur and Contemporary Moral Thought*, ed. J. Wall, W. Schweiker and W. D. Hall. 1–14. New York: Routledge, 1999.

Watkin, Christopher. *Difficult Atheism: Post-Theological Thinking in Alain Badiou, Jean-Luc Nancy and Quentin Meillassoux*. Edinburgh: Edinburgh University Press, 2011.

—. 'Thinking equality today: Badiou, Rancière and Nancy'. *French Studies* 67, no. 4 (2013): 522–34.

Webb, David. 'Michel Serres on Lucretius'. *Angelaki* 11, no. 3 (2006): 125–36.

Weinberg, Darin. 'Post-humanism, addiction and the loss of self control: reflections on the missing core in addiction science'. *International Journal of Drug Policy* 24 (2013): 173–81.

Wesling, Donald. 'Michel Serres, Bruno Latour, and the edges of historical periods'. *Clio* 26, no. 2 (1997): 189–204.

White, Hylton. 'Materiality, form, and context: Marx contra Latour'. *Victorian Studies* 55, no. 4 (2013): 667–82.

Whiteside, Kerry H. 'Systems theory and skeptical humanism in French ecological thought'. *Policy Studies Journal* 26, no. 4 (1998): 636–56.

Wilding, Adrian. 'Naturphilosophie redivivus: on Bruno Latour's "Political Ecology"'. *Cosmos and History: The Journal of Natural and Social Philosophy* 6, no. 1 (2010): 18–32.

Williams, Linda. 'Between Hermes, Gaia and Apollo 8: Michel Serres and the philosophy of science as communication'. *Critical Perspectives on Communication, Cultural & Policy Studies* 26, no. 2 (2007): 33–45.

Williams, Tyler. 'Plasticity, in retrospect: changing the future of the Humanities'. *Diacritics* 41, no. 1 (2013): 6–25.

Wilson, Raymond J. 'Metaphoric and metonymic symbolism: a development from Paul Ricœur's concepts'. In *The Visible and the Invisible in the Interplay between Philosophy, Literature and Reality*, ed. Anna Teresa Tymieniecka. Analecta Husserliana. 49–61. Dordrecht: Kluwer Academic, 2002.

Witmore, Michael. 'We have never not been inhuman'. *postmedieval: a journal of medieval cultural studies* 1, no. 1/2 (2010): 208–14.

Wolfe, Cary. 'Bring the noise: *The Parasite* and the multiple genealogies of posthumanism'. In *The Parasite*, ed. Michel Serres. xi–xxviii. Minneapolis: University of Minnesota Press, 2007.

—. *What Is Posthumanism?* Minneapolis: University of Minnesota Press, 2010.

Wolfendale, Peter. 'The noumenon's new clothes (part 1)'. *Speculations* III (2012): 290–366.

Wong, Michael Tak Hing. 'Towards a multi-layered discourse of the person: the Changeux–Ricœur dialogue and the challenge for neuroscience, psychiatry and theological anthropology'. Doctoral Thesis, Monash University, 2011.

Zembylas, Michalinos. 'Michel Serres: a troubadour for science, philosophy and education'. *Educational Philosophy and Theory* 34, no. 4 (2002): 477–502.

Zournazi, Mary. 'Cosmocracy: a hymn for the world? Reflections on Michel Serres and the natural world'. *Portal: Journal of Multidisciplinary International Studies* 9, no. 2 (2012).

Index